VANI SHED
KING DOMS

IRISH IN AUSTRALIA & NEW ZEALAND A PERSONAL EXCURSION

VANISHED
IRISH IN AUSTRALIA

NSW PRESS

Contemporary Photographs by Richard O'Farrell

KINGDOMS
AND NEW ZEALAND

PATRICK O'FARRELL
A PERSONAL EXCURSION

Published by
NEW SOUTH WALES UNIVERSITY PRESS
PO Box 1 Kensington NSW Australia

© P. O'Farrell September 1990

First published 1990

This book is copyright. Apart from any fair dealing
for the purpose of privates study, research, criticism or
review, as permitted under the Copyright Act,
no part may be produced by any process without
written permission from the publisher.

National Library of Australia
Cataloguing-in-Publication entry:

O'Farrell, Patrick, 1933–
Vanished kingdoms.

ISBN 0 86840 148 X.

1. O'Farrell, Patrick, 1933– . 2. Irish
— New South Wales — Sydney — History. 3. Irish
— New South Wales — Sydney — Social conditions.
I. Title.
305.89162099441

Available in North America through:
International Specialized Book Services
5002 N.E. Hassalo Street
Portland Oregon 97213–3640
United States of America
Tel: (503) 287 3093
Fax: (503) 284 885

Design/Production: Di Quick
Typeset by Excel Imaging, NSW, Australia.
Printed in Singapore by Kyodo Printing

CONTENTS

	Preface	vii
	Introduction	xiii
1	Kings Deposed? The Irish in Early Australia	1
2	Idiocy and Devilment	23
3	Prayer-worlds —	71
4	— and Priests	97
5	Colonial Irish: Themes	135
6	Variations: those other traditions	16
7	The First Generation	179
8	Dreams of Irelands	199
9	Politics	241
10	Death	281
	Bibliographical Note	302
	Index	305

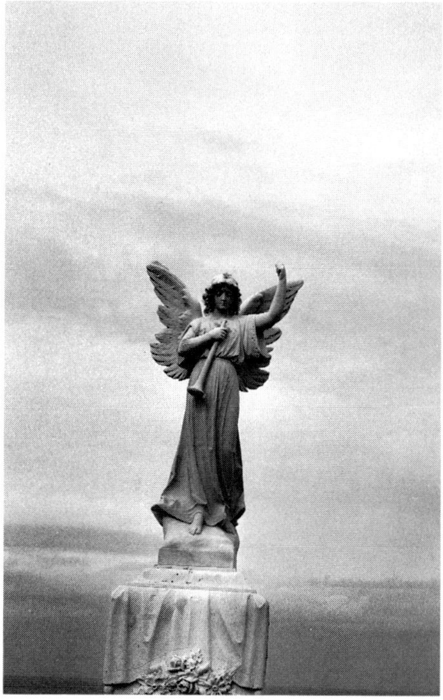

PREFACE

Had not my parents preserved the correspondence that is its core, this book would not exist. I much doubt that this was with a view to posterity, more a sentiment of their own casual remembrance, together with a lack of inclination, or need, to conduct a rigorous purge: what survived was incomplete, and a historian son was accidental. Nor had they any view of themselves as of historical consequence. This book is not intended consciously as a memorial. Perhaps it is, in effect, something of a general celebratory wake for the migrant Irish, but I intend it as a lesson, for present purposes which are mine. My parents are long dead, and, in the constrained tradition of so many migrants, I was present at neither death. I have visited their graves, but writing this book has been an encounter and communication much more intimate: in death as in life, they have enabled me to say what I wish, and I am immensely grateful for those freedoms.

This is a very personal book, and its judgments are mine. I am conscious that my cousinage, many of whom I have never met, may take a different view of some of the ancestral persons or events mentioned. To respect that possibility, I have in some cases avoided precise names in favour of generalities and minor pseudonyms.

I am particularly indebted to my wife, even more so than in regard to my earlier books. As with those, she offered detailed textual criticism, did the word-processing, and accompanied me on research expeditions, but in this case she added a particular dimension of insight and balance. The possession of a famous Irish name — Deirdre — disguises the fact that she comes from a background different from mine, sharing many of its basic values, but at variance, even at odds, with others: this has enabled her to offer angles and perceptions which have enriched or corrected my own stance.

All our children have contributed in various ways. Richard O'Farrell took contemporary photographs which not only illustrate the historical record, but which, in vital places, allowed me to enhance visually what I believe to be the mood and atmosphere of the book. The technical excellence of the family copying work is also his. Dr Clare O'Farrell did research in Melbourne, provided the translation from the French of Achille Lemire used in Chapter 5, and read a completed draft. Gerard O'Farrell undertook family background checking in Irish newspapers in the British Library in London. Virginia O'Farrell provided extensive research assistance in Sydney, and also on a visit to America. Justin O'Farrell organised materials at an early stage of research, and read parts of the final draft.

I cannot claim that my family saved me from myself, but I thank them most warmly for spotting errors and failings that do not now appear, and for their generosity in involving themselves in what was often, for one reason or another, an arduous enterprise.

In the category of valued critic, I also place Tony Cahill of the University of Sydney, who has read all of my books in draft since 1967, at great cost to his time and energies, and to my immense benefit. In justice to his scrupulous thirty-year scholarship on Cardinal Moran, I should note that he disagrees with my judgment of the Cardinal, especially in regard to 'aboriginal evangelisation': Moran was the only Irish bishop who took it at all seriously.

For professional literary reactions and advice at the highest level, I am indebted to Carl Harrison Ford and Roderic Campbell.

For the provision of source material, additional to that derived from my parents, I am first of all obligated to my aunt, Miss Chris O'Sullivan, now in her nineties, who has responded, over the years, to my various bothersome enquiries since 1970, about family history. Mr Pat Tully has supplied me, in long letters, with marvellous anecdotes about Irish Queensland. Mr Brendan Hanrahan, of Nunawading, has generously lent me typescripts of his parents' correspondence, and provided photographs: the Hanrahan material is now publicly available in the National Libraries of Australia and Ireland.

Miss Julia Moriarty has written to me at length about Irish Wellington, both volunteering information and responding to queries. My very substantial obligation to the Andrews family of Ballycrochan, Bangor, Northern Ireland, and to Dr Brian Trainor, now director of the Ulster Historical Foundation, goes back to my *Letters from Irish Australia* and now extends to the new material presented in Chapter 7.

I wish to thank all these generous people — and others to whom attribution is made in the text — for time and information freely given, and for permission to use it as I pleased. I hope I have honoured their trust in a professional manner, but such interpretations as are placed on this material are, of course, entirely my own.

My own university has facilitiated my work in various ways, but particularly through Special Studies Program leave in 1989, and through a prior succession of research grants made available by the Faculty of Arts. My colleagues both in the School of History and the Faculty have been unfailingly helpful and generous. I am also much obliged to the Humanities Research Centre of the Australian National University, where I was all too briefly a Visiting Scholar in 1989: Professors Ian Donaldson and Graeme Clarke, and their staff, gave me room, society and solitude. Nor can my wife and I neglect to acknowledge the hospitality of University House, a friend since 1956.

We visited New Zealand in 1989 to confirm (and at times correct) places and atmospheres. There I am indebted for help to my first university — Canterbury — and in particular Dr Len Richardson. Also in Christchurch, the Canterbury Public Library and the Canterbury Museum. In Greymouth I was obliged again to old friends, Martha and Arn Beck, Ward Rathbun, the late Ed Keating, and others who helped long ago — among many now dead, Marcia O'Neill and Jack Doyle. On this present occasion, I was also indebted to Miss Buckley of the Greymouth Public Library. In South Canterbury I wish to thank Mrs M.B. Scott of the Waimate Museum and the Waimate Historical Society and a range of family contacts, the Farrell family at Hunter, Mrs Topsy McArran (Farrell) of Lawrence, Dolly (Farrell) and Les Brown in Timaru, not to forget John Murray of Hamilton and Anne Byrnes of Melbourne.

In Australia I wish to acknowledge assistance from the Riverina Archives and Diocesan Archives, Wagga Wagga; Dr Malcolm Campbell; Jennifer Ridden; Eric and Elaine Rolls of Baradine, New South Wales; Professor Miriam Dixon of the University of New England; Philip Lee, of Longueville; and the following — Dr J. Jupp of the Australian National University; F.B. Higgins of Lavington, N.S.W.; Paddy Bastic of Maroubra, N.S.W.; and John Gralton of Ourimbah, N.S.W.

I am particularly grateful for the co-operation of the staffs of the Manuscript Room and the Photographic Section of the National Library in Canberra, and to the Braidwood and District Historical Society.

In Ireland, I am indebted to the Ulster Museum, Belfast, particularly Dr W.A. Maguire, and to Sir James Langham of Tempo, County Fermanagh; to the National Library of Ireland; and to Paddy Tully of the Irish Tourist Board. My former student, Dr John Kirkaldy, now in England, sent me a photograph of Borrisokane. I owe particular thanks to another former student, a previous Irish Ambassador to Australia, His Excellency Mr James Sharkey, not only for help with sources, but for the translation from the Gaelic in Chapter 2.

As a Director of the School of History's Community History Project, it is a particular pleasure to acknowledge the many local, parish and family historians whose valuable work has provided me with touches of colour and detail.

A book such as this draws on a lifetime of generosity, obligements and information provided by people and institutions too numerous to mention. The above list of benefactors is not to be taken as exclusive of those whose earlier help made possible the reaching of this point — and that in very basic ways: the facilitations of medical practitioners Professor Doug Piper, and Drs L'Estrange and Fevre come directly to mind. It is now nearly ten years (and four books) since I began publishing with the N.S.W. University Press: Mr Douglas Howie, Ms Di Quick, Mrs Frances Fourtounis, and all at the Press, have my warm respect and gratitude.

Alert readers may note an obvious omission from the kaleidoscope of Irish Australasian affairs reviewed in this book — the celebration of St Patrick's Day. Present considerations of space force its postponement to a future format. Similarly, this book is not a substitute for a long promised photographic *A Portrait of Irish Australia*. These remain works in progress, their completion subject to the usual human factors, and that over-riding law enunciated in the Irish tradition as 'God willing'.

I hope that no reader will escape from this book — noting its conversational tone, even its funny stories — with the idea that it was lightly written, an entertainment. True, no doubt, and despite my best efforts, the Irish have eluded me again, and this time, those closest to me. But I have, whatever the surface jokery, pursued them closely with all the seriousness and cunning I have at resource for that fascinating, harrowing, frustrating quest — and with a commitment and personal cost fitting to that strange ambivalence expressed by Seamus Heaney; to 'Feel dragged upon. And buoyant'. At moments I think I might have come close; a grasp of their coat-tails. Mostly I salute their inevitable escape, and welcome, as in magic shared, their vanishment again into mystery.

Patrick O'Farrell
School of History
University of New South Wales

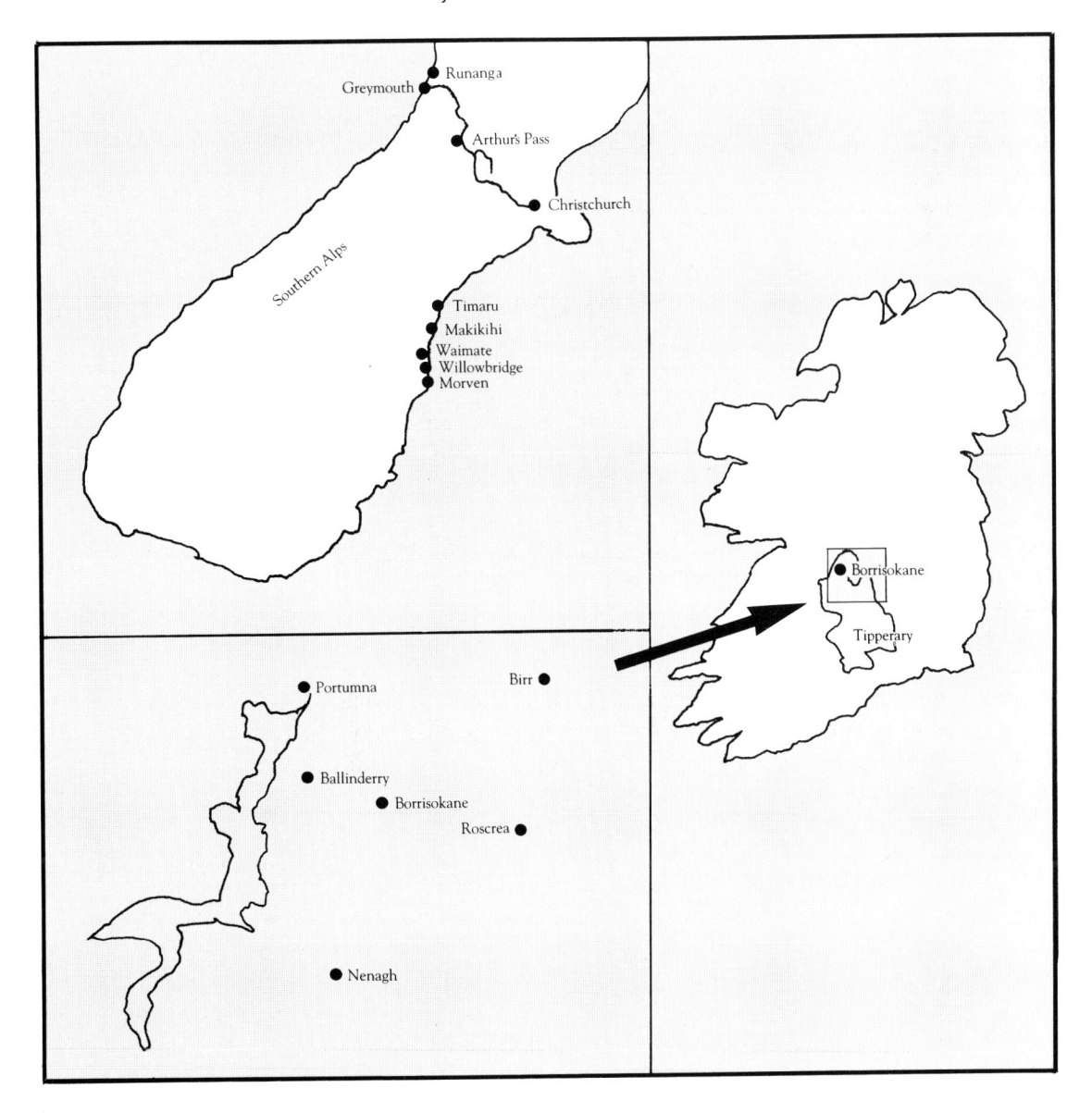

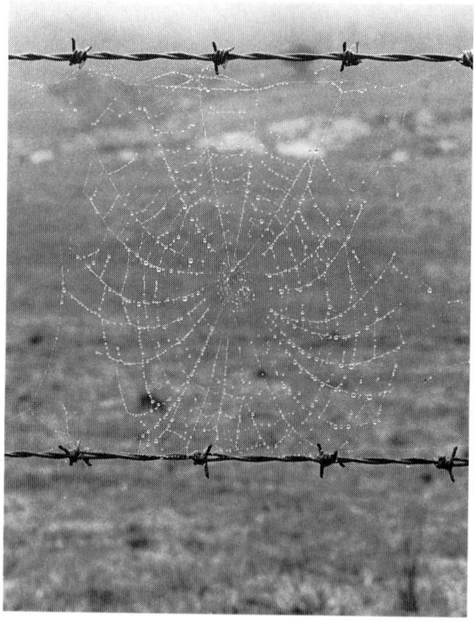

INTRODUCTION

How many books vie here? About what and whom? And why? One set of titled covers creates an expectation of oneness this reflective and refractive material denies. Its complementary planes, its range of harmonics and dissonances, conspire to separate, fly apart, escape into their different natural habitats — airy theory, earthy practice. Yet, to accommodate and contain this warring division is imperative to the sense and success of the history: the generalisation is lifeless and suspect without the illustration of the particular; the particular is meaningless or trivial without the setting of the broader context.

All very well. But to adopt a method, as this book does, of moving out from a small centre of particularity — two persons — into the wide territory of the general migration process is a very hazardous procedure. In which direction should one travel? Where does one stop? How to avoid becoming lost or breaking down with technical failure? The obvious answer is to take maps, set limits, define one's resources and destinations — and take the inevitable risks. First, what is the point of departure? Looking inwards, the book's structural core is a personal story of particular Irish immigrant experience in Australia and New Zealand, mainly in the earlier years of this century. This is (looking outwards towards and beyond the book's intellectual margins) merely a tiny case study on which a foray into grand and general migrant designs and processes cannot but precariously rest, however obvious and direct the connections. So, the reference, the supporting base, must be wider: an intermediate cast must be summoned. Other persons, other groups, other case studies are introduced.

But the book's ambitions are much more wide-ranging than anecdotal. The stories themselves are part of a greater story, indeed of several greater stories. They illustrate themes, exemplify processes, support arguments, sustain polemics. To choose which to pursue and how far, is a matter of hierarchies of personal importance and interest. Foremost here is analysis of one major process: Irish becoming 'colonial'. This occurred, not always, took place to different individual degrees, and adopted forms which often issued in kinds of dual personalities, a new colonial species both at home in, and foreign to, both old and new environments. Here is a variant on a standard ethnic experience, familiar from America's melting pot, and, of course, no preserve of the Irish. Resonances of that dislocating and melding process will be felt among migrants and migrant communities everywhere. I feel them myself, generated by that mildest of displacements, from New Zealand to Australia.

This transmutation, from immigrant to indigene, may be universal, the common knowledge of expatriate Greek or German, Anglican or Jew; but, here, the focus on the Irish is not a convenience, or based merely on personal ethnic origins. It derives from the historical fact that the Irish present in Australia and New Zealand offer those countries' longest, most substantial, and best case of immigrant interaction with the dominant English colonial culture, with a constructive dynamic outcome. This proposes inescapable lessons of creative assimilation to the present migrant scene. Such lessons are all the more pointed for the complexity and ambivalence of the Irish case: the Irish were locked in tense interplay with a majority culture they both detested and admired, better at the language than those who owned it, and equally determined to be both themselves and to fit in, conform. In their day, as new, abrasive migrants, they were to follow a pioneering assimilative path it would be dangerous and unhappy to ignore. Moreover, their example is not remote in time, but mostly within living memory — a virtually contemporary witness to the tried and traditional processes of immigration success. Here is a book about a fundamental aspect of the creation of a core Australia, which exists vitally still as quiet foundation to recent overlays.

Exists still. Too still, steeped in inertia and confusion, and under threat from the collapse of its structuring, more lately reduced to facade. The history of that foreign structure, intertwined with the translation from Irish to colonial, is another of the stories that compete here, the theme that gives its title to the book.

'Vanished Kingdoms' is a provocative and perplexing proposition when applied to the historical presence of the Irish in Australia and New Zealand. What kingdoms? When vanished? The obvious backward implication is that the Irish built dominions of their own within these British colonies, but that these are now crumbled and gone — an idea that might be thought to float dangerously within the hazes of romantic imagination. Can the history of these prosaic lands, their European beginnings heavily burdened with the rationalism of the so-called Enlightenment, be called upon to carry any meanings deeper than the secularised surface? Or bear the notion that a segment of their inhabitants harboured visions of empire far more grandiose, ambitious and spiritualised than those implied by the bootmarks of governors, soldiery and land-grabbers?

The story pursued here is partly that of a hidden history, buried by two centuries of the weight and self-promotion of an establishment, bolstered by both its supportive and detractive historians. Partly it is also the inversion of a surface story, an exploration of the other side of a triumph that once was: the Irish colonial conquest. The saga of that particular exercise of imperium is not a simple tale of invasion, displacement or slaughter of aboriginal peoples, settlement, civilisation — the presently accepted version of the public record of the flag-carrying power, Britain. All colonial societies are also constructs of mind and ideology, artificial value fabrications with imported rationales: dominant were those of Britain. Contesting that domination, or exalting it, or exploiting its liberality, were three types of Irish mind-set. The sustaining rationale of the Gaelic, Catholic Irish was their central myth, in the sense of abiding presumption, of repression and persecution: this myth was largely, but not entirely, dispersed by the 1916 Rising in Ireland and the years that followed it. The Ulster Protestant Irish lived with various forms and degrees of the Orange myth, that they were under Catholic threat. The Anglo-Irish were obsessed by their own political destruction as colonists by Britain in the 1800 Act of Union with Ireland, and determined that this would not happen in Australia.

During the First World War period all these questions were largely settled in both Australia and New Zealand: if there was repression it was ending, if there was a Catholic threat it was passing, if there was illiberality, it was on the wane. All these three nineteenth century Irish groups and their descendants had been living vicariously in and on Ireland, their impulse and momentum Irish, and all were overtaken by their own success in preventing, avoiding — if it was ever a possibility at all — what they feared. In essence what they feared was the suppression of their own ideally free identity, as they envisaged it themselves: gradually, experience of colonial life revealed its essential mechanisms — tolerance, equality, democracy, opportunity — and dispersed those fears. So fell the elements of Irish empire, lacking reason to further exist, and its dead hand dropped from the colonies' affairs. Not before time; for, only then could those colonies become themselves without the constant interrogation of Irish tests, Irish suspicions. Become themselves — but part of themselves was this habit of measuring up, referring to, metropolitan standards, a conditioning impossible to shed at a moment, its legacy twisted into the texture of independence.

This kind of terminology is instantly questionable, misty, grand generalisations as elusive as they are contentious. Yet parading a legion of illustrative particularities is both impossible and profitless: they will never be sufficient to convince the sceptical. What is possible is to tender as witness the implications of individual lives. This is the basic method of this book, and its major (but by no means exclusive) reference is to members of my own family and their friends. Predating, in the main, my infancy, and unconcerned with genealogy or completeness, it is neither autobiography nor family history, as I understand those genres. It attempts to use an accumulation of historical documentation, preserved by my parents, to illustrate, and above all to personalise in an intimate way, some major themes discernible in the Irish immigrant experience. It is not suggested that these are the only themes in that experience, or that they are exclusively Irish. Echoes of this particular immigrant witness may well reverberate in other expatriate cultures; but, in the Australasian context the Irish case has claims to being unique. Its significant size as a minority, its presence from initial settlement, its overwhelming Catholicity, together with its mastery of the language of hosts who were also its traditional oppressors — all this suggests an element both distinctive and crucial within the totality of immigrant experience.

The search for depth, intimacy, feeling, which is the objective of this book is a natural progression from the voyages I have previously taken into the subject of Irish immigration. In various expansions of *The Catholic Church in Australia* (1968, 1977, 1985) I dealt with the religious history of the Australian

Irish as Catholics. In *Letters from Irish Australia 1825–1929* (1984), I sought to enter the private world of a wide range of Irish immigrants, but mainly Protestants from Ulster, through their letters home. The Irish in Australia were revealed as a diverse people among whom, although Catholics were numerically dominant, major formative contributions also came from Ulster Protestants and Anglo-Irish. *The Irish in Australia* (1986) sought to survey the entirety of the Australian Irish immigrant scene to the present, advancing the argument that 'Until very recently the Irish have been the dynamic factor in Australian history, that is, the galvanising force at the centre of the evolution of our national character'. The emphasis of that book was on the Irish born rather than their descendants and on the nineteenth century rather than the twentieth. It celebrated a major neglected factor in the construction and character of Australian history, dealing with broad developments and major features.

These books were essential pathfinders in generality, in the overall scene, for the steps this present book takes nearer to home, nearer in time, place and frame of mind. Now familiar with those distant predecessors, who made my culture initially possible in these lands, what of my immediate origins and those of people like me, the Irish colonials, Australians and New Zealanders of Irish heritage?

Two years' residence in Ireland, with my family, in 1965–66 and 1972–3, amply convinced me that I am not Irish, nor accepted as such: there, I am properly, and happily for all parties, a friendly visitor. Yet, I am a product of the Irish tradition transplanted overseas — a colonial, a New Zealander of Irish descent and Australian citizenship. What then is my history — and that of millions of 'colonials' like me? It is only very partly that of Ireland and Catholicism: it is much more that of the process of these basic elements becoming 'colonial', responding to the new environment and thus becoming changed, something different and new. This was no straight forward or simple development, nor did it proceed at a regular pace, nor affect all individuals uniformly. Nevertheless, a glance reveals a large and momentous transition between the nineteenth century history in Australia and New Zealand of the Irish-born, and the culture in which I grew up, that of the 1930s and 1940s. That culture was residually 'Irish', but in a colonial way, and that realisation comes in retrospect: I was hardly conscious of it being Irish at all.

How did this transformation come about? How could I be so sure, in a first overseas generation, that I was not Irish — so certain of an identity which was firmly colonial? It was a question millions had unthinkingly lived the answer to. My Irish parents had lived and contrived the transition from Irish to colonial: they were the ones to interrogate. For their lives and outlook pioneered the colonial future rather than, as some Irish tried to do, recreated the past. They successfully, if with pain, made the creative links between an old and wise culture they brought in their bones, and a new world they joined and helped form. The outcome was a generation which was confident, free, self-possessed and at one with its colonial identity, if at times uncertain of what that precisely was, or what to do about it.

I make no apology for using my parents to testify in this way, nor for the comments I make on them and their world. I love them and am in their eternal debt: and I do them (and the place and people whence I came) the merited honour of taking their human achievement seriously. To the superficial view, these were small people in a small, remote, place, but I know of no better way to draw attention to the practical operation of migration's great themes, nor to the close presence of God in the world. I do not suggest that these people whom I knew best were either exceptional or typical. Each immigrant was singular, but is it too much to hope that these examples represent points to which others might relate, might accord some degree of recognition? At any rate, my parents are, in the ideal book of the objective historian, merely convenient vehicles for carrying relevant themes. Given that emphasis, the close family focus has been supplemented and broadened throughout by the use of other, both related and divergent, examples and illustrations.

A word on the term 'colonial' (some Irish used 'native' to make the distinction) and on the fact that much of the material has a New Zealand setting. 'Colonial' is used precisely when it denotes the settlers and culture of new territories connected with parent states: it is a term of convenience when it is used to take the descriptive emphasis away from terms whose structural balance is misleading — Irish-Australian, Irish-New Zealander. My quarrel with these terms is that they point back to the old culture, whereas the direction of this enquiry is forward; it is towards the formation of a new culture which is 'colonial' to the extent that it is derivative, but distinctive and unique to the extent that the derivation itself has a life and character of its own. The use of 'colonial' also obviates making inappropriate distinctions between Australia and New Zealand: earlier in this century Irish immigrants made no great distinction between the two countries, hardly more than was made between Australian States. Interchange was frequent and casual, particularly at the level of labouring men. It would be absurd not to recognise the different histories and characters of the two countries, particularly the greater English and Scots flavour of some parts of New Zealand, but equally silly not to be aware of their close similarity and relationship. This was particularly so of the West Coast region of New Zealand's South Island, the setting of much of this book: from the gold-rush times of the 1860s its proportion of Irish was roughly the same as Victoria's, and it had direct shipping, mail and news contacts with the east coast of Australia. In the more recent times of popular radio, Australian stations were more accessible at night than those in New Zealand.

It would be a foolish distortion if some of the tougher arguments of this book, advanced with reasoned care and supported by evidence, were taken as radically critical of the Irish and the Catholic Church. However, I am well aware that some believe the Irish beyond any human criticism and unlikely to deserve divine. Those who take the view that the Irish contribution to Australia and New Zealand merits only praise, may construe parts of this book as base ingratitude, or somehow morally destructive, or subversive of the decencies of history and proper social order, designed to destroy noble 'traditions and proud history'. It is appropriate to advert to this phenomenon at some length, given that it is a legacy persisting into the present, of the period and themes with which this book is concerned.

The champions of a perfect, or at least a superior Ireland, often appear to be moved by religious or moral nostalgia. They take the position — it dates back to the Venerable Archdeacon McEncroe in the 1850s (and he, of course, had a prior American career of conditioning significance) — that things Irish were, and are, a moral and religious protective, a bastion of religious faith and goodness, of sound spirituality. Their view is that the creeping form of decadence which they see as invading all society — including Catholic society — springs from 'abandoning and treating our Irish past with contempt'. Essentially their argument is that the Irish, historically, set permanently sound human standards, and that Irishness is criticised or shed at peril.

Such a position commands respect, in that its impulse is moral and its cast of mind concerned with values that have been lost. Moreover, it has been stung by expression of anti-Irish hostility both needless and unjust. However, insofar as

St Patrick Rules: the stained glass door to St Patrick's Church, Greymouth, New Zealand.

the champions of Ireland themselves desert moderation and sense, it is comforting to find that such reactions have been categorised long ago by the Irish novelist Honor Tracy, in, *Mind You, I've Said Nothing* (1953): 'If [Ireland] is criticised, [readers] are publicly furious and privately amused; if praised they are outwardly pleased while inwardly condemning the writer as a fool'. Tracy lists the predictable charges usually made against critics of the Irish. This list of charges, which the American anthropologist, John C. Messenger, expanded in 1977 to twenty includes: you are ignorant, a malicious liar, anti-Catholic, pro-English, haven't the Gaelic, don't understand the Irish — all marvellous, entertaining, invective, which nowhere engages real points at issue.

At issue are not causes, but effects. This book's emphasis is on the transition from Irish to colonial; its purpose, to analyse that process. Its concern is not to question the undoubted virtues and achievements of an Irish past — I have been proclaiming those historically since 1968 — but to trace its legacy into the Australian and New Zealand present; to jump from the great pioneering and missionary achievements, justly honoured but now long gone, into the real needs of a contemporary culture in confusion and crisis. However painful and disruptive, attacks on Irish hegemony, exemplified by the Manly movement for an Australian priesthood in the 1920s, sprang from a healthy rejection of the inferiority Irish rule and dominance were seen to represent. Did the French, so important not only to New Zealand Catholicism but to Oceania generally, exact such authoritarian loyalty to their memory? Moreover, the nostalgia tradition amongst the 'old Irish', particularly the priesthood — with the inherent assumption that this is their country, that they have built its Catholicism and to that extent own it — forms a curious base and continuum for a modern secularised version of that same attitude of proprietorship and superiority. Among some new Irish, visitors or immigrants, can be sensed something more than response to a welcoming place, rather something of the imperialist's conviction of precedence in culture and civilisation. Young Australia and New Zealand have an opposite reaction. The location of the championing of Ireland among the old proves the point at issue: that the edifice the Irish built and left has little or no meaning for the indigenous young — a situation too easily dismissed as ingratitude, or the well-known triviality of the younger generation. The real lesson is that the Irish built for themselves and to suit themselves. Young Australasia knows that, instinctively and practically: they have been force-fed a

St Patrick Rules: St Patrick's statue in St Patrick's Church, Waimate, New Zealand.

diet of ancestor worship, of those not their locational ancestors.

It is worth pausing, in this preliminary consideration, of the evolution of the colonial Irish, to consider the American comparison. From that republican vantage point, it can appear that the Irish in Australia were cowardly and derelict in their apparent lack of affection for 'the Old Sod'. An American clerical reviewer of *The Irish in Australia* was sceptical that the Australian Irish could have had such disgracefully little interest in Ireland, or had wished (gross betrayal) to conform to a British culture. But, conceding that this 'tendentious' argument 'may indeed arise from the data examined', it led 'to a conclusion seemingly unavoidable: that the career of Australia's Irish has been less than heroic and worthy of but limited praise'.

My own conclusion was the direct opposite. That career was often and widely 'heroic', mainly in quieter and more difficult ways than barricades and bravado, and nationalist sloganeering. And its social role as dynamic and generator of protest is worthy of the greatest praise — from an Australian viewpoint. That is the crux of the matter — the Australian viewpoint. The bald and open denunciation of emigrants as 'traitors' emerged in Ireland in 1910, but the judgement lay beneath the surface of some extreme nationalist minds much earlier, a coercive disposition which demanded total allegiance to some idealised version of an Irish nation, which the emigrant had allegedly deserted and thus betrayed. Such was perhaps an understandable position for resident ideologues whose first priority was Ireland, or for clerics who conceived of Ireland, not as a country, but a religious paragon or symbol. It was an impossible and destructive position for immigrants who had come to a new country, a new situation, which had its demands, its necessities, its viewpoint. To that challenge the Australian Irish responded magnificently. They were crucial elements in constructing a generous society, which was new, open, free and distinctive. In the main they achieved this without wallowing in agonies of exile or alienation, or being caught in the stagnancy, corruption and illusion that bedevilled the American Irish experience — or entering its dimensions of deferential hero-worship. There is nothing, for instance in the psychology of Irish Australia to parallel the didactic purpose of Patrick J. Dowling's 1988 publication, *California: The Irish Dream,* which offers brief biographies of seventeen Irish prominent in the development of California, and informs young Irish-Americans, 'whatever your station in life . . . you will find

A road to, or a road from? Galong cemetery, southern New South Wales.

a counterpart in one or more of the Irish characters in this book, someone to model yourself after in moments of doubt'. Such sentiments or responses appear totally unrelated to any element of the Irish Australian scene, where such instruction would appear, at best, ridiculous.

The almost obsessional seriousness of the continuing American Irish engagement with Ireland is rooted in historical factors and relative geographic closeness. It reveals a permanent duality or ambivalence, and a degree of dependence and deference, which Irish Australia did not have, or else quickly lost. It was, and remains, meaningful to speak of Irish-Americans. Not Irish-Australians. The hyphen has gone, if it was ever really there: Australians. This book is about the absence of the hyphen. Or in the jargon of the day, about assimilation: more simply, it is about the growth of a shared identity, shared with all comers, reasonably, and by choice.

On the personal level, I remain Catholic by religion and rejoice in being Irish by descent. But I am beset by those obvious questions, to borrow from the old catechism: who am I? where have I come from? where am I going? I know — and affirm — the orthodox theological answers to those questions, but I am vexed and perplexed about the historical ones. To me there seems a vagueness ... no, a gap, since the end of the nineteenth century. It was in that gap that my generation was born and its nurture formed — happy nobodies, caught between colonial mindlessness and Irish irrelevance. Both happiness and vacuity I put down to Ireland and its Catholic church. Blame them? For happiness and clear vision? Besides, I am too much of the earth for stone-casting. Nor will I subtract one iota of praise I have accorded earlier to those astonishing but now vanished empires. But I will, if I can, bring them to book to tax them with their sins of omission. Why have they left me thus, cheated and bereft? Is the fault mine that I am cheated of my own culture, bereft of majesty, besieged and abandoned in a world of disputatious dull dogs, short-changed in the currency of the spirit, when I should have had wealth?

So, this book is a question, not a complaint. Nor, despite its title, is it any exercise in nostalgia or blind regret. It is an affirmation of continuity: the past lives still. Another of those books, those intellectual and emotional purposes within this book, clamours to reclaim and release it. In this way.

In *Remembrance of Things Past*, that extraordinary meditation on the mysteries of time, Marcel Proust, in his journey towards Time Regained, finds rest and reason in an old Celtic notion.

> I find that Celtic belief quite plausible — the idea that the souls of those we have lost are held captive in some lower form of life, an animal, a plant or an inanimate thing, lost to us in effect until that day, which for many never comes, when we happen to pass by that tree, or come into possession of that object which is their prison; then those souls begin to stir, they call out to us, and no sooner have we recognised them than the spell is broken. Liberated by us, they have overcome death and return to life with us.

The construction of true History moves towards this kind of liberation, an exercise in close listening. Nor can we escape the painful conclusion that the search to free these souls is not a self-less act. Their passing into the realms of death has disordered and imperilled our own world. Our own journey of discovery, in which they rise up to greet us, is an excursion in pursuit of order and comprehensibility in our own lives, of which remembrance of them forms an integral part. It is not only those we have lost that are held captive in past time, but ourselves.

VANISHED KINGDOMS

INTRODUCTION

New life and old death. The Easter Sunday ceremony at the 1798 monument, Waverley cemetery, April 1989.

To fulminate against the growth and passing (too long delayed) of an Irish culture in Australia is also to be involved in measuring its richness against the asinine and empty poverty it left in its wake. To berate as irrelevant this culture's imposition on the colonial, to deplore its contempt for the local, is not to cease to enjoy it for what it was, at best. Rather, it is to protest in fear and insecurity at the spectacle of a society partly moulded in and by it: to be then cast adrift, without reach of a civilised shore. These are the standard colonial complaints against the departing imperial power, properly dismissed as puerile and cowardly in any political context. But here the context was spiritual and cultural, a difference of kind, and the dereliction and desertion were of a profoundly different order. The Irish disengagement from Australia and New Zealand was, in fact, hardly that. Much of the Irish embrace was permanent, an identificaton with things colonial that involved both in a relationship of possession and change. Theirs had never been a genuine or equal encounter with the land or its total society; rather, a narrow engagement with the segments of the pilgrim Irish who lived on its surface. Untutored — and deprived of example — in how they might construct a sense of wholeness in this strange, shallow place, these pilgrims cleaved to the superficialities of the desert, or made their peace with it as best they could. And when that immigrant army had perished in the wilderness, or deserted to it, or blended with its arid zones, and local recruits to Irish colours were exhausted, their self-appointed commanders — together with their green cause — were similarly mostly dead or departed. Their legacy was their absence, and a glorious and triumphal history, a time past. What they had built had become empty; or museums, or swollen with other lands' throngs. What they had uttered, and been, had drifted away in the babel of other men's tongues.

Those new Irish who came later, from the 1950s to the 1990s, were not their imperial successors, or set upon any similar civilising task. Rather were they sojourners, visitors, casuals, hived-off and happy inhabitants of their own particular division of multi-culture: they were a microcosmic reduction of what once had been, minus the conquering aggression and ambition, content to be permanently Irish while resident in Australia. These new arrivals, airborne, with money, and a ticket home in their heads if not their pockets, educated, with a republic of their own, self-confident in their identity and proud of their culture, were much like other Europeans, even the British. They were far distant in character, outlook, mission, from those Irish whose Ireland predated 1916, 1921. With independence, statehood, all was indeed changed utterly — for Ireland. But the mark of that old enslaved, imperial Ireland still lay heavily on the lands it had colonised, long after it had itself thrown off, in large part, the conqueror's yoke. The history of Ireland, pre-1916, weighs thereafter heaviest on those who most distantly inherited it; for, it was not their history, nor could they affect or change it.

The old Australian Irish, and their descendants, were, like Proust's captive Celtic souls, caught and imprisoned, but in an alien world's surrounds. Can a colonial passer-by, or descendant-possessor of those objects which are their prison, return them to life? In the hope of that return, and in their mingling with us, lies the beginnings of continuity, the bridging of gaps, the construction of a colonial culture with a sense of meaning and of ancient human roots, the reconciliation of Time Regained.

The mad, the sick, the imprisoned, the persecuted — there were the marginal elements of traditional society. But, in the nineteenth and twentieth centuries, marginality, the role of not belonging, was extended to a much larger, wider group, a group otherwise 'normal' — immigrants. Whatever it be called — emigration, escape, exile, expatriation — it was a process which did violence to a primal need for home and to feel at home. Even the most optimistic casting of the immigrant's ambition — to build a new home in the new land — carried with it the weight of loss and the constant abrasion of comparison, in its unspoken implication that there was, elsewhere, an old home and an old land. The disruption was inescapable: the immigrant was doomed, happily or otherwise, to be Janus-faced.

The assumption that the immigrant, virtually by reason of his or her immigration, will be forward-directed, disposed to be committed to his or her new 'home', is, possibly, a pragmatic necessity, a convenience of policy. It need not be the true situation, or at least, that most profoundly operative. Most likely this is so for those immigrants whose past was unresolved, that is, those who were, in some sense refugees: flight is the most traumatic of solutions and one that leaves the problem behind intact. Applied to the Irish, this dramatic terminology is traditionally associated with the exodus caused by the Great Famine of 1845–50; but the point, in milder forms, is relevant to the whole emigration process, pre-1921, that is, prior to Ireland's asserting control of its own destiny. So, for those who came to Australia from the Ireland of the late eight

The New South Wales town of Home Rule, near Mudgee, reduced, like the Irish cause whose name it carried, to a sign indicating where a history had taken place.

eenth century (the 'Kings Deposed' of this book's first chapter), freedom in Australia meant, not so much the opportunity to do something new, rather in their minds it enabled the liberation of the old. For all depended on the direction in time in which their mind-set was moving. The imposed discontinuity of convict exile did not necessarily invite a step forward, but a step back, now possible, into an old and historically contested continuity. Traditional knowledge was based on the principle of resemblance. The modern eye sees what is new (the penal settlement, a strange environment): it responds to the criteria of difference. The ancient Irish gaze fixed on what might be familiar, recognisable, old, most readily translatable into the idiom which they knew and for which they hoped — back home.

The cultural contradictions and confusion this bequeathed to subsequent colonial Irish generations are beyond any ready and general pronouncements. Imported reference points were the only verities. There was nothing local to challenge them beyond things so large and basic — land and climate — that they could only be ignored ... ignored until they forced their slow unyielding claims. So, in this shimmering vacancy, the new legatee colonial mind was focussed on aspiring to replicate, to improve on, home structures real or imagined, which were essentially restrictive, anti-new: colonial itself implied inferiority to metropolitan, as empty is inferior to full. Thus, the immigrant need to escape the old world is also a need to return, refer back, be reconciled, rebuild, be made whole with what once was. And all this breeds in descendants a similar need to escape and return, from their own points of departure — a process not merely generational, but profoundly preoccu

xxvii

French sketch of Irish emigration, in the usual place of farewell — the railway station.

pied with the search for some home place, one that ebbs and flows, or slips from focus and grasp like an ever-retreating mirage.

Little wonder that a century — or two — is a short time for the interactions of such painful and slow human processes to work themselves through to some secure resolution. Or that the concerns of this book are mostly with recent affairs and transactions, as these matters have clarified, consolidated, and come to a head in their natural term. To explain that maturing process. By federation, Irish immigration had ceased to be a contentious issue, although the question of the alleged disloyalty of those Irish already in the colonies was simmering, ready to explode in 1916. Controversy over Irish immigration had declined with the sharp fall in Irish migrant numbers, and with the swing towards concern with the erection of a White Australia policy. Ireland was exporting far fewer immigrants, and Australia's population fears were directed elsewhere. In their 1988 text *Sources of Australian Immigration History 1901–1945*, John Lack and Jacqueline Templeton find it unnecessary to refer to the Irish at all. It has been observed (most recently by the Chinese American novelist Maxine Hong Kingston) that, in relation to the public consciousness of immigrant groups, each wave of new arrivals generates hostility not only towards itself but to all previous such arrivals, reviving their feelings of unsettlement, tension, and insecurity. The newcomers spark off the old debates, rekindle the dead feuds, and create a situation in which the old arrivals feel compelled to emerge from their quiet settlement and assimilation to defend themselves yet again.

From the 1890s the Irish in Australia and New Zealand were spared the sporadic disruptions occasioned by the influxes of the previous century: the conflicts of the Great War period were over their role within the nation, not over whether they should be allowed to join it. The process of the Irish Australian development of a consciousness of confident belonging to where they were, was well under way before the end of the nineteenth century (if occasionally questioned), but the new century certainly saw it (ease in rightful occupancy and sense of equal ownership) confirmed, matured, and (save for 1916–21) unchallenged. That challenge, which sought to impose on Australia a narrow jingo Englishism, was firmly repulsed.

The second 'challenge' is much more recent, more general and less obvious. Indeed, it is hardly a challenge, more an erosion if seen negatively, an abrasive stimulus if seen in a positive light. It is the postulation, by some of those who do not belong to it, of a majority 'Anglo-Celtic' culture in Australia, that verbal amalgam which is both implicit compliment and term of insult and hostility. The compliment lies in the recognition of the achievement. The insult is in the hyphen, the failure to see what is Australian, what is whole.

What Australia and New Zealand have — and always have had — were colonial cultures (now a multiplicity and complexity of colonial cultures), each relating to its homeland in an increasingly tenuous and independent way. Historically, these cultures rapidly developed as characteristic, of their unique style, more what they had in common than what they held in difference, though these internal differences remained as tolerable diversities. Their growing commonalty lay in their occupying together a distant colonial place. It was this situation, its problems, its opportunities, its newness for them all, that brought them together as a distinctive people in a peculiar, particular, unique, place.

Here, then, is an exploration of the notion of colony, applied to Irish Australia and New Zealand: colony in the sense of plantation from afar, colony in the sense of new and separate growth, colony as state of free mind. And why the whole pursuit? An exploration with the purposes of Proust's wandering Celt — that its passage will stir those captive souls and their liberation will enlarge us, and make us, also, free.

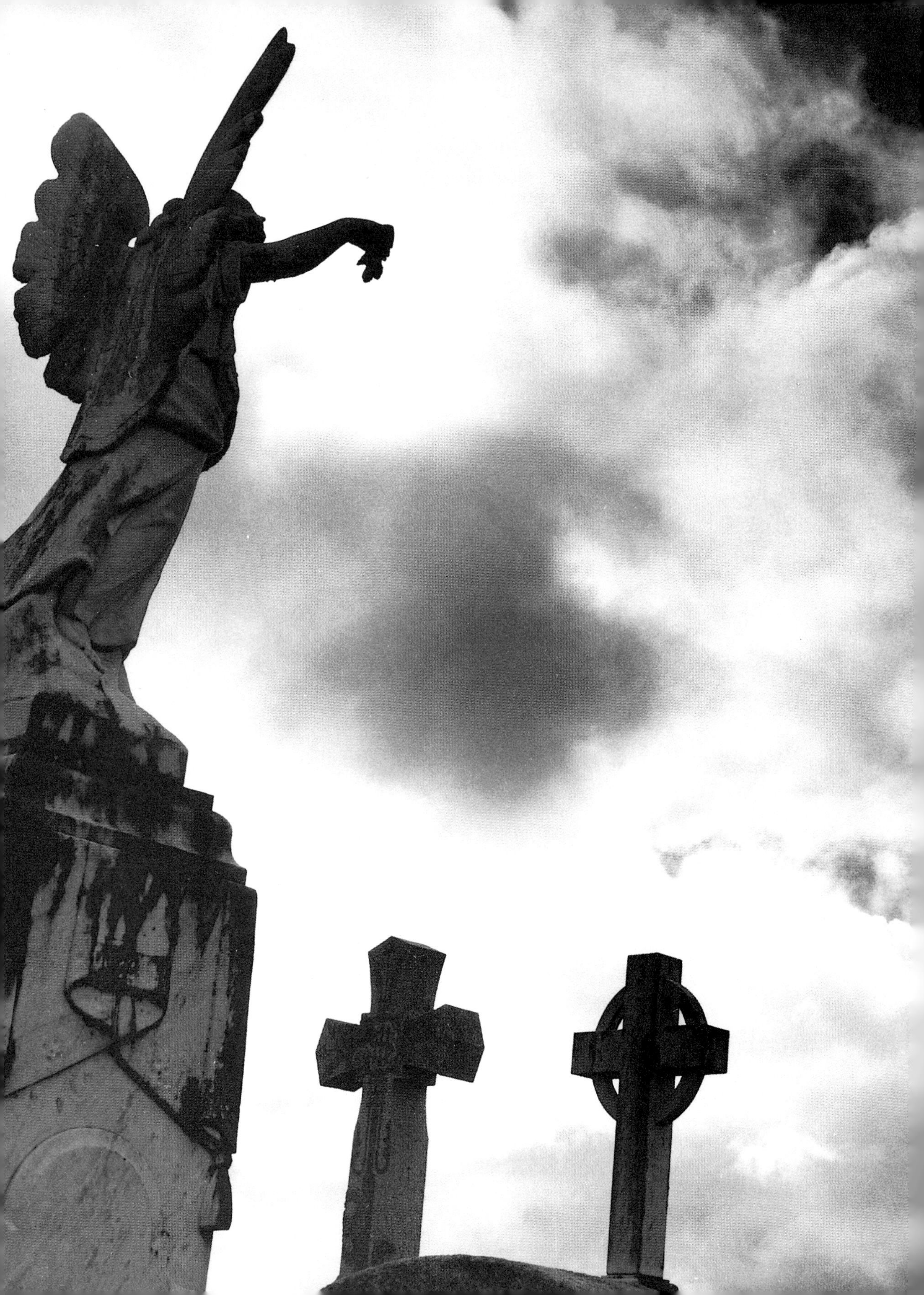

CHAPTER 1

KINGS DEPOSED? THE IRISH IN EARLY AUSTRALIA

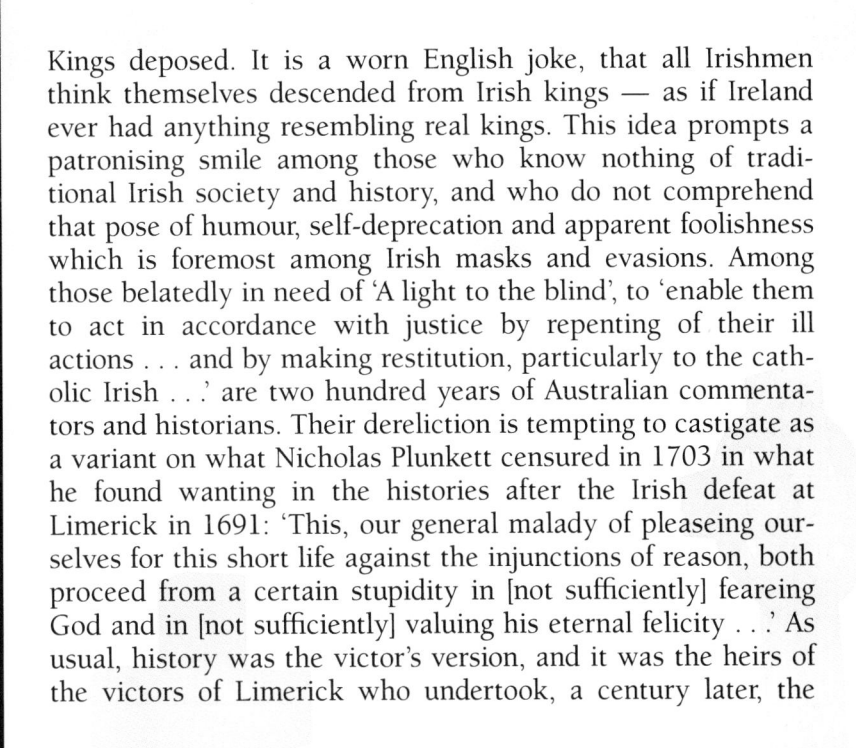

Kings deposed. It is a worn English joke, that all Irishmen think themselves descended from Irish kings — as if Ireland ever had anything resembling real kings. This idea prompts a patronising smile among those who know nothing of traditional Irish society and history, and who do not comprehend that pose of humour, self-deprecation and apparent foolishness which is foremost among Irish masks and evasions. Among those belatedly in need of 'A light to the blind', to 'enable them to act in accordance with justice by repenting of their ill actions . . . and by making restitution, particularly to the catholic Irish . . .' are two hundred years of Australian commentators and historians. Their dereliction is tempting to castigate as a variant on what Nicholas Plunkett censured in 1703 in what he found wanting in the histories after the Irish defeat at Limerick in 1691: 'This, our general malady of pleaseing ourselves for this short life against the injunctions of reason, both proceed from a certain stupidity in [not sufficiently] feareing God and in [not sufficiently] valuing his eternal felicity . . .' As usual, history was the victor's version, and it was the heirs of the victors of Limerick who undertook, a century later, the convict colonisation of Australia. In Australia historians insufficiently feared their English Protestant God (and more recently no God at all), and a blind stupidity in regard to Irish matters reigned, a condition arising, as Plunkett had perceived in his earlier world, not from a defect of the intelligence, but from a defect of the will. The traditional historical depictions (where they appear at all) of the Australian Irish, as an irrelevant underclass of pathetic peasants and stereotype rebels, are shallow to the degree of fatuity.

The proposal of a significant historical connection between Irish 'kingship' and early Australian settlement requires the support of some well-attested characteristics of the Irish emigration process, appreciated in the context of a basic and obvious fact. In contrast with the American situation, Australia at the end of the eighteenth century, at the point of its settlement by convicts — a quarter of whom were Irish — was a vacant land. For all the argument about the number and title of Aborigines, the aspect the country presented to the arrivals of 1788 and thereafter, was that it was unoccupied. Individual Irish reaction to this novel situation, and the challenges and opportunities it presented, was complex and various, but on the whole very positive — 'a fine country', 'the best country under the sun'. Complicating negativities came from two main sources — guilt and shame at their criminal transportation felt

Gentleman convicts at work and the convict 'centipede'. Port Arthur, Tasmania, 1836. (*National Library of Australia*)

particularly by 'gentlemen' convicts, those of education and social position, and the bitter resentment that some individuals harboured at what they saw as banishment from Ireland. That bitterness, in a form relevant to the 'kings deposed' argument, can be conveniently illustrated from the Irish experiences of W. Steuart Trench in the decade following the Famine. As organiser of emigration schemes on the estates of Lords Landsdowne and Bath, he saw himself as compassionate provider of free passages to far better lives in a new world. But his plans provoked wild anger, and a hostility based on a smouldering peasant belief that ancient Irish families would someday recover their forfeited estates, lands whose boundaries were known to the popular mind and were still being documented. Trench was astonished to discover, in popular circulation, a map published in 1846, which set out the kingdoms of the Irish chieftains from the eleventh to the seventeenth centuries: astounding delusions these, in the view of the nineteenth century English proprietorial mind. But, to tenants who occupied what they regarded as their own land, emigration meant that they were being finally cheated, terminally dispossessed of what they had held from time immemorial, by being driven to unknown and foreign lands across the sea.

Surely this is to over-dramatise a dreary and ordinary process, and, at any rate, these were hardly kings? Yet, dramatising their predicament was integral to much of the Irish encounter with the world, and some of them *were* kings — or near enough in Irish aristocratic status to entertain that self-estimate. Arthur Young's *Tour in Ireland (1776-1779)* reports on some of these fallen princes still living on the remnants of their own lands and style, commanding the residues of the structures of tribute and respect, once the hallmark of the entire Gaelic social order. Young's reference to such of these aristocrats who had dropped completely into the surrounding peasantry, is expanded by W.E.H. Lecky, in his very English history of eighteenth century Ireland, into romantic images heavy with literary conceit. Proud names which had graced the Annals of the Four Masters, were now to be 'found in abject poverty hanging around the land which had lately been their own, shrinking from servile labour as from an intolerable pollution and still receiving a secret homage from their old tenants'.

Whether the individual falls of these former Irish mighty took them down even further into activities deemed criminal and within the orbit of the transportation system, raises questions of particularities for future historians. But the evidence is

VANISHED KINGDOMS

Left: Evicted — Homeless. *Above*: 'Evicted —driven from the house we built.' The nationalist artist's version. *Below*: Eviction — the photographer's version, 1880s. (*National Library of Ireland*)

sufficient to be certain — and it is hardly surprising — that something, probably much, of their mental world came to early Australia. In *The Irish in Australia* I have sketched some of the reflections and expressions of the hierarchical structures of old Irish society that may be found in early Sydney and south-western New South Wales. The most particular and deliberate of these resurrections and reconstructions was that centred on the land holdings of Edward Ryan of Tipperary, transported in 1816 for fourteen years for assault and what amounted to riot, with fourteen others. From his emancipation in the 1830s, continuing even after his death in 1871, Ryan was the energising force behind an antipodean re-creation of an old Irish world.

> To describe with the staid term 'regional concentration' the Irish presence in south-west New South Wales is to diminish the reality to jargon. Here was the flamboyant creating of grouped and related family empires, adjacent and interlocking, the new dominions of the Ancient Kings of Inis Ailge, resurrected in New South Wales by the Ryans, the Corcorans, the Dwyers, and lesser lords. Here were Irish counties, whose coherence was certainly geographic and economic but whose stimulus was that of the Irish heart and mind. King of Galong Castle aptly describes Ned Ryan, his home not the Anglo-Irish big house, but in the style of the functional Gaelic culture that preceded it. His squatting acres were appropriate to an Irish kingdom, reputed in family imagination to be 100 000 square miles, a tract the size of Ireland. His personal style, gruff, quick-tempered, and his lavish hospitality fitted the lordly image, as did his patriarchal persuasion of many labourers from Tipperary to join him. His son, John Nagle Ryan, sustained the tradition: 'Everything was on a scale of barbaric grandeur not elsewhere to be enjoyed'. Barbaric grandeur — the phrase captures the flavour of these rough kings in their primitive vigorous courts.

Nor did the surviving remnants of the old Gaelic order abandon traditional obligations when dependants were transported to Australia as a consequence of service in their cause. Philip Cunningham, leader of the most significant convict rebellion, at Castle Hill outside Sydney in 1804, had been, in the Ireland of the 1798 rebellion, part of the rebel Irish network that eddied around the parish of Glin in Kerry, dominated by its ancient and famous Irish knighthood. That noble knight of Glin continued until 1817 to attempt, by petitioning local authorities and the British government, to retrieve his transported local retainers from Botany Bay — successfully in the case of Tom Langan.

Early Irish society in Australia — within its own internal

relationships — was a traditional Gaelic one, that is, deeply hierarchical, aristocratic, operating on ancient place, family and social distinctions. Such is a natural conclusion, however much this belated insight goes against the standard Australian mythology that all the Irish were egalitarian proletarians: this superficiality is the external English view, looking down. The Irish saw themselves as a distinct, complex civilisation organised on the basis of family structures and familial territories. The 1851 maps of south-western New South Wales, by the government surveyor J. Larmer, recording the Ryan and related holdings, were an Australian echo — indeed, realisation — of that 1846 Irish map affirming ancient territoriality that had so astonished W. Steuart Trench. There were hierarchies within and between the families of this traditional culture, and in Ireland itself its leaders (lost) and its values (hidden beneath the English overlay) were celebrated by an aristocracy of poets, whose poems were central to popular oral culture. Stripped of power, such Irish found identity in such poetry, whose spirit is captured in the title of a recent collection *Poems of the Dispossessed (1600–1900)*. The word implies other things those Irish brought to Australia: pride, resentment, the thirst for vengeance, and, of course, moods of failure and shame, a sense of loss, hopelessness, ruin, and sheer dogged refusal to further yield. This was a complex — and

1798 Memorial, Wexford, Ireland: an Irish Pikeman (*Bord Failte Photo*)

Ned Ryan's original 'Castle', Galong, New South Wales, now built into the Redemptorist monastery.

highly sophisticated — mixture; but the orthodox canon of Australian history, following the level of comprehension of the colony's first gaolers, has rendered this down to a primitive rebel yell, a low peasant violence. This assumption of primitivity has totally submerged any record of, or reference to that dimension of the Irish consciousness of themselves as being overwhelmed in the seventeenth century by a scum-tide of low-born traitors and infidels, whose very names were a bitter farce: the plebeian Cromwellian surnames — Black, Brown, White — generated contempt among an Irishry conscious of superior nobility. So, if at the foundations of Australian settlement the English colonisers judged themselves in Shakespearian terms as a noble breed, the traditional Irish view was that, whatever their power, here were social and cultural inferiors — 'a crew from the land of Dover', contemptible upstart nobodies. In contrast, the fettered Irish knew their genealogy, they knew who they were and where they came from: they were the subjects of — they were — kings deposed and banished.

What importance has this for early Australian history, that first phase of it — up to the 1840s — which is heir in part to Ireland's eighteenth century? It suggests, for the first time, a hidden Ireland in Australia's wilderness: not the criminal outcasts of a poor and primitive peasant mob, not just waifs and strays, the pathetic flotsam of a shipwreck that was conquered Ireland, but the survivors — however maimed and diminished — of a proud culture of great antiquity, with their own language, civilisation and value structure. Here had been dumped, as compulsory pioneers, representatives of a history untouched by either Renaissance or Reformation, medieval in outlook, continental European in orientation, with a poetry of loss and protest integral to their modes of thought — and each one of these vital characteristics at variance and conflict with the dominant English culture of the new colony. It would be hard to over-estimate the potential impact on Australian historical perceptions of any significant recovery of this long hidden dimension.

Why so long hidden, and hidden still? In part, for the reasons so long applicable in Ireland itself. Australia was an English colony. Its historians took — still take — an English view of appearances, accept English priorities, reflect Protestant value-judgments. The sub-world of Irish Catholics had no real existence for historians who wrote from and about the walled gardens of the establishment. The questions they asked, the issues they addressed, the troubles that concerned them,

Of Your Charity
Pray for
BRIDGET MARY BROWNE
AGED 87 YEARS
R.I.P.
MARY O'NEILL
RYAN
OF YOUR CHARITY
FOR THE SOUL OF
ANASTASIA HERBERT
AGED 60 YEARS
RYAN
FAITH
HOPE
Of Your Charity
FOR THE SOULS
OF BURROW

have been those of a dying British colonialism, matters of importance certainly, but at a tangent to the positive issues that have stirred ordinary Australians. The essential irrelevance, to Irish Australian issues at least, of the labours of Australia's historical profession has continued to the present, a situation exemplified in the publication in 1987 of the final, sixth, volume of C.M.H. Clark's *A History of Australia*. Prodigious achievement that it was, this masterwork remains a highly idiosyncratic testament from a once dominant Protestant elite, lamenting its own demise, and taken up with its own present confusions and torments. The only place for Irish Catholics in this establishment tradition, and in the labour-history Marxist and secular historicising that grew both out of it and in ideological opposition to it, was as members of the labour movement and, peripherally, of the Catholic church — real but only partial aspects of their full identity. So, the narrow professional structures of Australia's historical profession have squeezed out, as in the operations of some elite club, the wider concerns and character of the underclass: and that class has accepted, until recently, the WASP definition of both game and rules.

An expansion of Australian history, from the affairs of its dominant garrison into the environment of all that is human, is a by-product of the very recent concept of multi-culturalism. Consciousness of the immigration process itself as a formative cultural factor in Australia has long existed: witness the strand of hostility to Irish immigration that runs through Australian history since the 1830s. But the traditional prevailing assumption, formalised into government policy from 1947 to deal with the post-war flood of culturally diverse immigration, was that of migrant assimilation. This posited a single Australian entity and identity, which newcomers joined and in which they were absorbed. The old exclusivist concept of the one Australian self was one which rejected any idea of immigrant significance: immigrants became real, had meaning and significance, only when they vanished into the main body of society, that is, ceased to be their former selves (a proposition which is an obvious historical nonsense). This kind of supposedly monolithic Australia could have only one history, which could be written, only about and by those whose lives, values and concerns were at its alleged centre. That centre was defined strictly and exclusively as the domain of majority power, wealth and cultural orientation: Australia had meaning and significance only in relation to Britain, or in effect, England.

The multi-cultural view rejected this. Its application to the

The Ryan graves (centre) at Galong cemetery.

ethnically diverse situation that has transformed Australia since 1947 is obvious and inescapable. Applied to earlier times, back to 1788, it highlights in particular the Irish, and what becomes evident is its potential revolutionary impact, its radically solvent effect on the prevailing WASP canon: the previous orthodoxies need to be abandoned and Australian history re-conceived.

Central to this is the 'hidden Ireland' crucial to Australia's origins. This is to borrow the theme and title of a book first published in Dublin in 1924, Daniel Corkery's *The Hidden Ireland*. Its theme was the persistence, beneath the surface of British occupation, of a hidden Gaelic nation into the eighteenth century, preserved through a great literary tradition and popular poets. The question of the influence of both concept and book on the writing of history in Ireland itself is open to debate. Despite L.M. Cullen's indications that this influence has been considerable, it is open to suggestion that it was not until the publication in 1982 of S.J. Connolly's *Priests and People in Pre-Famine Ireland* that the consequences of the spillover implications of this insight for Australian history became evident. That the direct relevance of Corkery's work went unnoticed in Australia is hardly surprising, given the compartmentalising common to all historians and the particular blindness of Australian historians to the Irish dimension. In now accepting that relevance, Cullen's 1969 re-assessment in *Studia Hibernica* of the Hidden Ireland concept needs to be borne in mind, but this critique and qualifications bear largely on its place in Irish history, not on the general drift and question-generating capacities that constitute its value in the re-appraisal of Australian history.

With then, the general idea of a hidden Ireland in mind, roughly of the kind depicted by Corkery, let us turn to that most pervasive and entrenched of traditional myths about the Australian Irish — that they were all rebel underdogs, passionate for equality. This was the face presented to the overlords when the hidden Ireland surfaced, beneath notice save when troublesome — as in the various scares before and after the convict rebellion of 1804. Such was the view from above, crammed with erroneous assumptions that have become historical orthodoxy — that the Irish were levellers, undifferentiated peasantry, ignorant. In fact, they were strongly hierarchical, steeped in a poetic culture, and conceded no inferiority save that compelled by coercion and by their shortcomings in mastery of the language of their conquerors and gaolers.

Anonymous, and of stone. This Irish grave at Grabben Gullen, New South Wales, symbolised both absence from the historical record, and enduring presence in the land.

This linguistic situation does much to explain their absence from early Australian history. The Irish influence on English-language Australian folk songs, bush ballads and verse has been long recognised. One of the earliest such practitioners was Francis Mac Namara, a Corkman, convicted of larceny at Kilkenny in 1832, who styled himself in the Irish form, Frank the Poet. His best known piece, 'A Convict's Tour of Hell', written in 1839, has features familiar to those acquainted with the verse of the Hidden Ireland: an informed literary, classical and Christian reference, a strong touch of anti-clericalism, indeed a tendency to ridicule religion, and the placing of the poet on a level with the aristocracy, in this case, that of Heaven. It is written in English, in the style of the popular rhymester. Thus:

> Kind sir, I came from Sydney Gaol,
> My name I don't mean to conceal,
> And, since you seem anxious to know it
> On earth I was called Frank the Poet.

The exercise is sustained over two hundred lines and is full of incident and personages, but what it most lacks is literary quality. Mac Namara is a very poor imitator in English of a great Gaelic tradition, then exhausted for new invention but still carrying the momentum of its classics. One such, at a level of the ordinary to which Mac Namara's efforts might be compared, was Eoghan Rua Ó Súilleabháin's poetic order to Seamus Fitzgerald for a new handle for his spade, a bravura lyric performance which transforms the underdog into a figure of heroic art. Ó Súilleabháin, born in Kerry in 1748, died in 1784. It can be reasonably assumed that his poetry came to Australia, with a whole Gaelic oral culture like it. Reasonably assumed: because this is popular poetry which immediately predates Australia's white settlement, because Eoghan Rua was still quoted in Irish-speaking districts in Munster into this century, because many of those Irish transportees who came to Australia spoke Gaelic and had English — if they had it at all — as a second language, and because they came from a poetic tradition. Over little else did they have power, little else did they own, save the magic of words, their own words. Given all sensible qualification, and allowance for roseate depiction, Corkery's observation of the people of eighteenth century Ireland must have some truth for the Irish of early Australia. In the eyes of the authorities, here was a rabble of common felons and preachers of sedition. But beneath the appearances of

A convict chain gang in Van Diemens' Land (*National Library of Australia*)

Life on the Goldfields: a ball at Araluen, 1867. (*Illustrated Sydney News*)

ignorance and shiftless poverty was the proud tribe of minstrels and scholars, with their once kings and nobles, their obsession with family and lineage, their consciousness of old and superior civilisation.

Evidence? The possibility having not been raised, a search has hardly begun. A fragment from half a century later. In the 1850s, Father Maurice Stack of Listowel, County Kerry, was appointed to the Bendigo goldfields area in Victoria to minister to miners, many of whom, it is said, knew only Irish. Protestant miners threatened his ejectment, leading to a fight in which the Catholic Irish defended their priest and then took up a collection for him. He acknowledged this the following Sunday with a poem in which a Gaelic line alternated with one in English. Here it is, all in English:

> The full of a fist of gold from
> Tadhg Reaskavalla
> and twice as much more from the two rakes of Mallow
> Twelve ounces from Donal O Braon
> who has strayed far away from his native Asdee;
> Ten pounds and more from Peter Conroy
> that big-hearted giant from the banks of the Moy;
> A big yellow nugget from my friend John Higgins
> the pluckiest lad to be found in the diggings.
> There's no need for me to praise big strapping Fitzgerald
> God bless his two fists, sure they're harder than steel.
> I regret to have heard that Billy Rockett lost
> all the gold that he had through a hole in his pocket.
> Go you on home and don't you forget the collection
> [we'll hold] this forthcoming Sunday.

LAND RIGHTS NOW

KINGS DEPOSED? THE IRISH IN EARLY AUSTRALIA

This a light-hearted display of mild wit, but the alternate Gaelic/English construction, with interaction in rhyming between the two languages, is significant in several ways. Its bi-lingualism highlights the movement into English imperative in Australian conditions; its character indicates an audience which found it appropriate, and the verbal gymnastics demonstrate the paramount concern of the Irish poetic tradition with technique, with brilliance of style. The English emphasised content, the meaning, the message. With the Irish, the medium came first. Their delight was in the games that could be played with words, the effects that could be contrived by mastery of technical skills — the expression of a very different mind-set.

The existence of American examples, as late as 1900, of high quality poetic relics of the court culture of these dispossessed Irish, suggests the possibility of Australian equivalents. The emotions of alienation — the notion that foreign soil was mean or hostile — expressed in America, were common to the Irish experience of Australia. But, of course, the nature of the historical situation is against their discovery. Even in Ireland itself what is known of the hidden Ireland is fragmentary, partial, and the position of a subordinate, dying, and oral culture in Australian convict and colonial circumstances was radically more tenuous. Nor did Australia have the retrieval processes of a Gaelic revival, nor scholarly structures such as led to the Irish Folk-Lore Commission, to catch the vestigial traces of vanishing antiquities: and the few Gaelic scholars across Australia's history were interested in the culture of Ireland itself, not in its possible relics in Australia.

Yet, there are numerous incidents in the orthodox sources that permit, indeed invite, reinterpretation in line with the Corkery thesis. An example. Early colonial journals record Irish convicts escaping into the bush, with the idea, so they said, of walking to China. Was this merely the pathetic ignorance of simple men? Perhaps. The proposal and discussion of the absurd as though it were serious and real is a long-observed aptitude of the Irish; it is a variation on their beloved word games, a snare for the unwary foreigner, and an aspect of the clowning with which they masked themselves and expressed contempt for the stupidity of their oppressors. 'Why are we escaping? Tell the fools we are walking to China.' 'We found', wrote Captain Watkin Tench in 1793, 'the convicts

Inset: 'The Aborigines were not the only ancients who peopled early Australia'.

Harp and shamrock reflect the Australian scene, Galong, New South Wales.

particularly happy in fertility of invention and exaggerated descriptions' — which is not necessarily quite as simple a situation as is conveyed in the comment of today's historian Geoffrey Blainey: 'Never had so many liars been gathered together.' The demand for a prosaic and factual attitude to the truth was a cultural imperative not always accepted as necessary or appropriate by the Irish. Uncomprehending judgments of such variant behaviour attempt to cram these strange persons into foreign categories they do not in fact occupy.

Above all, the real Irish self, with its dimensions and echoes of exiled kings, was not a simple prisoner in convict Australia. The penal colony, and the immigrant Australia that followed it, was a school of reform and opportunity for the Irish in a way which has not yet been appreciated. Gaelic Ireland at the end of the eighteenth century was a society in dissolution. As Corkery puts it, the Lord of Misrule governed everything: it was a land of extraordinary slatternliness — slatternliness and recklessness. It was a climate verging on hysteria in which misery collapsed into laughter, in which the populace at all levels lived from day to day, and in which the governing principle was impulse . . . impulse to join the army, to emigrate, to resort to anarchic violence, explode into some kind of escaping action. Sheer mad impulse was behind much crime, and thus transportation. Here was a society in which the larger and longer disorder of foreign conquest and exploitation had leeched and corroded downward to produce a pervasive irresponsibility in family and individual, in which any abundance went with neglect. Disorder was a central principle of Irish life: they took fun in ruin.

The problems of this society were more complex than those of collapse. Below its surface of dissolution, the core of Gaelic Ireland was medieval, with little sense of measured time, and organised on a basis essentially feudal — that is, with a territorial aristocracy of family chiefs, and a society and economy based on land. It was not only in political rebellion against the English, but pitted against all that was new and modern, as being traitorous and foreign. It claimed a monopoly of the national spirit, of being Irish, and imposed on its emigrants — who were often its most energetic, innovative and prosperous members — a sense of guilt and a totally unmerited feeling of failure as they were involved in the powerful resentments of an old Gaelic order rebelling against its own destruction.

What did the early Irish, bond and free, conditioned by this ancient mental world, find in convict Australia? Orthodox historical investigation and debate has been concerned with the kind of definitional question asked in the lead article in a recent issue of Australia's premier professional historical journal *Historical Studies*: 'Free society, penal colony, slave society, prison?' Or to render this line of enquiry down to best-seller level, was Australia Robert Hughes's *The Fatal Shore*? Current revisionism has taken the position that such labels are unhelpful in understanding what was a unique society, but categorisation persists, as does the tendency to judge that society by present-day standards and modern expectations. But are such approaches, however appropriate as intellectual exercises, adequate to understanding one vital aspect of that historical situation: how it was viewed by its inhabitants, in this case, convicts from eighteenth century Gaelic Ireland? How did they see, and experience, this unique society?

The answer is: in the light of what they had left behind in Ireland and the projection of their unique, antique aspirations and dreams. Or, to step past the agonies of banishment, the dizziness and confusion, the perils and punishments: as an ideal Irish feudal society, a practical implementation of — indeed a veritable school in — the lost, poetic and tradition-familiar perfections of the old Gaelic order. Surely this is an absurd proposition to entertain in regard to what was, soft or hard, essentially a convict settlement? Negative, repellent images of convict society are natural to a modern mind situated in a liberal, organised, efficient and democratic society. But to those who came from disorder, anarchy and chaos, from a variety of personal bedlams, early Australia — at least beyond the constraints of the actual prison system and to an extent even within them — offered all the attractions and advantages of a disciplined society: order, security, productivity. The convict system, opening on to a ticket of leave and emancipation, seemed a marvellous resolution and quietude to many of the frantic victims of Ireland's Lords of Misrule, and so they testified in surviving convict letters. True, some rebelled even further against prison coercion to become permanent recidivists; and some, when freed, reverted to chaos: habituated in irresponsibility, they could not abide any organisation or settlement, and a disorganised squandering strain in Australian farming history witnesses to this tradition of prodigal neglect. But for most, the early colony produced a happy transformation. Its order was of a kind that — strange harmony of contrasts — aspired to traditional Gaelic Ireland's ideal: the penal colonies offered an ideal version of the customary system, one that was relatively efficient and beneficent.

This is why the Irish transportees in the main so readily conformed and embraced the system. When they recovered — those who did — from the trauma of their transportation, they became aware that, if they kept its rules, they were in an idealised form of the society that they had left behind, left behind not only in Ireland but in time. That this should be so, latent in the Irish mind, was not a reaction peculiar to Australia.

Half a century later, gold-rush California — it has been contended — had a related impact on the Irish imagination. In *California: The Irish Dream* (1988) Patrick J. Dowling devotes a first chapter to the myth of Oisin and Tir-na-nog, by way of introduction of the idea that California was not only El Dorado (the usual, but Spanish, dream word) but, more relevantly in the mentalities of Irish immigrants, the actualisation of the fabled Irish Land of Eternal Youth and prosperity. It was myth about to come true; and what followed by way of anticipation and disposition to reality, was conditioned by the initial marvellous vision: optimists' paradise, the mirage always on the horizon; pessimist's desolation, as reality proved a cheat. For a brief time Australia offered a kind of shadow vision of an order that had vanished in Ireland, existing there (if it ever had) only in the laments of the poets.

What these Irish saw was not what a modern eye sees — the harsh inhuman prison of English appearances. They saw a tightly disciplined social order of a feudal kind, hierarchically structured, with the lord at its head and his nobles and barons — in other words, the colonial governor, and his officers and administrators — graduating down the scale, in a system which depended on a mixture of force, patronage, punishment and rewards. It was a landed society and a rural economy. There were no, or very few, middlemen, those traditional exploiters of the Irish; and no levies of tribute. And it was a society starved of labour; thus, the bargaining power of the labourer was very great — again a sharp and beneficent contrast to the Irish situation. Or simply, here was a society whose structures and operation the Irish could readily understand; it was familiar to their imaginations and desires, as a reversion to their old tradition, rid of the deformities, malfunctions and disintegrations that had overtaken that world in Ireland (indeed some of these excellent features had never existed there) and open to their individual endeavours to succeed.

Moreover, those more lax dimensions of early colonial society, its roughness, its drinking, its informality, its remoteness, every aspect of its primitive pioneering disposition as a

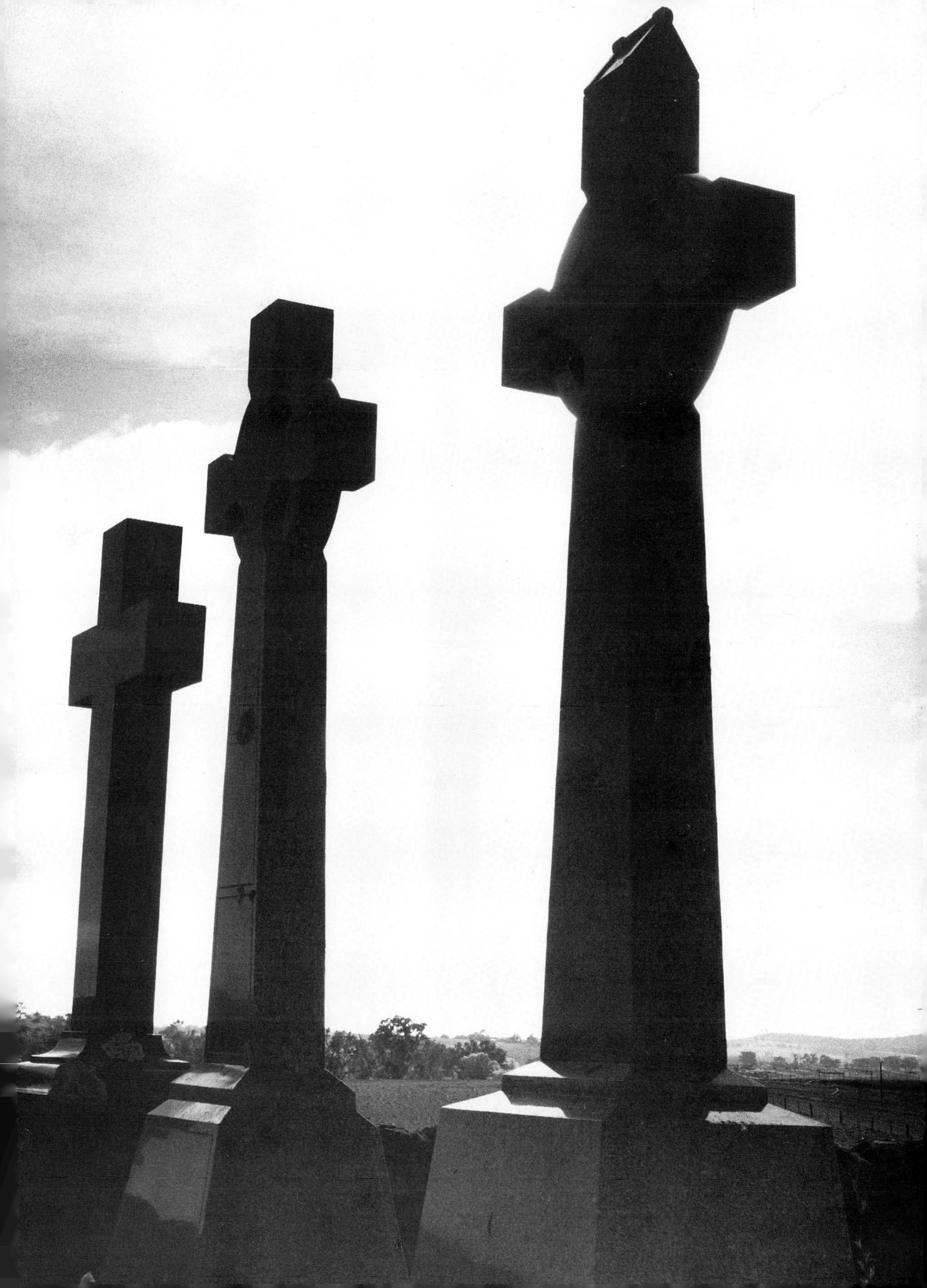

society, chimed in with the temper and style of the old Irish world. That style was epitomised in the kingship of Red Hugh O'Donnell in the 1590s, just prior to the 'Flight of the earls' in 1607 — that great symbolic image of the departure from Ireland into European exile of the last of the traditional Gaelic chieftains. To the English, what seemed like anarchy was fluidity, an aristocratic society characterised by mobility and a strong sense of family, where war had the elements of sport, and where Red Hugh was a paragon, as a contemporary chronicler had it, 'having large followings, holding meetings, being generous, joyous, roaming, restless, quarrelsome, aggressive . . .' Here, writ large and bold, was the style that enraged and disgusted the English — and took Ned Ryan's inherited and milder fancy at Galong, New South Wales, two hundred and fifty years later. The enemy of Gaelic Ireland was not so much the English as such, as modernisation. The invention of Australia allowed the Irish to step back again into their past, or rather, an idealised version of it, until the 1840s at least. Then, it was not the English who transformed Irish Australia, but new waves of anglicised Irish immigrants, equipped with the English language, English education, and an English view, caught from Daniel O'Connell, of the primacy of politics. And, of course, the 1840s brought the arrival in force of that other major agency of Irish modernisation, the Catholic church, dedicated to the death of pagan Ireland and of the pre-Christian civilisation that had sustained the old Irish world.

Insofar as it has been comprehended at all, the historical understanding of the Irish in Australia has been dominated by stereotypes generated since the 1840s by Irish nationalism and Catholicism. That has left virtually half a century, since 1788, as a kind of pre-history, unexplored. The contention here, at a point at the very beginning of the search for evidence, is that early Irish Australia was a strange reversional fragment of the Hidden Ireland of the eighteenth century and centuries before, a historically unrecognised protraction of antiquity into modern colonial times. The Aborigines were not the only ancients who peopled early Australia.

But these Irish were ancients with a dynamic difference, products of a mobile, restless society, liberated by Australian openness and possessed of the belief that all could be aristocrats in Australia, the land of free men. From their perspective, Australian egalitarianism — the proposition that all should be equal as men — was not a process of levelling down, the demolition of hierarchies and class barriers (the great socialist illusion), but the opportunity for all to level up, be aristocrats of an archaic kind, like Red Hugh — free-living, taking one's ease, restless, generous and so on. It was, of course, the great Irish illusion: all should be kings and behave like kings. Grand illusion indeed, and better by far than the search for the commonality of serfs. It was this optimist's illusion that was the gut attraction of the aristocratic Irish to the Labor Party (added to the obvious social and economic factors) and it was the spell of that illusion that mesmerised their descendants almost to the present. Only in that present were those would-be kings, hopeful bestowers of universal kingship, finally dethroned and disillusioned — their kingdoms had vanished, idealism sold out for money and power, bartered for popularity and the fashionable fix.

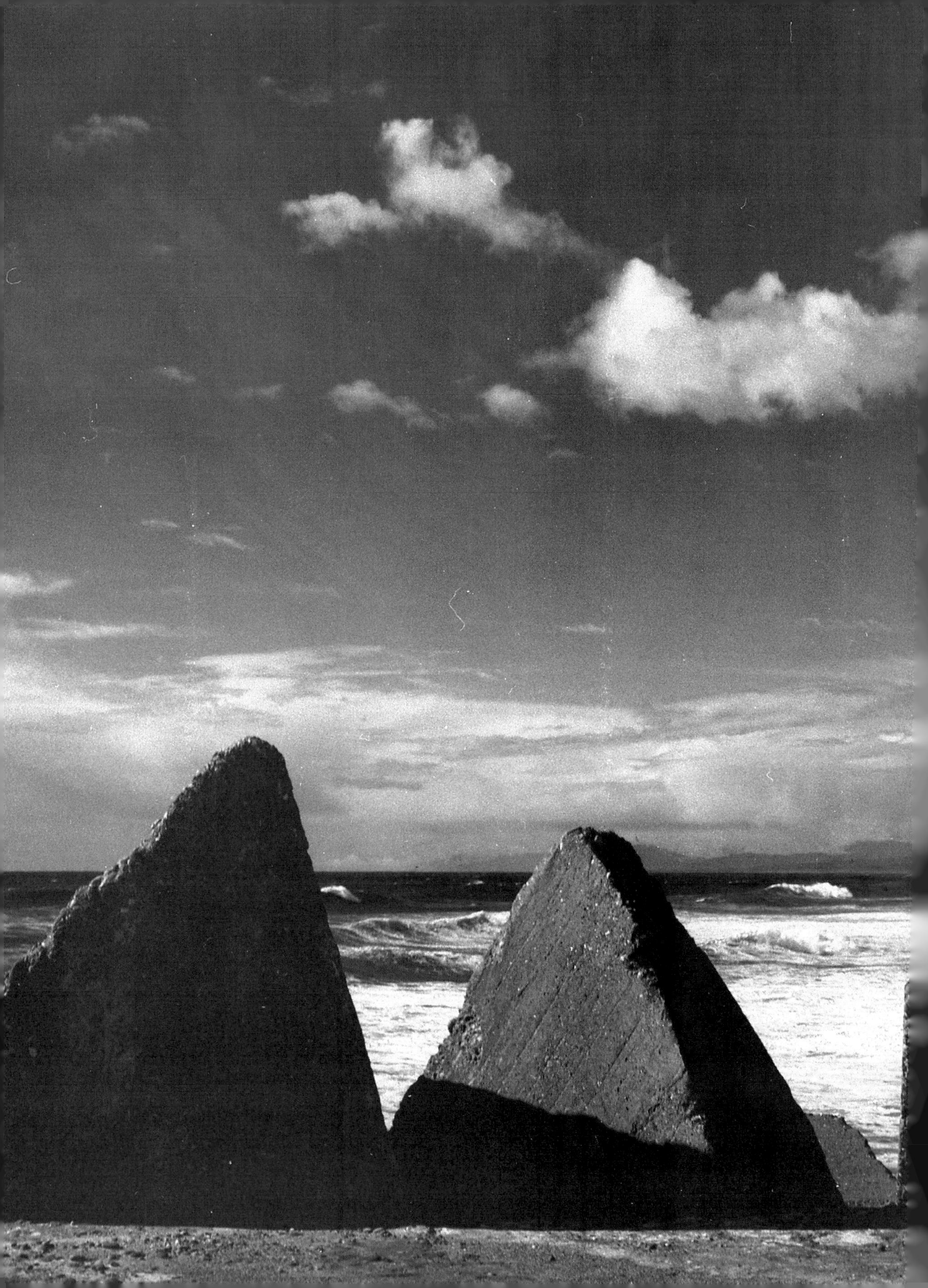

CHAPTER 2

IDIOCY AND DEVILMENT

On 15 November 1911 my uncle Michael Farrell (whom I never met) wrote from the small farming centre of Morven in South Canterbury, New Zealand, to my father to be (Dear Paddy), who was in Ireland. It was a long letter, each page boldly emblazoned with the official blue-enclouded heading of the Womens' Christian Temperance Union, with its motif of a be-ribboned globe, on which was inscribed 'All round the world our ribbon white is twined', with a curiously ecumenical bow, reading 'Every God and Home Land'.

Hardly predictable stationery to convey persuasion towards a lifetime's relocation, or answer the question of why come here to earth's end. Or was Ireland already in the mind earth's stagnant end, and the new, distant place — wherever it was — earth's start? Go, is the operative word in my immediate family case, Tipperary father and mother: some are great shakes for leaving, others for arriving, some stay still. Well before the twentieth century no one really emigrated first. There was always somebody before, if not to here, then to somewhere else — America, Canada, Argentina. Irish emigration was a continuous historical process with pushes and pulls, ebbs and flows, diverse destinations but, for the individual it

Greymouth, New Zealand, breakwater, 1981.

always began at some middle stage, some situation half-way through — and stopped. There were those who went before, but with and for that individual emigrant it ended. Colonial descendants were not Irish. Nor, soon or late, quick or slow, were the emigrants/immigrants themselves. They were less Irish or more, but undoubtedly different. The impulse, the invitation, to go, leave, was much more than that: it was the choice to be changed radically, and much of the surface scene of Irish colonial history consisted of the pretence that this was not so.

The Women's Christian Temperance Union notepaper was long a puzzlement. Was my uncle writing from some home for alcoholics? Certainly, the Women's Christian Temperance Union was strong and active in South Canterbury. Emigration was a serious business demanding earnest attention — so I once thought. Now I wonder what might have been the circumstances of that notepaper's mischievous thievery, the misappropriation of exotic, irrelevant and unlikely stationery being later revealed as a family eccentricity: silly juvenilia some would undoubtedly dub it. In fact, it was one of the expressions of the Irish mask, to achieve a confusing contradiction between medium and message, to place the beholder in a quandary; to both evade and score. So the zig-zag content of my uncle's letter is in triple counterpoint to its pretentious high-flown letterhead, and to the sharp see-sawing shifts of mood and tone (within an instant) — that startling ambivalence of part-game, part-serious pursuit, that Irish emigration had become. It was a mixture of grin and genuine sentiment, fun and dead earnestness, that had always lain at the heart of the Irish emigrant attitude, but which the miseries of the

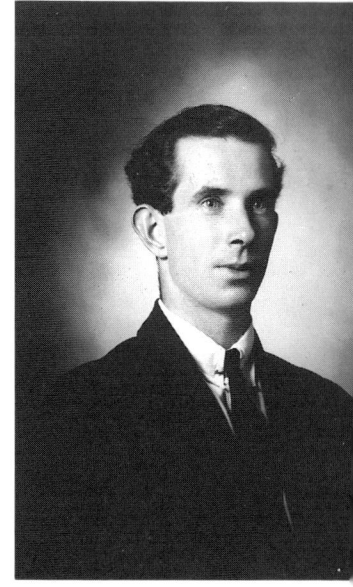

Paddy, in 1916.

Borrisokane, about the time of Paddy and Mai's departure.

nineteenth century had tended to crush or bury. (The Irish were fully conscious of developments within their own evolving emigrant history: certain behaviour modes were perceived as old-fashioned. When my uncle Mattie married in Ireland in July 1920, and left for New Zealand the next day, Father Matt Fogarty, family friend and priest in Rangiora, remarked to my mother: 'He was married to Nannie Calahan & then set sail for a far away land the following day. It sounds like old times, the sailing days'. Romantic perhaps, but now odd, and a bit questionable as matrimonial policy.)

As a setting for emigration, the Ireland of the twentieth century was significantly different from the famine-dominated half-century that had preceded it. The habit of emigration had become deeply ingrained in the whole attitude and outlook of the Irish people, a mind-frame which carried its own momentum. But the Ireland of 1900 was a much more hopeful and prosperous place, in comparison to the misery that characterised the period of highest migration, the 1840s to the 1880s. Then, in 1903, the Wyndham Land Act effected the beginning of a resolution of the fundamental, historic land question: tenants began to buy out landlords, using British Treasury loans. In seeking the stimulus behind continuing emigration, the nineteenth century image of starving refugees is no longer as meaningful, nor are overwhelming economic pressures generally. These still existed, but more often softened, and translated into their social manifestations, and personalised down into individual circumstances. Positively, and Ulster Protestant families were notable for this, emigration is seen as a family investment, an opportunity offered to, or encouraged in such family as were surplus to the farm; a setting up in some more promising foreign environment. Negatively — and this was the case in relation to my father — Ireland's economy had produced (a phenomenon exported in part to the colonies) a segment of marriages in which there were major age differences between an older husband and a younger wife. Such was Paddy's family, and when his father died, his mother married again — a common practice and often an economic necessity. Paddy disliked his step-father — again, something of a cliché situation, and one which altered his relationship with his mother. He was, then, (and his brothers and sisters with him) doubly open to the traditional Irish climate favouring emigration: he had no love for his step-father and his mother was being taken care of in the new marriage situation.

More than this, there must have been social intricacies,

nationalist ones: his father was a member of the Royal Irish Constabulary, a policeman. For that reason, the family must have been a little set apart, not only for the obvious reason — even the most popular policemen were distanced by their profession and role, and by their inevitable identification with the government of Britain — but because they were 'foreigners' to the district, and had the security and comparative affluence of government employment. Farrell was not a Tipperary name, but a Longford one, and it had long been British practice not to station police or military in their home counties. Whether Paddy's father had been affected by this policy directly, or it lay somewhere in the past, the policeman's lot — and that of his family — in the late nineteenth and early twentieth century Ireland, was inevitably not one of full and happy community integration.

As well, a tailoring apprenticeship in his late teens took him away from his village birthplace, Ballinderry, outside Borrisokane in Tipperary, to the nearest largish town, Nenagh, twelve miles away: he had already left his immediate home environment, was on his way. Or was he? Whatever the general stimulus to, or habit of, emigration prevailing in Ireland, whatever the attractions of foreign parts, in recollection it was one specific personal factor that took Paddy out of Ireland — dislike of his step-father. The mass continuing exodus that was Irish emigration attracts the broad explanatory generalisation — the economy drove them out, they were lured by gold, or land; the temptation is to lump all emigrants together. Yet, behind the big imperatives, the large themes, are the myriads of individual cases with their own private reasons or rationalisations. And their own choice of pace, swift or slow. The time that elapsed between Michael's letter and Paddy's emigration — two years — suggests that it was no automatic reaction, no impulse or foregone conclusion, but one requiring consideration, balancing, perhaps also the accumulation of a little money. Or was it, like so many momentous decisions in human affairs, made in an instant (the first encounter with step-father?) but long drawn out in implementation?

The year 1911 was modern times, with modern cautions and ambivalences. So my Uncle Michael's letter to his brother Paddy was not a simple encouragement to emigrate. He inquired how was Paddy's tailoring trade now his apprenticeship was over. Perhaps he now liked it enough to stay. Or was he impatient to begin 'ploughing the raging main'? If so, 'There is one thing I can assure no matter when you roam or whatever lands you view, you will never see a place like our

The Emigrant Stereotype — driven from home to happiness and prosperity abroad.

Nenagh. There is one thing I can tell you also, roaming beyond the seas isn't as nice as some people think'. Yet, against this: 'there is no doubt but you will do well in this colony. I am just telling you so as you will know'. The world held nothing like Nenagh (ancient farming town, secure in its past, familiar with friends) but the colony meant looking forward, not back. Michael had similar advice for others who might enquire if they should come out. Please yourself. 'For Paddy, a lot of fellows go mad after coming out.' Cody from Armagh drowned himself, he was so lonely: an English chap blew his brains out not far from here. As for himself — hospital: 'I got severe blood poisoning — very near did for me. I had a great time when I got convalescent. Had a good time with the nurses. They are hard doers' — a phrase more innocent in its flirting 1911 connotations than it later became. But tell no one of his illness, not a word. Met Tom Houlihan from Ballinderry: 'he's a devil, has travelled all over Australia'. What it was to be foot-loose and fancy free, a Ballinderry man roving the world, his freedom seeming virtually licentious, untrammelled by the normal; amazing devilry this appearing and vanishing, next heard of three places else. What example, what temptation! More Ballinderry gossip, fed back: 'I heard Molly was married to Mick Costello. I believe it's true. Were you at the wedding? For Heaven's sake tell me all about it when writing'. A cruel tease this surely — or another Molly: it was my mother's pet name. More local news: poor Willie Kealty was in the asylum, a fate that seemed to loom close and real and frequent in these tiny close Irish communities.

Back to the colonies. Michael reported that their sister Hannah had given up dressmaking. When, and in what circumstances she had come to New Zealand is unclear, but the change in her employment makes a general point: how often the colonies allowed an escape from some Ireland-imposed drudgery, the safe unimaginative employment that would never let you down — or let you free to be, or find, yourself. Hannah had begun a confectionery and fruit business in Waimate in South Canterbury, which, added Michael, is just the nice little town for you, Paddy, to start up in with your tailoring, and to keep me company. So much for the impartial please yourself pros and cons with which the letter began. Now it was, let's get the family together out here. No mention of course of parents: all detested step-father.

Tailors at work in Belfast, in a large outfitting firm, Marshalls, of High Street.

Remembrance of Nenagh. The imposing church is Anglican.

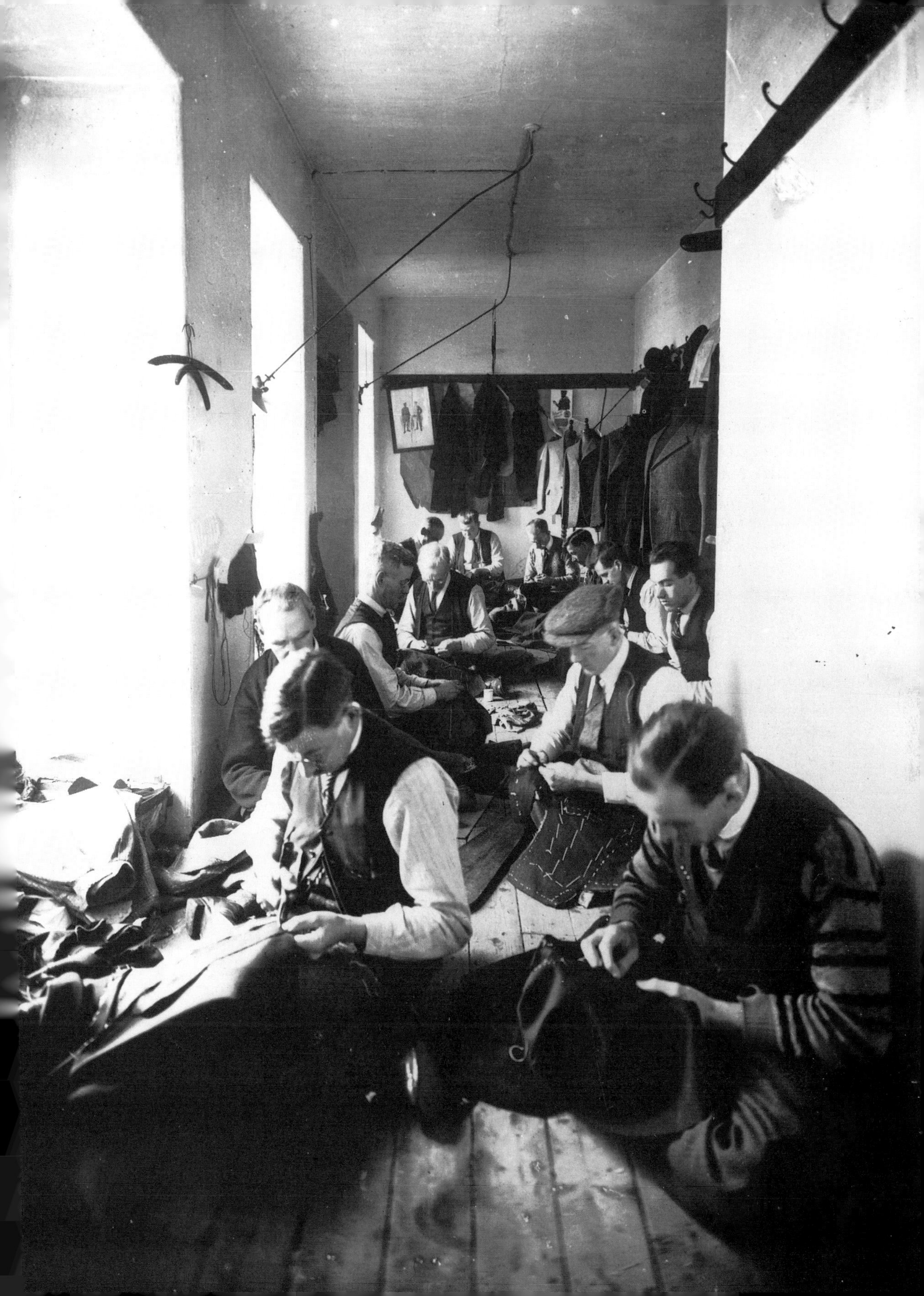

As for himself, Michael claimed to 'fairly colonised', in command of lots of colonial slang, which he relished with wonderment as a new language, most of it being electrifyingly obscene. 'The only adjectives I hear used in this colony are . . .'; and Michael spelt out fully for Paddy's instruction, the now predictable but then unprintable, four-letter list. The mildest specimen of this 'Fair Dinkum' (as the colonials say) verbiage was 'Balls up', a term whose wide descriptive popularity itself said something profound about the then colonial scene: situations meriting that label sprouted everywhere, but it was growth in contrast to Irish stagnancy. 'The Colonials' Michael observed, 'are a smart stylish set' — which sounded like the beginning of a compliment. The next sentence however, began with a demolishing 'but': 'But there are some fine fellows amongst them'. The distinctions were there and recognised, colonials and new chums, each with their views — and reservations — about the other. And they tolerated each other well enough. Yet, when it came to closer things — friendship, marriage — the Irish preferred their own, if they could; then other 'new chums', then the 'fine fellows' among the colonials. By the early twentieth century the crudeness and sterility of some aspects and levels of home-grown colonial society were very evident to newcomers from richer, more refined — and less secular — cultures. For the Irish this was no false superiority, since they were rich indeed in that area in which the colonials were poverty-stricken — in the possession and use of words. They spoke, and continued to speak, different languages. Casual obscenity was not to the taste of either my father or my uncles (let alone my aunts!). So their style and vocabulary set them, in a colonial working world of limited adjectivity, just a little apart. What attracted my uncle's notice of colonial obscenity was its utter strangeness, its astonishing monotony, and its outrageous coarse vigour, its total lack of restraint or inhibition. As a performance it compelled a kind of admiration and a degree of amusement on first encounter. But as a language of daily encounter or expression, it had nothing to recommend it to people who loved words and were masters in playing with them. Paddy enjoyed whimseys of the kind attributed to the universal Irish loquacious engine-driver Flanagan. Upbraided by the railway authorities for sending back telegrams of staggering length and wordiness to explain the mishaps that plagued his journeys, he reported his next derailment thus: 'Off again, on again, gone again, Flanagan'. This story — or rather, construction — amused my father perhaps excessively, but it had nuances and implications

Paddy in self-portrait, probably just before he left Ireland in 1913. In the background, holy picture, broken crucifix, the foreground, books, pen, inkwell — deliberately posed, a little out of focus, the camera on timer.

I did not appreciate at the time: the triumph of the fool, victory in the war of words, popular poetry. It could have been set to music.

Michael's letter continued. The harvest would soon begin, with a welcome bob an hour for a few months. Michael would have a chat with some of the local tailors to try to set up a job for Paddy on arrival. He would also, he thought, probably arrange for the two remaining members of the family, Matt and Madge, (Margaret) to come at the same time. 'But don't be in the least hurry, Paddy. You scarcely ever see the 'Old Dart' again once you leave it.' For whatever reason, Paddy did not hurry. It was two years before he acted, and he never saw Ireland again. As to Matt and Madge, nothing was done immediately. Matt decided to try out (unsuccessfully) a vocation to the priesthood, and war intervened. It was not until 1920 that Matt and Madge joined the rest in New Zealand — Michael, Jack, Hannah and Paddy. Another brother, Jim, was a Jesuit priest, to serve much of his life, and die, in 1932, in Australia.

Paddy appears to have left Ireland towards the end of 1913. He was employed as a tailor by Ballantynes in Christchurch and lived in private lodgings — it was the day of the widow landlady. The letters that followed him from Ireland, from his brother Matt, are curious mixtures of frivolous information and internal turmoil as Matt tried to resolve his own future and cope with (in Paddy's going) the removal of almost the last vestige of his former family situation. So, who was at what dances, who was chasing what girls, what marriages, and various messages and gossip, were mixed with his repeated resolve to attempt the examination for entrance to the Jesuit Order at Mungret College, a subject he had discussed with Paddy before he left. Obviously emigration was the occasion for serious family discussions on subjects otherwise rarely entered, and it may have been a disagreement over Paddy's assessment of the genuineness of Matt's vocation that explains the uncertainty and coolness that pervade these letters. Paddy had seen his older brother enter the priesthood at the same college: perhaps he sensed that his younger brother's commitment was not of the same kind and said so. Whatever, preoccupied with his own spiritual affairs, and obviously uncertain of where he stood with Paddy, Matt's letters were confused and contradictory. He recalled shared past incidents in terms of 'Them was the good old times', at the same time as promising 'Well Paddy there are better times coming'. While he hoped Paddy was liking New Zealand 'fairly well', he was obviously very dubious about that as a prospect: his own cast of mind shrank from the whole emigration process, its disruption, its committal to unknown foreignness, its relegation of the 'good old times' to distant unrepeatable nostalgia. Realistically, in his then mood, there were no 'better times coming'; they had all been used up. Yet, failed aspirations to the priesthood behind him, married the previous day, he left Ireland for New Zealand in 1920. It was a sensible, indeed the only move: the taint of 'spoiled priest', as the contemptuous Irish phrase of the day had it, would have clung to him in Ireland, to produce alienation and bitterness. (In New Zealand, his religious past unknown or disregarded, he made his own way to the northern settlement of Pukekohe, where, eventually as a substantial farmer owning several farms, he lived a happy and productive life. He had ten children and died in 1973, a loved local identity. He and Paddy were never close.)

It was Matt's translation to New Zealand in 1920, with Madge, that brought the wagster Michael back into my father's surviving correspondence, via a letter passed on from Jack: its keeping signified its status — intimate family business involving money. Michael had since joined the police force and had married, in 1917. Either or both of these steps — or was it merely the passing of the years since 1911? — had sobered him, in the sense of imparting a seriousness formerly absent, unadorned by jokes or fun. His subject was the mechanics of getting Matt and Madge Farrell to New Zealand by assisted passage and how to share the cost (£26 each) between the family already there. Michael had begun the formalities, and proposed that he pay one fare and the others — Paddy, Jack and Hannah — share the raising of the other, which they would send to him, as he was in touch with the Immigration Department. It was a testy letter, impatient with a lack of communication from the others, but mainly impelled by his admittedly intense feelings of personal unsettlement. He was under orders for transfer, but had no idea to where. He dreaded a South Island posting: he liked the North. His preference may have been climatic, but it draws attention to the sense of separateness felt within the two islands towards each other as almost foreign countries, certainly remote and different environments. It also brings into view the curious dispersion of the Farrell family across New Zealand. True, several were loosely grouped in South Canterbury, but Paddy was on the West Coast, and Matt was to elect to go to the North. They had not emigrated to live in each other's pockets. They had had enough of that in Ireland — the men in particular — and the colonies gave them the opportunity and space to maintain an

Michael the policeman, in Wellington in the 1930s.

independent distance from each other, in fact, distances so great in terms of the money necessary to bridge them, that the brothers, North and South, hardly ever again met.

It was obvious from Michael's letter that he thought Jack, in particular, had been shirking his duty to assist these last family members to get out of Ireland: 'Matt is fairly clever & would do well here'. He also believed that he (Michael) had done more than his share in that regard. As oldest brother, and one of the three pioneer family members in the colony, he had provided passage money and nomination for those who followed, although the money was by way of loan. He was the lynchpin of the Farrells' New Zealand operation, prime mover and go-between to officialdom, seeing his responsibility as gingering up the family to do what he thought it ought, and be where he thought best for its welfare. Not surprisingly he had come, over the years, to resent his own role and feel impatience with his brothers. They, in turn, saw things their way, and were averse to having big brother tell them what to do, however worthy the object of his instructions. It is doubtful if Paddy's enthusiasm for assisting Matt was particularly intense, given that Matt had gone his own way into a false career start. As to Madge, it was always problematic as to whether marriage prospects were better at home than in the colonies. Anyhow, how was Michael so sure they wanted to come? Back in 1911 he had got the idea that it was best for them to leave then, and ten years later he still had this conviction stuck in his head.

That Jack seemed tardy in offering his share may have related to such questions. Certainly, it was not meanness of spirit. He was the most generous and gentle of men. But he was gripped by an obsession, quiet but going to intense depths, with the ownership of land and was caught up in its practical consequences. He had already married, in Waimate, the local born daughter of earlier Irish immigrants — Anne, one of twins, fey, simple, a natural smiler — and embarked on the ownership of a succession of South Canterbury farms. Each was a little less primitive and rabbit ridden than the last, to culminate in the 1950s with a property at Hunter of substantial size and wool-boom wealth. It was not wealth or status or possessions that Jack was pursuing, but (he was the idealised Irish stereotype in this) the sheer love of the ownership of one's own land, the feel of it ploughed, crumbled in the fingers, the sweep of it in a vista, the sight of it stocked with sheep, the satisfaction of good crops, the independence, and all of this achieved against ups and downs, in a battle against

Jack, on his Hunter farm, c1950.

climate, pests, the economy. In 1920 he had just begun that struggle, at that teetering stage dominated by mortgages, banks, and Dalgetys, that giant of stock and station agents that loomed over his and so many other colonials' farming worlds. Thirty years later (and the photographs show nothing different from the beginning) Jack's farm was indistinguishable from any other colonial farming enterprise: nothing Irish about it, nor was his national origin a matter even of awareness in the district in which he lived. In contrast, his brother Matt, whose passage he was being called upon to assist, was to maintain an Irish identity and reputation, to the degree of sentimental stereotype, to his death. Is this the difference between the Ireland of 1910 and that of 1920, with a 1916 rebellion in between, a revolution in national pride and consciousness? Is it a contrast between a South Canterbury used to the Irish and a Pukekohe not so accustomed? Or merely a difference in the style of the two men? Whatever, Jack was the more natural, instinctive colonial, and in 1920, with his own farming venture just launched, there were slim resources to respond to Michael's importunings in the emigration cause of Matt and Madge.

Paddy's circumstances in 1920 were different, but no less pressed for ready cash. He was about to get married and had bought a house, The brothers were persons of very different styles, their responses to the colonial environment as various as their personalities. Jim, the Jesuit in Australia, was the quiet but assured man of religion, firm, God-absorbed, demure. Matt, who tried to follow Jim's path was, at this stage, confused and in search of himself. Michael seemed in danger of becoming P.C. Plod, his talents and sense of fun crushed by his uniform and big boots: life had become a serious business.

To pause at this point to consider the shrinkage of the outgoing Michael. Strange how the colonies — or was it the demands of a new adult life and responsibilities? — dissipated the fizz and dimmed the spark of Irish people initially ebullient, a diminishment notable more in some than in others. Some black Irish carried their moods, and simmering violence, wherever they went, a heritage of dark temperament and pugnacious disposition. But other Irish, at first all bubble, rapidly grew quiet, serious. It is tempting to suggest the reason as sheer fright, the panic of waking to the reality of displacement from familiar Ireland to 'this mean sod', a process documented in an American setting in 1900 by the Gaelic poet Padraig O hEiageartaigh (1871–1936). In the poet's case it was the shock of the drowning of his son that wrung from him the anguished curse on his foreign location, and the plaint, 'The world grinds me'. That awakening to the misery of being alone in a strange place, exposed to the grinding action of the world, could come less brutally, but no less destructively to the lightness of the inner self. Perhaps, too, the colonial environment, on longer acquaintance, was a leaden weight on those unable to carry it: the airy wit and subtlety of Ireland floated on itself, the shot of humour prompting the response of fellow players who knew and enjoyed the game.

Colonial life was too thin, too diverse in the large, to sustain the pursuit of fun, or a good crack, save in occasional enclaves and gatherings. The 'fun' of colonial life was larrikinish, heavy-handed, thoughtless, crude. It was a bog into which the lighter Irish variety, unsustainable without its own air, inevitably sank. Take the diversions of the 'Kelly Country' in northeast Victoria in the 1870s, as noted by the historian, D.

Faction fighting in Ireland, in the 1840s.

Morrissey. Regular brawling, mixed with drinking sprees, were sometimes organised into 'King Hit' contests, to test masculinity and allow for wagers: one such contest resulted in a death and the attempted suicide of the blow's inflictor. Not to suggest that this type of violence was any colonial invention; it flowed naturally from derivation in Irish low-life. So did the as yet unexplored contribution of Irish rogues to Australian life, those whose natural métier was trickery, 'shonkery', and activities bordering on and entering into the criminal — a domain occupied not merely by the lower grades of confidence men but by some of the luminaries of the legal and political fraternities.

But missing from this fun — the fist in the mouth, for love; the cunning, jovial swindle; the high-stepping wastrelry — was much representation of the top of the range: that is, wit, verbal gymnastics, ingenious jokes, and harmless tomfoolery.

And so Michael became, at least on the surface, less than himself in that way. A loss? Yes. But more an exchange: gone may have been the fun of Cork (that curious and city-inappropriate phrase) but come had a variety of colonial things — a future, a family, dignity, independence.

As to Jack, he had already developed that silent, worried smile and absorbed squint into the hazy distance that marked the colonial man of the land. He had lifted his vision from the demarcations and boundaries of Irish ditches and bogs, to the horizons of infinity and the stretch-marks showed in his eyes: wherever it was, far off, he was going there, slowly. He dressed accordingly. To all casual appearances he was a colonial labourer save on Sundays, town days, race days, where his best was excellent quality crumpled. Presentation, style, was not what he was about. And appearances — the waistcoat, the collarless shirt — were deceptive: his manner said that he was in charge, of himself, and of his farm. He wore the greasy remnants of a dressy hat, never the Irish labourer's cap. A generation later, his own children sensed the clarity of his purpose, to carve a small empire, to live a full life on the proud boundaries of his own land. His quiet dynamic and iron ambition spoke out in their recollection, in contrast to the aimless ordinariness of their own children. Looking up to him as Dad he had seemed ordinary beyond notice: looking back, he was the force without which the centre did not hold.

Hurling, the real thing, with modern protective headgear. An All Ireland final in the 1970s. (*Bord Failte Photo*)

Right: Remembrance of things past: the Borrisokane Hurling Club, c1915.

Hurling romanticised. A sketch from the 1840s.

Right: Paddy's own photograph of a hurling match in Ireland, c1913.

IDIOCY AND DEVILMENT

Back Row—J. Cleary, T. Hough, M. Heenan (Goal); G. Gleeson, W. Foley, J. Egan, D. Kelly.
Front Row—M. Heenan, J. Guilfoyle, P. Fogarty, W. Kelly, W. McKenna (Capt); J. McKenna, W. White, W. Fogarty.
Photo by Paul Flynn, Nenagh.

And Paddy? My father was symbolically but ironically the archetypal Irishman, maimed from the start — by hurling, the Irish national game. It was not the great hatred, little room, of Yeats's famous poetic reproach to Ireland that maimed him, but the sporting expression of the Gaelic revival, that had welled up in Ireland from the 1880s. Born and brought up in Tipperary, the home of the hurling revival, that ancient Irish aristocratic game whose legendary past was associated with violence and death on the field of play, his story was that he was too good, too fast, to be allowed to prosper. With that deliberate malice and casual idiocy that was one of the less endearing facets of the rougher Irish character, his ankle was intentionally smashed by a hurling stick. In May 1908, when he was seventeen, he spent a considerable period in St Vincent's Hospital, Dublin, for the repair of the shattered bones. The outcome, whether of the injury or the surgery, or both, was a permanently shortened leg, a surgical boot, the use of a walking stick for the rest of his life, further operations, a lifetime of sporadic pain — and condemnation to a sedentary trade: he became a tailor, something he did well, but never really liked. He thought he might have done much better with his mind, had he had the opportunity. The intimate relationship detailed by W.E. Mandle between the Gaelic Athletic Association, which controlled hurling and Gaelic football, and Irish nationalist politics, particularly in the form of the Irish Republican Brotherhood, raises the question of Paddy's possible involvement. Unlikely at seventeen, perhaps on the junior fringes, yet . . . the Association by 1908 was so much a front organisation for the revolutionary extremists that, particularly in Tipperary, it must have been virtually impossible for players to be unaware of this, whatever their personal involvement. And certainly my father's team were formidable men. His friend Matt Fogarty, soon to enter the priesthood, sent him in New Zealand a thoughtful memento of the environment of the infliction of his disability, a photograph of the Borrisokane Hurling Team. Good old Matt, soon to don the mantle of a sententious if distant family friend, assuming that elevation to priestly status gave him room and title to pontificate. Which it did. Paddy's resentment of the airs of the Irish priesthood was a matter kept *en famille*.

So, the Gaelic revival which so transformed Ireland and laid the basis for its independence, worked otherwise for my father. It restricted his life and cast his work as sedentary, with a little time to think about things, and a workshop environment classic to the tailoring trade internationally, that is, talk and more talk, inevitably about working conditions, about politics, about the state of the world.

Not that tailoring was unusual among the very few Irish who were able to enter the skilled trades. In the 1850s Henry Mayhew's classic study of London labour found Irish tailors significant in the workforce and, they continued to be so well into the twentieth century. Indeed, it was from London rather than direct from Ireland that most Irish tailors moved on to establish themselves in the colonies. There, they shared the independence natural to their trade as well as a spirited degree of open criticism of the proficiency of less able practitioners. Julia Moriarty recalls Irish tailors in Wellington in the 1940s warning their customers against an Irish newcomer who made trousers too short from waist to crutch: 'sure they cut off ye're water' was the dire prediction. Paddy was often scathing of the work of others he was asked to alter, or even remake. Such variations in skill were human, but they were exacerbated by the existence of two levels in the trade, an 'honourable' sector, and sweat shops: the sweaters paid a labourer's wage, the best establishments, twice or three times that. It was a trade in which one could take pride, with styling from the *Tailor and Cutter,* the trend-setting English magazine (whose elegant models were a source of wonderment to me), the choice of the best (English) materials from the Christchurch importers, and several fittings: then, being locals, the customers would be encountered in the street in the finished product, in the normal daily round. With a business run in part from home, this engendered more than commercial relationships, as clients stayed to talk, or drink tea, or sample Paddy's home brew. Each was a walking advertisement, and test of workmanship. He even invented, and patented, a dust- and moth-proof suit bag. A curious trade, small-town tailoring: it swiftly made Paddy an intimate part of the community because he was responsible for how so many of its members looked, women as well as men (it was the day of the ladies' 'costume'), and across the social divisions.

Having been compelled to it, Paddy made a virtue of it. He gave a smart performance of the act that his disability was no hindrance, and capitalised on his tailoring expertise to advertise himself as the best dressed man in town, the snappy dresser incarnate. An early courting post-card photograph to my mother shows him sculling on Christchurch's Avon River, in velour hat, winged collar and bow tie, well-cut suit of his own making — very much the poised and confident young man taking his sporting ease. Nothing of the stereotype Irish

VANISHED KINGDOMS

Left: Rabbits were shot and snared more for skins than meat in New Zealand. In Australia they were a significant item of diet: selling rabbits in Gundagai, c1914. (A.C. Butcher collection. National Library of Australia) Note C.F. Cullen, tailoring shop, behind the cart

Right: S.T. Gill's 'Irish Emigrant'. (*Mitchell Library*)

Below: Paddy on the Avon River, Christchurch, c1915.

unkempt, or scruffy, more towards the archetypal dandy of the day. Not that this was not also part of the Irish scene, particularly in Dublin. Dashing, handsome men with a flair for wearing quality clothes and accessories were a distinctive part of the sartorial parade. S.T. Gill's well known 'Irish Emigrant' portrays the casual colonial variant of this style mid-century: looser, more informal, closer to the eighteenth century modes, but still the self-aware handsome man using clothes to convey an unmistakable message of being a force to be reckoned with, not to be taken lightly, respected. Into age, not only Paddy's clothes but their accessories — gold rings, large inscribed gold pocket watch with conspicuous chain — were part of the performance props. Real props were the variety of walking-sticks, with gold or silver ornamentation, a necessity masquerading as stylish affectation. The walk was as erect and the pace as brisk (even aggressive) as the limp would let it: from a distance the limp seemed a swagger. He looked a man of pride and substance, which he was, though not financially. Even the sport was tailored. Paddy had a succession of snappy American repeating rifles, carried at the dip, squire style, which he used to stalk West Coast possums for fun, and the profit on their skins. When holidaying on Jack's Canterbury farms, rabbits filled the same role.

All this, and what is to follow of this story, seems far away in time, historical. Not so. Paddy's family, and that of his wife, Mai O'Sullivan, were modern migrants: many of their direct colonial descendants are still alive, indeed one of themselves, in her nineties. This modernity placed them far distant in motivation and Irish cultural background from, say, the Famine migrants, or indeed those up to the 1880s. Moreover, their attitudes to family, to extended kin, to property, and to provision for descendants, were very different from many of their immigrant predecessors, and particularly from Irish Protestants, even from the same Irish area.

The most substantial study of Irish family migrant transference overseas so far attempted, is Bruce S. Elliott's 1988 analysis of 775 Protestant families who emigrated to the Canadas from North Tipperary (many from Borrisokane) largely between 1818 and 1855. This reveals a very tight chain-migration situation, rigorously planned and managed by patriarchs, overwhelmingly rural and directed towards land ownership, and characterised by families that were extremely close and given to intermarriage with cousins and located in the colony in close proximity to each other. They were a closed group of related families, defined by their Protestantism, their comparative Irish affluence, and their determination to improve, or at least preserve in the colonies a privileged status that they felt to be under threat in Ireland. In contrast to this stability, closeness, and meticulous organisation, the Farrells — and the Sullivans — seem to be less examples of the stereotype of the typical Irish immigrant family, than a loose assemblage of casually related individuals, with individual realisation rather than family interests a first priority. Their migration was not a smoothly running chain, but an erratic one; they migrated not in the kind of tight phalanx of families characteristic of the Tipperary Protestants, but as a separate single family unaccompanied by parents, which looked to itself and not to wider kin or related families. And they married, not into a cousinage, but into the wider colonial community, some partners being Irish, others not. Then there is the elusive matter of disposition and outlook. Elliott's 775 Protestant families 'settled down' in Canada. They produced few wanderers and became rooted in the land.

The Farrells' impact and commitment were much lighter: some pursued the soil, others did not. Perhaps it was a matter of Irish history. The Protestant haves were determined, and had the resources, to remain colonial haves; the Catholic have-nots had become accustomed to having little, and found freedom and virtue in colonial transience. Or perhaps it was simply a matter of colonial period. By the twentieth century the best lands were long gone: pioneering had a different — harder — face. The Protestant Andrews in Gippsland from the 1880s (the subject of Chapter 7 of *Letters from Irish Australia*) were eventually defeated by land which was not economic to farm: determination, and hard work were not enough. But even they were far less land-oriented than those who had preceded them and much more inclined to wandering and adventure. Unlike their Tipperary Protestant precursors in Elliott's study (some of whom had come to Australia and New Zealand), they emigrated without parents — indeed, in a sense, were escaping from them. That, they had in common with the Catholic Farrells. But with the Farrells the breach with parents was almost total (in contrast with the frequent correspondence of the Andrews), the emigrant goals more various, far less well-defined, the family links looser, more occasional, no less warm, but strongly tending to a determined individualism which came close to the anarchic. Unlike their Irish Protestant brethren, early emigrants or late, they carried with them a certain irresponsible devilment in their style and air, a latency that something unpredictable might happen, might escape, explode.

Then, there was the matter of destination. It is an easy — and false — assumption that the traditional family mechanics of chain migration implied closeness in all things, an edifying togetherness in amity and warmth that pervaded the whole spirit of such family entities. A moment's reflection should dispel such generalisations as illusory. Some very few families may have achieved total harmony, but most contained tensions of some sort or degree. The emphasis on the family as a conceptual entity, and as an economic unit, has often masked the realities of fluctuating relationships, dislikes and feuds, and simple personality differences. Crudely, the family had its uses, and, in most cases, its demands on basic loyalty and responsibility, but it could also be a constricting liability and irritant. For some, probably most, its chain-migration facilities offered not much more than a utilitarian means to the end of eventual personal independence, and to their choosing just that degree of family closeness in both physical distance and intimacy that they wished, and could control to suit themselves.

So, initially, the advance guard of the Farrell family, Michael, Jack and Hannah, had gravitated towards South Canterbury. This area was already known as one of obvious Irish concentration. In a train journey undertaken in the early 1880s, W. Spotswood Green remarked on what he had observed between Christchurch and Oamaru:

> The homes of Irish farmers were often conspicuous amongst the others by the mud walls and the thatched roofs, exactly similar to the homes of their fathers, only that they looked cleaner, and the whitewash and neatness of the surroundings were pleasant to see.

Indeed, the town of Timaru — which still retains to the eye echoes of older Belfast — was, in 1880, the scene of a sectarian confrontation, prompted by an Orange Order march, which drew the opposing Micks or Pats from as far away as Waimate: or so it was recorded in the satiric poem 'The Siege of Timaru' by the Irishman, Thomas Bracken.

But the connection was much closer and more personal than this general atmosphere. The Farrells' mother's brother, Peter Byrnes, also of Ballinderry, had emigrated to Willowbridge, in South Canterbury, a generation earlier. Also in the area, at Pleasant Point, were friends of the Sullivan family, known from the previous Sullivan stay in Timaru in the 1880s and 1890s:

these friends had recently made a return visit to Ireland. Such connections were important, but not necessarily decisive in determining the direction of emigration. That was confused by the fact that, by the end of the century, many Irish families had connections worldwide. Specific destinations could be a matter of matter-of-fact and unexpected pragmatisms, such as shipping timetables and deals. (Julia Moriarty's mother, with two sisters and a brother, came to New Zealand as a result of a price war between Cunard and Norddeutscher-Lloyd: Cunard's discount meant that their uncle, a bushman in Masterton, could afford the four fares as a job lot).

Willowbridge, a few miles from Waimate, like Koroit and its district in Victoria, had an economy founded on the potato, and its adjunct the pig: 'Koroit canaries', the Victorian locals named them for some obscure reason — perhaps their squeals dominated the local bird-song. This was, for the Irish of both colonial places, a familiar and sporadic agriculture, which fitted that pattern of idleness and intense spurts of community labour the Irish so enjoyed: all hands, including women and children, were involved in the digging and bagging. It was also open to the occasional fiddle (mild skirmish in the unending war between farmer and city merchant), rocks and rubbish finding their way mysteriously into stitched bags. In this economy the Byrnes family had achieved success, to the degree that their eventual family home at Willowbridge was still, in the 1950s, known to the lesser extensions of the family as 'The Big House' — in the reverential and resentful Irish manner. This was partly an absurd and pretentious misnomer, in that the family was not Anglo-Irish (the traditional occupants of 'Big Houses' in Ireland) and the house was by no means large. Yet, apart from what the label had to say about the importation into the colonies of slavish imitations of the Irish class system, the house did have some of the classic feature of the genre, on a scrawny miniature scale. It hid behind a dense, high hedge, harboured formidably unmarried daughters, was dominated by an irascible old patriarch, and (characteristic of a sub-group of such Irish edifices) appeared to radiate an atmosphere of gloom and standoffishness into its surrounding district. It constituted a significant local presence, but one neither approachable nor happy.

It was to this family, with its farm economy of potatoes and wheat, that Jack came from Ireland as a farm labourer; Michael also, with Hannah close by in Waimate. The two men soon left the Byrnes's employment, to go their own way, but also, it seems, because the autocratic atmosphere was not to their

Right: Potato pickers at Willowbridge, 1920. (*Waimate Historical Society*)

Below: Potato pickers at Willowbridge, a generation later, 1953 — mechanisation, army surplus tunics, no children, one Maori worker, colonial cockiness. (*Waimate Historical Society*)

IDIOCY AND DEVILMENT

Vanished Kingdoms

The 'Big House' in diminished present reality.

Left: Willowbridge, the sign a relic of the demolished railway station, Luck's road pointing in the other direction.

Below: The departure from Greymouth of the first continuous rail link to Christchurch, via the newly opened Otira tunnel, 7 August 1923. (*University of Canterbury Library, Christchurch, Gordon Howitt West Coast Photographic Collection*)

liking. In the colony they need not endure what they might have had to in Ireland. The history of the Waimate area has been published in 1983 as a substantial (363 pages) book, in which Peter Byrnes appears once, in a list of committee members to build a Catholic school in 1916. He was not a man of substantial local holdings or reputation; not the 'Big Man' to fit the 'Big House', save, it might appear, in his own estimate and within his own family and Irish Catholic community.

Madge, arriving from Ireland in 1920, joined Jack and Hannah in the Waimate area, and was soon married to Peter Byrnes's son, also Peter, but known as Sam. They lived in a small house at the end of the main property. Jack was already married, Hannah soon to be so. Although they lived at some distance from each other, their relations were close and frequent: older children were exchanged to help as housekeepers during sickness or family crisis. With Madge and Hannah, their Irish world of light-hearted idiocy and devilment took on a darker tinge, as they married into a world of colonial primitives, the society of men who worked hard but who were, if not naturally lazy, inclined to take their ease, and who, especially when loosened by drink, harboured stores of violence and resentment. Their own husbands laboured on the fringes of this harsh and unrefined farming world, which at times burst in to engulf their families in various kinds of unpleasantness. Madge was the more sensitive to this lonely and vaguely threatening desert of rural poverty. At first she was terribly homesick, both for a home lost before she left, through her mother's remarriage, and for the familiarity of Ireland itself. Then, as her family grew, she was fearful for them, even of them — fearful and tearful, prone to laugh and cry at once, in a terrible moist grimace, while simultaneously wringing her hands in utter anguish. It was a quasi-theatrical performance, completely natural, and deeply distressing to watch. Here was a pretty, delicate woman, powerless and petrified in the face of the wilfulness, laziness and careless waste and destruction wrought by labouring men: men basically good-hearted, generous, often fun, but large, strong and irresponsible, habituated to tea and beer, and condemned, just as she was, to the coarse idiocy of rural life, hating it, waiting for the Big House to die.

Vain wish: death revealed that all was sham and shell. The property was sold. The little house that had looked up to the big up the road was razed completely, its site indistinguishable from the green of any paddock, not a trace remaining of Madge's agonies or Sam's ambitions, the farm vanished, the children scattered to towns and cities. Here was some South Canterbury translation of a bleak, frustrative Irish short story, with a touch of the destructive Carleton madness, where all was locked in a downward spiral, out of control. The casual colonial images of bright sunny decay and dereliction crowd the remembering mind. The expensive aluminium preserving pan, essential for jams and preserves, left by unruly children in the yard, flattened by the truck whose driver — seeing it — was too lazy, too arrogant, too brutal, to turn the wheel. The harvest slumbering over a scorching race-day, deserted, to be spoiled by the next day's rain. And that next day full of black cursing, and yarning and card-playing (euchre) and boozing and sleeping and work not done. Ah, Madge, Madge, oh, dear God, dear God: her own keening invocation accompanied the long drawn-out funeral of this prodigal poverty.

South Canterbury became the other pole of Paddy's world, but he avoided doom-ridden Willowbridge. He liked Jack at Arno, Hannah at Makikihi; stability, order, cheerfulness, quiet: Willowbridge was unpredictable, a little scary, a place for a day's courtesy visit. But South Canterbury was the *other* pole: Paddy's world had to be his own world, not a mere family extension. First, the job with Ballantyne's in Christchurch, a big tailoring shop with the largest store in the city. Then, not Waimate, but Greymouth, the opposite direction, across the Southern Alps. In 1916 Greymouth was a remote, isolated settlement, then barely fifty years from being virgin bush with a very few Maori inhabitants, until opened up, fitfully, by gold then coal. The rail link with the east coast was incomplete, leaving a gap bridged by a hair-raising coach trip across Arthur's Pass. All travel was something of an unpredictable mountain adventure, and frequently dangerous or quite impossible, owing to gale and flood. The average annual rainfall was 102 inches. More, from the viewpoint of Paddy's trade, the inhabitants were few, and of a class not much in the market for gentleman's suitings. They were mostly miners, sawyers, and labourers, and their employment fluctuating and uncertain. There, Paddy began day work in the small shop of George Kear — four tailors — and for himself, until all hours of the night, in a workroom at home.

At a first glance, Greymouth seems the reverse of the emigrant's dream: hostile, unpromising, friendless. Why choose to go there? It was an adventurous, unpredictable place; challenging, a bit crazy, a place on the edge: such was the flavour of the ideas and stories that were to keep cropping up in Paddy's subsequent correspondence. In the parlance of this day, not

A usual Greymouth scene: the Grey River in flood in 1890.

his, 'it was way out'. So, it was the reverse of Irish boredom; its isolation, the reverse of Irish closeness and claustrophobia (though it had an indrawn oppressiveness of its own); its youth, the rejection of Irish antiquity; its close-pressing, harsh, and jagged bush, the antithesis of Irish softness and plains. So, Paddy sought the place that met his need to find and embrace the extreme antipodes. In the old world turned upside down, he would seek and affirm his success by rejecting what had rejected him. Jack wanted, above all, land, and went where it was. Michael wanted security: the police force filled his need

Greymouth: the centre of today's town.

for that. 'Emigrants' is a cohesive, grouping word. 'Searchers', 'seekers' might do better, and 'settlers' when and if they found what they wanted, if they indeed knew. Each had his own demon to exorcise, to pursue where it led. Ireland was a repressive place, not merely in its political circumstances but in its terrible weight imposed on the psyche of the ordinary individual. For many of them, for 'emigrants' substitute 'escapees', a word which has something of the wild edge and dynamic which drove them from Ireland, and also in the new land. The romantic image of Ireland features its warmth and positive human virtues, but more the point of the life experience that motivated the Farrells was the old man's tirade recorded by the playwright J.M. Synge, early in the century, in Mayo: 'I don't know what way I'm going to go on living in this place that the Lord created last, I'm thinking, in the end of time; and it's often when I sit down and look around on it I do begin cursing and damning, and asking myself how poor people can go on executing their religion at all'. Despite good will and a long-suffering decency, many thinking Irish contemplated their situations with anger rather than resignation, and lost their respect, even their love, for the place that crushed them.

That place, the one that devoured them contemptuously and spat them out, seems to have been the wider, disembodied entity, called 'Ireland', real in its way, but more a way or level of conceptualisation, a general condition, than what they understood as 'home'. 'Home', the particular area of attachment, happened to be in Ireland, and consisted of a particular affection for, and loyalty to, a small group of people — immediate family and close friends — and a certain limited area or specific place. In the case of the Farrell and Sullivan families, this was a group of villages and towns in north and central Tipperary; Ballinderry, Borrisokane, Nenagh, Birr, Roscrea. Dublin or Cork, other Irish places, were irrelevant to this commitment: these were virtually foreign places, some totally unknown. To encounter in the colonies another 'Irishman', from some other county or region, was a matter of very mild interest. To transfer, as the Farrells did, their whole 'Irish' family to the colonies, was to relocate there the larger part of what 'home' meant, its human constituency. Sure, the place was different, but the most important people were the same, facing and sharing the same environment. How did 'Ireland' fit in to this scheme of things? Answer: it didn't. Or if it did, only in general or marginal ways. Or in a fashion too deep, too buried, too integral to the core of self, to be articulated: it was the character and stance of the spirit.

Paddy's home brew, being sampled by the author, 1937.

Paddy as property owner, Puketahi Street, Greymouth, 1919.

On the surface, practicalities ruled. In 1920, when Michael began organising the importation of Matt and Madge, Paddy had not long begun the purchase of a Greymouth house. For all his adventure-seeking, he had more sense than to go into this unfamiliar wilderness alone. In August 1919 he had borrowed £270 (at 7%) from Mrs A.M. Revington, a local hotel-owner, for the purchase of a leasehold property in Puketahi Street. He had paid it off by mid-1923. The house was in view of his forthcoming marriage, and he thought its acquisition great fun, posing for the camera on the verandah, in the relaxed role of Southern Planter, plantation owner complete with tame palm frond; or is it as some imperial Bush Bwana? No matter; it is the half-joking air of ownership and frontier command that counts: the forest wilderness of the Southern Alps then virtually lapped at his door. And it was a very basic colonial domicile indeed, pokey, ill-built, timber already loosened by the earthquakes endemic to the region, intended — ah, those migrant intentions — as a first stop. Circumstances made it a last one. The keen photographer in him committed it to film: 'I began here' — the migrant recording his steps for his own satisfaction rather than to impress others. There were no others. The camera itself was part of the act, the instrument of a style, a distancing device, an assertion of mastery, non-involvement, superiority: the participant-observer manipulating and controlling the world. Here I am, a boy from Ballinderry, carving out a destiny on the edge of nowhere, the jungle just outside, with the Winchester in the hallway, great mountains looming, everywhere strangeness. And, says the posture and the grin, I can cope very well indeed.

Part of the coping lay in becoming a colonial handyman, a do-it-yourself expert. Paddy built or repaired everything: shoes, roofs, plumbing, electrical wiring: his greatest technical achievement was a lavatory cistern, fashioned from sheet copper. And, of course, he was an expert home brewer of a

Paddy and Mai's wedding, Rangiora, October 1920; Jack best man, Chris, bridesmaid.

heavy beer, akin to Guinness. This was on a large scale, using a 80 gallon cask and finings supplied by the local brewery manager. This yielded over 200 bottles, half of which went to the Marist brothers. Paddy was a social drinker. The beer oiled the constant talk of an unending succession of loquacious and thirsty visitors — politicos, priests and brothers, tailoring clients, friends, neighbours, visiting relatives.

The jack-of-all trades activity was aimed at saving money — the town did have the services he provided for himself — but it was also much more. It was a response to a colonial challenge, an affirmation of competence and versatility. It was another affirmation of the escape from Ireland, with its rigid demarcations of role, social class, trade and behavioural expectation. Such a range of work — from menial labouring to respectable skilled, to the white-collar aspects of his managerial and political activities — went against all Irish employment conventions. In Ireland such a mixture was unthinkable. Here was another Irish prisoner the colonies had set free. The tailor turned ditch-digger or carpenter or journalist could occupy all of these roles without a colonial eyebrow raised, as long as he filled them proficiently. Indeed, a reverse process was in operation. In Ireland for a man to stoop to tasks beneath his agreed status would be to demean himself, to forfeit community respect. In the colonies the man who could do anything and everything was more of a man, not less. It was a liberation of talents and challenges on which Paddy thrived.

Paddy was married to Mai Sullivan in Rangiora in October 1920. Why Rangiora, north of Christchurch? Because this was the parish of his Borrisokane friend Father Matt Fogarty, ordained in 1917 and sent to New Zealand. There were seven people at the wedding, and three congratulatory telegrams, all from Waimate, where Mai had been working in a hotel. Jack, looking awkward and over-dressed, was best man. Mai's sister, Chris, was bridesmaid. She looked superior and wise beyond an occasion of which she disapproved: Mai could have done better. A small group of isolated and lonely exiles, huddled together against a cold world? Or a warm, intimate close assemblage, centred in celebration on church and priest? By report, probably a bit of both. Proud and frightened Mai had written home to Ireland, after a long silence, to the nuns she knew in Borrisokane to tell them of her engagement and ask for scapular medals. The nuns were surprised to hear from her and could hardly fancy her married 'so young'. She had dropped out of their lives in 1914. Time had stood still for them but she was twenty-six. Sister Agnes responded: 'I am sure you will make a good little housekeeper and have a bright and happy home', a banality reflecting the orthodoxies of the times. As it happened (where had she acquired them?) Mai had other and much more advanced ideas on the female role. Sister Patrick was much more in tune with life's realities when (with the scapulars) she sent the hope 'that you will be very happy as well as lucky in your married life'. Hope and luck, these were grand things to have. To be so wished by religious from home was important to Mai. It was a benediction necessary to maintaining equilibrium, for settlement in the future. If the nuns knew, approved, and wished her well, then, whatever the outcome, everything would somehow be alright. Mai, in the great adventure of marriage, sought anchors in the lives of those who had embarked on another kind of life-long commitment. For her, the Mercy nuns spanned the world (as indeed they did) and went beyond it. To preserve relationships with them, as she always did, was to maintain her part, her different, individual part, in the divine network. It was a feminine, female thing, a mysterious sense of solidarity. Married to God, married to Paddy — very different worlds they might seem, but they were linked through God, and Mai perceived that link in a strange intuitive way, the way of loss and gain. These nuns were women whose loyalties and perceptions were not complicated by other husbands. They alone could supply that clear female echo of God that Mai in her very different circumstances so much still wanted to hear. For Mai it was a case of: not to be a nun, but to know that nuns might be.

Mai O'Sullivan (O'Farrell) c1915.

So Mai and Paddy were married in 1920 and (in those days) that was that. They had known each other in Ireland. Mai lived in Borrisokane, one of a family of eleven; Paddy came from Ballinderry, a village a few miles away. But they had been in New Zealand for six years before they married, moving in a tiny microcosm of the old society, set in the wider context of the new. The effect of the colony was not to widen their deeper emotional world so much as to constrict it to the emigrant fragment of the old. At the same time, their going disrupted the world they left behind, and in the same areas of passionate sensitivity — matters of the heart. Between Borrisokane and this far colony crackled the electricity of love, loss, and marital might-have-beens, sparked by correspondence which sometimes held little else but news, or enquiries, direct from the world of romance. But it was a world falling apart and lapsing into a profound emotional unsettlement. The old warmth, the flirting, the giggling at dances, was in the past — casualties of emigration ... and of war. Lonely friends, Maggie Moran in Mai's case, his brother in Paddy's (writes Matt in February 1914: 'I suppose you have a nice little mot spotted out there now. Give her lots of sugar candy & chocolate') fed remorse for possible romances left at home, pressed for details of new ones abroad, and dispensed news of marriages, marriages. Maggie conveyed coy messages from boys once known. James Hacket said Mai was 'a very nice little girl', Joe Naughton sent 'best love' and Pat Fogarty was lonely for want of Mai's letters. By early 1915, though her perspective was still one from the viewpoint of matters romantic, Maggie was reporting on an Irish society already beginning to dissolve under the corrosion of war. A good many chaps from around Borris had gone to join up; one was already back on sick leave. By November 1916 her letters were not only a catalogue of boys joining the British army in great numbers, 'anxious to do their duty', but also lists of female friends who were now Red Cross nurses in London or Dublin, or working in munition factories in England. 'So you see May — what a stir the War brought on poor Borris?'; a much bigger stir than 'the insurrection in Dublin on Easter Week. Wasn't it terrible? and all the poor creatures who were killed'.

Stir indeed: the Great War, before any Rising, had torn old Irish society apart by dispersing the young, female as well as male, unpeopling Borris. Those who returned, returned changed. Those who stayed, lost the dimensions of their youth. The wilful and adventurous, who, like Mai and Chris, had used their restless vitality to leave (early in 1914, before the deluge) in the classic emigrant tradition, found from afar that the secure and firm ground from which they had just stepped was now awash with treacherous currents of change, swirling, uncertain. They were now truly adrift. The traditional act of leaving had implied the rejection of the sameness, stagnancy, of what was left behind, but it also implied, at a deeper level, a reliance on the old order remaining unchanged, a dependence which was a comfort and a confirmation in the emigrant situation. But why leave if the old regime was no longer itself, and all those who were expected to stay at home to make it itself, had suddenly departed elsewhere? Viewed from near — but also particularly from afar — the human situation central to concepts of place, specifically the unpeopling of Borrisokane,

Mai, in South Canterbury, c1915–16.

A photograph sent to Mai from Borrisokane: local boys as soldiers, one girl.

in this outbreak of goings and comings, was bewildering and deeply unsettling.

'Poor Chris', (it was always to be poor Chris) 'I think', observed Maggie Moran on receiving a first letter from a colonial Chris, 'she has as much life in her as she ever had, although she seems to be lonely. She says that they sometimes call her 'The mad devil', all the sport she used to spend at home and at dances'. (Chris recalled, in 1988, these dances as

Dancing on the road, Glendalough, Country Wicklow. (National Library of Ireland)

being often the traditional crossroads assemblies, the focus of a district's youth, resort of musicians who sprang up like grass from the gathering itself. Paddy, lame, denied dancing, had his own fiddle, carried in hope to New Zealand; but no crossroads dancing there. And it was dying, even then in Ireland suspect to a puritan clergy.) 'The mad devil' was tamed, by colonial lack of company and opportunity. Who would have thought that the price of being better off, of the great colonial opportunity, was to be less happy? That the cost of escaping from a suffocating crowded stagnancy was to be miserable and lonely? That the toll of full employment and ample hard work was to be at the expense of the hidden benefits of idleness — time and energy for dancing? Who amongst these hopeful, crazy emigrants would have believed that they were entering a life less full, less lively, than the one from which they had so eagerly escaped? True, the old order — or disorder — was vanishing in Ireland itself. The dances of war and death put paid to that. And true for you, 'tis a matter of gone, alas, like our youth, too soon. But the passing of the dance, the abrupt shock of loss of all that dancing meant, became an obsession, tedious even, in the passage of correspondence. What era of youth spent so much of its thought and time recalling, lamenting, in painful long-distance correspondence, the dances of yesterday, vanished, never to be repeated?

'Do you remember the dances we had at Cleary's?' Maggie quizzed Mai. Of course she did, forever after (they all had 'the fun of Cork', a phrase unintelligible to me as a child: corks were things for bottles). 'I was speaking to Paddy Cleary from Birr one day last summer. He wanted to know all about your going away, he said "he was very lonesome after you" — a comment probably as reflective of the passing of that era of fun and dance as of the end of a particular romance. For end it had. Lamented Maggie: 'They hadn't a dance at Cleary's since.'

And Maggie was desolated by the loss of her friend, her Irish world of company, and gossip, and support in the bewildering encounter with boys, shattered by Mai's emigration. 'There was no truer friend than you', she wrote, 'I never found anyone as good since you left. I have to do all the "knocking about" by myself. Folks often say to me "Oh; how are you getting on without poor May". Poor May, Poor Chris. It was a stock description, but it carried its sigh of pity and regret nevertheless. Poor anybody on whom misfortune fell, or who was seized by some disordered impulse, such as the desire to leave home to pursue the dance of youth and life where, surely, it could not be had. Pity the deluded, 'mad devils' like my

Angels: familiar furnishings of the Catholic mind.

mother and Chris, who had abandoned their homes in some crazy search for something better, for excitement, for the unknown. Given another year or so, the stir of war would likely have spun Mai and Chris out of dull Borris into nursing or munitions or whatever — elsewhere: but hardly so far or so finally. New Zealand, like Australia, was a land of no return; to go there meant the death of youth. It cut off, as with a single blow, that innocent devilment that had been young Borrisokane pre-war. It was about to vanish, but those who had departed were not to know that, even though their going contributed to its end. Neither my mother, nor especially Chris, who never married, ever quite recovered from what they regarded as being thus deprived and cheated. They had abandoned a frivolous and happy girlhood, which they imagined as whirling along in their absence. Whose fault? It was mostly illusion; but, to the extent that they were wayward and determined to leave, it was their own. But who was to have warned them that, in terms of warmth and subtlety and lightness of human touch, the colonies were no Irish village?

And, as further Irish female complication, there was that other life, that life of religion, which always beckoned good girls, as an alternative route to happiness and fulfilment. Of a mutual friend who had entered the convent in Birr, Maggie Moran told Mai, 'I think I never saw or expect to see anyone so holy or nice looking. She was like an angel. I wasn't a minute speaking to her when she mentioned you and Christina and said how sorry she felt for you going away and that you were very sincere, and she was very fond of you'. Compliments from angels, approval from the godly, regrets at the parting of good people, were not lightly borne, nor without confusion, particularly when presented with a bewildering mixture of news from the other pole of the female-experience world — men, money, the fast life. Maggie was equally euphoric in her gossip about Chris's lost loves and abandoned romances. In Dr Heenan, who was now dispensary doctor in Shinrone, Chris had 'lost a fine chance. Do you remember one time she was with him at a dance in the Courthouse. Chris was great sport no doubt'. And of Tom Fogarty, home last summer: 'I never saw such going of cash, motors, dances, dinners etc. etc. Where on earth did he get all the money? He was great "gas" while he was at home'.

All was unsettlement. Maggie hoped to emigrate. Mai encouraged her, but she could not make the step. Perhaps better to try to settle down at home. Chris remained the victim of her Irish romantic success. No one met in the colony came up to expectations or recollections; the locals seemed boors,

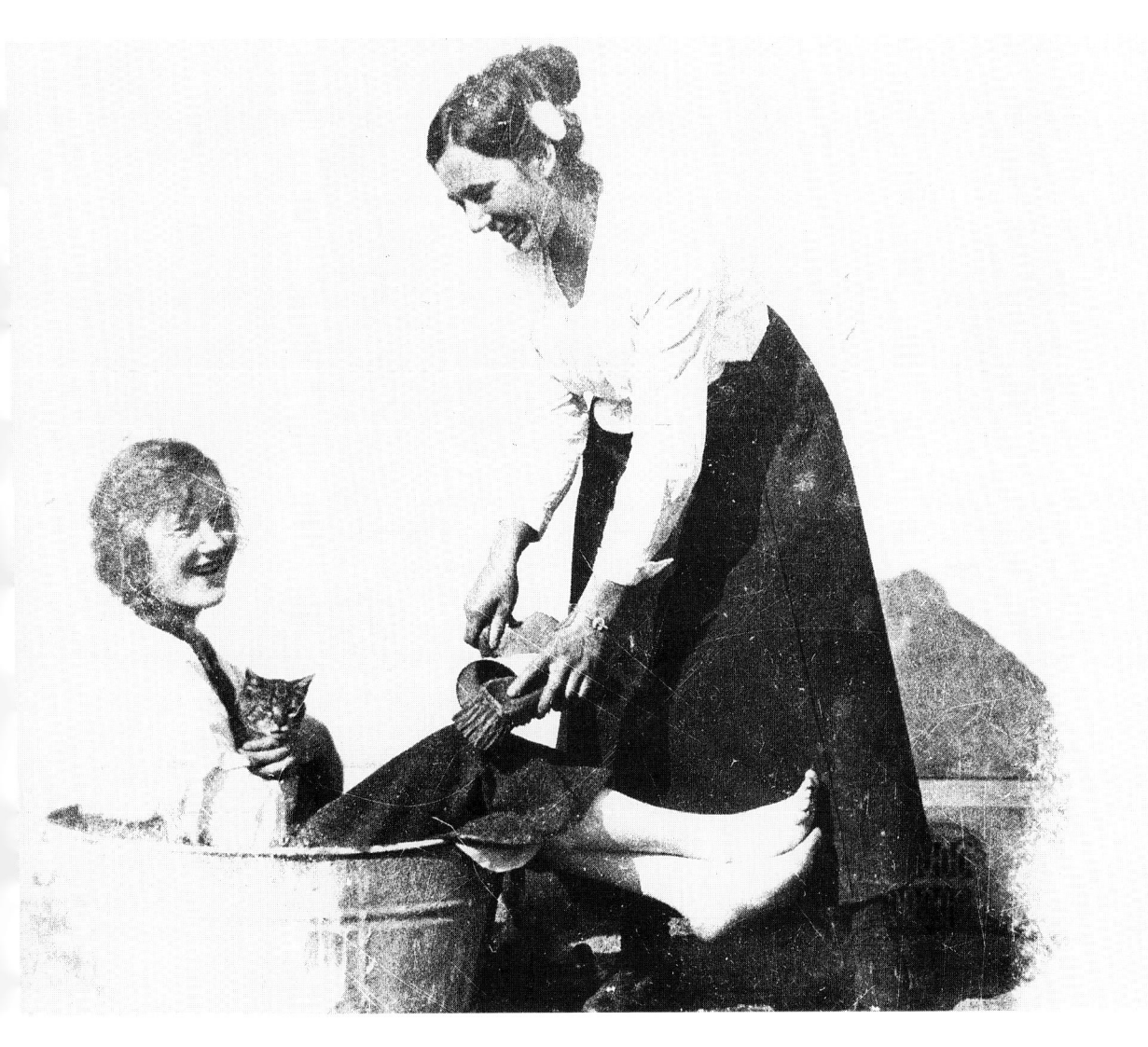

Mai and Hannah, being silly, having fun for the camera c1915–16.

cheap, no fun, dull dogs. Nor (sisters differ) was she an easy companion for Mai; too bossy and critical, too overbearing and impatient. So Mai developed a close friendship with Hannah Farrell, Paddy's warm and easy-going sister. 'Poor Han' (poor again) was a 'brick', chatted Maggie, who had been 'great chums' with her in Borrisokane: 'it is well for you, May, to have her, as ye will keep up each other's spirits'. And, 'I don't pity ye much when you are near each other'. Pity? What a reversal. The stereotype expectation had been that it was those left at home that deserved pity. The emigrant had sailed forth to fame and fortune leaving the sorrowing remnants and rejects behind. But now, time and time again, it is the emigrant who is in the role of the deprived, the lonely, the object of compassion. The basis for such a judgment is clear. They were lost to the family that was Ireland. Yet, mark the terminology — a 'brick', 'great chums': anglicisation had bitten deep into central Tipperary. The old-fashioned 'ye' remained — still does, and Hannah was to use it all her life — but while the growth of the Gaelic League said one thing about Ireland, enlistments in the British army said another. And while Pearse was right in saying that my parents' generation was desperately in need — from the nationalist viewpoint — of 'redemption', he was also wrong, in that the consciousness of being the true home and headquarters of the Irish family had revived in Ireland. Where, before, the focus had been on the great ships that had taken Ireland's humanity far away, now Ireland itself had become the great ship, with emigrant men and women overboard, piteously lost from a vessel that had regained its way.

But it was a vessel steaming in new and different directions and the signals it sent were verging on distress. At both ends of this attenuated female correspondence was the miserable refrain, worded by Maggie Moran, 'we never have any fun anymore', counterpointed by an absurd feeling of termination, of the end of innocence. Concluded Maggie: 'I didn't go into the Convent since last June. What do you think of that, May? I think I got very wild although I was bad enough before'. Wild not to visit the convent, not to maintain those social contacts with the nuns, by which their religious life percolated down into the community? Surely this is farcical rebellion, a trifling departure from the old mores? Yet, for all its ordinariness, its triviality, here was revolution in microcosm: the break up of the old society, its rejection and fragmentation. It was a process that moved those at home both to pity for those who had left, in their excitement and wilful ways, and yet also to sadness for themselves, diminished with what remained, regretting and not regretting the passing of a social order, in which dancing and boys and gossip and visits to convents and nuns as friend, had all formed an integrity of enjoyment and set the boundaries of life.

A girls' world this was, though many of the people who inhabited it were well into adulthood in age. It was a happy world, without major evil or the corrosions of sin, a world where people prayed for each other and truly wished each other well, a place of friendship and fun. No wonder its girls were reluctant to leave it behind. Was it merely a glad space of life between child and woman, constant to all historical times? In part, though, such a space was absent from much previous

The stereotype emigrant's farewell.

history and had narrow class delimitations. Nor can it be separated from religion at its socially constructive best, whatever the negativities of other aspects of that religion might be. Whatever, it was a world about to collapse and vanish, and these are people caught in its vanishing, pulled by the forces of spaces and times beyond any controlling or even comprehension. All they knew, and that emotionally, is that they were in the grip of a dissolution.

So the ties stretched, lengthened, snapped. By November 1916 Maggie was reconciled to the end of the correspondence when a letter from 'my poor dear May' arrived. 'I was quite sure May that I would never hear from you again and my heart was sad with the thought . . .' Then the old news welled up, the intricacies of an Irish village. The uppish Kennedys had moved to a stylish house, but 'at homes' (an English practice anticipated of persons of upwardly mobile pretensions) were 'pleasures unknown to the "Kennedy family". They could not give a cup of tea with a good heart. The people over there are disgusted with them, they are so very ignorant'. 'Ignorant' was the favoured dismissive term of Irish social casting, just as 'very nice' was its opposite, the predictable term of high praise Maggie applied to the Clearys. They also 'knew their place', a virtue crucial to the esteem of the opinion of Borrisokane. 'Son' (pet name for one of Mai's brothers) was so endowed, that is, imbued with a proper sense of his own station, his rightful position in the town hierarchy; he was 'nice', unpretentious, had no airs, was himself.

Of course, Maggie also reported on gossip of the heart. She had had 'many a change of fellows' since Mai had left, but the selection was drastically restricted by the depredations of war and the growing pull of Dublin city. 'Lovely looking chaps' were hard to come by (appearance in boys was very important) and by and large the old days had gone: 'Very little sport now May. No stir at all, times are rather dull'. Their mother had hoped Mai and Chris 'would come back to Erin' last summer. Would it be this? Or never? Maggie gushed, 'I prize the photo that you sent me above all earthly things'. And in a society centred on religion there was clerical news. Maggie reported on which priest or nun had moved, and on the coming of religious strangers.

Here was the ordinary inconsequential fabric of life, the texture wearing thinner as the Irish scene changed with goings, marriages, deaths. What was curious was the absence of parental correspondence: both Mai and Paddy had mothers still alive. Yet, they impinge only indirectly, by report from friends, and then seldom. Emigration seems to have opened — or perhaps confirmed — a gulf between young and old. Did the parent see the young emigrant as effectively dead to them, with those who remained exhausting completely family priority and interest? Was it seen as family disloyalty to have left, or as departures welcome and quickly forgotten in situations overburdened? Whatever the reason — it might even have been a matter of literacy, or at least fluency — it was the young, those of them left, who wrote from Ireland to their emigrant friends and relations. Obviously, they had increasingly less to say, their information dwindling in relevance and meaning as the years swiftly eroded common ground. What could Maggie Moran know of Mai's life in New Zealand beyond the other friends that had gone there? The best of friendships was doomed to shrivel and diminish to bland Christmas cards and dried shamrock mementos for St Patrick's Day. Then, from 1920, after six years, nothing. There was nothing left to say.

Chris, in 1920.

Male and female: the contrast in reactions and responses to the colonial environment is a recurrent Australasian theme, as is the conflict occasioned by their interaction. From the oral history of one of the most famous of Irish Australian pioneering families, the Queensland Tullys, whose history is entwined with that of the Duracks and publicised therewith, come stories (via the curiosity and humour of Pat Tully) that illustrate this contrast in purpose and vision, and illuminate the harsh crudities of pioneering life. Pat Tully's rationale for his collecting activities, and his retelling them to his children, is that the births and deaths and ships' registers, and tales of overlanding too prodigious to comprehend, are 'dry bones'. He wanted to know the 'real character' of his Irish ancestors, how they functioned as people, their foibles and faults. His sister finds some of these tales horrifying, revolting even, and grossly embellished in the telling to gain effect. To which his response is, that his sister might be a bit of a snob.

But it is not snobbery which is at the core of the female rejection of such outrageous crudities, more a sense of what assaults such incidents are — assaults against the building of a world of refinement and civilisation. To protect that initially flimsy, fragile structure, epitomised in their doilied drawing rooms preserved as sanctums in outback shacks, they were prepared to fight vigorously to suppress what was ugly and coarse, primitive and demeaning. Both their sensibility and sense told them that such crudities warred against the gentler, polite lifestyle they were seeking to create against a harsh world. They were quite prepared to ignore, pretend, even lie, in order to protect and further their vision of how things should be (as distinct, being also realists, from what they knew they were). Added to this was a growing sense of the reputation and dignity of family as the years went on and clan numbers and their acres grew: the tendency to clean up, glamorise, was irresistible as grass empires were built.

It was significant that it should be 'an ancient crone' who asked Pat Tully if he knew that his relation Pat Scanlan had died in the 'loony bin'. The question was mischievous with phraseology, and probably malice, left over from a primitive age of Irish village gossip. He asked his Aunt Maria, who flared back 'That's a horrible cruel wicked thing to say about anyone. How dare they say a thing like that about one of the family. Who told you that?' But Pat persisted elsewhere, to find from a friend, in her eighties, that, while acting as executor for a will, Pat Scanlan suddenly leaned over the solicitor's desk and gave him a terrible bite in the stomach. His informant paused to consider her recollection, then remarked: 'You know, Pat, he *could* have been a little bit odd'. Patently, wide latitudes were available in judgments of mental health. In the view of the norm general among his associates, Scanlan's behaviour inclined more towards eccentricity. It was the way he was, a bit odd.

While there is a good deal in the cliché proposition that the cornerstone of the Irish Australian family was 'herself', women were not the only arbiters of acceptable social behaviour and talk. Patsy Tully enforced strict decorum in his house. His brother, Frank, was talking of prison life in Ireland and how prisoners much enjoyed their 'twist' (chewing tobacco). Where did they hide it? someone asked. Frank supplied an answer, whereupon Patsy brought his fist down with a crash on the table: 'No more of that', he thundered, 'I'll have none of that filthy talk in my house'.

But outside the patriarch's domain and control, eddied a scurrilous Irish company, small in size but spectacular in social impact, that even the Tullys regarded as 'bog Irish' — cunning, venomous of tongue, chancers waiting for something to turn up, dirty-minded and at their worst with drink. Dinny Skehan was one such, married into the family. Drunk at the Euromanga (western Queensland) races, Dinny went around waving a fistful of notes, shouting, 'And I'll back Patsy Tully to outrun, outjump, outfight or outf — any man on the course'.

He was confronted and admonished: 'Dinny that's a scandalous thing to say. You know that Patsy Tully is a most moral man. He would never be unfaithful to his wife and would never enter into a competition like that'. 'All right. All right', said Dinny, 'we'll leave the effing out'. Strange, coarse tribute, and acknowledgement of the dignity of the patriarch. And it was Dinny who was at the centre of the 'short grave' story allegedly behind the naming of his own home place, 'Jack in the Rocks', a dreadful expanse of bare basalt hills, redeemed only by the spring it contained, the only water for miles. Because of this, it became a mail staging post and supported a pub run by Dinny and his wife. One summer, an overnight coach passenger died, demanding a prompt burial in the fearful heat. The grave, hacked out of rock by rum-fortified locals, was too short. 'Send the bloody women home,' ordered Dinny, picking up the cross-cut saw used in making the coffin: the shortened version and the pieces removed were tucked in the grave: thus, 'Jack in the Rocks'. Aunt Maria Tully would never speak directly of Dinny: her lips tightened if his name was mentioned; his wife was 'poor Mary'. But Mary, perhaps affected by the contagion of her consort, had a formidable command of the rough style and authority needed to cope with pub life, from casual fornication with maids to the drunken violence endemic in a frontier hotel. Aunt Maria recognised in Dinny a constant, uncontrollable threat to the decency and propriety she valued. His doings were not only an affront in themselves but the generator of legends, which spread widely among unruly and delighted men, to the erosion and disruption of decorum and good order.

Dinny's gross behaviour provided male leadership of the most subversive kind in the age-old Irish version of the battle between men and women. His antics fed an underground stream of male rebellion, which bubbled joyfully apart from, and below, the level of respect, conformity and control the females exacted and secured. The sexes occupied different roles and worlds, whose impingement on, and awareness of the other, was too subtle and complex to be categorised by appearances but whose character resembled nothing more than a bewildering and highly sophisticated game, with rules known fully only to participants.

Dinny, of course, was far from the only culprit, whose outrages might be turned into good stories. Such stories whose essential truth — they were often so true that it did not matter if they were true or not — went to the hard heart of pioneering reality. They were cruel, violent, unforgiving — and yet did something to tame and reconcile their subject matter. From the opposite perspective to that taken by the females, men sought to master the hardness of their environment with joking words, stories that would share and, thus, soften the harshness, and subject it to the release of amusing tales. The Irish belief in the magic of words was used to earth the tension of the bizarre and the evil. Or, obscenity was introduced as a shock tactic to deflate the pompous or to create diversionary entertainment in a dull world; sometimes it was merely to allow a local character to live up to his disruptive reputation. So, there was the time a Labor politician came to visit Euromanga. His host was Frank (Wampoo) Murray, the local storekeeper, who held a meeting of support in his store. As chairman, Murray ended the meeting by asking: 'Now, is there anyone who would like to move a motion for the honourable member to take notice of?' Down the back was an old reprobate who had earned the nickname 'Scandalous Jack' (a tag which attested to community opinion of his behaviour). 'Yairs', he said, 'I move that the honourable member be f--d'. Fastidious Murray was appropriately scandalised. 'Oh dear', he said, 'this is dreadful. What can I say'. But the politician was equal to the occasion. 'It's all right Frank', he said, 'but if anyone seconds the motion I'm getting out.'

Such crudities were harmless light relief in all male gatherings, bringing the house down with mirth in places starved of

Basic entertainment, Station hands playing cards, cribbage. (*National Library of Australia*)

entertainment, where life was all too real and earnest. There was an expectation that local characters would perform to ginger up some solemn occasion. Sporting occasions could be expected to generate more spectator skulduggery than the central contests themselves, given that they invariably attracted substantial wagers as well as involving local reputations. So, his horse involved in a very close finish at Euromanga races, Patsy Tully silenced the uproar with: 'Let no one say a word until the Judge speaks, but anyone with half an eye could see that the Tully horse won clearly'. And so his friend, the Judge, ruled. But other stories have a different edge and atmosphere, where good-natured deflation, coarse tomfoolery, or self-interested trickery, have slipped into a kind of sly, merciless, cruelty. Take the tale of 'Brumby Jack', in the horrors from drink. He was crawling around in front of the pub, on his hands and knees saying: 'I'm a cattle dog. Who'll sool me on to a horse?' There was a line of horses tied to the pub hitching rail, and a bloke called Crosin, pointing to an evil-eyed flea-bitten grey, said: 'Well, go and skitch that one'. Brumby did so and was promptly kicked in the face. He lay on the ground for a bit, groaning, his face bloody. Crosin eyed him and then said: 'Garn! Why don't ya yelp, ya bastard?' This bitter, cruel anecdote had a humour as uncaring as the environment from which it sprang: it was violence inflicted deliberately and without compassion on the weak and foolish. If Brumby Jack could not master his liquor, he was fair game.

But the violence that simmered just below the surface of this primitive outback society was seldom gratuitous and malicious. It was usually sparked by good cause, by provocation. Illustrations abound. Patsy Tully's father was informed by a visiting Englishman that he, as an Irishman, was neither socially nor intellectually the Englishman's equal. 'This is not Ireland you bastard' was the reply, accompanied by the production of a stockwhip with which he chased 'the smelly Pom' off his land.

These are tales, light enough in the telling, which have another dimension, one that throws the mind back to half a century before — to the Victorian world of the Kellys. That was a community in which primitive violence and agrarian outrage simmered in very 'Irish' forms, mixed with a degree of litigiousness and hostile police-public relations also reminiscent of Ireland. But a later time, and more space, contrived a Queensland Irish scene less vicious, more distant in spirit and atmosphere from that sinister Irish-reminiscent shadow of land war that had so darkened the Kellys' Victoria.

What is remarkable is how little of the terrors of the Irish land scene spill over into the colonies. For a unique Australian example of the classic Irish landlord-threatening letter, election motivated, Catholic-generated, anti-Orange, one has to go back in time to Kiama, New South Wales in 1859: '. . . the sun will not shine on your Orange body in August until we quarter you and burn you like a damned heretic dog . . .'. More generalised if no less intense was the desperation, frustration, unchecked wildness and sheer evil that had gripped the Kellys in the 1870s, though that itself was highly localised. By the turn of the century in Queensland, primitivism, crudity, lack of civilising restraint, were still the rural vices and were long to remain so, there, as elsewhere in the colonial scene. But the Irish-related elements had dropped out. The Irish rhetoric and historical reference which had so inflamed Kelly's Jerilderie Letter no longer made sense, in the colonial context, nor were they any longer widely known or intelligible. Even the powerful colonial reality that was Kelly had been sanitised to fit convenient myths — and diminished to equivalence with a boxer. Testimony from Irish areas in early twentieth century northern New South Wales has Kelly already in the standard heroic mould of champion of the underdog, persecuted by police, on a gameness par with — how tame and banal had come to be the linkage — the Irish-American boxing champion, John L. Sullivan.

Pat Tully's tales are colonial tales, in the Irish tradition and spirit. They are truths, embroideries and fabrications generated by a people of Irish birth or descent in their encounter with a new environment. The 'Irishness' lies more in the delight in the absurdity and incongruity, and in the telling, than in the content. These are stories in the Irish style, coarsened, brutalised, colonialised, but telling, revealing of humanity, value-ridden, as Irish stories are.

Many of these tales came back to Pat Tully via their absorption by the Aborigines, who were often part of the audience to the extraordinary and gross behaviour of white people — in that remote region, so often Irish. For all that these ancient cultures had in difference, they had much in common, not least the encounter with an unforgiving and hostile place, which yielded accommodation only to those who could match its challenges. These challenges were basic and stark in the dominion of the Tullys, with its heat and sand and drought. As such, that territory evoked from those who attempted to inhabit it, the extremes of reactions to cope. Some few soured in its primitivism, and lapsed beyond toughness into cruelty

Some mild idiocy in Gundagai, New South Wales. A couple of locals turning on a Wild West act in front of Ryan's Store. (*National Library of Australia*)

and hardness of a kind with the desert they fought. Others sought to endure and enjoy, and the coarseness of their behaviour and humour put them on equal terms with an environment they had to tame and then master. Others again were determined to civilise a wilderness — some priggishly; some with sense and fortitude, nobility elevated to high courage, courage shot through by pride. They were not to be bested. All these responses to a daunting, impossible land were based on one central resolve: not to be broken; defeated perhaps for a while, but broken, made less than a man — no. Thus the contempt, the degradation, served out to 'Brumby Jack', the make-believe dog: he had surrendered himself to the tyranny of drink.

The stark deserts of Tully country exhibited in extremes what was to be found in much milder forms everywhere in the Irish immigrant world of the Australasian colonies. In one form or another, tough places, strange people. Too much has been made of worn images of the 'sorrowing exiles' and 'banished patriots'. Well before the end of the nineteenth century a people renowned for their healthy idiocy and unconquerable devilment were making the deliberate choice to exchange an ancient, peopled civilisation for the loneliness of bush and sand, or some lesser variant and mixtures thereof. Seen thus — and many of the lesser spirits remaining at home saw it thus — the whole emigration thing was a mad, imbecile adventure, perilous and unsure. Indeed. But escape is those things. The individual heart may be a turmoil of impulses in which the need for security wars with that for liberty. And it may not see the present with truth, or foresee the consequences of the future with insight and accuracy. But if Ireland seemed a stifling prison, and strange, alien lands offered the promise of liberation; for that heart the choice is already made. It is on its pilgrim way.

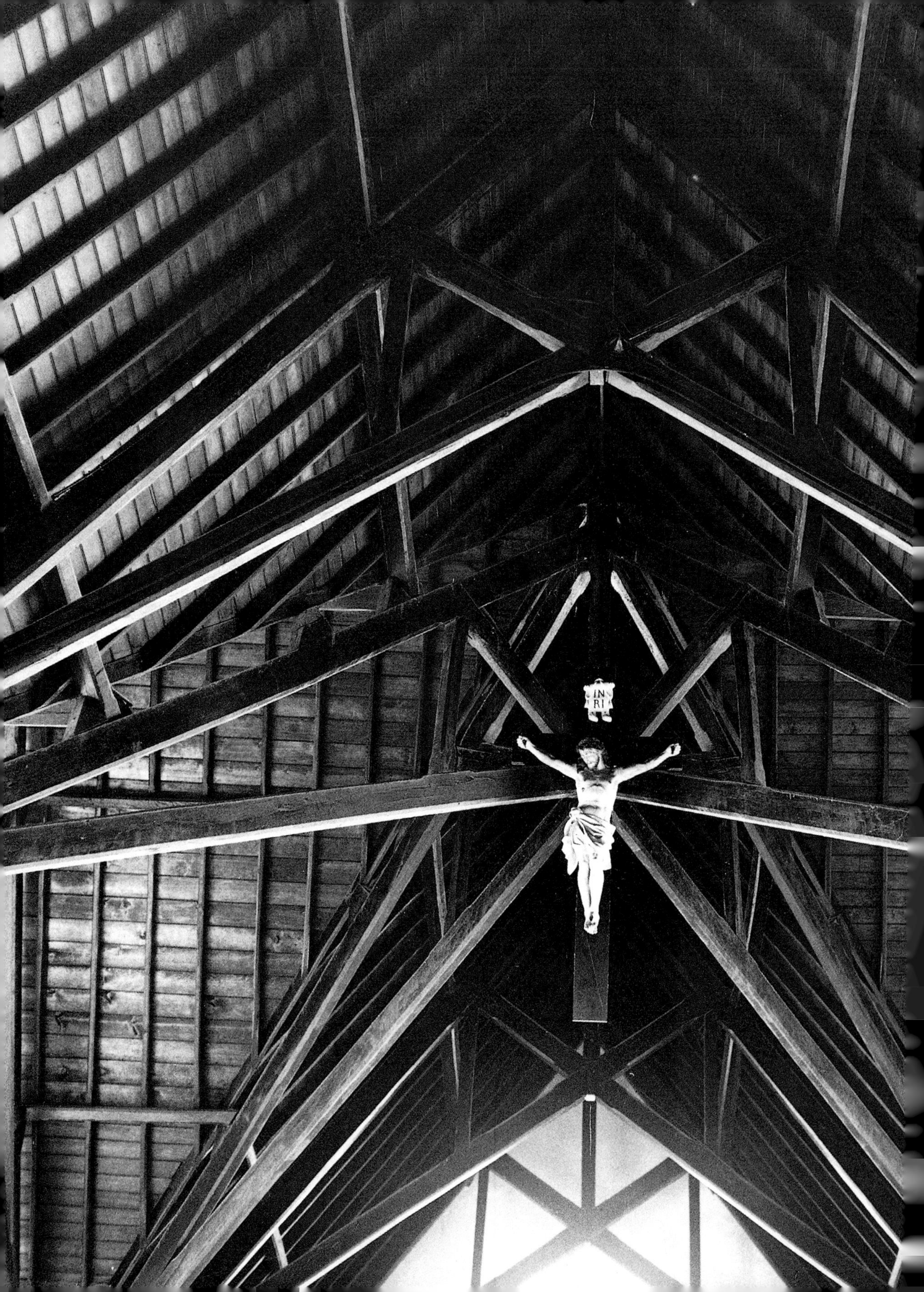
INRI

CHAPTER 3

PRAYER-WORLDS

On the eve of my mother's departure from Borrisokane to New Zealand on 7 March 1914, her parish priest, James Meagher, gave her an inscribed, bound, *Selections from the Publications of the Catholic Truth Society of Ireland*. This was an upmarket version of the priest's traditional open-air blessing of emigrants, immortalised by the illustration in the *Illustrated London News* of 1851. It was also a gesture congruent with a clerical Ireland increasingly aware, since the 1890s, of what it saw as the baneful effects of popular secular literature on a now educated public. (The tradition of seeking the Irish priest's blessing on leaving home persisted. I received a book when I visited Monsignor Long, on my parents' instruction — it would hardly have occurred to me — when I left Greymouth for university in foreign Christchurch in 1952.) In my mother's case in 1914, perhaps Monsignor Meagher had a job lot of these sombre, purple volumes for what would have been a frequent purpose. They were stunningly irrelevant and arcane in content. Yet, that very mystery and unreality was a comforting link with the stylised, grandiose religion of the day, one which presumed, not today's pathetic and vacuous childish-

Interior of St Patrick's Church, Boorowa NSW

The priest's blessing: Irish emigrants leaving home. (*Illustrated London News*, 1851)

ness, but rigorous intellectuality without apology, a religion of power and scholarship. So, the book contained eight pamphlets, six of them high brow bravura pieces: Pope Pius X's strictures on some errors respecting the rights of Democracy, particularly in relation to the French 'Sillon' movement, (what was that?); Unknown China (from a Catholic viewpoint); heavy Gaelic revival erudition on Clonmacnoise (the ancient Irish monastic centre); Saints MacArten and Dymphna (of similar antiquity); and the Origin, Symbolism and Use of Holy Water. Mai could well have studied this latter tract, as holy water (with some obscure brands and rare collector's items) was standard equipment in her household, with the practical dimension, beyond Irish application, of being openly regarded as a legitimate resource in case of fire, a major hazard in our wooden house. It was this light-hearted blend of respect and frivolousness that made Mai's piety endurable and entertaining. Holy water was a popular gift by mail, or on the return of those few wealthy enough to have been to Lourdes, or later, to the Irish shrine at Knock. It was accepted with real gratitude and reverence and used liberally, particularly in situations of childhood ailments which carried off others not so steeped. I was, and am, happy to be so sprinkled, and to subscribe to its 'holiness', however defined, but it needs little reflection to ascribe most benefit to its symbolism as an expression of caring. Like so much of that faith, the gift of holy water, its sharing, its bestowal in droplets on the young, was a gesture of commonality and love, affirmation of the one belief. So was flicking it out of fonts into the faces of other juvenile church-goers; or pouring the main supply on some potentially dangerous household conflagration — the tumbled candle. Silly or serious, it was all God's mysterious world.

Mai's Catholic Truth Society volume also contained two pieces of pious light fiction designed to combat the secular equivalent, which was flooding into Ireland from English presses. They were Mary T. McKenna's *Maureen Doherty; or the Story of a Trinket* and K. Gaughan's *Mike Hanlon's Mother-in-Law*, which began: 'Whisht, whisht, alannah! sure I know 'tis hard on you but if a man doesn't get comfort and pace in his own house, he'll stay out av it an' who's to blame him?' Such antiquated stage-Irish dialect was out of keeping with my mother's time and taste — and social class: the 'whisht, alannah!' school of Irish speaking had retreated into the domain of the popular novelist as a stylistic device to denote the lower orders. Nobody of Mai's acquaintance spoke like that, unless to parody it as absurdity, such as the impish Irish priest stationed in Greymouth in the 1950s who invariably announced his arrival in our house with 'How ar ye livin'?', shouted and set in a large, inane grin, to the ritual amusement of all present. But, despite its outmoded language and its thatched cottage ambience, *Mike Hanlon's Mother-in-Law* was heavy with obvious morals: the necessity for household frugality and tidiness on the wife's part, thrift in cooking and clothesmaking; for the husband, abstinence from drink. These, encouraged and engineered by a wise mother-in-law of the 'whisht, alannah' type and generation, were the keys to marital prosperity and happiness.

The moral in *Maureen Doherty*, an upmarket tale, was similarly evident, if disguised in the garb of popular romance. She is a doctor's daughter, who, on his death, is forced to take employment as a governess in England, among an aristocracy outwardly genteel but, beneath, wastrel and lascivious. She meets an Irish stranger on a train and, after mild and predictable vicissitudes, they meet again, marry and live happily ever after. However rich and attractive might seem the immediate Englishmen, wait and marry the genuine, noble Irish.

The content of such religious pulp fiction points to the dangers apprehended as most likely to face the young. Its moral weight fell most heavily on the women, as the decision makers, the creators of environments, and the power factors in such stock situations. That such pious fiction was usually written by women, often under male nom-de-plumes, may account in part for the emphasis on the female as the dominant actor, but it is also both socially reflective and formative. Mike Hanlon's drunkenness is in reaction to his wife's sloppiness; Maureen Doherty resists temptation, bides her time, and chooses the Irishman. The male is the reactive, dependent figure whose destiny is mapped out by female decisions. These are stock situations, fictionalised. The fact that real life outcomes were often opposite to those encouraged by the fiction (drink situations usually got worse, Irish married English) did not alter the location of the dynamics of sexual politics and initiative. Women ruled — in their own way.

One clear way they did so in the new century was to affirm their own independence, both from the Irish low-life represented in *Mike Hanlon's Mother-in-Law* (they were going to do better than that) and from traditional expectations of the female role. They were going to have some innocent fun and adventure. Such as migrate to the other side of the world.

So, my mother, where she had been before. Bridget May Sullivan had been born in Timaru, in South Canterbury, New Zealand, in 1895 of Irish parents. Her father was a painter — of houses — from Tipperary, her mother was from Limerick. They had been married in Temuka, just north of Timaru, in 1881. Some time in her childhood the family returned to Ireland — reason unknown, but probably inheritance of property — to Borrisokane, and a similar painting business. Why her parents were in New Zealand remains a mystery; perhaps there was some connection such as Tipperary Protestants had built up with Canada. Certainly, it seems likely that her return to New Zealand, to her birthplace, would have been to the company of people known to her family, perhaps even to herself as a child. And perhaps it was the stock colonial joke reaction to 'Bridget' that caused the abandonment of that name, and the adjustment of May to Mai — a discreet exercise in self-improvement? Yet, such an interpretation goes against the aggressive addition of the 'O' to Sullivan, the adoption of an Irish form common in the Gaelic revival and directed against the English stripping of such names of their aristocratic format. But not going too far off course, not back to the original Ó Súilleabháin. So, pretty and perky, Mai O'Sullivan,

English and Irish; Molly to very close friends — maybe.

All this was not shame at Irish origins, although Chris's haughtiness might give that impression. It was in fact the opposite, pride in being Irish, but rejection of those Irish elements which were in fact coarse, crude and dirty, or stereotyped as being so. Mai soon found that colonial crudities easily outdid the Irish, with barefaced casualness. An earthy illustration makes that point, with a religio-cultural contrast that goes deep into the nature of the two cultures. The lavatory arrangements at her sister-in-law's (Madge's) farm at Willowbridge were the usual country ones, a dunny not far from the back door. On one holiday visit, Mai found that the door had fallen off and that nobody had bothered to replace it, through sheer laziness, and through seeing no need. Indeed, the absence of a door was itself a convenience, as a glance down the path rather than a walk to the door, could immediately ascertain, if it was in use. Such was the colonial practical view. It was of no consequence that the dunny's position in relation to the back door meant that all visitors — other farmers, the breadman, whoever — could also note, indeed could not avoid, seeing any occupant. After being confronted with various strangers, Mai was moved to protest, which she did with an outraged grin, borrowing familiar words from a devotion she practised frequently, the Stations of the Cross, the tenth station, where Jesus is stripped of his garments: she felt, she said, exposed to the vulgar gaze of the rude and scoffing multitude. It was an apposite complaint, its every word a hint of her real feelings towards such barbarism and want of respect, its religious format adopted naturally and without irreverence, and its presentation in the tone of a joke, a laughing matter. It was a masterpiece of her own cultural declamation, translated into the style, though hardly the language of the natives. The door was repaired with good will, however eccentric the request was regarded, and the incident, with its weird verbiage, absorbed into local lore, to be trotted out to the wonderment and entertainment of other natives.

Weird verbiage: the country cousins were not much given to churchgoing. Not least because, in the days before cars, distances were formidable and services in their nearest church could be on as little as a monthly basis, as a scarce clergy took scattered churches in turn. But for those in towns, like my mother, the position was very different and the church, school, convent complex became a focus not socially different from that in an Irish village. Set service times and a pedestrian mode of locomotion — a few cyclists, hardly any cars —

Church in a paddock, in the middle of everywhere and thus nowhere; alive on second Sundays only. The Makikihi Catholic church, church to the Farrells and the Whites.

meant that coincidences of route drew worshippers together casually, well before they entered church. They talked there afterwards, as did their farmer counterparts, and shared the walk home. But what distinguished these frequent churchgoers from others was their constant immersion in prayer language. A related point is often made in regard to the impact on the English language generally of the Authorised, King James version, of the Bible. Those Catholics whose religious practice went beyond the mere attendance at Latin Mass entered a world of rosaries, sermons, litanies, and ceremonial prayer structures, such as Stations of the Cross, or burial services, which were replete with the beauty and complexities of words, lovely obscurities teasing to the intelligence and music to the tongue. Why should the Blessed Virgin be —

> Mystical Rose,
> Tower of David
> Tower of Ivory
> House of Gold

as her litany had it? And, of course, such Catholics were drawn, as all Christians of that generation, into the drama, personal to all, of the great battle against Satan and all his works and wiles. All this, religious considerations quite aside, was an immense enrichment of both imagination and vocabulary. What is now often dismissed as empty piety and ritual, was in fact a mental and intellectual expansion, taking the participants away from the poverty of their origins and into the real world of luxury and white and gold, and to participate in the conversation and company of the angels of God. This was a world to which they instinctively knew they belonged. This was what made the colonials lesser. They had no language for this internal real world, except what they borrowed from the Irish or French. For a time they made it their own, but it was not natural to them; for them, it was a borrowed key to heaven, which they came to misplace, then lose.

They lost also the concepts of quiet and the easy sense of God's relaxed company, things long gone before the noise of Vatican II. The Irish talked to God as almost equals, friendly deference, a posture inaccessible to colonials without concepts of holy places or divine sociability. Authority or anything to do with the sacred made the colonials ill at ease: their God was remote and none too approachable. They could not manage that curious balance between solitude and society that makes the person whole. Their imported, inherited religion offered it to them in devotions and beliefs that sustained that natural tension. Adoration of the Blessed Sacrament, on hourly roster, compelled solitude and contemplation, introspection as refreshment in a sacred place, God's closer reality within the distant noises and smells of other external realities: children shouting in the church yard, tennis being played, or juvenile cricket, the tang of varnished church pews. Even the outside,

Puketahi Street, Greymouth c1950. Mai's Catholic parish is strung along the mid-background, which is the other side of the town block: from the right, church, convent, convent school, to the middle — Brothers' school — then Brothers' house and technical school. (*Greymouth Public Library*)

filtered world was a familiar church-oriented world of parish environment, and the everyday world that seeped into the church was thus sacralised, cleansed, made bright. Was the worshiper alone? Yes. And no. The sustaining belief that transformed loneliness, conferred dignity on the lowly, and imparted both confidence and a sharp consciousness of good and evil, was set out in a simple, even banal, hymn:

> Guardian Angel from Heaven so bright
> Watching beside me to lead me aright
> Fold thy wings round me
> And guard me with care . . .

The sense such believers had of being not alone, even when alone, gave them the benefits of a personalised security company of benign comfort and invincible strength. Perhaps God was busy with other things and more important persons, and His plans for you were pinching tight, but He had sent His personal emissary to look after you, only you, always: you would always be in divine, special, individual care. Of course, two thousand years ago He had died for us all, but that was a long time back and hard to fathom. To have one's own delegated angel was another matter. How could one not be friends with a God who would do that?

Such were the rock foundations of Mai's religious world. Fools would say she was credulous — she and the millions, Irish or otherwise, like her. She knew what and who she was, and where she was going. But it would be absurd to claim this was a singular or even completely individual achievement. Her Irish generation was meshed into a powerful religious network, which stretched to Australia and New Zealand; indeed, it was particularly influential there, in ways both profound in effect and ambivalent in outcome. Nor was it merely the Irish priesthood alone that controlled the nature and direction of this religious and cultural initiative. Indeed, without massive help, the priesthood may not have sustained that task of imperium. In the new century, earlier, from the 1880s, with the influx of Irish teaching orders, male and female, the lay Irish were pursued for their own religious good not only by their priests, but by these religious teachers often working to that end through the children parents placed in their charge. And whereas the priests were relatively few, and often virtually itinerant, or socially remote, and frequently, in the new century, old, authoritarian, cranky or eccentric, the nuns and brothers were numerous, young, and omnipresent — and

'Guardian Angel from Heaven so bright.'

through their pupils, a close influence in Catholic homes. Father Matt Fogarty of the Borrisokane hurling team married my parents, but the relationship was distanced by his sense of elevated priestly dignity and authority, an Irish-derived stance which, while not particularly marked in Fogarty, in other priests contrived an alienation from the laity tutored generally in egalitarian colonial ways. The nuns were different. The Sisters of Mercy who had taught Mai in school, and with whom she had later been a pupil-teacher in Borrisokane, had been long (1882) established in Greymouth, not just the Order, but some of the very nuns from Borrisokane and nearby centres. There was even a family connection. Sister Fabian was Peter Byrnes's sister. Some of these nuns were not only former teachers but, from a younger generation still, Mai's former school friends, family acquaintances. And some of these, contemporaries, were to long outlive Mai, into the holy, balanced, wisdom of their nineties.

These already were, or soon became, close friends to Irish women like Mai, looking for familiar responses and a shared unspoken commonality in the colonial wilderness. It was, of course, a friendship with strict limitations, in a context of mild religious invigilation, but it was exactly what Mai wanted: women who knew and cared. Nor did former teachers back in Ireland neglect to write, and to urge visits to maintain contacts with the nuns in their colonial convents. Despite her being with her sister Chris, Mai was lonely after arrival, lost without familiar context. She wrote to Sister Patrick in Nenagh who responded (14 July 1914) with understanding and encouragement, and those kind, moral compliments that coerce benignly towards the good: 'I have the feeling that you never can be otherwise than good. Therefore you will always succeed' (marvellous optimism for the wider vistas of life, but no invariable rule for the immediate short run). Mai had been a student-teacher, but had now joined the seemingly irresistible march towards colonial practicalities and money-making. She had enrolled in a course in book keeping and accounting with one of the commercial colleges so popular at the time. It was a liberated colonial thing to do, a break with Ireland, and a piece of individual, personal initiative of which she was very proud: the overblown ornate diploma proclaiming her secretarial proficiency was framed, and dominated her sittingroom wall until her death. Her announced decision to take up book keeping met with Mother Patrick's approval: Mai would enjoy that; 'you were always so good at figures. Do you remember the fine long sums you used to get through?' The fostering of enjoyment was

Above: The Mercy order in a class-room situation, Christchurch in the 1950s.

Right: The Carcoar, New South Wales, Convent School. Nobody idle — tennis players watched by embroiderers. (*National Library of Australia*)

not something usually attributed to the stereotype of nuns, nor pleasure in the abandonment of teaching for less noble, safe and worldly pursuits. The stereotype was wrong, being the angry, distorted picture of those whose lives led them away from conventual values, or of those who were unfortunate enough to encounter neurotic misfits unsuited to the religious life. Sadly there became too many of these, as the ladies of Ireland's nunneries accepted coarser materials to cope with the insatiable colonial demand to teach the Catholic young. But the advice of Mother Patrick was wisdom and openness, not coercion or prohibition: keep up your studies and try not to neglect your music: 'You had a taste for it and would get on well'. It was the best kind of advice, that attuned to discerned talents and recognised preferences. What it could not take account of was circumstances. The piano was a bourgeois instrument, unknown in the farmhouses of Mai's relations, beyond her own married means; it was the furniture of the rich and of convents. Besides, it was like Paddy's violin, which was also to languish unused. The colonies were not the home of minstrel boys and warrior bards; they were not lands of song. They were lands to be pioneered with hard work and long hours, their music rough and crude, with lyrics as loud and unsubtle as the people themselves. People who were themselves Irish or of Irish descent, whose vitality and impulse demanded musical outlet, exhibited modest (or immodest) colonial inventiveness. When the traditional imports had been exhausted, they tended towards the lower end of the lyrical repertoire — 'Bullshit Bill', 'Damn and Blast and Bugger the Cat', on to the more recent low-life of 'The Balls of Bob Menzies'. Undoubtedly all masterpieces of folk art, in their place, which was not the convent.

For the colonial Irish, most of them, if there was to be music at all, it was not to be the piano, but the fiddle, or the Jew's-harp. To move from Mai's genteel aspirations, back across the Tasman and to an earlier time, the Irish urge to dance and sing had found an expression as a dimension of the life of a man whose history was to impinge on the lives of Mai and Paddy — indeed, of all New Zealanders. From that basic popular Irish colonial farming tradition, the battler tradition of harsh rural poverty, came Michael Joseph Savage, to become New Zealand's first Labour prime minister, from 1935 to his death in 1940, saint of the New Zealand common man. Born near Benalla, in Victoria (Ned Kelly country) in 1872, of Irish Catholic selector parents, in conditions of rural desperation that mirrored those of the Kellys, Savage's reaction to struggle and

A heart-felt musical moment in a concert at the diggings. (*National Library of Australia*)

The standard portrait of Mickey Savage beams from the sitting room wall on Hannah White (Farrell), Makikihi c1950.

injustice was the opposite to Kelly's bitter violence. His determination to rise wore a sweet face, and took a lighter form, in a household where poverty was constantly lightened by dancing and song. His mother played the Jew's-harp, the only luxury that was constantly replaced when broken. After supper, family music, and lessons in the Irish jig and reels, as soon as the toddlers could walk. Savage remembered this as a source of joy, and carried the urge to stepdance throughout his life. In his teens he gave exhibitions at Benalla sports meetings, with occasional concerts of stepdancing and Irish jigs, sometimes exuberantly on top of a barrel.

Into the warfare of New Zealand labour politics Savage carried the echo of his mother's Jew's-harp and his father's violin and the vigour of the Irish jig. And occasionally, in private as aging politician, he managed a few steps of those intricacies and leaps that lift the heart and lighten, for the moment, the world's weight. Briefly in the late 1890s, Savage had worked at North Yanco station (now the town of Griffith) for that other type of Irishman, millionaire Sir Samuel McCaughey, whose New Zealand counterpart he found in the first prime minister he was to face across the floor of the House, William Ferguson Massey — hard, bigoted Ulsterman. McCaughey, whose technical farming innovations and philanthropy ensured him a place in history, disliked Catholics and unionists, favoured

Ulster Protestant workmen, paid low wages, ignored the unwritten law of country hospitality to swaggies, hunted off trespassers, and radiated fun and joy not at all. He died, unmarried, in 1919, bequeathing nearly £2 million to various causes. Savage did not stay long at Yanco. From 1900 to 1907 he was at the gold mines of Rutherglen in Victoria, where he took up socialism and met the charming happy-go-lucky Paddy Webb — to be another political associate of Paddy O'Farrell. Webb persuaded Savage to come to New Zealand in 1907. Savage's farewell at the Rutherglen hotel epitomised popular colonial Irishry. After the speeches, there were two-and-a-half hours of recitations, songs, and political discussion. And no doubt some dancing: Mick had been local dance organiser and Master of Ceremonies since 1904. The rumbustious politics of Irish dancers was about to descend on dour New Zealand to create an atmosphere into which both Paddy and Mai were eventually to move.

Sir Samuel McCaughey.

Savage and his like had origins in a different Ireland from that of Paddy and Mai: his father had been an 1850s post-Famine, gold-rush immigrant to Victoria. Half a century of Irish history separated the handed-down Savage experience and outlook from the Ireland Paddy and Mai left in 1914. That fifty years had seen the transformation of a primitive, peasant Ireland into a country still rural, but with a growing middle-class with skills, education, aspirations to refinement, and a culture increasingly anglicised, and Catholicised. Savage, and those of his generation of immigrant ancestry (the 1850s to the 1870s), were the heirs of the transported traditions of pre-modern Ireland, before widespread education, before railways, before Cardinal Cullen launched the devotional revolution that made the Irish a nation of practising Catholics. Paddy and Mai were the products of these radical changes, part revolution, part overlay: they were modern Irish, their style, their disposition, that of tending to Catholic ladies and gentlemen in the English tradition rather than pointing back to the traditional ways of the pagan Gaelic peasantry. Of course, they were legatees of both traditions and formative influences — the matter is one of emphasis and direction; but whatever the conflicts and ambivalences, their fundamental decisions of the self had been made. Catholic had subdued pagan, gentleperson had overridden peasant.

At some cost. The music of life that they wished to play and hear was in the style of Thomas Moore, the melodies of emotion and refinement. But the natural Irish cadences of the colonies were raucous and beery, or heavy with false sentiments of rebellion and violence. Paddy and Mai were out of tune, at variance with the crude, popular beat.

So their music died, that which they had in them to give and enjoy. Though not that deeper music of the spheres, which Catholic hymnody hinted and in some moments echoed. Nor did they lose their attentive hold on that elected silence, which in Gerard Manley Hopkins's intuitive spiritual recognition, sang to these prayerful ones, and was, in last resort, the only music they cared to hear. Mother Patrick's genuine interest and practical advice to Mai flowed on naturally to spiritual wellbeing and the preservation of those social links likely to preserve and foster religion: 'Are you near a convent? If so,

Street musicians in Perth, Western Australia, c1920. Violin, tin whistle, plus harp suggest an Irish trio. (*Hassell's Australian Miscellany 1921–22*)

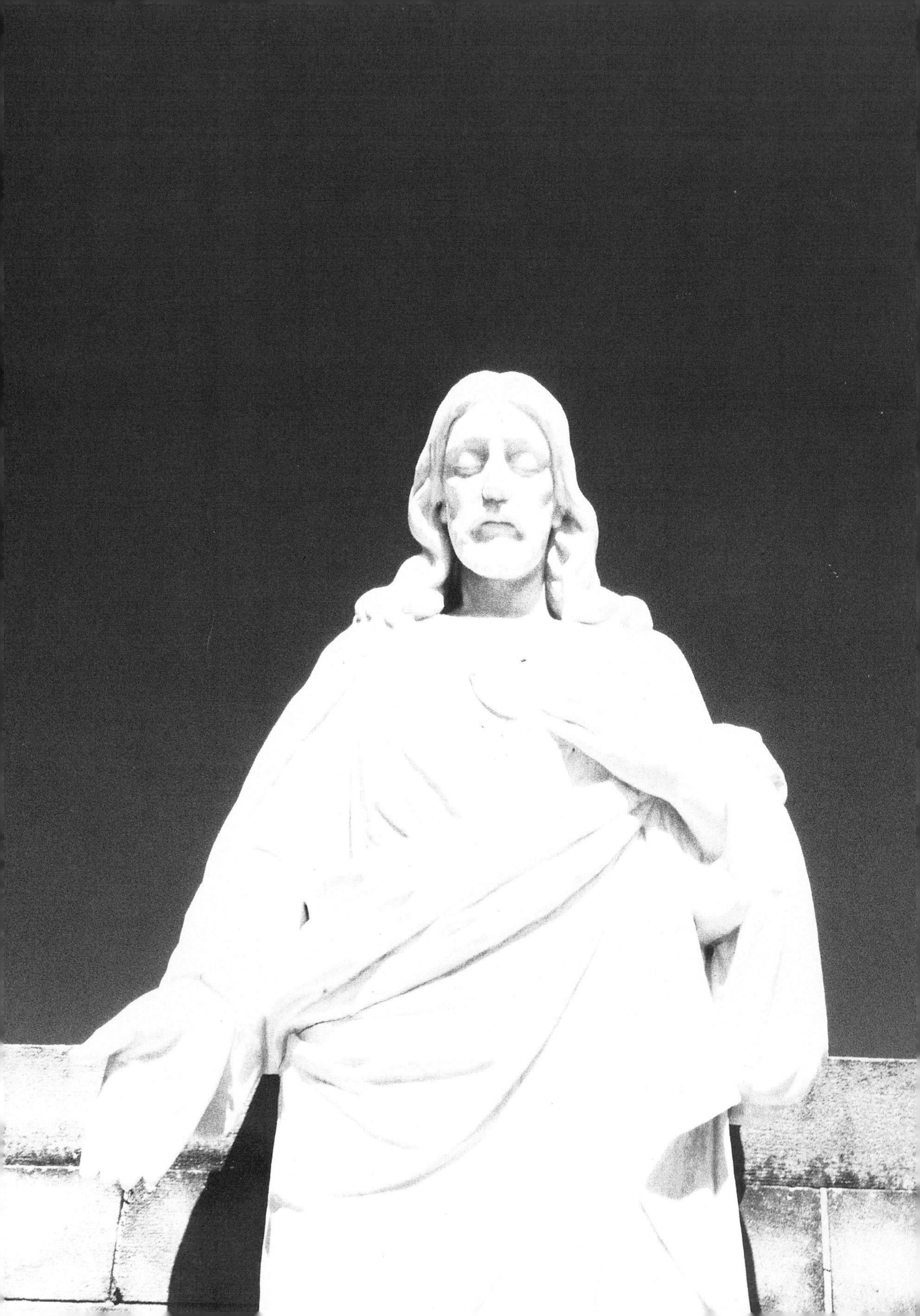

The traditional depiction of the Sacred Heart

would it not be nice for you & Christina to attend the meetings of the Children of Mary. It would keep you in touch with the sisters'. It was a long letter, considered, personal, and generous; testimony to the influence of teachers well beyond their present pupils and immediate geography. No surprise in that; teachers, religious and secular, will always live on in the minds and memories of pupils. But less common is to find documentation within the laity of such direct and positive conformity to lines of life set in school, and followed, without deviation, until death. For, the prayer book Mai most used, that most crammed with holy pictures and memorial cards, was the *The Little Treasure of the Children of Mary* to be had at the convent of the Sisters of Mercy, Limerick, which she received when admitted to the Children of Mary in Borrisokane on 24 May 1912. This sodality was especially designed for keeping in touch with ex-pupils and its *Little Treasure* was imbued with advice and instruction, which occasionally lapsed from encouragement of the child-like, into spasms of the childish and prurient. An example was its injunctions against reading which might prove 'fatal' and its condemnation of 'all romances, in which are mingled intrigues, more or less capable of exciting the passions'. Such strictures were applied 'with much stronger reason to songs of the same nature, the melody and harmony of which render them more seductive'. As to 'balls, theatres, &c., where virtue seldom escapes untarnished', the theoretical Child of Mary preferred 'the ineffable sweets of recollection'. Not so in practice, save among the pathologically scrupulous. Mai was perfectly capable of making the distinction between child-like virtue and innocence, and incomprehensible adult juvenilia. She and her friends continued to dance, sing, and goggle at silly romances, as did the rest of young Ireland. It was not Catholic religious absurdities which quietened the songs and dance, but the heavy weight of colonial life and its pervasive, chilling, contagious Protestantism. Romance went on through popular literature — Georgette Heyer, Daphne du Maurier, other love-smiths long forgotten, smouldering mildly on the bedside table.

At the time of becoming, at seventeen, a Child of Mary, Mai was already (17 February 1907) a member of the Apostleship of Prayer in union with the Sacred Heart of Jesus and of the Arch-confraternity of the Blessed Sacrament. These devotions she continued until death and they were openly proclaimed, notably the Sacred Heart, with plaques and pictures in all rooms of the house. French-Irish piety, focussed on the Sacred Heart, and the Little Flower (Sister Thérèse of the Child Jesus and of the Holy Face), was at the centre of Mai's devotion, even before that saint was beatified. Each of these three commitments — Child of Mary, Apostleship, Arch-confraternity — entailed a complex and onerous programme of daily and weekly prayers and devotions. They imposed a set of spiritual duties which returned specified indulgences, and offered promises of support and spiritual merit from a worldwide network of masses, prayers, and good works offered by other members, sometimes specified numerically (100 000 priests in the case of the Eucharistic League, around 1910) but obviously, in the case of the larger international lay organisations, to be counted in millions.

Much has been made, since Luther, in rage and ridicule, against this numerical religion and its calculator mentality. But often its more ludicrous aspects were not unappreciated by many of its zealous practitioners, who had only half a bemused eye on its absurd and meaningless mathematics (in eternity, what did a year off Purgatory mean?) but had a very clear view of a sense of subscribing, in this way, to an international commonalty of God's creatures, and of the security of a ritual homage and supplication widely shared. It became fashionable to scoff at the search for comfort and security through religion, by those who thought they had found security and comfort in medical advances, or meaning in other gods than Jesus. But Mai's was a generation before these delusions. While their lives as immigrants were in one sense a great adventure, in another they were embarked on a great rift, and in every sense, one full of risk: they could, at any time, go mad, get sick, or die. They needed, and had, an area of certainty, a sense of ultimate care. They had no doubts about God or His power, or of the intercession of His Blessed Mother, in the absolute intimate core of their daily lives. Such sodality memberships enlisted them as volunteers in an international holy brigade, affirming in silent unison their proud and humble adherence to a Catholic culture that knew no distinctions or boundaries. Along the pew, Mick Fogarty, solicitor, apex of town power and wealth, and his sad wife, from whom beauty had passed, swore the same allegiance as lowly Conrahan, day labourer with large brood. Alone and bleary after sleep, 'Morning Offering' they mumbled and knew that millions elsewhere were intoning the same or its equivalent, earlier, later, or at the same time: 'O Jesus, through the most Pure Heart of Mary, I offer Thee all my prayers, work, and sufferings of this day for all the intentions of Thy Sacred Heart'. Interiorised it was, but outgoing too. Precious little about Satan (that seemingly Protestant demigod) either, though he was certainly there to bear in mind, and a focus of sermonising at public mission rallies. But most private prayer was an affirmation of the creature's identification with the will of its creator and a plea for help from a loving God in a hard world. Today, as with every day, there would be work and suffering; hopefully, too, a joke and a bit of fun, and if they could not make sense of it (and, sometimes, who could?), then leave that to God, the Sacred Heart, His Blessed Mother.

All this was no weak search for protective comfort, or evasive self-indulgence despite its paraphernalia of talismans and ritual. It was stark, practical realism in the face of a God that did exist and a world full of uncertainty and peril. It was a piety, an upright way of life, that stood firm, made common cause with others, radiated its warmth and strength, and had tangible practical effects. In 1951, writing from Rome to my mother and father on the occasion of his ordination as a Dominican priest, my brother acknowledged that he had learnt the beginnings of piety from my mother, a sense of social responsibility from my father, and from both, the ability to distinguish between what really mattered and what did not. Not a great man for emotion, or floribund devotions to pasty-faced saints, my brother knew that his own difficult and dangerous birth in 1921 had taken place within a cloud of beseeching to the Little Flower. He thus made it an early duty as a priest to say mass at her shrine in Lisieux. A gesture to my mother? In part. But also an act of common cause. Dominican intellectuals such as Saint Thomas Aquinas were not the

Devotions in progress in Braidwood, New South Wales, the 40 Hours' Procession, 13 April 1915. (*National Library of Australia*)

only saints worthily in Catholicism's Pantheon, and the wise man made peace with them all.

Yet, this is to idealise, perhaps more than a little. Inscribed in gilt lettering across the base of the choir loft of the Braidwood (New South Wales) Catholic Church are the curious words 'My house is the house of prayer'. Whether this be reminder or admonition, there leaps immediately to mind the famous biblical denunciation of which these are the first words, followed by 'but you have made it a den of thieves' — Christ's shout of rage as he drove the money-changers from the temple. Did the Catholics of Braidwood-Araluen, drunk on gold, need reminding of their proper priorities? Their world contained temptations of avarice and worldliness unknown in more settled times and climes, where the apparatus of religion was less new, more established.

Colonial crudities grew there also. The gentle civilised touch of the Irish nuns, which so confirmed Mai's piety, was often missing in those they recruited, and more generally, in the ranks of those lay women of Irish descent, whose unmarried status and surplus energy drew them towards the church as helpers, acolytes, outriders, emissaries far more demanding and tyrannical than the religious obligations they claimed to represent and promote. Family friend, good-hearted, Julia Greaney was one such. Bossy, be-furred, superior with the residue of timber-milling — or was it gold-dredging? — wealth, sweeping into the house with righteous organising force, before whom all quailed. Visiting Ireland (for the first time?) in 1932, Julia was entranced by all she found. That was a world stood still at the exact point of her imagining: a wonderful realisation of her dreamworld, created in her receptive mind in the colonies by priests and nuns of great piety and soft, lilting voice, peopled by prayerful peasants, with thatched cottage back-drops. Do I wake or sleep? 'No wonder,' she wrote to my mother in November, 'I am asking myself occasionally if I am really in Ireland?' To which my mother's — and particularly my father's — answer would have been — no, you are not: you are in Julia Greaney's wealth-insulated romance-construct, with rosary-bead garnish; try winter in a Tipperary mud hut. Why this spell, this extraordinary enchantment experienced by the visitor?

Briefly encountered, the Ireland of the 1930s appeared changeless in the best sense, the clocks stopped at dreamtime, the natural charm of both people and places caught in a time-warp of never-never land. To the sympathetic visitor, or the briefly returning emigrant, it was like opening a door into the

A world stood still. An old Irishwoman accompanied by children and washing tub, Tempo, County Fermanagh, 1899. (*Ulster Museum, Langham Collection*)

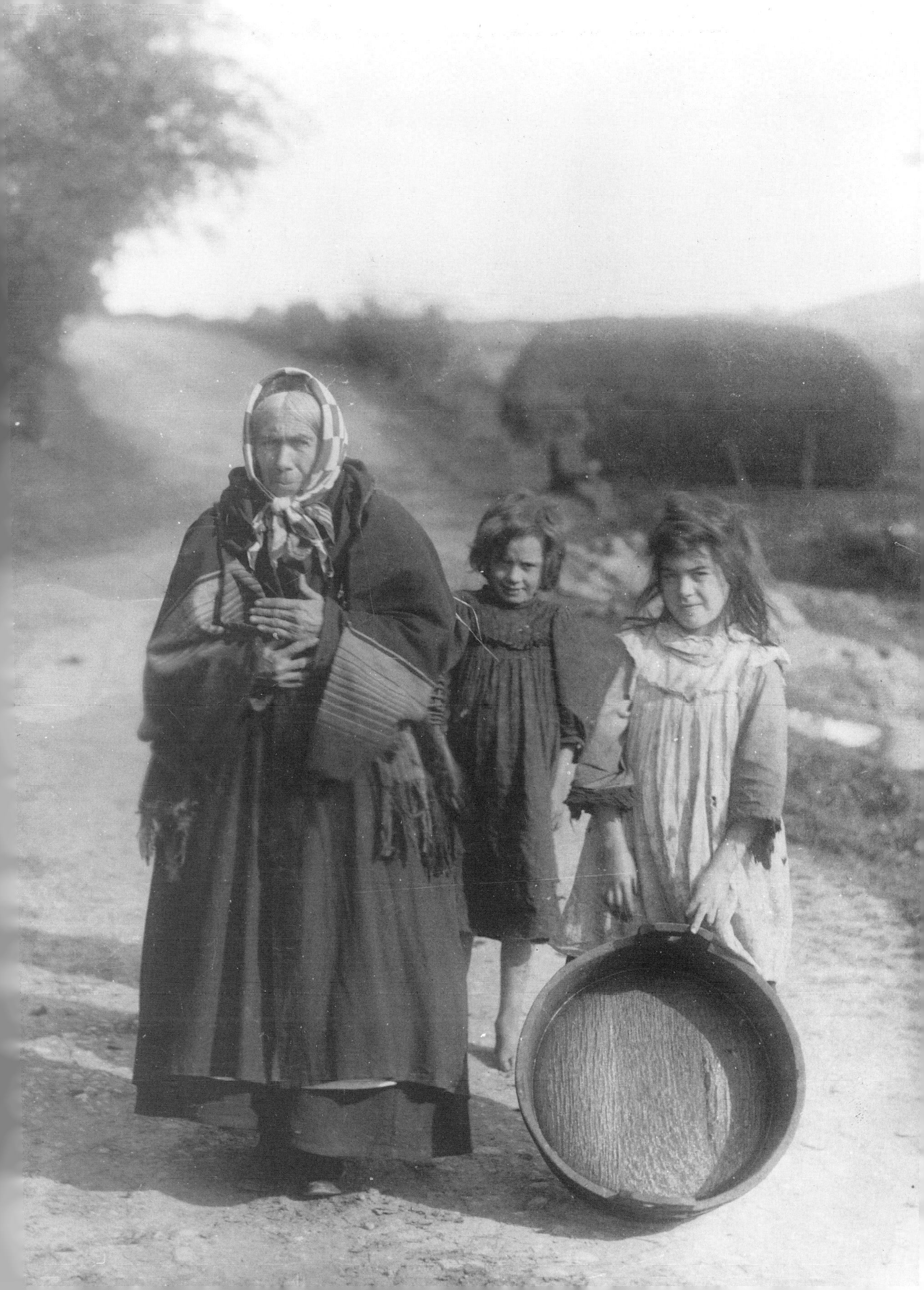

past, their past, youth again, the world that was lost. It seldom occurred to such observers of such static wonders, that static too often meant stagnant, and that Ireland could not drop out of the modern world just to please entranced tourists. Nor did Julia Greaney see the inconsistency of her colonial enthusiasm when, bursting with the wonder of her encounter with ancient Ireland, she could conceive only of modern mediums as equal to the demands of communicating her enchantment. 'I wish I could broadcast everything, it's impossible to write it all.' Undoubtedly friends such as my mother were subjected to Julia's broadcasts, and re-broadcasts, on her return. After all, such unfortunately penurious emigrants were a perfect audience for such enthusiastic (and codded) Irish travellers' tales, a phenomenon which did little to increase my father's love for Ireland, but did not displease Mai, for whom they revived memories. In the meantime Julia Greaney had a vital religious transmission to make, by mail. For the Catholic devout, the lay religious professional of the day, much of Ireland's charm and astonishing emotional impact, came from the centrality and casual prominence of religion in its social life and character. Coming from a society constipated by Protestantism and repressed by secularism, Australasian Catholics experienced the openness of Irish Catholicism with amazement and — if they were of Julia Greaney's enthusiastic religious kind — a shock of delight. No apologies or quiet religious ways seemed necessary here. And Ireland had recently discovered a new potential saint, the timber-yard worker Matt Talbot. His death in 1925 had revealed that, to subdue his flesh, he had so long and tightly worn heavy metal chains around his body and limbs, that they had become embedded in his body, the flesh growing over them: his story is a clearly recollected part of my own religious childhood. Talbot, a reformed drunkard, was another example of 'the little way' associated with Saint Thérèse — the sainthood of ordinary, obscure people. Long before his death, he was known locally as a saint, being a daily mass-goer and communicant, eating little and engaging in long fasts, achieving total immobility in prayer. Julia Greaney had made the pilgrimage to his Dublin house, and with a ruthless religious enterprise and determination totally characteristic, engaged in some minor looting of the shrine, for the good, of course, of others. She instructed Mai:

> I'm enclosing you a little piece of Matt Talbot's bed. I visited the house where he lived for the 26 years preceding his death. Please give the bigger portion to Jack Keating & tell him he is to take good

care of it. (Matt will be canonised some day.) He is to give a piece to Maggie [a crippled relative].

Jack Keating no doubt got his larger portion, but the smaller splinter remains, bound to the original letter with purple thread. My mother was probably at a loss as to what to do with this investment in future sanctity. What did she think of holy Matt's frugal furniture being whittled away by hordes of pilgrims for distribution in slivers around the Irish world? Did she know that his bed had an iron frame? The only wood was two planks laid across it with a block of wood for a pillow. Perhaps the wood was renewed from time to time in pace with the depredations of pilgrims. Perhaps other visitors were less relic-rapacious than Julia Greaney, less agog with the need to possess something of a saint. After all, Ireland had many, and even more martyrs, legions of them, religious and political, if such a distinction was meaningful. Sanctity was the order of the day, the breathing atmosphere, in this strange land; itinerant colonials, on hasty visits, whatever their Irish descent, comprehended this hardly at all. All they knew was that they, the colonials, did not have it. Therefore, greedy for the good, bring back a piece, steal it with good faith. But, like the fresh green shamrock that flowed out of Ireland by mail in time for St Patrick's Day in Vancouver or Valparaiso, it died en route, a sad, flat skeleton of a former self.

Mai in New Zealand, and Julia Greaney, and all Catholic colonials, shared a radical religious disadvantage — the very place, whether it be Ularu or Surry Hills. One of Mai's sisters had married a *garda* — an Irish police officer — who was stationed at Kilmovee, a small village not far (14 miles) from that factory of the miraculous, Knock, in County Mayo. In the 1930s three of their children, ranging in age from six to nine, with two other children, claimed to have seen, on two separate occasions, an apparition resembling a statue of Our Lady of Mount Carmel, in the belfry of the local church. Word spread quickly and a large crowd assembled from afar. Nothing happened, but the incident was given sufficient credence to reach the local press, and the clipping was sent to Mai. None of her own children aspired to this level of demonstrable holiness. Nor did the potential of our surrounds. Kilmovee was a picturesque village with an imposing church, within the atmospheric aura of Knock: it was a likely enough place for a holy picture the children had often seen, brown veil, hands joined in prayer, to come to life. What the vision testified to was, at least, the appropriateness of the setting (the children often

The Ireland of shrines and grottos. The blessing of the grotto of the Immaculate Conception, Leitrim, County Down, 26 May 1929. (*Ulster Museum*)

played in the churchyard) and the natural furniture of their imaginations, living in that larger factory of holiness that was Ireland, with its production line of priests, nuns, brothers, prayer books, holy cards — all the paraphernalia of religion. As to Greymouth, and every rough colonial settlement like it, it was new, unformed. Its religious structures were an afterthought, plonked awkwardly on the land in designs copied from depressing, lacklustre Irish originals, buildings which aggressively, indeed resentfully, proclaimed their foreignness. They did not belong.

And not belonging, these structures were temporary to that place — ultimately to be vacated, demolished, put to other use — oddities on the surface, not the sustaining places of deep roots. Nor did the Irish themselves do much more than pass across the surface of the land en route to life and death.

Paddy Bastic of Maroubra, New South Wales recalls a practice of some Sydney Irish in the 1920s, which makes a profusion of points about the Irish colonial process of superficial transplantation. In the colonies religion served an enhanced, social function: mass was the common set occasion which drew a locality's Irish together, for prayer — yes, but for much else. So, the Woolloomooloo Irish met for mass at St Columbkille's. Then, those from Clare — a large proportion — assembled at 'Clare Hill' (so they named their usual place) in the Botanical Gardens, there to gossip and picnic, and exchange information about available work. Bastic's uncle was a coal and timber merchant in the Loo, whose deliveries made him an authority on servant and handy-man vacancies: he got Bastic's mother a job in service to Judge Cohen. So, mass drew together those who saw themselves not merely as Catholics but also as people from Clare, and sent them on to an Australian public place, which familiarity led them to claim and name as their own. Nothing sacred about it, or other than a convenient point to meet, and attracting a name which has vanished with the practice it witnessed. Totally colonial; temporary, ironical, characterless, matter of fact, secular — but why name it at all? To sacralise this foreignness for the occasion, to confer something of the magic of home place.

'Clare Hill', as a spot in the Botanical Gardens, was both a pretence, and an appropriation. Natural, amusing, trivial, a curiosity, but a foreign incursion nevertheless, and a rejection of what was patently not Clare. And an avoidance of engagement with the local spirits of place. Whatever mystery or apparitions these colonial lands possessed, flitted at the fringes of the bush, or shimmered in distant heat haze. And the mind's accoutrements and senses did not suggest that these presences, half-apprehended, or fleeing from the corner of the eye, had anything much to do with the traditional apparatus and arts of Christianity. Coming from a land of bridges between earth and heaven, and where representations of the supernatural, the divine, and the blessed, might — just conceivably might — become real, alive, acting among men and women, the Irish found their new lands inert, lifeless, no external support or sustenance for that which so powerfully lived within. It was a lack they could endure and survive, given the resilience of their personal spiritual resources and their unwillingness to venture into the alien, local deserts of the soul. Their children were far less fortunate or protected, and all the more vulnerable to the perils of emptiness, because of an Irish priesthood to whom the problem of colonial place had no challenge or meaning.

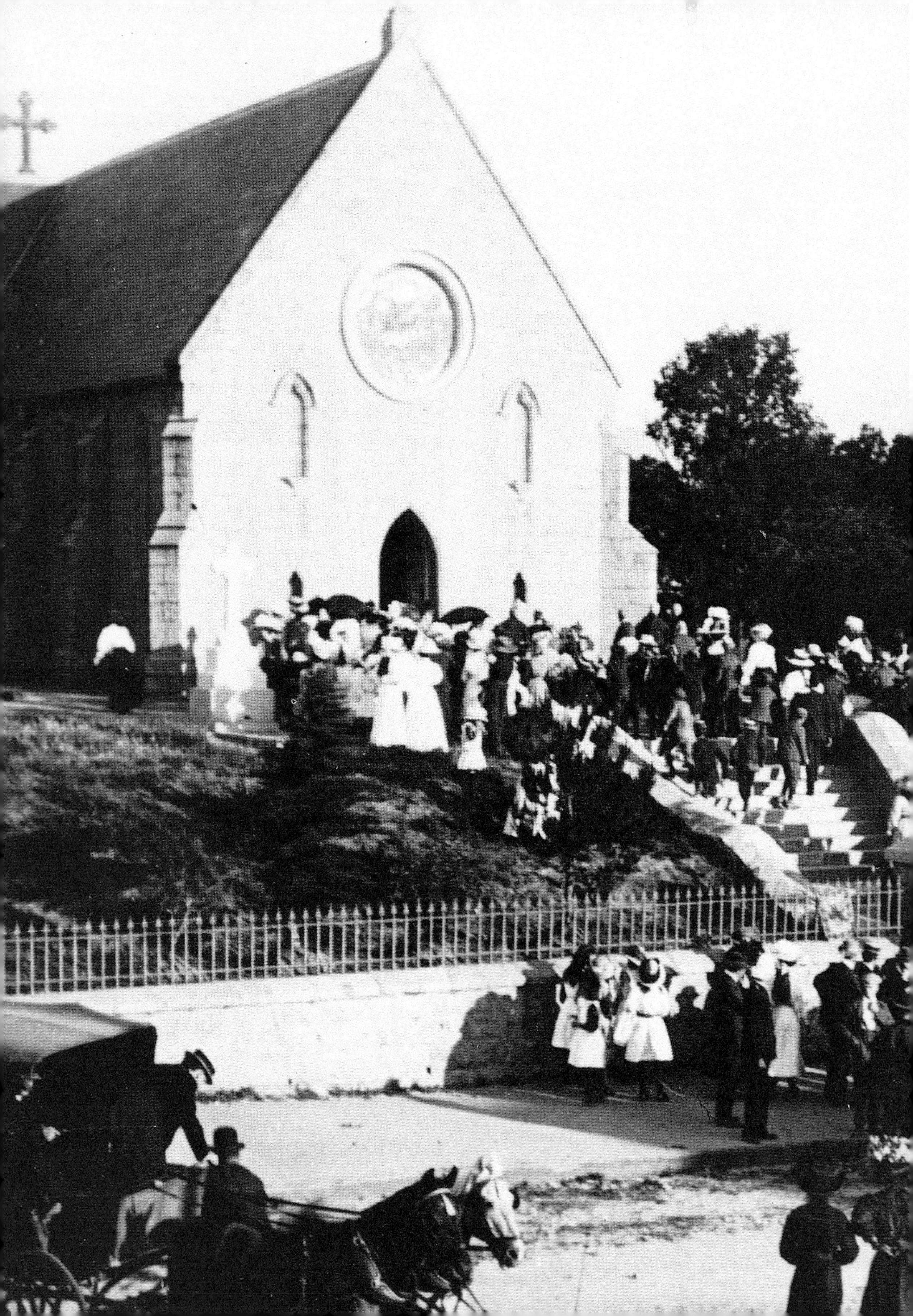

CHAPTER 4

— AND PRIESTS

My father's older brother, born in 1884, was a Jesuit priest, something Paddy made little of, though their letters indicate a warm and easy personal relationship, in which it was their friendship and family feeling, mutual concern, that was obvious, not any difference in religious status. That concern was, on James Farrell's side, a real interest in his brother's trials as a family man in a strange land. Paddy's worry was James's delicate health, which eventually saw him transferred in 1921 to Australia (Riverview, and later, Sevenhills), diagnosed as tubercular. The climatic change was beneficial and James spent ten productive years in Australia: still, he was a mere forty-eight when he died in 1932. Whether of his natural personality or a consequence of his health, James was a quiet and sensitive man, urbane, affectionate and selfless.

> I need your prayers Paddy, that I may have the robust health which a worker in Australia needs. Of course the great thing is to try & please God with little work or much as He wills & help me to do that whatever happens. I am very happy I need not say & will need a long life to thank God for so much goodness. I hope you are taking care of your health. Mind you are not made of steel. I trust

St Bede's Catholic Church, 1910. (Braidwood Historical Society)

in God it is possible to take an odd rest. Mind I was once young and foolish & thought I would stand anything and last forever. I know better now. I do hope that Molly is keeping strong — I take it for granted of Tim & the little cherub! [Mary]

So he wrote in September 1927. Jim was, in the Irish vernacular, 'a lovely man', 'nature's gentleman', whom a compassionate, warm priesthood and a deep identification with the things of God, fitted like a glove. Others — not over many — were similar. Greymouth's own parish priest of that time, Irishman James Long, was of that non-intrusive, self-witnessing kind. But others were the reverse, essentially clerical thugs, whose bullying crudity was both an unfortunate reflex and their contribution to the coarse primitivism of the less civilised aspects of the colonial environment. Because of that very aggressive affinity, they gained a certain popularity, or at least awe, among those to whom they ministered. Irish bishops, in both Ireland and Australia, were aware of the problem. Dr Moriarty, as college president, stated it clearly in the 1850s, towards the beginning of the history of that prodigy of Australasian and American missionary production, All Hallows College in Drumcondra, Dublin. It must be contrived that 'the rude and vulgar boy from the country is changed into the saintly priest'. Such were the raw materials. And the transformation was often made. But often it was not. Or, colonial circumstances were often such that 'the rude and vulgar boy' reverted to type. In fairness to the Irish, but irrelevant to Australia, it was a difficulty with which the French church was also familiar, experienced there in the contrasts between country and city priests.

Father James Farrell, S.J., in Sydney c1925.

There was another problem. Drumcondra House, in which All Hallows was established, had a grim place in Irish nationalist history. It was reputed that in the 1798 rebellion croppies were hanged in the chestnut tree named 'Pompey', which stood facing the mansion, 'whispering its secrets', as the All Hallows historian evocatively puts it, 'to generations of All Hallows students until it succumbed to old age in 1952'. Coming from the Irish class and places they did, these students tended to be a strongly nationalist lot. In 1871, for instance, they erupted into a noisy demonstration of displeasure when Cardinal Cullen's anti-Fenian pastoral was read to them at dinner.

So, to put it at its mildest, All Hallows men, by and large, were disposed to be Irish nationalist and tended to be a little uncouth — a generalisation unjust to many, but making a vital point for the future of the colonies. They (again the unfair broad brush) lacked the courtesies, refinement, sensitivity and, of course, the capacity to be aware of that lack. The priest best known to Paddy (and his Jesuit brother) was Father Matt Fogarty, ex-hurler, friend from Borrisokane, who had officiated at his marriage. On a return visit to Ireland, Fogarty passed through Sydney, but made no effort to contact James, leaving him hurt and bewildered when he discovered this. It remained on his mind, and he wrote to Paddy to see if he could throw any light on the inexplicable behaviour. Was it avoidance of the uppish Jesuits? Some personal matter? Probably — Paddy's response does not exist — it was mere thoughtlessness: better Sydney fish to fry. Paddy's opinion of big, bluff, patronising Matt Fogarty is not recorded, but it may be reasonably supposed. Paddy's hurling background may have been relevant — the Gaelic Athletic Association harboured a strong anti-clerical streak — but more likely his judgment was formed by a natural cynicism allied with a keen ability to separate person from profession. Respectful but wary of priests, he was easy with them, but firmly of the view that as a class of person, they lacked certain vital, realistic information. They had no idea of the value of money; did they think it grew on trees? And many of them were inclined to silliness and bullshit (rubbish was his word), which they expected a docile laity to believe, and might even (God help them) believe themselves.

It so happened that in 1951 Father Matt Fogarty was also visiting Ballinderry in Ireland (his and Paddy's birthplace) when the newly ordained Dominican Tim (Paddy's son, my brother) arrived to visit that place and Irish relatives. In a letter to Paddy, Fogarty went into raptures about this, claiming the colonial Tim for Ireland's own and attributing to Tim ecstatic reactions to his land of racial origin. 'He is enjoying Ireland to his heart's delight . . . [and is a] credit to his name race'. But this was not Tim's then experience, which was much more complex, nor in any way his racial claim: he saw himself as a New Zealander. And Paddy was well aware of this directly, from Tim's very candid correspondence. Nor was a lyrical enthusiasm in keeping with his estimate or experience of much of the Irish element which then, and for much later, dominated his own Australian province of the Dominican order. He found too many of them tricky, obstructive, narrow-visioned and rigorously authoritarian, wedded to the sluggish and selfish possession of power (rather than its use) and contemptuous of mere colonials. Holy, prayerful — oh, yes. Men of God, sure. But as human beings, Irishmen, those other things as well.

However, to Father Fogarty, the priesthood in the person of colonial Tim, was a condition of bliss, welcome as a newborn babe, whose arrival was describable in similar effusive and unrestrained terminology. 'He is a grand young priest God bless him ... It is an unspeakable joy for you & you have every reason to be righteously proud of your brilliant and holy son.' And here he was, returning appropriately to visit the land of his 'name race', which, as Fogarty saw it rosily in 1951, well before economic revival associated with Sean Lemass as Taoiseach, was teetering on the verge of transformation into a temporal paradise. 'Ireland is going ahead ... in leaps and bounds. Prosperity is written across the face of the country in capital letters. So is Peace and happiness'.

This was a priest's eye view, characteristic of that unworldly superficiality and lack of realism that was Paddy's main criticism. It illustrated a strange dichotomy that had grown in post-Famine Ireland; that many priests lived in and experienced a very different world from that of their flocks — the parable of the Good Shepherd carried an unfortunate nomenclature of ministry seen from the viewpoint of those who occupied the role of sheep. The priestly encounter with reality had become genuinely different. Their Ireland was reverential, benign, generous in lifestyle, and secure, and they could not conceive of it as being harsh, hostile, degrading or mean, save as some evil and very limited aberration. Their present closeted experience was bolstered by a mental self-image which attached to themselves the tradition of the eighteenth and earlier persecuting centuries, when the reality for priests had been harsh indeed, even to martyrdom. The outcome was, in many cases, a double insulation from the world around them. For they failed to comprehend the present condition of their own country and people; they saw themselves as heirs to the popular priest heroes of mass-rock and hedge school, defiant of penal laws, invested with the authority springing from tradition and self-sacrifice. The reality was, however strong the religious bonds and structures they declaimed and administered, that their social position and lifestyle were bourgeois and, however unconsciously, their social models lay within their own profession and class, the respectable Victorian (Anglican) clergyman. The determination to emulate and outdo (in an aggressively Catholic way) these competing paragons of

— AND PRIESTS

The priesthood in traditional view: celebrating mass in the cabins of the poor.

Below: The priesthood in Australia, in touch with all, but a little above most. Father P.T. Donovan of Gundagai, in front of the Royal Hotel, with Colonel Ryrie and David Bruce. (*National Library of Australia*)

religion, expressed in elevated social class and refined living style, removed many priests from the orbit of their smelly flocks and from insight into their basic concerns and predicaments.

As to Ireland in the 1950s, the fact was the Irish were fleeing their own country in numbers unprecedented since the calamitous 1880s. Nearly half a million departed in the 1950s, to leave the Republic with a population of 2.8 million in 1961. Father Fogarty was living in some clerical dreamworld and the reason is not hard to seek. As Ronan Fanning has observed: 'The Ireland of the 1950s was . . . much more identifiably the Ireland of the 'twenties than the Ireland of the 'sixties'. Fogarty had stepped back into the land of his youth, possessing now vastly elevated clerical status therein. Dominican Tim had recoiled in colonial shock from a land where, even ten years later, in 1961, 43 per cent of private dwellings had no piped water, and 35 per cent had no lavatory facilities whatever.

By 1951, when my brother was ordained, the colonial prestige of the priesthood still remained theoretically high, especially among those brought up in the Irish tradition, such as my mother. To have produced a priest was testimony to the Catholic quality of a family, a kind of visible guarantee and proclamation of spiritual superiority. A priest's parents were, whatever their economic circumstances, a special sub-branch of the aristocracy of lay Catholicism, meriting privileged places at appropriate church functions. Mai was conscious of this status and privilege, the more perhaps for being, in part, denied it. The central public proclamation of this link with the service of God was the ordination ceremony. In my brother's case this had taken place in Rome. His ministry was not to be in home territory, radiating prestige, but in distant Australia. Besides, the great *mana* was generally waning, and Paddy's attitude was necessarily more practical and less enraptured than Mai's: apart from anything else he had a brother a priest. The nineteenth century Irish secular priest had been a family asset in more ways than spiritually; or in promotion of status. Many were the financial support, to one degree or another, of the family to which they belonged. Many were affluent, some rich, and the trip home to Ireland was a feature of the priestly life not available to the ordinary Irish emigrant of that time. This situation did not apply to the members of religious orders, who took vows of poverty, chastity and obedience and whose families were expected to assist in a long and expensive theological education prior to ordination. Such was the position with Tim, reverting at twenty-five years of age, from paid employment with the public service in Wellington to a position of partial dependency on a family economy never flush, and becoming less so, consequent on Paddy's growing illness. Pride demanded the burden be carried and all requests met, but if priesthood in the family was a source of satisfaction and joy, it was also, up to ordination, a worry and a strain.

By this time, the 1950s, Paddy was thoroughly 'colonialised', with little respect or affection for the Ireland he had left, and which still remained virtually unchanged. Unfailingly polite, he would listen respectfully to the lyrical praises of Ireland enthusiasts, and accept with seeming gratitude second-hand Irish magazines such as the humorous *Dublin Opinion* — which remained unread. It was an expected emigrant part and he played it well, rising to heights of sparkling thespian brilliance as he endured the Irish priestly pipsqueaks that came to the parish as curates and found in Mai such a gullible, admiring audience and provider of afternoon teas. Half his age, they patronised him with 'Paddy', and took liberties through crass ignorance. Their gentlemanly parish priest knew him better, treated him with friendly respect, sought his local political advice, and generally tapped his common sense.

Moreover, Monsignor James Long had, by the 1950s, put in a generation of service to the parish — since 1921 — and was universally loved and respected, his soft and refined brand of low-key Irishness and patent goodness being the secret of his popularity. His story of steadfast, long, dedicated, and strikingly genuine priesthood was repeated in various forms throughout many parishes in Australia and New Zealand, to the gratitude of a laity that recognised spiritual value when they got it. In such cases, the Irishness was usually incidental to the priesthood. Less happy were the situations in which the reverse seemed to prevail, and a loud, strident Irishness, often accompanied by what came across as authoritarian contempt for congregations, dominated the relationship between priest and people. Such situations extended into the 1950s a style and stance common in the nineteenth century, but sadly out of place a century later. Such priest practitioners — and many of them were young — demonstrated to colonial congregations that they had forfeited the right to be deemed other than foreigners. These priests, and their domineering Irish clericalism, were speaking to generations long dead and buried in Australia and New Zealand. Alienated, but enduring respectfully, the new colonials waited in vain for that illumination that would wed spirit and morality to the soil of their own new world.

The explanation for this alienation goes back into the nature and history of the construction of the Irish clerical empire. The power of the priesthood in nineteenth century Ireland can neither be denied nor reasonably criticised. It was a face of emergent Irish life that did much that was beneficial — indeed, crucial — for Irish civilisation, both religious and secular. Within Ireland itself, the priesthood stood forward as an agency of social control, which was venerated, loved, respected. At the same time, though to a much lesser extent, particularly in the public domain, it was feared, resented and criticised. The possession of power bred in those over whom it was exercised, a natural ambivalence of reaction. More so was this the case as the church both warred against, and cooperated with — as suited its religious objectives — the English state, for the allegiance and morality of the common people. In a real sense, this interaction of high politics took place in isolation from the mainstream of society, which, as the 1916 Rising among much else witnessed, had its own objectives and dynamics, quite apart from the designs of church or state.

Such it was in Ireland. Much more volatile and unpredictable was it in the colonies, despite their seeming docility. There, the tendency of the church to become a total and enclosed cultural institution, with its own self-absorbed law and life, became much more marked, for a variety of obvious reasons. Ministering to only part of a total population shrunk its concern to that part; this took the priesthood away from, or put it at odds with, the wider social involvements which were necessarily imposed on it by the postulated, virtually total, Catholicism of Irish society. For the same general reason — the pluralist and secular nature of colonial society — docility and subservience were postures easily adopted by a colonial laity. Easy because, at first, in pioneering circumstances the priest was infrequently and casually encountered. Then, when they were established, firm clerical structures were islands in a secular sea, and thus relatively easy to escape from. Or rather, to exploit the analogy, the church was a Sunday island, visited by those who voyaged weekdays in secular seas; for that reason, people were quite prepared to accept Sunday's rules and defer without question to the island authorities — for a day. After all, Monday would see them off again, free sailing. So, colonial Catholics had the best of both worlds, the familiar apparatus of salvation on call, but freedom from any real clerical interference. More, the surrounding climate of Protestantism was ultra-sensitive to any signs within Catholicism of 'priestcraft', or incursions of pretentious clerical power, or lay excessive servility. Thus, any potential for extreme clerical power-mongering was, in a strange way, checked by the mere existence of Protestantism, and this monitoring presence protected Australian Catholics from possible duplications of what was at least believed to be the Irish situation. The worst of colonial Catholics appreciated this liberty for low reasons. The best of them appreciated it for reasons that went to the heart of a pluralistic and anti-theocratic theory of the appropriate limitations of church power.

Julia Moriarty's Irish father encapsulated the poised subtlety of this view of church-state relations in his marvellous instruction to his Wellington colonial offspring: 'Children, let us thank God for Oliver Cromwell'. No doubt he was saying, at one level, thank God for raising up a great Protestant scourge to harry the Irish into that blazing intensity of Catholic devotion that was to sustain their religion across three centuries of deprivation and persecution. But he also meant — thank God Ireland was not a Spain; thank God that the church was not also the state; thank God our experience was of the poverty of religion, not its opulence; thank God we Catholics were pitted against the state and not its servile creatures, or its emissaries; thank God our tradition was one of intensity, contention and anarchy, not blandness and indifference; above all, thank God we are free! And in these British colonies — where the shade of king-killer Oliver Cromwell still walked abroad as distant hero in the British tradition — doubly free, courtesy of his spectral presence.

This droll and cynical intuition of the unintentional benefactions conferred on then-unthought-of colonies by Ireland's darkest stereotype enemy, was an insight denied many of the serious-minded Irish, notably the clergy itself.

Apparent docility and subservience, the smiling face of gratitude and compliance, cups of tea (and stronger), generous collections, were a source of manifold confusion and misunderstanding, to the extent — and that was considerable — that it rested on an act played out by the laity (or some element of dutiful schizophrenia). It led to a stance by the Irish colonial priesthood based on false premises and the unthinking assumption of authority. Remarkably durable though this morality play was, it was inevitable that a performance so reliant on pretence and unreality should eventually collapse and fall apart, with great and enduring damage to both religion and society. These illusions and malfunctions were at all levels and within all varieties of the Irish priesthood. Prodigies of

The usual Irish view of Cromwell's activities: the massacre at Drogheda, 11 September 1649.

self-sacrifice and missionary endeavour were no substitute for comprehension of the evolution of a new colonial culture and some effort to relate to it, rather than the re-construction of, the pantomime rehearsal of, some make-believe fragment of Ireland.

At all levels priests were an exclusive club, or rather several clubs: of bishops, of the various religious orders, and of secular priests mainly from All Hallows. This was inevitable, given shared training, profession, education levels and status. But clubs are properly defined as organisations for keeping others out, and the consequence was isolation and stagnancy in social attitudes and awareness, in the midst of a strange, new, and rapidly evolving colonial civilisation. Nor were these Irish clubs at one with each other, despite their common geographical origins and shared profession. They were divided by rifts of class and clerical status, and by tensions between secular priests and religious orders.

Put aside for the moment the pioneering phase, and the later era when Irish priests struggled with English Benedictines for possession of the Australian church. Begin consideration with the reign of Cardinal Moran from 1883. Begin assessment at the top. As the Irish Augustinian, Bishop John Hutchinson, remarked in 1886: 'His Eminence in Sydney is very anxious to have everybody and everything under his thumb. However flattering this might be to him, I believe it would be not at all good for the Church in Australia'. Here was Irish clerical insight straight to the point. The Augustinians' Australian historian, Father Michael Endicott, likens Moran to the armchair general drawing campaign lines on a map, while woefully ignorant of terrain or resources.

Moran took the imperial view, seeing Catholics *en masse* even where they did not exist. The wilderness, even when unpeopled, was to be tamed, Catholicised, brought into religious order. Facts were subordinate matters; people also. What mattered was the grand design of Irish Spiritual Empire. Irish? Well Roman-Irish, the imperial ambitions and mind-cast of that city, allied to competition with the pretensions of Britain. The Roman training of Moran, his Irish episcopal colleagues and appointees in Australia, made them highly political. They were deeply into power: administrators, manipulators, clubmen, inveterate meddlers, a tradition which they bequeathed to a host of more recent Australian successors dominant within the very recent past. These were Irish, but not of a kind with people they represented themselves to be, and whom they led, from above and often against their will: they knew what was good for the Australian Irish. But they were not Irish like them, but Roman Irish, a group of church professionals, with all the cunning and wiles of the masters of the administrative machine, a caste to whom religion was all life. What was wrong with that? It could be argued, to the glory of God, nothing at all. All was very much right with it, in its time and place. But its legacy was the machine. The rationale of the machine was its efficient relevance to the religious situation. That situation, of an Australasian Catholic camp modelled on Ireland, had always been a contrivance, a bit of play-acting, but when its props fell bare — the 1960s saw the last of them jettisoned — what was revealed was the irrelevance to Australasia of Roman-Irish religion. Nothing had been done to anchor the realities of this religion to the Australian or New Zealand earth. These professionals had preached to the converted, and those they believed ought to have been converted, that is, the Irish. With the death of the Irish, so also withered that brand of religion tailored, it was thought, to them. Let the tragedy, the great omission be put in bland priest historian's words. 'This hibernian mentality emphasised maintenance of those already Roman Catholic, to the almost total exclusion of activity towards those who were not ... It was more than a historical accident that the presence of a hibernicised Catholicism was paralleled by the absence of Aboriginal evangelisation': — thus Michael Endicott, who chronicles how 'possibly the greatest opportunity for Aboriginal evangelisation in far north Queensland slipped by' through financial factors 'not necessarily insurmountable'. The machine, in mode economic, had faltered.

Broader than this, but embracing and explaining the Aboriginal dereliction as well, was the great failure of imagination that lay behind Irish episcopal authoritarianism in Australasia. In contradiction to that stereotype that has the Irish the dreamers of the world and the English the pragmatists, it was the English Benedictine Archbishop Polding who devised, entertained and pursued great Australian religious dreams. Polding's dreams were Australian not merely in location, but relevant to land and people, religious dreams that embraced not only the Aboriginal, but embodied his aspirations towards a common identity expressed in 1856: 'by a name swallowing up all distinctions of origin, we are Australians'. Erratic, highly problematical, dreams that failed. Nevertheless, they were visions of expansive humanity and religious wholeness anchored in a deep appreciation of the nature of Australian colonial reality and what subsequently might be made from it.

They stumbled and failed because he had other dreams more personal, more monastic, to which the cultural was secondary, and he had faults and shortcomings, which impeded their implementation. But, above all, he also had enemies, opponents, clerics who conscientiously believed that Australia could achieve no salvation which was not Irish. Polding was opposed, out-manoeuvred, subverted, defeated, by those determined that his wider dreams must be brought to nought.

At its rigid episcopal worst, the Irish clerical mind could not conceive of any circumstance or challenge that was not defined by Irish experience or Roman prescription. Even Roman prescription, on the imperative necessities for missions to Aborigines, hardly touched their minds, so full were they of Ireland. To themselves, Moran and his episcopal lieutenants, disciples of Cardinal Cullen all, were generals fighting in remote Australia, the previous Irish war. That war was that? In 1852 Cullen had been appointed Archbishop of Dublin to redeem Ireland from its sins and negligences. He had contrived, in the aftermath of the great Famine, a devotional revolution which turned a patchily indifferent lay Irish into fervent practising Catholics, and imposed discipline and order on a wayward clergy and church. In this improving crusade a young Moran had been heavily involved. This was the battle he set out upon again in Australia thirty years later: redeeming the Irish. He was merely increasing and better organising the pressure. The Irish campaign to create an Irish Catholic Australia had begun long before. Commenting on what had occurred at the consecration of William Lanigan as Bishop of Goulburn in June 1867, Polding went to the heart of the basic (but Irish-unrecognised) anomaly: 'At the consecration ... there was a dinner and ... speeches after, which I am sorry to say contained much to inflame. It might have suited the atmosphere of Dublin, but here was sadly out of place'.

Out of place — it was a phrase that summed up a major theme of the distinguished, sacrificial and splendidly energetic history of Irish Catholicism in Australia and New Zealand. Illustrations abound, are legion, are woven into the tapestry of Australian Catholic life: the Irish flag (presumably the harp) which fluttered over the laying of the foundation of the new St Joseph's Church in Launceston in September 1864; the state of mind exhibited by Dean David Griffin, ordained in Carlow in 1921, died in Bega, New South Wales, in 1955, who had 'an almost pathological anti-British streak in him — the sight of a Union Jack was for him worse than the proverbial 'red rag to a bull'. And so on: fine in the atmosphere of Dublin; here, sadly out of place.

Australia, whatever the pretences and make-believe, and however many colonials were christened 'Irish Catholics' by Irish clerics or hostile denigrators, was not Irish; and the Irish and their descendants were only part of the religious scene and the basic religious problem. Australia was a different place, a different people, and at a different time in history. Like so many generals of limited competence and imagination, trained in fighting old and previous wars, Cardinal Moran's generalship stands indicted for leading cavalry against tanks, for his big guns pointing the wrong way, for his contempt and intolerance of allies: Irish-Italian relations were a sorry story, as were his relations with other Christian churches. Behind the prodigious façade of building, activity, Congresses, pomp, energy and expansion, lay neglect and inanition, the failure of the Irish to attend to any culture other than their own — and what they claimed as their own, that claim itself being a denial of colonial personality.

Worse still was the hostility and frustration meted out to those perceptive but subordinate Irish in the field who could and did see the wider problems and urgent needs. The Augustinian John Hutchinson engaged in the mission in far north Queensland, found himself ill at ease at the 1885 Australasian Plenary Council, with a constituency almost entirely Irish, but hostile to him. Most of the council members were trained in Rome, he in Ireland. Most of them were secular priests, openly biased against religious orders. Moran was in full sympathy with both of these prejudices and their outcome in dismissive self-rectitude. Added to this opposition from his fellow countrymen within Australia, Hutchinson felt himself and his Australian mission grossly neglected by his own order in Ireland, despite its initial commitment. 'We felt that we were more or less forgotten, the legion of the lost ... I'd say they were negligent in sending us men ... from neglect and lack of knowledge.'

'Neglect and lack of knowledge' were not words which featured in the Irish-generated depiction of their own Australian role. Hutchinson was writing of his colleagues in Ireland but his criticism applied also within Australia. Not surprisingly, big Irish stars were in the cities, and the thinness and top-heaviness of the Irish Australian church became more evident, the smaller and more remote the diocese. The more ambitious and the powerful gravitated towards the cities in a natural interaction between their abilities and the fact that power was

Some of Bishop Hutchinson's 'legion of the lost'. Two Augustinian priests in front of their presbytery, north Queensland, c1900. (*Father M. Endicott*)

both exercised and seen to be so in the cities. Essentially their government, their point of legal reference, was Propaganda College in Rome. Ireland was their home, and that of their friends and fellow ecclesiastical power-brokers; it was their gossip-conduit, patronage and person source, and psychological prop. The church, and Ireland, gave them their joint identity. But they could have been located anywhere, could have been residing at any one of the many other outposts of Irish spiritual empire — Calcutta, Newfoundland, Buenos Aires, as well as New York.

The dream of Irish empire, so patent and forthright in Cardinal Moran, was in him religio-political; its stimulus was the obligation to shoulder the Irishman's spiritual burden to redeem the wider world and, equally, the desire to both compete and make common cause with the world civilising mission of England. Historian that he was, with massive scholarly publications to his credit, Moran lived again Ireland's medieval redemption of the then-known world from barbarian darkness; this time the Irish travelled in Victorian England's splendid wake — advantaged (marvellous Christian paradox and contradiction!) by the very power that had oppressed them, a mission spearheaded by the forces of the Famine Queen: oh, divine dispensation! Crucifix followed flag as in Christian empires before the English: the Irish 'white man's burden' was the True Cross.

Contradiction and ambiguity too, in that the empire of the English was both inspiration and persecution. On the one hand, it offered to the Irish the triumph of expansion; on the other, it inflicted a crime of national dispersal. For the Irish to travel with it, it was both an exile and a boost to self-confidence. In an imperial age it was vital to the Irish that there be two Irelands, home and abroad. This nurtured egos, fed ambition and sense of purpose, provided an outlet for mission, and expressed the mixture of urges, both selfless and domineering, that made up the complex that was Irish evangelism. It would be a superficial and sentimental view that overlooked, in the product of Irish missionising, the hidden elements which were proud and imperial, and which swung the achievements of the Catholic clergy into line with those of those administrators of empire, the Anglo-Irish, and those of the determined frontiersmen of a Protestant God, the Ulster Irish.

The historical exercise of relating all this holy jingoism to Cardinal Moran, or Bishop Moore's injunction in Ballarat in 1888, 'not to forget . . . the Holy land of Erin, because to forget Ireland . . . is to take the first step towards the loss of the Catholic Faith', or Archbishop Mannix's remarks to exactly the same effect in 1924, relegates it to a more or less remote historical distance, an antiquated curiosity. In fact, such spiritual imperialism had an elaborate and argued 'philosophic' base, widely and often declaimed, but nowhere more cogently than in the Australian Catholic Truth Society pamphlet *The Vocation of the Celt* by Father Robert Kane, S.J., around 1910:

> . . . there is not now left one single nation, thoroughly, profoundly, and emphatically Catholic except one. That one true Catholic nation is Ireland . . . Ireland has been chosen by God's supernatural Providence to be the vanguard of his Truth in her battles against the errors of the modern world.

It is a position in no way buried in forgotten history. The themes of Irish spiritual superiority and mission to lead the world were recently and ambitiously the political stock-in-trade of Ireland's foremost twentieth century political figure, Eamon de Valera, whose enormous influence, and reflection of major elements in the Irish mind, did not end with his death in 1975. De Valera's contribution 'Ireland's Call to the World' in

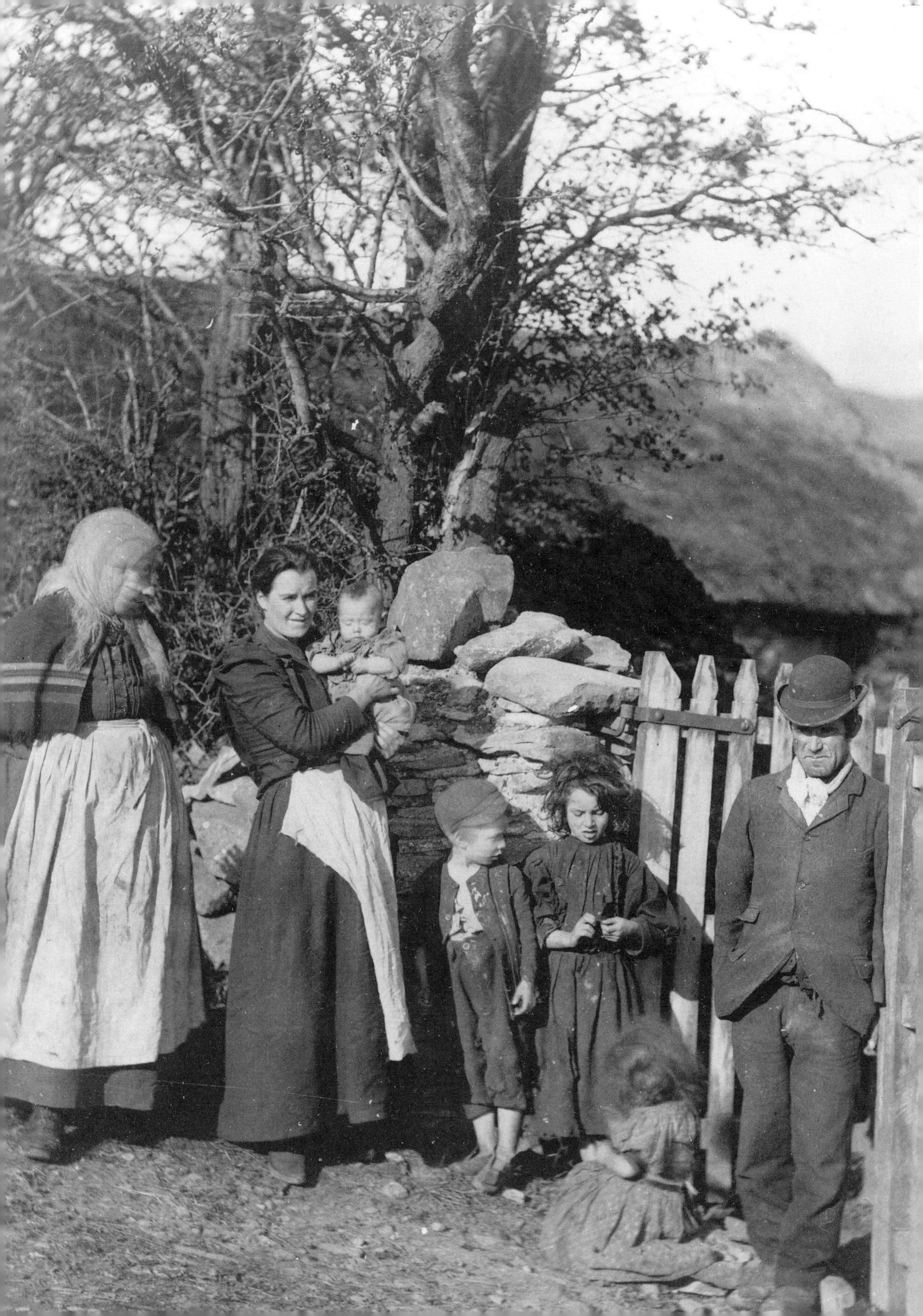

A 'Paddy' in an Irish setting. A Killyculla farmer and his family, Tempo, County Fermanagh, 1899. (*Ulster Museum, Langham Collection*)

the *Young Ireland Reader*, stresses that 'she alone can give ... special qualities of mind and heart' and reviews Ireland's unique history and culture to conclude that 'her dearest hope is that she may humbly serve the truth, and help by truth to save the world.'

This extravagant terminology, and the whole idea of the triumphant might of the small and the humble, and their salvific role (the Irish meek inheriting the earth) resonates in Australian Irish history at least from the 1880s. The French priest and observer Jules Lemire picked up its strident echoes in 1884, confronting Protestantism, he believed, with the thrilling contradiction of the Irish lowly rising up to become conqueror of all:

> And Paddy, ridiculed because he will eat dry bread in order to have his children in the parish school, Paddy the labourer, the believer, stands before them like the ghost of an enemy they cannot conquer, who affrights their selfish repose with the threat that his convictions will triumph, because they are the truth that rule the world.

Lemire was lyrical also about the place accorded priests in Paddy's humble vision. For these people ('worthy of the sight of the Angels') their priest was seen as 'religion incarnate', 'the most exalted, the most estimable person in all the world'; they wanted to see him 'living like a man of distinction, a gentleman', seeking to 'afford him that affluence, that distinction, that comfort, which are the stamp of the aristocracy, civil and ecclesiastical'. In 1888 Jules Lemire's priest brother, Achille, had experienced another emanation of this, when arriving with the Bishop and Irish priests at Ballarat railway station:

> ... we fell into the arms that a whole people stretched up towards us. And this people acclaimed us, folded around us and swept us along with them. We were the homeland for these good people. We were the family. We were everything they loved down here. The emotion was indescribable.

Heady stuff. And in some priests this fed a lordly arrogance. Thus Father Slattery in January 1868: 'How poor, how ignorant are these creatures in Pambula'. Some priests stopped there, with a proposition, in the 1860s, probably beyond contention. But many, the best, went on, as Slattery himself did, to add: 'yet they are full of faith. "Blessed are the poor" etc.'. The

Lemire brothers had, by implication, identified the opposite poles of Irish priestly destiny in Australia — that which offered them a role as family, and that which accorded them a role as aristocracy. In a levelling age and in an egalitarian country, the role of aristocrat was dangerous ground to attempt to occupy. And this was so whatever the natural inclination, indeed, whatever the justification in terms of social class or disposition — indeed again, whatever the demands of 'Paddys' determined to set up and serve at the court of a religious nobility: the 'Paddys' would not last forever and would be succeeded by cynical sons. Nor did the family role have a realistic future, for the same reason: the original Irish family would pass away, and with it the welcoming sense of 'the homeland', defined as Ireland. The colonial definition would change so as to render the old family appurtenances foreign.

So, whatever role priests chose had a short future in reality. Pretence and the momentum of habit or inherited role-playing could, and did, extend its life marvellously. What might be called the Moran, Mannix, de Valera mind-frame, the certainty of spiritual superiority and of divinely designated right of religious leadership, dazzled many of those colonials exposed to it into a paralysed sense of their own inferiority and a willingness to be led by such self-assured great men. Such Catholic Australians were willing to cast their own unique history into an Irish mould; to see the fights of boxer Les Darcy as Irish, and those much later Sydney Stadium verbal fights, against communism, as Irish too — Rev. Dr Paddy Ryan versus Edgar Ross, communist, editor *of Common Cause*. Ryan, reminiscence has it, 'had the touch of an educated Irish chieftain', a Sydney Mannix. Echoes indeed of vanished kingdoms, brave Irish battles.

Yet, boxing was never a significant sport in Ireland, as communism was never important in Irish politics. So powerful was the Irish spell that it could generate deference to an Ireland that never existed. To arrive at the painful point at long last, these clerical administrators were men who knew everything and, at the same time, nothing. They knew how to govern, and St Johns, Newfoundland, or the Cape Province were much the same; for, the descriptions of spiritual need and the pleas for priests that arrived at Dublin headquarters from Buenos Aires and from Sydney were almost indistinguishable. But if they knew the problems, and the general outlines of their convinced solutions (more priests, tighter regulation, Catholic education, more Irishness), few of the generals knew the actual ground. If (the pioneer excepted) they passed over it, it was with feet that

Maynooth College, County Kildare, the premier Irish seminary for secular clergy. (*Bord Failte Photo*)

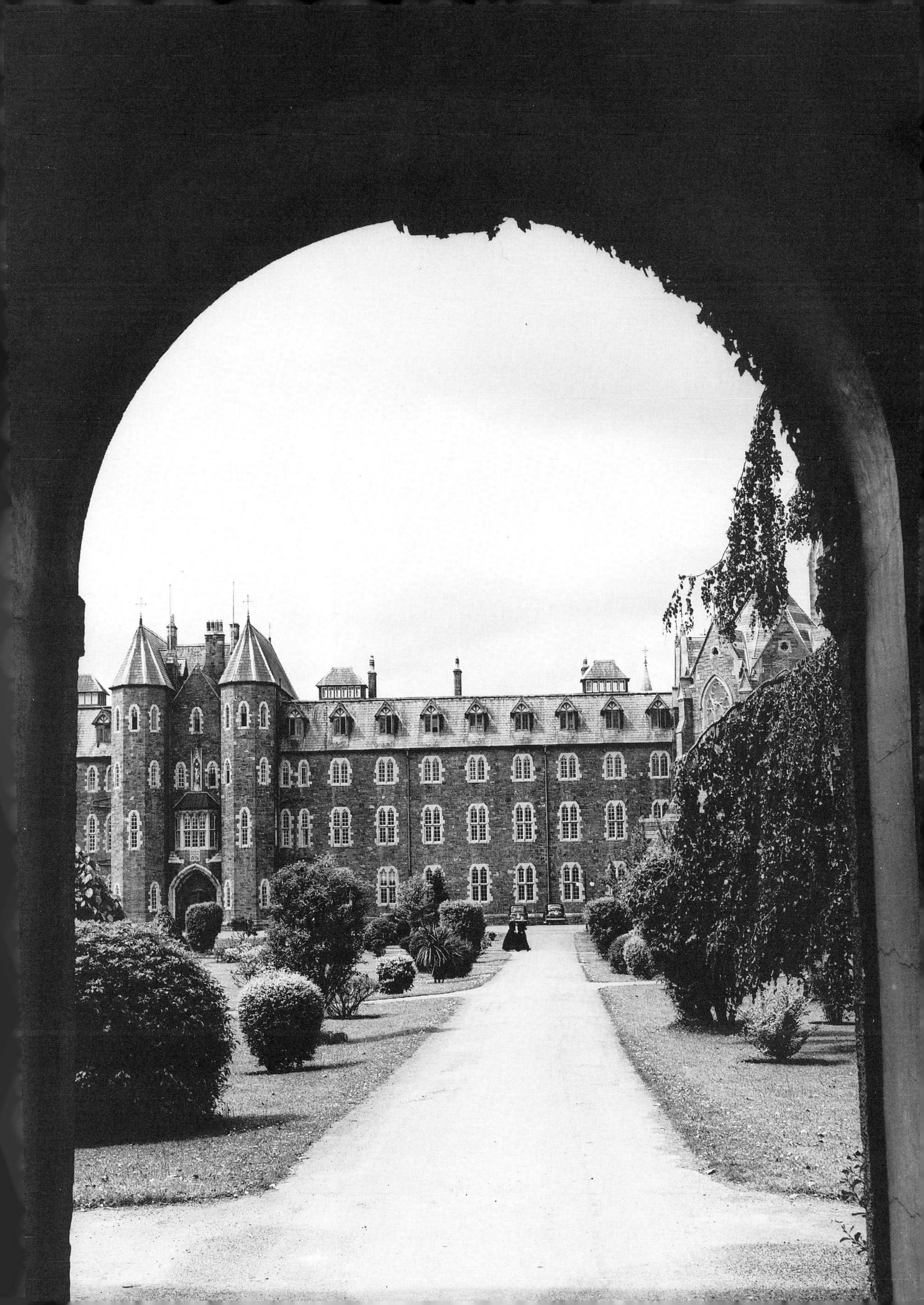

hardly touched the soil; it was in triumphal progress, with retinue, cheer section, and pre-arranged devotees.

So, who occupied the religious ground? To exploit the imperialist imagery, it was local patrol officers, who organised the natives. The problem was — their quality. Beneath the episcopal aristocracy were the rank and file of the clergy, most of them trained at All Hallows, Dublin — a good half of the Australian missionary total, says the college historian Father Kevin Condon. This meant certain Irish things, notably a lesser level of education, and aspirants from a lower social class than that entering Maynooth and other seminaries. To paraphrase Father Condon, the students were limited in background and education, the college education was neither academic nor scientific, but charismatic and religious; the community life was undisciplined. Certainly, it imparted the then Irish Catholic way of life, but it derived its remarkable vitality from a world of poverty and dispossession, and was energised by a deep-rooted nationalism that pervaded its products' missionary world. All these characteristics spelt future problems for the distant society to which they were exported and on which they were imposed. Particularly was this so as that new society expanded and developed apace and, with the death of the Irish-born, acquired a local-born population and character various, diverse and unique. Ireland, by comparison, dwindled in population in little over a century from eight million to under four million.

In a sense, to note all this is simply to record how things were, and where willing and available priests came from. Yet, the question of the suitability of such priests to their new environment can hardly be ignored. The case of Bega, provides some perturbing evidence of what can hardly be viewed as lovable eccentricity. What is to be made of the story told of Dean Gunning, All Hallows graduate of 1885, priest of Bega 1905-33? Hearing of the school children's planned excursion to see the first aeroplane land at Bega — late in 1928 with the aviatrix Amy Johnson — he burst into the school, pointed his blackthorn stick at the Sister's nose, and said: 'If you take those kids down to see that bloody heathen thing I will deal with you': no excursion. Other Bega Irish priests locked latecomers out of mass, or effectively locked them in, by terrorising those who attempted to leave early. Another believed an outlying church sacristy was haunted and refused to sleep there. Others forbade dancing; a not uncommon prohibition elsewhere. To borrow modern parlance, it seems unlikely that it was only Bega that got the crazies.

The marvellous achievements of Irish missionary endeavour, and the eternal indebtedness of other countries to that ministry, spiritual dynamic and personal self-sacrifice, cannot signal the end point of evaluation. The historical process, and religious tradition, is continuous and ongoing. Beyond those matters noted by the All Hallows historian, or the parishioners of Bega, lie further obvious questions and conclusions. Some of its products were not good enough for local Irish consumption but would be adequate for rough distant missions. Some of those who entered were full of missionary zeal and self-less dedication. Others selfishly foresaw a free-ranging and lucrative living in some pleasant and untrammelled colonial backwater. All these various possibilities, positive and negative, proved to have basis, and had outcomes with consequent impact on the various colonial environments in which such men were placed.

From the beginning, the late 1840s, there were episcopal complaints about the qualities of some of these priests. Such complaints were at times trivial — their table manners, or a generally uncouth bearing. At times they were more substantial — that their ill-educated insensitivity made them unacceptable to the aspirations and temper of an increasing genteel or sophisticated laity — and, at times, quite serious (quite apart from the normal human quota of weaknesses such as drunkenness, sexual problems, mental illness). In her forthcoming study of the Presentation sisters at Coonamble New South Wales, Sinead O'Brien remarks on the extraordinary behaviour of the two local priests towards the nuns, refusing to attend a fund-raising school concert because it would take money from their own pockets. Mother Synan reported Father Clancy as saying, of the nuns' fund-raising efforts: 'they are doing us great harm for they are getting what is our right'. Clancy even ridiculed the nuns to their pupils. Such rivalry was scandalous to, and divisive of, the laity, with the majority sympathetic to the nuns, as teachers of their children. It was a situation difficult for a remote bishop to control, and he was often insufficiently aware of it. What he was often very aware of — priests were better able to press their grievances than nuns — was inter-clerical disputes over parish boundaries, which were usually in reality wrangles over sources of revenue, collection money from affluent centres. Such conflicts were frequent, and at best, unseemly.

All this is hardly surprising. Baser elements of human nature vied with the sacrament of Holy Orders as they always will. And there is another way of interpreting and evaluating the coarseness and crudity of the All Hallows products and some Irish generally — that, particularly in the outback, and well into the twentieth century, they suited, indeed fitted like a glove, the harshness with which they were compelled to deal. It is a case which Pat Tully makes, in detrimental contrast to their modern counterparts: 'It was not only the Irish laity who were rough and tough. The priests were even more so . . . '

The colonial mission in primitive mode. Herberton in North Queensland, 1884. A photograph sent back to Ireland by Father J.D. Murray O.S.A (*Father M. Endicott*)

Even more so? Therein lies the problem. Tully's stories to illustrate this are equivocal. They tell of priests who spurred themselves into the scriptural highways and byways, represented in Tully's experience by the remote mustering camps of western Queensland, there to remind, in the hard ways of desert men, wayward Catholics of their duties and to administer the sacraments. His stories tell also of some of the cost and casualties. The Tullys had their own station chapel, where a procession of clerics over the years — men who were falling apart under stress — retreated into the wilderness to escape and 'lick their wounds'. Most of these were Irish, many — and the acidity of his recollection is significant — aggressively, even scatalogically sectarian: priests unaware, or uncaring, of their radical religious disharmony with the social environment. Here Tully's stories become harsh, unamusing. They reflect a priesthood impervious to local human values, clerics assuming a commonalty in raucous, offensive bigotry where it did not exist, and conducting what amounted to personal persecutions to gain, not only the way of the Lord, but the satisfaction of personal pride and will.

So the Redemptorist from Ulster telling the tale of the Belfast Catholic Irishwoman, in great pain in hospital, approached by a Presbyterian minister with an offer to read from his 'little black book' to be told crudely and graphically to use it otherwise: 'Hadn't she the Faith, Pat, the Great Faith, and the hatred of heresy!' The same priest horrified, seemingly at some kind of desecration, that Tully should extend a meal and the hospitality of the bush to an Anglican Bush Brother. And Father Pat, very lax with his language, but strict on his view of doctrine. A parishioner had died who had been generous to the Salvation Army: the local officer arrived, to ask if he could assist with the funeral: 'Get out, ya bastard. We want no unskilled labour on this job'. Father Pat, in the pioneer tradition, would ride an unbroken colt twenty miles to a dying man; and, as a powerful fighter, he would dispense rough justice with his fists to a local wife-beater and thug. Father C. was in similar anti-Protestant mould. He would never say Mass for a deceased Protestant, in a community where Catholic and Protestant were often close friends. Careless Catholics he harried mercilessly and publicly — and famously in the case of one trapped in the station-yard WC, who had his sins (bad women) recited to the bystanders until he emerged to confess. A Charleville priest, cited to his bishop by twelve of his parishioners for visiting a certain house too frequently, read back their letter at mass and retailed all the scandal he knew on each of the twelve, suggesting they were ill-equipped to cast the first stone. Was all this the way to civilise a community, win its respect and confidence, reveal the beauty of holiness to a plural society?

These were performances natural to a primitive nineteenth century Irish Catholic village; as areas of Australia — even remote ones — moved further towards shedding any vestiges of resemblance to such an Irish society, the more out of place, outlandish, repellent and repugnant, did such theatricals become. So it was recognised in the hearts and minds of men and women. But in deference to God's representatives, rather

Below: The O'Connell Statue erected in the grounds of St Patrick's Cathedral, Melbourne, not in the commanding public place desired, nor completed until 1891.

than in cowardice, their tongues toed the traditional accepting line of silence. Sad parting of ways, as popular culture secretly lost faith in the relevance of that kind of religion.

Above all else, the element in the priesthood which was Irish nationalist introduced a basic complication and misunderstanding. The success of appeals in Australia for Irish famine relief, visiting Home Rule delegations, and the like, bred amongst the clergy a very false impression. They should have taken more note of the scant and tardy support evoked by the John Mitchel Fund in 1874 or even of the Daniel O'Connell Centenary Appeals in 1875, which in some cases dragged on for twenty years before reaching their objectives: the Melbourne statue is an instance, in Australia's Irish heartland. The reality was that a very large element in Australia's Irish clergy — even Daniel Mannix — was out of kilter with their laity without realising it: out of kilter even with the Irish-born laity, not to mention the Australian-born. They assumed a sympathy for and identity with Ireland, which did not exist. That they should do so is easy to understand. They talked to, or at, their laity, from a height and distance; they listened only to themselves in their own company. They came from Irish villages: they simply did not know how to think of themselves in relation to Australia and Australians, and it was easiest to just remain Irish. But with a difference. The Irish village or town mounted its own scrutiny and tests, which inhibited some kinds of priestly behaviour and imposed its own disciplines. Too often the Australian posting held no discipline and possessed no tradition, to the inflation of priestly authority and the indulgence of those clerics — happily, comparatively few — who were in Australia to make big money or, and these were more numerous, to build big houses for themselves and their religion.

Moreover, despite the claims to complete identity, they came from different Irish sub-cultures from their laity, cultures which intersected at various times and issues, and then drew apart. Thus, the clergy were by tradition and training more European and more anglicised than their laity, until the Gaelic revival and various strands of Irish nationalism, mainly cultural-religious, contrived a strange reversal of role late in the nineteenth century. Then, when the laity were galloping headlong towards modernisation and anglicisation, the clergy were rejecting those things as corrupt and irreligious. And while the nineteenth century began with the clergy a social, cultural, and educational aristocracy, which largely remained the case in the persons of the hierarchy, by the end of the century the ordinary priesthood was dropping behind the social-class position of an increasing number of their laity. The priests had become the peasants, a situation they were not likely to admit, even if (again it was unlikely) they recognised it.

Further, they assumed that Irish birth, even Irish descent, meant shared attitudes in everything. A common religion to them implied, unthinkingly, a common attitude to Ireland and things Irish. They overlooked a fundamental difference in commitment and orientation. They were itinerant, missionary, visitors. The laity were permanents, residents, settlers. The priests' homes, that is, their families, mothers, were in Ireland; they returned there periodically, some quite often if they had the means. Those in religious orders were members of Irish provinces, that is, simply posted for some set period to the

Dr Arthur Hanrahan, with a large Australian cat.

Australian station. Their priest friends were Irish, and very often their lay friends also were if social class permitted. Dr Arthur Hanrahan, a medical practitioner in South Australia, moved naturally with Irish Jesuits; they were at home with him, knew the same Dublin families, were of the same moneyed class. They expressed delight in 1916 that he had chosen an Irish wife: contempt for colonials was diminishing, but Irish with social pretensions (and some Irish Jesuits had ample of those) still had no doubt about which was the better quality article. Hanrahan himself gravitated in any crowd to where he could hear a Dublin accent, which his ear picked out unerringly. And Hanrahan found the whole Australian thing an adventure, something of a romance, an experience to be viewed from above, from the outside, as an exteriority. In this he was just like so many of the priests — above, not part of. And did not the locals note this? That the Irish Jesuits hosted the Irish Hanrahan, and vice versa? That these priests were outsiders? All totally natural and human; but all also alienating and divisive. Even that old King, Ned Ryan, had no doubts where his future lay — in Australia. That did not stop King Ned parading his household and persona in Irish regalia, a pattern of behaviour which was standard polite practice in the Irish Australian community, but which was also the source of great clerical misunderstanding, error and presumption. The standard local welcome arch, for visiting clerics from Polding to Moran and well into this century, proclaimed *'Céad Míle Fáilthe'* (a hundred thousand welcomes) and the lay speeches were full of affirmations of loyalty to 'the Old Land' — and the new. Note, 'the Old Land', not 'Home' as was the English usage — and the Irish clerical. There was a 'world of difference' (an exact phrase in this case, not a cliche) between the two terms, which the clergy failed to notice. What of the fulsome Gaelic greeting? A performance by way of token proclamation of origins and differences, sincerely meant, and to be respected, but not indicative of some full-blown affirmation of some Irish policy of Thorough.

Nor did these Irish clerics, not seeing or sensing the difference, have any occasion to ponder why there should be one. A very little thought might have discerned that, beneath the green trappings and clichés and docility and the apparent deference, this was not an Irish laity. These were people who had left Ireland for something Ireland could not give. Not just for prosperity — that was to see skin-deep. But for what went with that: freedom, security, confidence, independence, a whole range of attitudes, styles and outlooks the clergy did not encounter in Ireland, and simply did not recognise in what they automatically presumed was Ireland once again — because, arrogance of arrogances, they were there. Wherever they were, was Ireland: the English had taught the insolence of imperialism better than they knew.

Cardinal Moran fell victim to, and expressed with startling clarity, this petrifying illusion of the duplication of Ireland in Australia, when he first visited Boorowa, New South Wales, in 1885 to visit the Mercy Convent (now vacated by religious and in use as a private dwelling). He saw, was dazzled by, all the externals — the church of St Patrick, nuns under the mantle of St Bridget, schools, priests, Total Abstinence Association. He proclaimed that 'it seemed to him as though some privileged town of the dear old West [of Ireland] was by magic wand translated to this new world to be set as a brilliant gem in the crown of sanctity of the Holy Church beneath the Southern Cross'. Boorowa a privileged Carlow (Moran's birthplace) or Thurles? Castlebar translated? This paralysing delusion was anticipated and repeated a thousand thoughtless times around Irish Australia and Irish New Zealand as a new world was crammed by an army of priests into the mental constricts of

St Patrick's Church, Boorowa, New South Wales. Could it be the west of Ireland?

Another Moran opening ceremony. The convent at Braidwood, 21 November 1909. (*National Library of Australia*)

the old. That Moran, prince of the church, scholar, man of missionary vision, energetic architect of a new non-Benedictine Australian church, could see only Ireland when he beheld Australia, was imaginative blindness of major proportions and profound consequence.

Did he pause to think how such settlements came to sprout such Irish nomenclature and religious apparatus? His unthinking assumption was that they arose spontaneously from the very ground, the inevitable outgrowth of pervasive Irishness. In fact, they were the outcome of automatic clerical decisions, that a church be called 'St Patrick's', that Irish nuns be invited; these were obvious decisions certainly, familiar ones, unexceptional to the laity. But they were external constructs, not natural local expressions. (Such local expressions were few. It is unlikely that Moran knew that his famous green, penny catechism, approved by the 1885 Plenary Council was known by children and parents as 'Cardinal Moran's "funny cuts" ').

That an acquiescent laity, or that section of it closest to the priest, should accept such Irish externalities and names was natural. They knew nothing else, there was nothing else; and it it unlikely that they cared. It was the priest's decision anyhow. What they did not know was that from the seventeenth to the nineteenth centuries, the papacy had been at embarrassed pains, from time to time, to distinguish the orthodoxy of international Catholicism from the very different and peculiar local variant that had developed in Ireland. What the Catholic inhabitants of nineteenth century Australia thought (if they thought at all) they were getting by way of religion was unadulterated core Catholicism. What they were really getting (in worst case extreme circumstances) was the religious vagaries and political imperialisms of a tiny island off the coast of Europe, a narrow localism which expressed Irish history, Irish attitudes and Irish interests. Given no choice, they could sense and see the value and virtue of that. Such Irishness was a distinguishing identity, valuable as a device and rallying point for colonial purposes, some anchor against loss of self until they found their feet or could swim in strange water. To the laity, their Irishness had a transitory social and psychological role. Its value was as a bridge to their new identity, to be used en route. Their priesthood took it to be a permanent condition, an enduring edifice to be shored up, aggressively asserted, managed as if it were in Ireland.

That the priesthood had a religious case is undoubted. Part of their campaign was, indeed, properly a follow-up to Cullen's Irish war against the people's indifference, non-practice, indiscipline. And part of their vigorous defence of their laity against external attack was necessary and appreciated, in little things as well as large. When, in the early 1880s (the story is Sinead O'Brien's), the Coonamble Public School teacher took to treating his Catholic pupils with contempt, ridiculing their 'Irish ways', christening them 'Paddy' or 'Irish Judy', he may have been mad or drunk, but the bishop's retaliatory instruction to withdraw all Catholics was enthusiastically welcomed. Yet, was there not some other possible response, less total, less extreme? Defence too often escalated into full-scale attack, and that onslaught was prone to sweeping up, on the way to savaging the enemy, all other traditional Irish bogeys — England, Protestantism, proselytism, landlords, what ever came to mind — simply translated, relevant or not, to the colonies. Translated: Moran's word, Moran's essential policy. It won him the appearances of an imitation Irish church, but did it lose him, and those who followed his lead, the enduring elements of a thriving local-based religion?

This was the broader insensitivity in which was set the narrower assumption that the laity shared the clergy's Irish nationalism, in its varying degrees, up to the 'fervour' (nationalist as well as religious), embraced by the graduates of All Hallows. It took the Manly Australian priests' union and the Australian repugnance to the Irish Civil War of 1922–23 to dint this assumption. Even then, the realisation that Irishness in politics might be unwanted in 'Irish' Australia had a very limited carry-over to any general Irish clerical questioning of the popularity of the Irish religious style or leadership. Nor was the matter ended by such apparent landmarks of Australianisation in the Catholic church as the appointment of Cardinal Gilroy as archbishop of Sydney in 1940, or the death of Archbishop Mannix in 1963. Even into the revival of Irish political issues by the Northern Ireland conflict from 1968, almost half a century on from the great disillusionment of the Irish Civil War, priests — presumably Irish — were in some Australian areas still introducing contentious Irish topics, and influencing, indeed dictating, opinion on them. Consider the raw comments made in a 1970s interview by a socialist dairy farmer in south-west Victoria, on his devoutly Catholic sisters:

> Like, take the IRA. Now last year they were all in favour of it. They thought she was a great thing. But now all of a sudden she's no go, and if you so much as mention it you'll get a clip around the bloody ear. Yes, there's been a write up in *News Weekly* I wouldn't mind betting, as to how she's a Marxist show, and nothing to do with the Catholics. Like, I reckon that's what happened — either that or the priest's said it to them, telling them they're not to have anything to do with it. They all take the bloody thing . . . like me sisters and all the rest, they all take it, the bloody *News Weekly*. Christ, you'd think they hadn't a thought to bless themselves with other than what Santamaria and the bloody priest put between their ears. Yes, a lot of poor priest-ridden bastards.

Hostile, embittered reportage certainly, saying something resembling the facts of Irish clerical authoritarianism into the 1970s, used in relation to Irish topics and locations foreign to their congregations. How far this distanced such priests from people who slept through or rebelled against such irrelevance is impossible to say, or whether that distancing and its misuse of power and position harmed the seedbeds of faith; but its negative function lay in far more than its being an obstacle or an irrelevancy. The assumption of the existence of an inherent, local born, Australian Catholic Irishness, and the protracted campaign to impose or defend it from the 1920s, when it was under question by men — clerics — of good will, took its clerical champions into their most serious area of culpability. This was the failure to locate the Catholic faith in a real Australian cultural setting. The consequence eventually was that, to some products of the Irish-conditioned religious system, it would seem a cultural excrescence, a wonderful, exotic imposition, which felt foreign and weighed heavy. Good reason (or excuse) to reject it as an imperialism and authority out of keeping with personal and cultural independence. What saved the Catholic religious essence, for those who saw beneath the Irishness, was the reality of the buried international dimension, the other roads it implied to universal Catholicism, and the adamantine strength of its spiritual qualities. The religion of which it offered one national variant survived, but damaged, diminished, and still adrift in the land that had given that variant so long a tenancy.

French clerical commentator Jules Lemire saw such dangers as early as the late 1880s, at the zenith of Irish hegemony, in views published in 1894. For all its marvels of Australian achievement, he saw to the heart of the flaws central to the then vibrant Irish missionary church, faults whose 'consequences become each day more damaging. They have no practical sense of perseverance or tenacity of purpose', grave faults 'liable to compromise the success of a venture'. Theirs was 'an Irish Church', 'isolated', which 'must escape from this Irish circle that confines it'. 'It is not enough to do what was good enough in Ireland, to hold to Irish ways.' The Irish priesthood must move out of its narrow orbit, into the general community, in a spirit of courtesy and trust.

Lemire found this priesthood rough and authoritarian, many of its members in Australia because of their inability to find parishes at home rather than moved by any missionary vocation or intention. They were hard workers, with big hearts, but full of harsh reprimands. They got away with it, provided they used an Irish accent and Irish expressions of reproof. They were instinctively repelled by coloured people, whom they regarded as inferior. And above all (and Lemire uses the word) they were — 'foreigners'; and 'foreign clergy, useful as they may be, constitute a danger or at least a weakness, for a Church cannot be assimilated into a country unless it can support itself'. It was imperative, urgent, that they be replaced, by Australian-born clergy.

Lemire was highly critical of Moran's efforts in that direction — St Patrick's College seminary at Manly; it was too large and unattractive, he thought, impracticable, an exercise in the Irish grandiose. And 'as a general rule the churches are vulgar

— AND PRIESTS

St Joseph's Catholic School, Boorowa, taken early in 1900s. Irish in shape and style, but Australian in materials — brick, corrugated iron, picket fence. (*National Library of Australia*)

with neither style nor distinction'; and, again, they were 'foreign'. He was particularly critical of St Patrick's, Melbourne: 'The huge mass of dark, melancholy stone which rises up to the pure, dazzling Australian sky needs some touch of joyfulness. The structure is in painful contrast to the local colour, to the gaiety that surrounds it. Some people . . . see the outward severity of their church a constant and serious lesson for the frivolous people of the city'. Lemire disagreed with such a view. Churches, he believed, should not be like this, symbolising public censure and religious barrier, radiating gloom. They should assimilate in architecture to the climate and the light, be at one with the environment. 'Gothic architecture belongs to dark skies and the shady fields of our countries. It is out of place under a bright sky or among Australia's gum trees'. Out of place — that phrase again; Polding's phrase and like his, to be, not so much brushed aside or derided but

Lemire's joyless, painful, contrast: the spires of St Patrick's Melbourne.

simply never heard — not audible above the loud self-confident bustle of Irish clerics going about their redemptive business among their own countrymen and those they pretended were their own countrymen by virtue of descent.

Yet even there, for all his admiration of their spiritual services, Lemire would not concede that these Irish clerics were true missionaries, starting from scratch. The nature of their potential congregations gave them a head start, a massive advantage derived from centuries of deep, ineradicable faith. Commenting on the effect of the sudden passing in Australia from 'wretchedness to riches', he contended that:

> Morality has collapsed, smothering under its ruins the practice of religion. To be fair, however, it should be admitted that the Faith has not been completely lost to these victims of isolation or sudden wealth, since they still remained Irish. For it is unthinkable, not to

— AND PRIESTS

say impossible that an Irishman born in Ireland should ever become impious or Voltairian. He will take to drink, commit crimes of passion, but he will never coldly deliberately renounce the faith of his baptism. On his death bed, he will . . . never refuse to confess his sins and be reconciled with God. The fact of having been born in Ireland of Irish Catholic parents is for him, so to speak, a kind of eighth sacrament, whose special effect and grace are to preserve his faith.

But this is to speak of past times — the gold rushes — and a dying breed: those born in Ireland of Irish Catholic parents, a qualification Lemire reiterates. All others (and by 1894 most Catholics were not of Irish birth) were in grave danger of perishing in a religious vacuum.

It was those priests, fortunately there were many, who most moved away from braggart 'Irishness' who did both priesthood

Perhaps Father Lemire would have approved of the Mediterranean look of the church on the coast at Gerringong, New South Wales, a reflection in white of sun and sea — but the white is a relatively modern presentation of a building named after Mary, Star of the Sea.

and people best service, those whose luminous Catholicism most abstracted from the Irish origins and circumstances. It was these 'gentlemen of the cloth', like Paddy O'Farrell's frail and ailing Jesuit brother, or Paddy's saintly parish priest, whose religion left colonials and Irish alike most free to be themselves. It was the bullies and the boyos who did most harm, either in evoking similar thuggery in colonial environments open to such coarseness or sectarianism, or by driving away, or stilling, the forces of independent creativity in religion, refinement and individuality. This is to say nothing of their failure to build or encourage such things.

From such strictures, the contradictions and ecclesiastical aristocracy of Moran and Mannix offer them partial exception. It was Moran who instituted the three intellectually high-powered Australasian Catholic Congresses of 1900, 1904 and 1909, the quarterly *Australasian Catholic Record*, which still thrives; and he identified himself with those core developments of Australian history, federation, and the labour movement. It was Mannix who discerned the threats to Australian life that lay within conscription and communism, and who embarked on, and encouraged, effective means to combat them. Such engagements with the mainsprings of Australian experience were of the greatest importance, but they were, necessarily, interventions from outside, the perceptions of those who did not belong: impositions of external authority rather than the promptings of self-awareness.

Residual ecclesiastical authority (bequeathed in part to colonial clones) collapsed in the 1960s; when that happened in the years immediately following Paddy's death in 1950, there was little left of his Irish generation's colonial acquiescence and perception of religious essentials. Gone was the trained patience and perseverance, the habit of quiet, the granting of respect for office, the sufferance of fools. Colonial religion was left with the Irish variant of the legacy common to any departing imperialism: large, imposing, useless buildings, a colourful and burdensome past, and the problem of what now to attempt to construct specific and appropriate to themselves. It was left also with a host of disruptive and confused deserters and supporters from the old regime.

The imperial legacy is clearly set out in Aubrey de Vere's anthem for All Hallows:

> Hope of my country! House of God,
> All Hallows! . . .
> That race of God that conquers earth — . . .

'Large, imposing, useless buildings'. The Greymouth Mercy Convent, 1989. The hoarding reads 'Stage One. Restaurants & Function Rooms. Maximillians. Stage Two. 50 Luxury Accommodation Units'. The building was still vacant, the transformation not having commenced.

Evangelisation conducted with such racial confidence, and in such a spirit of masterful imperialism, no doubt did wonders for the revival and sustenance of the imperial power itself, expressing its need to rule, its dynamic ambition, its sense of superiority, and its identification with the will of God. The Irish were the instruments of God. But what was the effect on the colonised, those on whom this Godly army was quartered? For all the self-sacrifice of the conquerors, their goodness and good intentions, their spiritual grandeur, the effect lay in much the same range of reactions as that induced by more earthly imperiums. It lay in mindless acceptance, slavish imitation and abasement, sycophancy and parasitism, sour rebellion, destructive hostility, and obsession, either with the preservation or the abolition of the old regime, which even in its vanishing remained the measure of all things. Or if the military image be rejected as harsh and unfitting, and the softer authority of fatherhood be substituted, here was a step-parentage which, however worthy, noble and dedicated, had prevailed too long, and deprived its care of its vigorous, unique, youth. It remained to be seen how such a dispossessed progeny would cope on its own with the demands of maturer age.

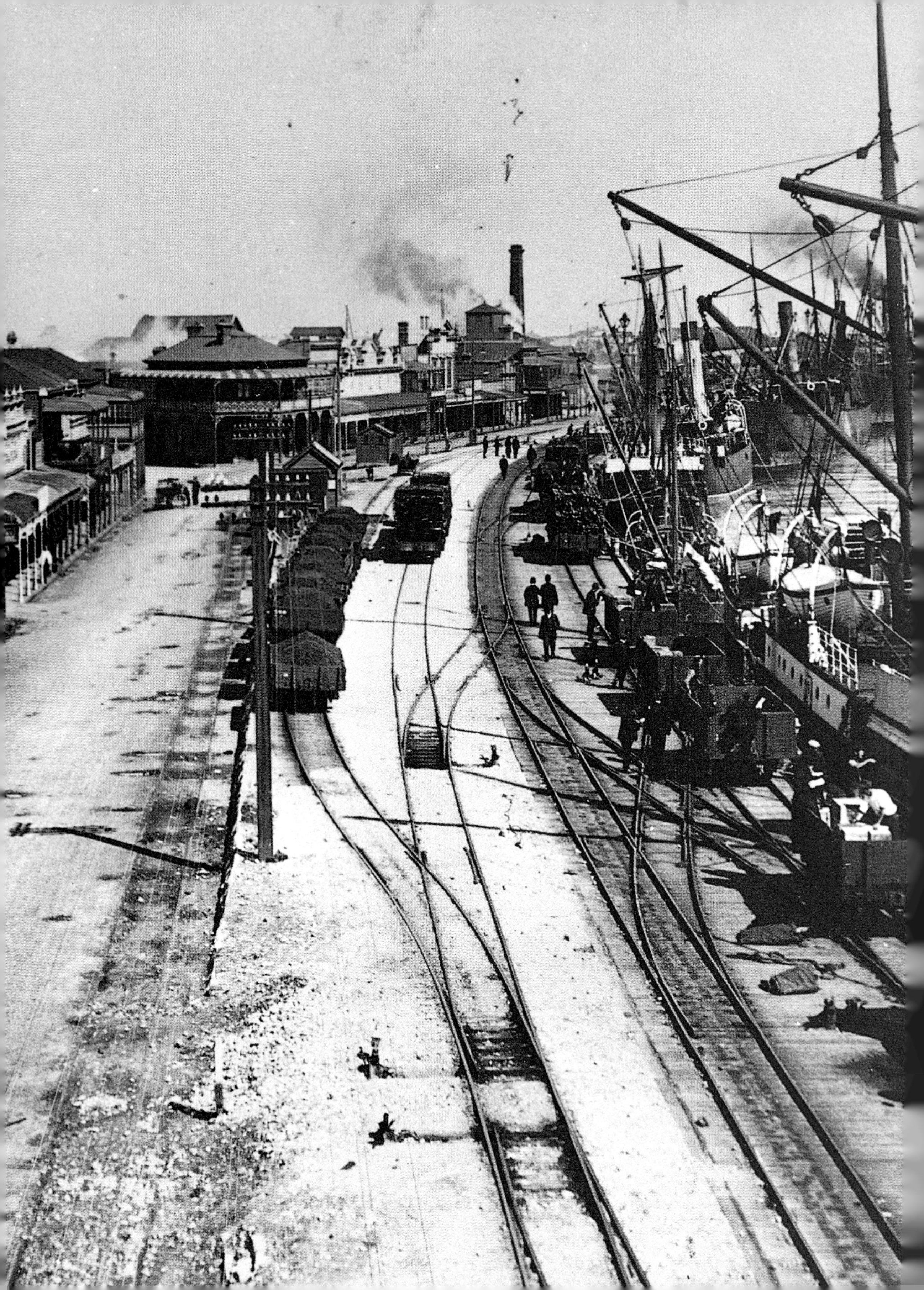

CHAPTER 5

COLONIAL IRISH: THEMES

It is self-evident that the Irish emigrant came from an Irish culture — or rather, to be importantly exact — from that phase and variety of Irish culture which existed and prevailed at the time and place in Ireland from which the emigrant departed. As Ireland moved into the twentieth century, this culture, already subject to major religious division, became increasingly more complex and contradictory, as the pervasive influences of anglicisation were challenged by the forces of the Gaelic revival. How much of an individual's cultural environment was Irish or English depended on a range of factors. There was location (the west was in marked contrast to anglicised Dublin), social class and education, access to railways and the communications they enabled, a host of variables, and, of course, personal attitudes to the cultural resources on offer. Given a choice, some preferred Gaelic mythology or the classic English novel, others the novels of Canon Sheehan, others the penny dreadfuls or pulp romances of the English publishing houses. It is, thus, absurd to attribute a common standard 'Irish' culture to the Irish immigrant of, particularly, the post-Famine era, and again especially in this

The Greymouth waterfront, about the time of Paddy's arrival in 1916 (Canterbury Museum, Christchurch)

century. Yet, some degree of common ground can be clearly assumed in the major categories: for the Catholic majority there was the apparatus of Catholicism; for Protestants, the Bible. For Protestants there was a far more anglicised Imperial heritage; for Catholics, their own history, with a strongly nationalist emphasis and a heroic structure.

My parents illustrate both the mainstream and the complications of this process. Paddy always harboured a reactive edge against things Irish, as well as a loyalty and identification. With little time for reading until his health deteriorated later in life, his preference was for the ultra-English, the aristocratic eccentricities of Osbert Sitwell's *Left Hand, Right Hand*, the pukka imperialism of John Buchan. How much this had to do with the stock available in the local Carnegie Public Library, thirty years of colonial conditioning, the unremitting seriousness and political or religious obsessions of such Irish books as were available, and Paddy's foremost preference for a good yarn of whatever origin (he devoured James Fenimore Cooper's Red Indian tales, plus Zane Grey and Clarence E. Mulford) — all these influences are hard to disentangle. Or perhaps they are not. The core of his reading, the basic food of his imagination, was the frontier. The British and the Americans were the experts on that, in fiction and fact: Sir Ernest Shackleton's *South* (1923) and Frederick O'Brien's *Mystic Isles of the South Seas* (1921) kept shelf company with the adventure novels. Or — to explain what might seem cultural betrayal or rejection — he read about on the grand scale, in actuality or invention, what he had himself attempted in minor key.

The cultural and literary legacy of Ireland was intense domestic introspection, political and religious, the exploration of that convoluted close atmosphere from which Paddy had designedly escaped. It was hardly likely that he would return to it for recreation, or even illumination. He knew it too well already. Somebody passed on to him the Irish satiric-humorous journal *Dublin Opinion*: he never read it, preferred the *New Yorker* or *Punch*. Paddy shared the characteristic noted in the Wellington Irish by Julia Moriarty — bookish, but interested in much more than Irish books; their world was now wider and they were interested in many aspects of it. When in Ireland, that country fully occupied the span of a normal vision. The further one moved away, the more one became conscious of what crowded into the periphery of sight. That could be excluded only by a deliberate narrowing of focus onto Ireland. Normally, from a distance, Ireland became part of a

Mai's old home in Borrisokane in 1965. The rough-casting and ornamental fence were recent additions of questionable merit, proclaiming the then owner's increased affluence.

much wider scene and things formerly unknown attracted attention: the world opened up. The typical colonial attitude, at its healthiest, was no cultural cringe. It was a looking outwards, an openness, in contrast to the way in which Ireland was introspective, obsessively gazing inwards. No, Paddy's reading and the caste of his imaginings, followed his character and inclinations into adventures on the uttermost rim of civilisation. In the black rainstorms that hurled so often from a tumultuous Tasman into a Greymouth huddled in creaking timber and tin houses clinging to the foot of a mountain range, it was easy enough to cast oneself as an intrepid battler at the world's edge. Lashed by the elements, pitted against forces that might sweep one away, yet warm and secure in the inner sense that this conflict and stand, and only this, was real; this was being alive. To test the nerve by inhabiting and thus mastering this primitive outpost, to hold it against the onslaught and the odds, was to sustain victory over self. In the biblical language of the day, it was to make the stone the builders of the old land had rejected, the proud cornerstone of the new.

Surely to comment thus is to inflate this process, to glorify the ordinary, inchoate impulses that formed the identity and sense of self of common men and women? In climates the reverse of Greymouth's sodden gales, countless other immigrants spun off by their homeland took their stand against forbidding and challenging environments. They did so with the same sense of response and self-assertion, the same glow of excitement when confronted by hostile bush or desert, the same determination to prove in themselves that spirit of enterprise which the old world denied. For such immigrants, engagement with the new world, the combat with its environment, left little energy, time, or disposition, to dwell on the irrelevant old.

Colonial adventuring is a theme which stretches back deep into Irish history in forms both military and settlemental. As early as the sixteenth century, the Irish abroad were a significant part of Ireland's history, and on a worldwide stage. Irish priests and soldiers could be found everywhere, notably in the seminaries and armies of France and Spain, and wherever exotic those imperialisms spread — Chile, Argentina, Venezuela. The subject is a vast and complex one, its central adventuring and missionising impulse overlapping to various degrees with the ordinariness of more usual emigrant life. Real life examples of Irishmen at the adventuring fringe flood to mind, one close to home in Peter Dillon of Vanikoro, arriving in

Calcutta in 1826 aboard his ship *St Patrick*, with two Maoris he had dubbed His Royal Highness Brian Boru, Prince of New Zealand, and his aide, Morgan McMurroc. More within popular general acquaintance is what might be called the Fitzcarraldo syndrome, to borrow from Werner Hertzog's film. This portrays Brian Sweeney Fitzgerald, Irish Latin-American adventurer, rich on rubber, who sets about building a flamboyant opera house on the bank of the Amazon, and then embarks on a fantastic scheme to haul a steamship across a mountain range from one river to another. This is done through dense tropical jungle, with prodigious human effort and bizarre engineering, to the accompaniment of recordings of operatic arias. It is a tale of a man part practical idealist, part artist and dreamer of grand designs, part inspirer, part mad; a cultured obsessive nomad at war with the primitivism of the world's jungled rim, and in tension with his extravagant ambition and his own, and his environment's, limitations. Fitzcarraldo is the Irish frontier adventurer at a crazy extreme, but his was a direction in which many Irish colonists were moving in much smaller, less hazardous, ways.

Macho stuff? Not at all. What was being pursued and liberated in such colonial environments was personal freedom, the flowering of individual identity, and that was a process involving male and female alike. Alike, within social constraints and role-modelling certainly, but within a related heroic mould. Both Irish men and women recoiled from the dull ordinariness of their former lives and rejected the idea that such tedium was their ordained future. Looking in (as I did) from the accustomed open, sparsely inhabited, expanses of the frontier, to me the Irish writer Frank O'Connor seemed to have captured, in *Domestic Relations*, the wonderful essence of an Irish household world. How my mother would enjoy this evocative re-creation of a world she had left and whose memory she relived in terms of the fun of Cork! She hated the book — too real; its subtle sharpness had the bite of a remembered rat trap. Fond memory was best enjoyed without such shivering literary anchors to stop its floating. Like Paddy, Mai preferred freedom; in literature the open, grand designs of family saga, Galsworthy, Sigrid Undset. What is significant is not their imaginative, romantic preferences, shared by millions other than Irish, but rather their avoidance of reliving the literature-distilled encapsulated experience of their homeland. For them this was too dark a mirror. Those who were dazzled by it were others: foreigners, subsequent colonial Irish generations whose experience was not direct, and some of those Irish whose socio-economic class and education placed them in an English rather than an Irish cultural world.

But for the ordinary refugee and adventurer, it was heroes and heroines. Paddy had a range that amused him. Some, like Deerfoot, Indian brave, inhabited worlds of forest and tracking not too different from his own environment. Some, like the incredible Sitwells, appealed through their flamboyant, aristocratic individuality. Mai took her heroines more seriously, and from the Irish and religious traditions: Saint Thérèse, the Little Flower — but saints were in the remote category. Ireland had a strong female literary and political tradition with which Mai identified, not actively as participant, but strongly enough to copy out, and keep, newspaper articles on the notables of that facet of the Irish world. Her particular interest was 'Eva' of the *Nation* (Eva Kelly, wife of the 1848 rebel, Kevin Izod O'Doherty). A star-crossed lover, married to her dream hero, renowned for sentimental nationalist poetry, dying in colonial Brisbane in 1910, Eva was one of three women — the others being 'Speranza' (Lady Wilde) and 'Mary' (Sister Mary Alphonsus) — who had written for Thomas Davis's immensely popular newspaper, the *Nation*, in the 1840s. They were thereafter immortalised in Irish nationalist mythology, their stories being retold journalistically from time to time. My mother's source was probably Eileen Duggan's women's column in the *New Zealand Tablet*, an Irish Catholic religious weekly based in Dunedin.

Mai's interest was in the romance of these women's lives, their role and predicaments as active women, rather than in their nationalism. But basically, whether it was in regard to these women's poetry, or their femininity or degree of independence, it was love that interested Mai, love between men and women: what it was, what it should be, and in particular, how it should be in her own marriage. Grand questions of women's place in the modern world were subsidiary to that very personal question on whose answer her future would be based. Just before her marriage, in an essay, 'Love defined', which she gave to Paddy, Mai set out in her own hand what she understood love to be. She signed it, with no attribution to any other source. Is this the product of an education at the Convent of Mercy, Borrisokane?

> In a strongly virile man, love towards a woman is, in its essential qualities, naturally selfish. Its keynote is, 'I need'; its dominant, 'I want'; its full major chord 'I must possess'.
> On the other hand, the woman's love for the man is essentially

unselfish. Its keynote is, 'He needs; 'its dominant, 'I am his, to do with as he pleases'; its full major chord 'Let me give all'. In the book of Canticles, one of the greatest love-poems ever written, we find this truth exemplified; we see the woman's heart learning its lesson, in a fine crescendo of self-surrender. In the first stanza she says: 'My Beloved is mine & I am his'; in the second, 'I am my Beloved's, and he is mine'. But in the third, all else is merged in the instinctive joy of giving: 'I am my Beloved's & his desire is towards me'.

This is the natural attitude of the sexes, designed by an all-wise Creator; but designed for a condition of ideal perfection. No perfect law could be framed for imperfection. Therefore, if the working out prove often a failure, the fault lies in the imperfection of the workers, not in the perfection of the law. In those rare cases where the love is ideal, the man's 'I take' and the woman's 'I give' blend into an ideal union, each completing & modifying the other. But where sin of any kind comes in, a false note has been struck in the divine harmony & the grand chord of mutual love fails to ring true.

Molly Sullivan

Typical scene, typical weather: Greymouth about the time of Paddy's arrival. (*Canterbury Museum, Christchurch*)

Her own words, or copied sentiments she subscribed to? Whatever the origin, so much for the myths of Irish prudery and the alleged unsophistication of country girls.

Within a few months, the idealistic theory was to be put to severe practical test, not by any sin or falsity, but by other less dramatic and ordinary interventions. The scholasticism of the essay had not provided for Mai's health, and her revulsion from Greymouth and the West Coast of New Zealand.

Paddy found there the life he enjoyed; independence from his brothers and sisters, a taste of adventure in a rough and untamed place, and a gamut of new acquaintances, plus new and absorbing interests, a house, a job, unionist activity and the Labour Party. Mai was confronted by the reverse. All her friends, especially Hannah, were in South Canterbury — in those days an expensive, two-day distance across a terrifying mountain wall. Any new friends were Paddy's, a strange lot of dark and silent folk who seemed of a piece with their coal and timber economy and their incessant grey rain. They oozed suspicion of flighty, uppish women ('G'day, missus' they would grunt) with ideas above an agreed local station, which reflected a worker ethos, a legacy of hard times, and a grimy coastal platform held hard against storm and sea. Or so it all seemed to a newcomer from sunny, bright Canterbury.

Mai found making colonial friends very difficult (though she was eventually to have many, and they beyond praise). She simply could not understand these standoffish un-bubbly people. Thus, always a family person, she swung back even

The Greymouth economy: the coal trade c1914 (*Canterbury Museum, Christchurch*)

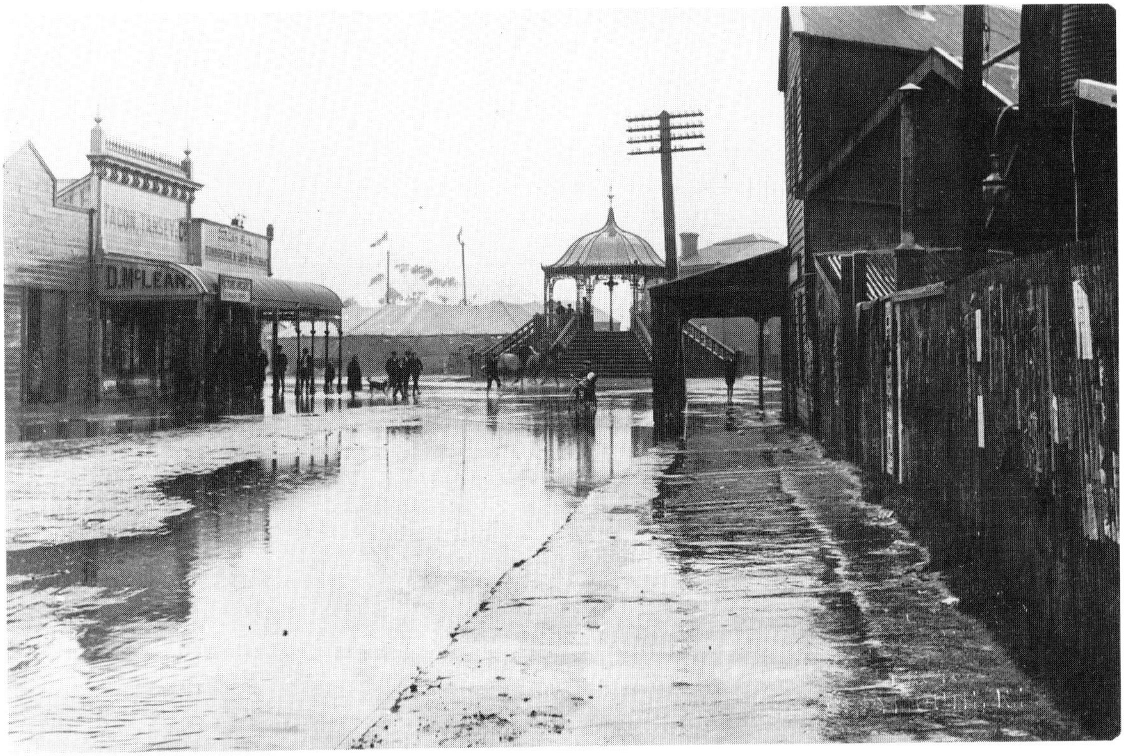
D. McLEAN.

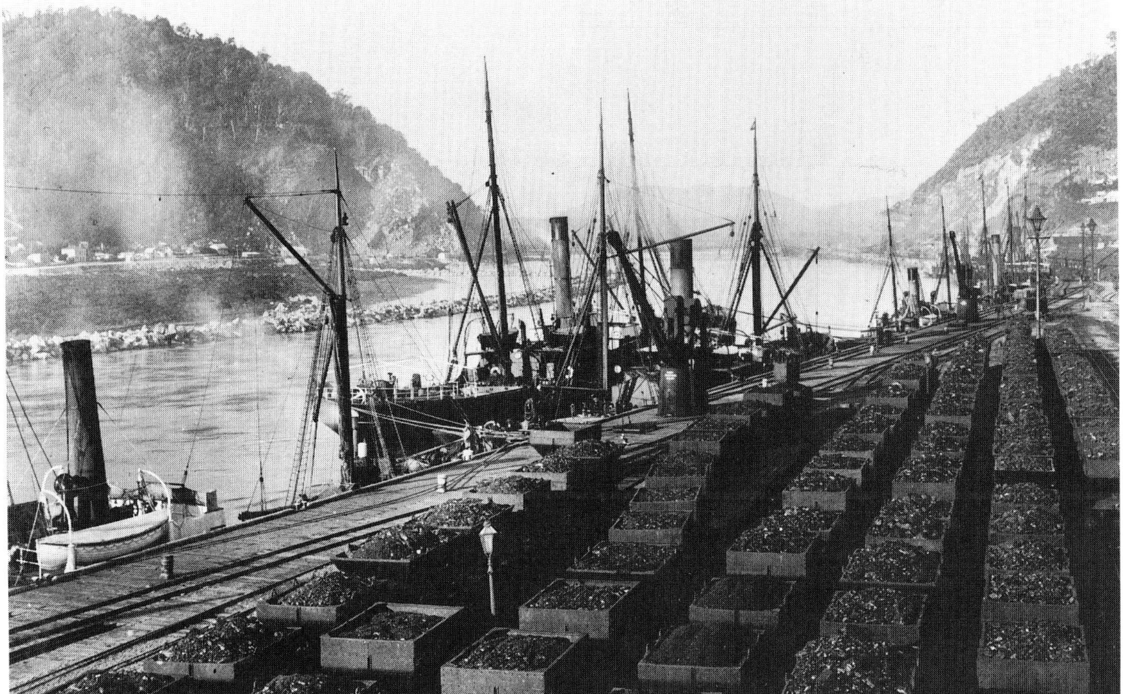

more strongly to dependence on the South Canterbury Irish brigade she loved so well, a movement of the mind that made the Greymouth situation harder, lonelier, and postponed its resolution. In the meantime, locally, she turned to the Greymouth church, not in any impulse of religious zeal, but simply in terms of the familiarity of Irish priests and nuns. To these she turned for the warmth of friendship and understanding she so passionately needed. Mai's is an extreme case. She had been tipped unprepared into the closest and most complex of working communities, that of coal miners, situated at earth's inaccessible end. Testimonies to the impact of this environment tend to cluster around the mine at Denniston, some miles to the north of Greymouth. Said the English trade unionist Tom Mann: 'That place seemed to me the most completely shunted off from civilised society and from humanity generally I had ever seen'. But one of the first women to arrive put it in less stilted terms: 'Well of all the places God had made, this beats all'. Greymouth was better, but only if one had seen Denniston, or Blackball, or Runanga, or other mining centres.

But the cry to God to confirm the nomination of this or that place as the most inhuman and soulless the immigrant had ever encountered must have arisen from countless remote places and times across the whole colonial scene. And in such contexts the consolations of religion might seem warm indeed. Not out of piety, or even out of the need for society, but from something even more basic: humans huddling instinctively together against what they felt to be the forces of nothingness, which would suck them into voids of deserts or mountains, and depersonalise and destroy them. Hence, the popularity of priests and nuns — familiar, fellow-travellers across the face of a hard earth. Persons of religion might understand without words, words which might sound like betrayal, or cowardice, or admission of mistake, but were none of these: they were the plaints of loneliness and bewilderment. And even the Greymouth house. Like the environment and its people, it seemed primitive. There was little furniture, some rooms not yet papered, everything rough and temporary. Not that she did not make an effort. Virtually upon her arrival, in went the sweet peas, gesture towards softness and colour against a grey world, addendum to the inevitable vegetable garden. They flowered in her absence, as Paddy described them, 'simply exquisite now, just a mass of blooms that beggars description'.

But what to do, how to cope, with this barbaric place? Mai fled. Married in October 1920, in January 1921 back in South

COLONIAL IRISH: THEMES

Canterbury, in Struggler's Flat as she called Waimate, staying with Paddy's brother Jack, and with his sister Hannah, or Annie as the colonials preferred to shorten it, who was now married to Harry White, a labourer for a farmer at Arno. This hasty and mysterious departure from Greymouth caused much local comment and insistent questioning directed to Paddy. His correspondence with Mai and doctor's visits in Waimate point to a threatened miscarriage. Did Greymouth acquaintances

Runanga emerges from the bush c1914.

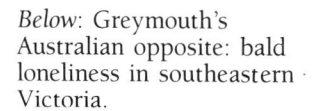

Below: Greymouth's Australian opposite: bald loneliness in southeastern Victoria.

and neighbours know? Probably not: Paddy and Mai were private people and recent arrivals. The reaction to Mai's precipitate leaving (to be cared for by old friends) was so inquisitive and unsympathetic as to suggest ignorance of the circumstances. (Taking ill at this stage was an immigrant's nightmare. An unknown environment, a new marriage, no friends, a house barely habitable, a husband working late hours, without money to pay for help — and pride conspiring against asking for it from strangers.)

Much of the apparently solicitous enquiry had a hidden, sly edge, aimed at people thought above themselves — too private — and that particularly from the Irish. To remark that the colonial scene and circumstances blurred former social distinctions among the Irish, whose home environment was riddled with complex hierarchies, is a generalisation which skims over a process which was often awkward, painful, and loaded with malice, however healthy the eventual outcome may have been. The process was harsh and coercive to the extent that it imposed the crude upon the refined, and forced together those who would have instinctively avoided each other in Ireland. Greymouth's element of Irish bogtrotters resented Mai's distancing herself, her reserve and timidity, and what they took to be her airs. 'Thinks she's too good for us does she?' — and they made her pay. Irish social structures and placement depended on a host of factors, historical and intangible, which were irrelevant in the colonies. There, money and power was what drew respect, perhaps strength and physical prowess. Otherwise, all were deemed equal and expected to perform so, or to pretend to perform so.

Mai's problem, however, was not as simple as the onslaught of an unfamiliar and unwelcome egalitarianism. It was more the sense of a loss of known place. The structures of the old world conferred a hierarchical order, and communicated, in a multitude of subtle ways, the individual's socially acknowledged place and role. That old world breathed wordlessly 'This is where you fit in', a message generally accepted. In contrast, the colonies were chaos, nobody knew where anybody 'fitted in' — they didn't care — and the comfortable machinery for slotting persons into categories which determined treatment and response, hardly existed. This was not an ordered society, but a jumble of unknown individualists bouncing off each other in random unpredictable ways — or so it seemed to Mai, who was initially bewildered, distressed and lost in this strange human jungle.

On the other hand, Paddy loved this jungle or, at least, knew how to survive in it. Writing in February 1921 from 'Angel's Abode' (one of his numerous extravagant glorifications of the humble 13 Puketahi Street), a first letter to Mai since she left, he confessed his initial misery, then his better thought 'that you would benefit so much by the change that I was selfish to be miserable about your being away'. The change? It was a generous view. She had been in Greymouth only three months, in South Canterbury much of the previous years. Paddy had braced up his feelings 'until such time as you want to get back'. The problem was, she didn't. To him, yes (he was fun) but to Greymouth and its unfriendly primitivism, no. This is an aspect of colonial marriage little appreciated. The beloved, met and married in an environment of familiarity and friends, might, at some male whim, or at the dictates of a pioneering economy, whisk off his spouse — or is the truer word, drag? — to some remote and repulsive outpost, devoid of romance, or the amenities which might make female life and work endurable. And all on the assumption, probably seldom surfaced in the male mind, that marriage vows subsumed all such situations. It was a time when they usually did, but the strain they were asked to bear was well outside the normal 'home' experience. The colonies offered some environments beyond the imagination, and at the limits of tolerance, of Irish country girls. In Mary Durack's descriptions of the 1860s, Sarah Tully's mad cross-country rides across their Goulburn property, taken on the impulse of frustration or anger, are in the same category of the bursting urge to break free, though in Sarah's case it was from the oppressions of close living, not loneliness. Fortunate was the young pioneer woman who could saddle up some lively horse and vent her feelings of imprisonment in the movement and danger of some wild ride.

Paddy enclosed £2 (half of all he had) and promised to send plenty of bush honey. This was part of the constant trade in family produce that criss-crossed the Alps thereafter. And then he plied Mai, most injudiciously, with Greymouth news, and the reported doings of his friends. The combined Trades Unions had held a picnic at Totara, to which he would like to have gone — with her. Two thousand people packed a train with three engines hauling it, seatless passengers spilling out to stand on the open-air platforms at the end of carriages. His tailoress colleague, Kate Spencer sat on a platform on a billy can she had brought to make tea, a sight which prompted Paddy to vulgar functional comment. Later, Kate had tumbled over somebody's push cart on the sports field, and exhibited patched bloomers. This was not the kind of crudity to which

Mai warmed readily, but she was to learn to accept it wryly as part of the colonial scene.

She was to learn also to contribute to that colonial domestic economy of frugality, born of economic need and limited availability of goods, which saw sugar bags as door mats, or made into carriers for pegs and tools, stockings woven into rugs, swatch books from Paddy's tailoring samples taken apart to make patchwork quilts, and white flour bags used as linings for clothing — and drawers. In Australia the Dalton's flour mills at Orange, and Crago and Tremain of Bathurst, each with their distinctive badges and names printed on their bags, got unsolicited advertising on the washing lines of the 1920s and 1930s, in a manner immortalised in crude verse:

> See the lady's britches fluttering in the breeze
> With Crago on the backside and Dalton on the knees.

The Greymouth family economy also included poultry, half a dozen fowls in a hen house, built by Paddy, at the bottom of the garden. Traditionally, poultry rearing was an Irish farm woman's occupation, directed towards sale, not household consumption. In the early twentieth century agricultural reformers found it impossible to induce Irish men to take it up. Transition to the colonies changed all that. Although the task of feeding was shared (and given to the children), the hens were essentially Paddy's, kept for fresh eggs for family use, with surplus not sold, but given away. That eggs, or surplus garden produce, should be given away, indeed pressed on friends and neighbours, obviously reflects a domestic economy much more prosperous and abundant than that of Ireland, abundance which in turn wrought a psychological change. Whereas the Irish domestic economy tended to be strictly policed and meanly administered, the largesse of colonial production allowed for generosity and expansive giving. Such gifts, of produce of various kinds, were met by similar gifts in return, but these did not take place in an atmosphere of exchange or expectation. The gifts were free, spontaneous, and unpredictable. Even in the bestowal of a few gooseberries, or a jar of pickle, the less constricted, open-handed colonial atmosphere spoke through.

Why the sex-role revolution, in running the Greymouth Irish poultry farm? Mai was a lady, an Irish town-dweller, a cut above the small-farmer class whose women dealt in eggs. So much for an Irish explanation. As for Paddy and 'women's work', the domestic economy came first, and colonial judge-

Mai, snapped by an amused neighbour, in Paddy's clothes, for the purpose of repairing the shed roof.

ment thought less of roles. Less, not nothing. When Paddy fell seriously ill, and heavy 'man's work' could not be avoided (local practice was to deliver large loads of coal and wood loose in the laneway next to the house), Mai donned Paddy's work clothes and cap as a disguise, to create the impression among passers-by that she was Paddy, or had employed a handyman. This ruse was part of an economy, but also part cheeky game, thumbing the nose at conventions and expectations against which Mai instinctively rebelled. Not always successfully. She resented the 'men's talk' situations which often developed in a household frequented by political or clerical visitors, and was not above intervention to assert her presence. But not frequently.

In 1921, at the beginning of marriage, this all lay in the future. The immediate problems were a dangerous pregnancy and a revulsion from Greymouth, and from the very plain tales from those rough hills supplied by Paddy in his correspondence. Crudity she actively disliked. Nor did she much care for the casual wild escapades to which Paddy was addicted in the company of hare-brained friends, mostly Irish but some not. Bill Greenhill, who ran a carrying firm next to Paddy's tailoring employment, and thus could offer the mobility of motor transport, was one such. A man whose aura of bluff authority masked a straight-faced drollery Paddy found most entertaining. The same with big George Phillips, a Waimate bootmaker, with whom Paddy may have travelled out to New Zealand. These men, powerful, apparently stern and serious, were persons always good for a laugh and an adventure. Irish or not (Jim was), they had mastered the art of the mask — the trick of appearing what they were not — to the confusion and discomfiture of such colonials as became their prey, and to their own private delight. Their dual personas provided them with infinite resource. Discovered in some buffoonery — or lawlessness (drinking out of hours most usually, or speeding) — the mask of respectability, dignity, and sombre public responsibility dropped instantly into place, to cast aberrant behaviour in some completely different and explicable light. Bill Greenhill was always dropping in on Paddy, in the evenings, to suggest 'a run up country'. Paddy described one such to Mai. It began with a major tyre blowout, without a spare available, entailing two hours of repairs in the freezing Brunner Gorge: Paddy had forgotten to bring his vest. Then, all the lights failed. They borrowed some kerosene from a local resident and rigged up a lamp. Following that, in need of refreshment, Paddy noted — 'thoroughly oiled ourselves inside at

Mai, at back left, carrying Tim, on one of Bill Greenhill's (on right) picnics.

Paddy Curtain's Pub'. Then, off home in good spirits — but not before colliding with a bus 'on a nasty turn outside Kaiata'.

This would have been regarded by Paddy in 1921 as a good night's entertainment, though some of Greenhill's other expeditions on the precipitous northern cliff road to Punakiki were more in the category of sheer terror. But nothing disastrous ever happened and Greenhill's trucks regularly transported loads of friends to local picnic spots, with all aboard clinging to makeshift seating erected in the flat trays. Initially, Mai regarded the likes of the Brunner Gorge night ride as dangerous madness, though residency in Greymouth was to develop in her an inclination towards similar stupidities, particularly if they were directed towards attendance at distant race meetings. Besides, translated to Greymouth, even the more formal orthodox entertainments tended to lapse into chaos.

Paddy reported to her that the stage show *Gold Diggers of 1921* had been to the town, and that he had been told that 'the crowding was awful, hair down & blouses torn and gasping for breath . . . it was like a wild beast turn out in the Opera House lobby. Three women I am told fainted & had to be carried out'.

'Wild beast turn outs' in the wooden ark which was the grandly-styled Opera House, continued into the motion-picture showings of much more recent times. At weekend performances burly members of the Beban family, who owned the facility, were stationed, with torches, at strategic spots in the auditorium, to attempt to quell the frequent disturbances and eject offenders. Drink was minor among the causes of the rowdyism. More to the point was the inadequacy of the accommodation to the demand, in a town starved of entertainment, of colour, and of something to do. So, houses were always full and many were turned away. Factions identifying themselves with outlying towns, or suburbs, or the main religious divisions, were necessarily seated together. And all was pervaded with the belief that the actual entertainment provided was only part of a total occasion, to be enlivened by the audience as participants, when opportunity offered. This volatile mixture was not attractive to the respectable, or those who simply wanted to see the show. It was not until much later, and the provision of another and more civilised auditorium, that Mai saw much of the dream-weaving entertainment she loved. At her arrival, in 1920, the worlds of colour and music and dreams operated under the rough and jostling tyranny of the frontier.

So did other Greymouth things. Paddy sent her some satiric verse, cut from the local paper, about the notorious Greymouth water supply, 'populous with living creatures' and heavy with sediment. The verse suggested that turning to beer was the only solution. But Mai knew, from only brief acquaintance, that many of the inhabitants had already done that. Her new house was at the top of a significant street incline, sufficient to exhaust passing homeward-bound drunks, compelling them to rest in the gutter and to convey their feelings about their predicament and life in general to all sleepers in the vicinity. Some required aid or directions, and were given it, whatever the hour. They were, by residential definition, neighbours, or at least people known.

Then Paddy turned, in his correspondence, to another of Mai's least favoured topics, the consequences of Greymouth's lack of a sewerage system. 'The night man still makes the night beautiful with musical tinkling and oriental odours, and by the dormant attitude of those responsible for the sanitary condition of this town, it looks as if he or his successor will continue to do so when the writer of this is where the weary are at rest & the wicked cease from troubling.' Nor was it only the night man who polluted the night. His horse was prone to

Paddy, on some bush outing. The beverage, despite the bottle, is probably cold tea, the usual drink on such occasions.

bolting, with disastrous results to cargo and much noise and shouting, creating alarms which most sleepers linked with fire as they awoke.

In a timber-built town fire was another of Mai's constant fears, horrifically fed by Paddy in his next letter. He seldom attended the frequent night alarms, but seeing the glow to be in the direction of Kear's tailoring shop, he rushed to this particular one, at 4 a.m. Arthur Bustard had been kicked out of home, and was sleeping where he could find shelter. He emerged from the burning building, his clothing all burnt from him, save for his shirt collar, still on fire around his neck, collapsing on the street asphalt, melting into it as his flesh fell from him. He died almost immediately, Paddy added — after smoking a cigarette, which he requested from a bystander. 'It was sad', commented Paddy, 'he was a kind of ne'er do well & perhaps it was for the best', though he thought that the family that had banished him would be weighed with guilt. Perhaps: it was a hard world, with death, in mine or timber mill or between railway wagons on icy shuntings, a commonplace. But the cigarette incident, surely that, even for Greymouth was totally bizarre. Was it a memory of the World War trenches, real or imagined, then close in time; of ritual behaviour when about to die? But where were the prayers, the priest?

All this Greymouth news, from low life to the casually terrible, could hardly have conveyed an enticing return prospect to the recent victim of a near miscarriage. (At least it omitted an earthquake, which was another occasional visitation in the area, usually rattling windows, but also capable, as the future was to prove, of spilling chimneys down the tin roof and twisting the house frame.) Nor did the peculiar behaviour of the neighbours inspire confidence. One Saturday Paddy was working in the front of the house when Mrs Greenhill asked him if he had any bread to spare. He told her to take what she wanted from a large loaf he had out the back. But she took the whole loaf, leaving him with only a remnant of Christmas cake, to eat with ham, for the next two days: the cake had survived until February because it had made Mai sick and had been deemed inedible. It was all he had in the house. He had expected Mrs Greenhill to ask him to Sunday dinner but she

At least the house was clear of the recurrent floods, such as this, of 1988 (*Greymouth Public Library*)

did not, and he was too proud to ask. Nor did anyone else invite him to meals.

Was he becoming a pariah, shunned because he had been deserted? It was only a few weeks after Mai's departure before the pressures of the Irish village in its transported colonial form began to close in on Paddy and compel him to subterfuge and exasperated avoidance of his tormentors. 'By the way', he told Mai, 'Greaneys enquire for you regularly, damnation regularly, in fact they talk of nothing else — what you should have done, what you should do and all the rest . . . So I don't go hither much now'. All he did was work, seven days a week, to combat loneliness and to make money. The Greaneys were not the only inquisitors: 'It was funny how the fact that you had left got about. I sure got some rare old barrack and get it occasionally yet'. But no invitations, or food dropped in to help: he felt he was 'getting back to the savage state fast', having forgotten to fast on Ash Wednesday, never making a bed, settling for cold showers rather than bothering to heat water.

When he had received no mail from Mai for a month, the tone of Paddy's letters changed to hurt and anger. Their understanding was that she would be away for a month, and write when she felt like it, but now his impatience showed, under the pressure of loneliness and worry, and the duress of nagging enquirers, whose solicitude he sensed to be false, even malicious. He took to inventing letters and news from Mai to satisfy the constant curiosity of his interrogators. No doubt he could sense, though he did not tell Mai, the local vultures circling to pounce on the corpse of their marriage, could smell their scepticism, and see their disbelief in his evasions and inventions. Still no one invited him for a meal. They would bide their time to see what eventuated. If Mai returned the talons would be sheathed and it would be smiles and innocent delight all round. All would explain their neglect of Paddy as respect for his privacy, or his obvious busyness with work, or their claim to believe that others were looking after him with meals, or that they were just about to invite him. If she did not come back, Paddy's fate was obvious — ostracism perhaps, but more likely a chorus of I told you sos directed against Mai, and a deluge of smug intrusive sympathy for Paddy. Whichever way it went, the community would have won — and certainly Mai's defection to South Canterbury put it to the test. If she returned, the community triumphed in her implied acceptance of it: she had submitted to their rules, joined, however loosely or reluctantly, this band of strange outsiders riding hard and

Jack Murphy's view from the church porch, taken in 1989: was it better in 1921?

proud on the Tasman rim. If she stayed away, pulling Paddy back to Waimate or not, she had chosen the soft option, was demonstrably unfit for the tougher going, a weak sister. And the community could take pride in its being an élite company, above any la-di-da refinements and city sophistications, its own hard superior world apart, to which the unworthy and effete could not aspire to belong.

Paddy had no doubts. Even his angry letters were full of news and jokes. Self-pity did not come naturally though he lapsed into stage-Irish sentiment when it did ('Dearest Molly Bawn', 'mavourneen'). Clowning around was more his forte. His most heated complaining missive to Mai (no doubt enclosed in a properly addressed parcel, probably of bush honey) was addressed to '(Missus) Molly O'Farrell' ('Missus' being an aggressively egalitarian colonial form of address, favoured by uppish and off-hand tradespeople, and particularly detested by Mai), 'c/o Bullock Crap Flat, New Jerusalem, Jericho.' This last was probably designed more for his brother Jack's ironic eyes. The droppings which buried any prospect of a New Jerusalem were undoubtedly those of rabbits.

As for news, the biggest was that the French Marist Fathers were leaving the West Coast to be replaced by Irish secular priests, one consequence of a long delayed outcome of Cardinal Moran's manoeuvring to staff New Zealand as well as Australia with the Irish. What good news for that mainly Irish congregation. The opposite: the Marist going was greeted with bitter regret and a sense of loss. Paddy attended their last mass. Many wept: 'they knew what the Order has done for the Coast in the days gone by. I was damned near doing a weep myself'. Farce saved the day as it did so often with the Irish. Heavy emotion switched to laughter with a piece of trivial silliness at the back of the church. Male cramming of the back porch (which had a good view over the town) was an ancient Irish religious custom, resulting from late coming, and facilitating early going. 'While communion was on, Jack Murphy who was standing longside me, was looking out the door with his back turned to the altar. One of the Horans sang out "You are looking the wrong way Jack" & everyone in the porch nearly exploded. It sounded so funny & Jack did a right about turn in double quick time & looked a fool to be sure'.

The French priests had something of a the madness of the ordinary lay Irish to whom they ministered. This colonial madness took the form of selfless missionary dedication with the French priests (and an identification with the savages — Irish and otherwise — they found). With the Irish laity, it expressed itself in that crazy wandering independence which drove them to absurd places at earth's end. More, the Marists, with their French nonchalance and sense of an international spirituality, exuded a quality of matter of fact acceptance of, and commitment to, the rough primitive land. That won them enduring local affection and deep respect. This was enhanced by the fact that some of these Marists were in fact Irish, notably Dean Carew, Greymouth's parish priest from 1884 to 1917. Tipperary born, the Dean was a forthright scourge of those of his clerical fellow-countrymen — not Marists, but Irish seculars — who featured in the frequent drunken incidents that disfigured West Coast religion and local priestly reputations: too drunk to say mass, or conduct burials, drunk in the streets and so on. An Irish laity loyally did its best to protect such Irish priests from the disciplinary consequences of scandalous conduct, but did not approve it. Such incidents pre-dated Paddy's Greymouth arrival, but were part of recent lore.

In contrast, the Marists, whether French or Irish, made natural that stunning equipoise between God's presence (and theirs) as being a big thing, the greatest and only meaningful truth, and God's presence (and theirs) as a little thing, casual, the thoughtless breath of life. The high-level church politicking, which stretched back into history and into machinations reaching the Vatican bureaucracy, ... the more immediate clashes and power struggles between the Marists and Irish secular priests, centred mainly on the Christchurch bishopric, all meant little to the laity who bore the consequences; other than that the outcome was not welcome at the time. On the very day of that last Marist mass, Paddy was on another of Greenhill's maniac picnics. 'We met old Pere Aubrey [the last Marist priest] on the Ten Mile track, tramping back over that wild country after saying mass at Barrytown. He had his coat off & over his shoulder & was hitting the track great'. His dignity was in his soul and the track he was hitting was God's. Coats off and hitting the track were not the salient features of some of the Irish priests who had been, and were to come. Some were men of great holiness, even of significant scholarship, but often they also held exalted notions of their roles and were in active rejection of the common countryman's touch that marked the aristocracy of some of the Marists.

In fact, with the coming of Irish priests, the clerical–lay division tended to widen and to formalise. This is hardly surprising. The French were Catholic priests: the Irish were — Irishmen, not merely convinced that the Irish way (by them defined) was best, as the diocesan historian kindly puts it, but that it was the only way. Among their own countrymen they felt it incumbent to assert their superior place, to make their religious point through hierarchy, authority, distance. Lacking the foreign mystique of the French (and their wonderful, seemingly careless, natural arrogance), the Irish sought to substitute — the heavy hand, the hard clerical hat, the distant smile and bow. The lax pioneering days were over, with their strange Frenchmen. Time now to erect a distant replica of Ireland in the 1920s.

Mai returned to Greymouth in March. In August she was back in South Canterbury again, this time staying with the Phillips family in Waimate. She was ill with the pregnancy which produced my brother Tim, on 12 September 1921. Both mother and child nearly died. For several months she 'lay between Life and Death', as her sister put it, not told of the death of her own father. In appalling weather conditions of flood and washouts of road and rail, Paddy made a nightmare trip to Waimate. Eventually all was well.

Mai's return to Greymouth in March 1921, evidently pregnant, instantly transformed the ominous social climate that had clouded Paddy's life. She came accompanied by sacks of

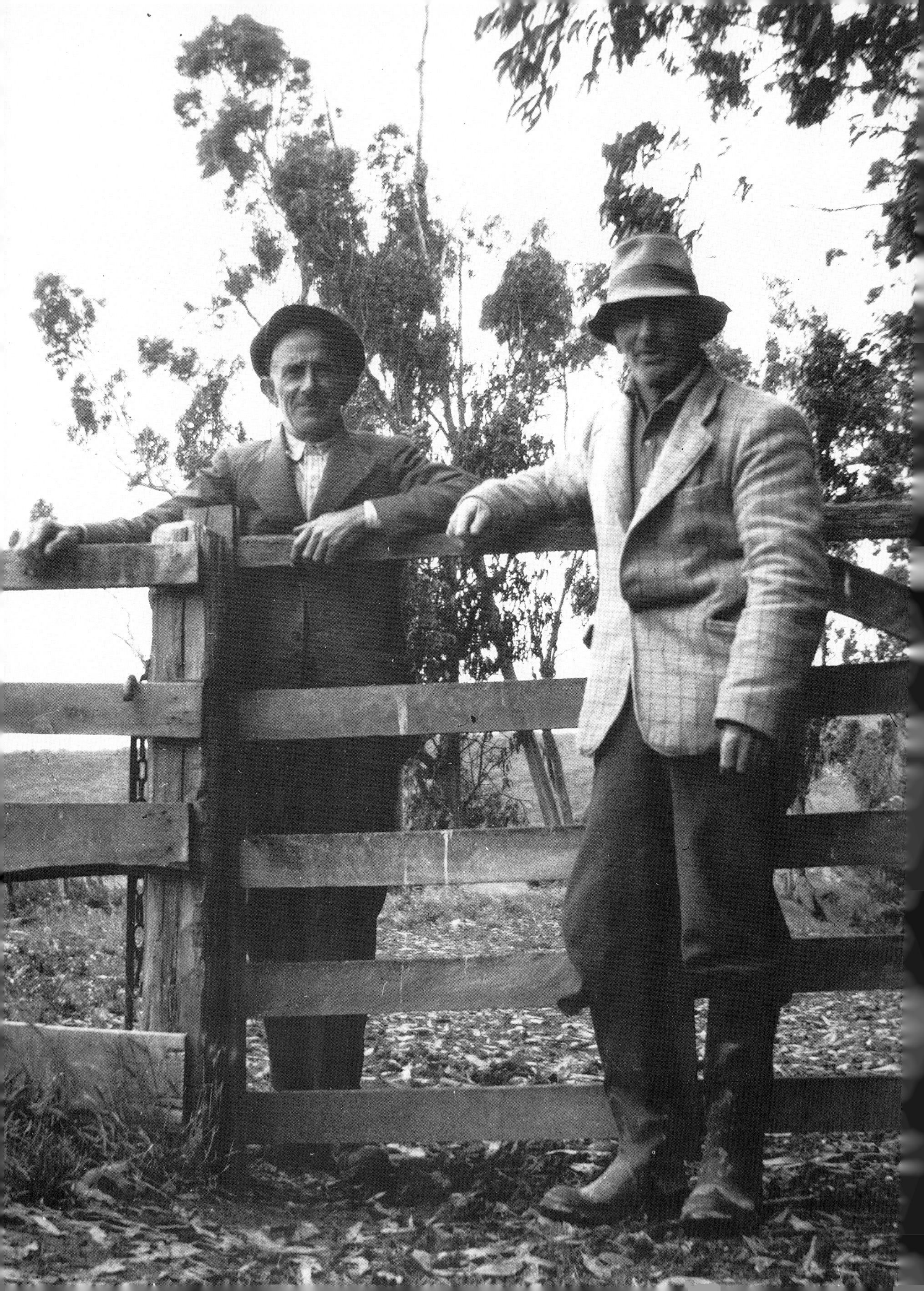

Paddy with Jack, at the Hunter farm, c1950.

spuds from Jack. Stone fruit from South Canterbury crossed honey, gooseberries and blackcurrants (and, of course, tailor-made suits) from Greymouth. Jam interchange proceeded apace. And they had solved the problem of Greymouth tongue-wagging. Paddy would visit Mai when he could. Loneliness? Mai had brought back the violin he had left with Jack: music was a friend and companion. Above all, Mai was now held to have joined the Greymouth encampment: to have accepted was to be accepted. When she went away again — deviant behaviour now accepted in compromise — Paddy was showered with meal invitations and gifts of food from Julia Greaney, several families of Keatings, neighbours, workmates. The problem now, with his self-imposed, frantic workload, his union activity, and his Labour Party meetings, his membership of the Hibernians, and the stepped-up church activities of Irish priests trying to outdo the French legacy, was how to make time to avoid offending these kind people who demanded his attendance at their table. That little Irish village on the edge of nowhere, in its strange context of admixture of English and Welsh, and Scots, had accepted these newcomers, partly on their own terms. They were always just a little apart, a little unpredictable and foreign, given that South Canterbury dimension, family and Irish though that was. At the heart of this process of acceptance was not Irishness or Catholicity, but allegiance to place, a colonial place, with its own unique character and history. Some basic identification with that particular geography, an essential loyalty however reluctant, or qualified or confused, was enough to gain admission to this little group of remote colonials and to take up an accepted role in that new-born community.

And having been accepted, the isolated O'Farrell family, when children arrived, added to their real wider family — which was distant, elsewhere — an honorary immediate family of local aunts and uncles, by conferring these titles on family friends. Such friends accepted the titles gladly and filled the role to the extent, in some cases, of becoming indistinguishable from real kin. Especially for the many unmarried, the honorific filled a real need in their lives: the need for nephews and nieces to inspect, to follow their fortunes, the need to give presents, to be at birthday parties, to be part of a family. So, from nothing, Paddy and Mai built an artificial family in Greymouth, which, to a child, blurred with the real one encountered on South Canterbury holidays.

The world of innumerable aunts, real and honorary, could be separated out and evaluated, and then with exceptions, only on the basis of whether they were married or single. The married ones (mainly Paddy's sisters and sisters-in-law) were soft; the unmarried, hard. Soft meant indulgent, warm, forever cooking and baking, everybody's mothers. Hard? A various and formidable gaggle. There was stern 'Aunty' Kate Spencer, tailoress and tough Labour stalwart with some private means from a small farm, shares, and a trade in blackberry wine, good for £1 each Christmas and 2s 6d on special occasions, all delivered with a hatchet face, inspiring terror and gratitude. Then, the real Aunty Chris, demanding and insistent on family rights, or what she thought were rights, always with an eye to the comparative and hierarchical. So, in 1930, instructing Mai to arrange with her children, what another of their honorary aunts received from her real nephews — a letter a week to Chris.

Possessing a strange pride as well as a vacillating sense of haughty shame at her Irish origins, Chris above all other relations, endeavoured to maintain the constricting social ethos of the Irish village, with all its subtle social distinctions, snubs and snobberies, all its rigidities and pettiness and pretence. She relied heavily on mail from 'home' — Ireland — and in Wellington, where she worked as the millinery buyer for the largest department store, her social acquaintance was very substantially female Irish. Eventually, in the late 1930s, she visited Ireland, borrowing a large sum from her employer to do so. This gave her the Irish reputation of being affluent, indeed rich, which she enjoyed in so far as it demonstrated her success to her Irish family, an impression she later paid for in years of penury meeting repayments in New Zealand. In fact, she had gone to Ireland with no real intention of returning to New Zealand, but she found the Irish situation a repeat of that which had forced her out in 1914 — no suitable work. Her New Zealand employer was happy to lend her the return fare and to have her back. Why? Chris had panache, style, metropolitan assurance and aplomb, which might grate on immediate family, but in the business of choosing the stock and selling hats in a large department store, it was an invaluable merchandising asset. She could model a hat and fit it for a colonial customer in a way that gave them the illusion of a glimpse of the exotic world of high fashion that existed in mysterious London and Paris.

While Mai lived perforce in a colonial world, pulled into it by marriage and particularly children, Chris, and single Irish

Mai, with Tim, in the Greymouth back garden, c1925.

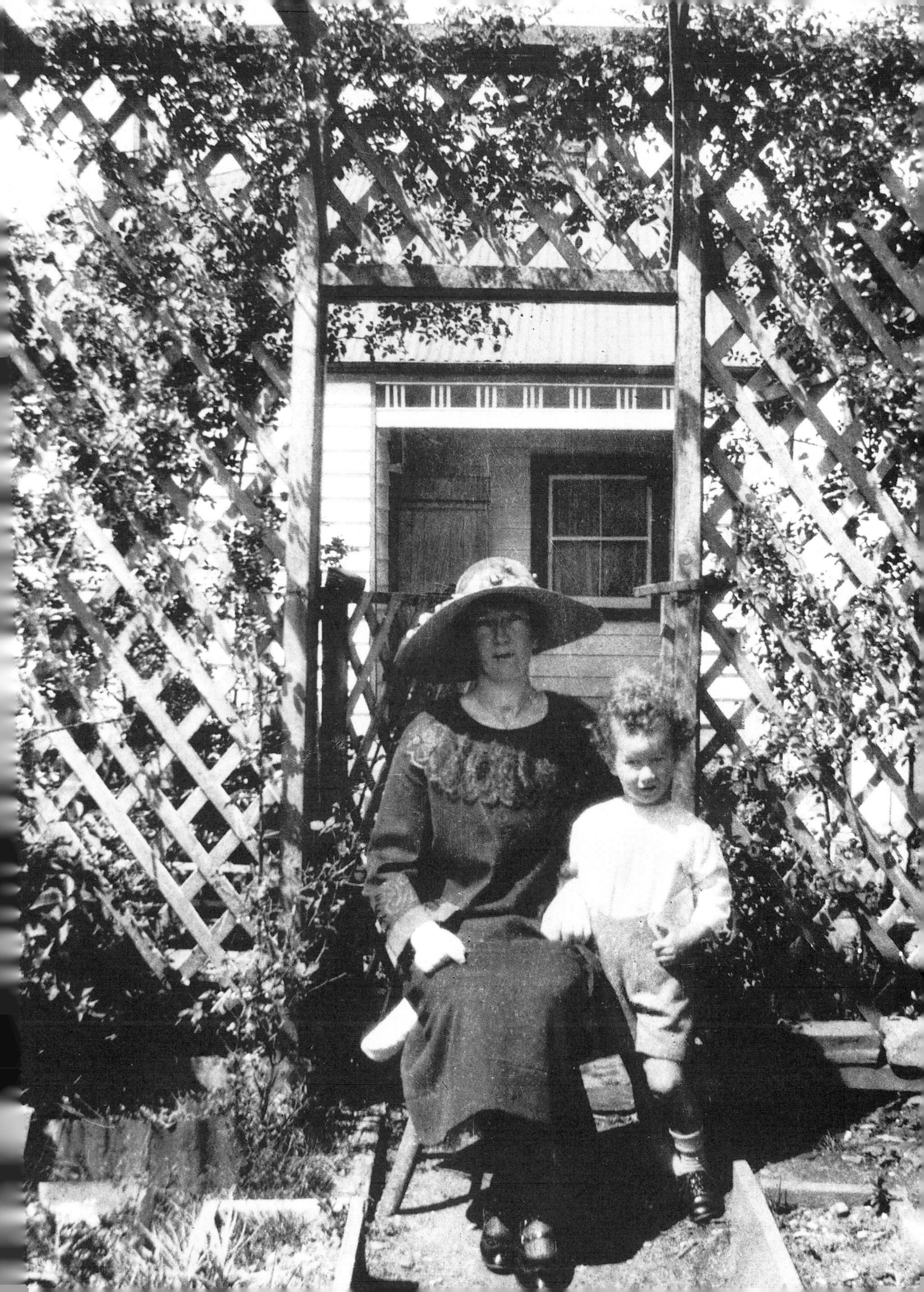

women generally, could remain to some extent disengaged from intimacy with their environment. Their world remained their own, consorting with their own kind, still mentally focussed on 'home', and often very critical of colonial ways and persons they encountered, usually through their married sisters. The criticism was natural enough: the colonies had not lived up to their greatest expectation — marriage — and they invariably blamed the colonies, and the inferiority of colonial men, for that. As to Irish men in the colonies, these were seen as the dregs of Ireland, and, at the same time, traitorous marriers of Protestants and English. Single women were in the vanguard of those who championed all things Irish. Yet, they seldom returned: they knew where they were better off. Their reasonable affluence, being single, usually in good work, or with family incomes bequeathed by fathers, lent them a certain freedom and superior style denied their married sisters. They dressed well and went to the races in groups, haughty in their cheap fur stoles, in which the clasp was the imitation fox head's sprung tin mouth, biting the tail.

Chris, with stylish hat, 1937

Such were the appearances, and in better times. The Depression was bitter for Chris, long unemployed, eventually starting as a 'slushy' for the firm in which she rose to be millinery buyer. One golden deed shone through the bad years. At a worst hour, out of the blue, came £3 from Paddy, probably a bonus from a lucky horse; never forgotten in a relationship where superficial abrasion overlay a deep loyalty and support for family. And one golden friend, Julia Greaney, just as haughty, just as broke, tramping Wellington together looking for jobs, both full of pride, close to a giggle or tears, eyes sparkling with challenge — the Depression female variant of the indomitable Irishry.

And in a hazy background, a dream aunt, Kit, in America, New York. She was unmarried and had some ordinary if 'respectable' job — in Macy's? — but she was the allegedly wealthy one, having taken on the aura of that mythical land of power and might, where all were predicated rich and successful. From her came exotic small gifts, never before seen in barbarian hemispheres save in the wonderland of glossy magazine advertisements — Whitman's Sampler Chocolates, perfumes: taste and smell of a world of luxury of which she was presumed a full citizen. When she died alone in 1960 of cancer, she left Mai a tiny legacy, the first independent money Mai had since her marriage. For all that her modest circumstances must have been obvious, Kit was invested with the reputation of greater means and substance than all other

O'Sullivan family members. Something to look up to. Something to be wondered at, in awe. No envy or resentment. Just further testimony to the overwhelming, indeed stupefying power of Irish illusions about America.

It is hard to escape the conclusion that, however successful, or however reconciled to the nature of life as being — everywhere — hard, and full of the varieties of pain, these Irish emigrants held Ireland in a place of blame. At basis, their attitudes were not those of lachrymose sentimentality, nor

Aunty Kit, in America, 1946

Hands on hips, mistress of her own new world, Mrs James O'Brien of Braidwood c1880s (*Braidwood Historical Society*)

affection, nor esteem, nor even acceptance of the Irish spiritual superiority preached by the clergy. No. Rock bottom was an angry indignation that they had been forced out, cheated and deprived of what was theirs by right of birth. No matter how voluntary the going, or how apparently eager, no matter if the whole situation could be sheeted home to Britain, or family circumstances, or whatever, the core of it was — at the last,

Ireland had done them a great wrong. While nationalists in Ireland might rant against emigration as being desertion, betrayal; but, looking back, especially over a long span of years, it was those emigrants who felt betrayed, thrown out, rejected, deeply angry.

Such feelings were often confused, contradictory, seldom coherently expressed, and often only partially admitted to the self. It was no small thing to acknowledge what might seem in distant retrospect (the compulsions then being forgotten) a major mistake, or to consign a lifetime as an immigrant to the realm of regret. Yet, consider the answers of an aunt to the question of a child (not myself) as to why she left Ireland for New Zealand. One of the answers was (she knew the correct one) that there was no work; others paid her passage. The other answer was mythical: there was a potato famine at the time. The 1920s? Both answers said the same, at different levels of perceived experience: Ireland drove me out. As did Paddy's response to the question of return: 'What has Ireland done for me?'.

There was in many immigrant Irish people, in age, loneliness, and felt distance from 'home', the ache for a shared role, a shared victim's role. Whatever the impulses or circumstances that took them away in unthinking youth, in age (or earlier, in disappointment), they reverted to the role of a persecuted people, driven out by the hard times of which the Great Famine and the flight to America were the universally dominating facts and myths. So, the mind performed its own justifying inventions. It said: for me to have left Ireland to come here to this place, strange to my dying bones and dimming eyes, for me to have endured a colonial life, primitive and boring, there must have been a famine — yes, a potato famine, not the big one that lingers in the memory's memory, but another one, particular to me. Famine was the emigrant's validating myth. And, the mind said, I die at one with all other of us victim exiles, we banished Irish, united the foreign world over in loss and lament. Here was a valuable, consoling fiction. These wandering, wayward, sociable Irish, were determined not to die alone, strangers in a strange land.

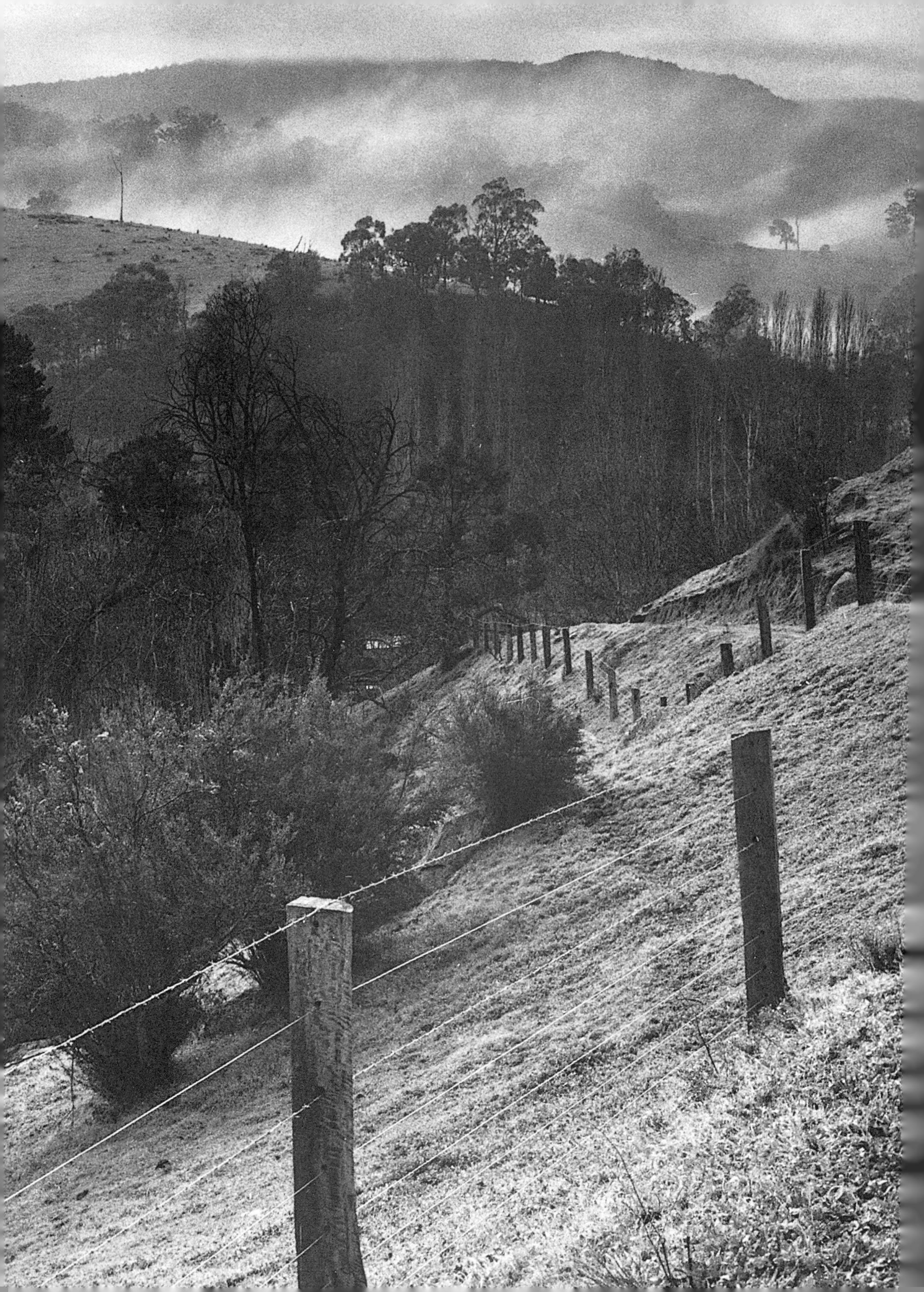

CHAPTER 6

VARIATIONS: THOSE OTHER TRADITIONS

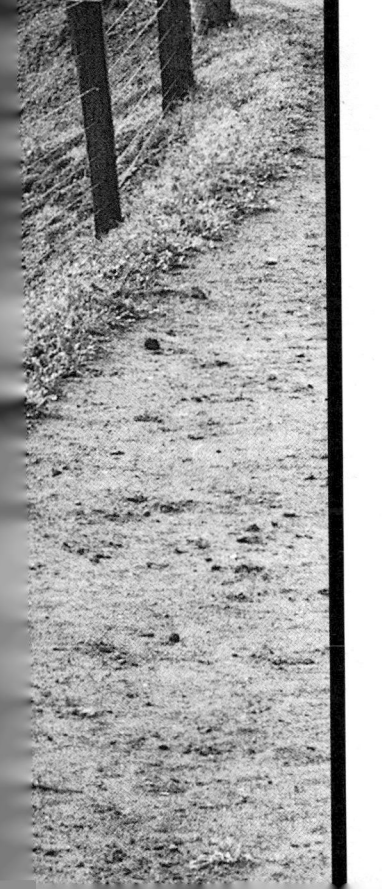

Writing to his father and mother from Aden, en route to Australia, on 31 October 1887, William Andrews, Ulster Protestant versed in the Bible, remarked 'The Red Sea is far larger than ever I thought it was . . . The Israelites had a long walk when crossing from Egypt to Pallestine [sic]'. It was the type of comment Paddy O'Farrell, travelling a generation later and from that other Ireland, would have made as a silly joke, the kind of smart remark that would humanise the sacred book. It is doubtful that William intended it so. That it should occur to him at all — Paddy never forgot (but neither did William) the labour of the swarms of 'darkies' coaling the ship at Suez, from sacks on their backs — evidences the power of the Bible in his education and imagination. For such Protestant travellers to Australia, the Bible was their mid-east travel guide, their key to a feeling of instant familiarity with that holy part of the geographic world. In their imagination's eye, and in those vividly coloured Bible illustrations, they had entered the hot, desert world before, and that aspect of Australia came as no surprise to them.

The Andrews story has been told before, or rather, partly

Tambo crossing, Gippsland, Victoria, home district to John, Hugh and James Andrews, a photograph taken in 1987

Above: The Andrews family and relations gathered in Ireland in the 1880s. (*Public Record Office of Northern Ireland*)

Left: The house at Tambo Crossing which Hugh Andrews was eventually to build on the land John had pioneered, photographed in 1987.

told. The vagaries of circumstance and further documentary discovery can now allow an addendum, more detail, and a dispensing with anonymity: they are the 'Maxwells' of 'The Fortunes of a Family' in my *Letters from Irish Australia*. The details given there are exact, save for their name and place. They are the Andrews family of Fairview Farm, Ballycroghan, just out of Bangor. The Andrews family lives there still, in exactly that place, as they have for two centuries. As such they represent a strange emigrant reversal. Whereas the families of Paddy and Mai (and millions like them) dispersed into new lands, and have vanished from the Irish lands which were once their homes, the Andrews (the immigrants were the five brothers, Hugh, John, James, William and David) have vanished from Tambo Crossing, Gippsland, Melbourne, Ballarat, Western Australia — all their Australian haunts and settlements. They remain, after a series of Australian disasters, circumstances, twists of fate, only in the Irish place whence they began.

That is only one of the curious contrasts that seem to distinguish the two traditions, or rather that well up, as baffling questions of difference, from the detail of tiny case studies. It is the Andrews who dream of Ireland, whose minds most frequently turn back to their homeland with both anguish and pleasure. They also note that disposition in their acquaintances. Of the senior Mr Reid at Yackandandah in Victoria, Hugh Andrews observed in March 1884, 'I think he thinks a little long of the old home. With little to employ his mind with, his thought will naturally turn homeward'. Naturally: but Hugh thought it unhealthy. Emigrants could sense it in each other, that distraction, absence of present mind, quietness, lack of zest, a contagion of loss the young sought to avoid, and did, through the compulsory therapy of hard work. Age and affluence — the Reids were substantial Australian landowners — made the elder Reid a vulnerable target for the arrows of the recollected past. But so were the young Andrews, despite themselves: plagued by dreams, riddled by worry and presentiment, as well as nostalgia. Susannah, at home in Ballycrochan, wrote in mid 1889 to her brother John (solitary in the Tambo Crossing bush, which he was clearing as a farm) of her alarming dreams of him, seeing him ill, close to death — which, unsuspected, he was: in April 1891, aged twenty-nine, he haemorrhaged to death in a few minutes in his bush hut. But then, in August 1889, John comforted his sister and confessed his own dreams, which blended Australia with home, but were hardly less fraught with anxiety. Patently he lived in a dreamworld ridden by emigrant guilt, and tenanted by the vivid reincarnations of the family he had left.

> I hope the next time you dream about me that it will be something pleasant, something that won't make you think I am ... ill, that won't keep you worrying your soul out. I find that if I have a feed of beef at tea I am round the world a dozen times before morning and keep mixing Australia with home. One dream I had was that I was home again & that I had no money & was in great distress how to get back to Australia. I often see you all as vividly as if it were reality. Not long since I was subjected to a good scolding from Aunt. I cannot remember what it was about but I do remember that I knew the voice to be the same as of old.

To put all this down to 'a feed of beef at tea' was in harmony with John's dietary fixations, but his brother William, at Barnawartha in northern Victoria, was caught, waking and sleeping, in the same shafts of blinding recall and dreams of transcendent intensity. In February 1888 he told his father and mother:

> ... tell him [a friend] that I can see them all as plain as if I was there, and I can remember the roads better than when at home ... I dreamt on Xmas night that we were all at home every one of us and could see them all seated around the table. If there is such a thing as spirits meeting they did it that night.

Obviously, the roads that William travelled in Australia were overlaid in his mind by another pattern, deliberately recalled, no doubt as anchor against strangeness and the drift that pulled at and eroded the emigrant identity. He clung tenaciously to what he knew, places and people, in the deepest foundations of his being. Later, he was able to turn to thoughts of home, and the letter writing which inevitably generated such thoughts, with some sense of pleasure and comfort, a feeling of moving closer to familiar things, but it was William and his wife and family who returned permanently to Ireland in July 1892, to manage his aged father's farm.

To leave their parents and sisters in Ireland, as the Andrews boys did, was to establish a substantial complication in the emigration process, both emotional and practical. The complete break eventually made by the Farrell family, and those many like them, who left neither family nor property behind in Ireland, created a distinctively different attitude towards both new and old homes. The Andrews maintained a substantial and continuous correspondence, which, if suffused by warmth and affection, was also a constant source of distur-

Above: A view, in 1987, of the farm at Barnawartha, Victoria, where William and Susanna Andrews had worked in the 1880s.

Right: William and Susanna Andrews, sharing the milking at Barnawartha, Victoria, 1880s. (*Public Record Office of Northern Ireland*)

bance and worry, and guilt. As their parents aged, and as the usual variety of problems arose, of illness, or farm prices, troubles of all sorts, reports from home were full of such difficulties, involving the boys in a paralysing tension and pulling their minds and concerns back into a country which they had left, and gladly so. The dispossessed, those who had left Ireland with nothing, had the advantages of no such ties, no such barriers to full, uncomplicated, commitment to the new lands they chose. In contrast, increasingly the Andrews correspondence, until William returned, was full of Irish farm prices, Ballycroghan labour problems, Irish weather — in relation to crops — and after he returned, with Irish politics. Simply, the realities of their family situation, split between Ireland and Australia, dragged the Andrews boys, in mind and spirit, and eventually in physical fact (William returned in 1892, David later) back into Ireland. Their position, powerless at a distance in the face of Irish family crises, caused them distress, frustration, impatience, and eventual hardness of heart: one endured that for which there was no remedy, one closed off that part of the self that suffered in sympathy with kin in Ballycrochan.

Yet who could do that with total success? In letters from Australia, William raged to his mother and father about the exploitation he believed they were suffering at the hands of those they employed: 'It is the wages that keep you down & you work far too much to give to lazy fools'. He chafed at a situation in which he believed his parents were at the mercy of rogues and loafers: if he were there, things would be different. If he were there. William resented those who did not emigrate as lazy and gutless, those whom he believed were spoiling Ireland — for his parents, and through them, for himself in Australia.

Put crudely, the contrast of the Andrews and the Farrells suggests a consideration opposite to the expected. Those emigrants who cared most about what happened back in Ireland ought to have been, according to the nationalist canon, those from the Gaelic Catholic majority. Yet the fact was that these had often cut or had severed for them, all connection with Ireland, leaving neither family nor property. They had no longer any stake in that country, many not even the connection of correspondence, or even public news. Those with family remaining in Ireland, with direct interest in property and land there, and with strong links via frequent correspondence, tended to be the Ulster Protestants, the Anglo-Irish and more affluent Catholics, particularly those in the professions, lawyers, doctors, priests. It was they who remained most vitally

An Orange procession in a small Irish village: Tempo, County Fermanagh, 12 July 1900. (*Ulster Museum, Langham Collection*)

interested in, and informed about, Ireland's day to day affairs.

So, to the Andrews family, Home Rule was not or not only, an abstract consideration, or a matter of high principle, as it was to many of its Australian enthusiasts. It was a direct and practical family matter, and their opposition was firmly grounded on personal involvement in the situation so created. In March 1908, William, long returned to Ireland, sought his brother James's views on Home Rule. The family had never been enthusiasts in the Orange cause, but it behoved James, even in Australia, to keep up with what was going on. While Catholics had long taken Ireland as full of general lessons of what must be avoided in Australia, by way of exploitations and oppression, so had Protestants, from Ulster in particular. For the truth in these matters, or rather, analysis of the nature of possible threats to the freedoms they valued, James relied on the *Watchman,* a militantly anti-Catholic newspaper, edited in Sydney by that Ulster Presbyterian Orangeman, Reverend Dill Macky, Australia's foremost anti-Catholic controversialist of that intensely sectarian time. Part of James Andrews's reply to his brother in Ireland was to send him a couple of copies of the *Watchman* 'which will give you some idea of what is going on'. Ever vigilant on Ireland, in a detailed fashion few ordinary Irish Catholics were bothered to be, James assumed that he, in Australia, with the aid of Reverend Dill Macky, could illuminate the Irish situation in which his brother actually lived. Here was conclusive testimony to his degree of informed interest and confidence in his judgment from afar.

> You ask my opinion of home rule (Rome rule) . . . if the Priests keep agitating as they are, Ireland is likely to experience trouble, & should they succeed in getting home rule, or to be correct Rome rule, it will I fear be impossible for a Protestant to live under it. It may not be granted them for sometime to come but it is slowly working up to it.

Why had William sought comment? Because, James assumed, he was thinking of selling out if the threat looked like becoming an actuality:

> . . . you have an idea of making a change should Home Rule become law . . . I would forewarn you to be careful what you say to neighbours or anyone else who [are] likely to be buyers, as it might injure the likelihood of selling at a good price. The plea of ill health would be better than to say you feared home rule.

What happened in Ireland — or what might happen — reverberated intimately through the Andrews family in a way simply not matched amongst the Farrells, or those many like them, to whom the years had made Ireland remote to the point of vague generality or even vanishment.

And, of course, the empire had similar contrasting degrees of reality. Hugh Andrews's Australian-born son, Jack, left the Tambo Crossing farm to enlist in the AIF (Australian Imperial Forces) as soon as he was twenty-one years old, in December 1916. Hugh remarked that 'Jack looked on it as a solemn duty, and hard as it is for us all we could not have wished otherwise. It is the brave men and boys, not the shirkers, that are saving the Empire'. So said Hugh, but Jack was in the Australian cynical and critical tradition, no empire yes-man. He had visited Ballycroghan and met his Irish family, and his cousin Susie, just before becoming involved in the final hostilities in

Jack Andrews (left) with some of his A.I.F. friends. (*Public Record Office of Northern Ireland*)

France. He wrote to Susie in May 1918 about the aerial combat he had seen from the trenches:

> It is a pity that those responsible for prolonging the war didn't have to put up with what our brave airmen go through or even the sight of it. I saw a plane take fire (in a fight the day before yesterday) at a terrible height, & after falling in flames for about a thousand feet the two scorched men left it & it was positively sickening to see them fall spinning in the air, although very probably they were both dead shortly after leaving the plane.

Jack considered General Haig's praise for Australian efforts in stopping the German offensive of March 1918, 'a bit more "Kidstakes" to cheer them up to box on more'. He was neither impressed nor convinced: 'bullshit' was not a word he would have used to his cousin, but that is what he was thinking.

With Jack, the Andrews had moved into their Australian generation and into the colonial values, attitudes, and questioning of authority and tradition, which is a cliché of that transformation.

A further curious contrast remains to be observed, a matter of religious style and expression, hardly surprising in view of the structure of differing faiths and their contrasting understanding of the role of ministry. The Ulster Protestant style affirmed the nearness of God to the individual, and did so

Protestant Christianity without ornament or intermediary. The Elim Pentecostal Tabernacle, Hunter Street, Belfast, 10 April 1935: nothing to come between the creature and the Word of God. (*Ulster Museum*)

publicly in a manner not natural to the Catholic. Used to mediated prayer through the priesthood, or silent private prayer in their personal lives, God and his intervention in the world seem almost a Catholic embarrassment, hardly a topic for conversation or correspondence. It is the Protestants who are open about God and His will, to the degree of respectful claims of familiarity. The Catholics are reticent in religious matters, which seem, on a surface view, not to be part of their intimate lives. As the correspondence conveying John Andrews's death exemplifies, the Protestant encounter with God was felt to be direct, and death's spectators savoured the very moment of the soul's departure. William informed his brother and his father of what had been told to him of the detail of John's last moments:

> He gave a little throw of the breast & the soul departed from its tenement of clay to pass through the Golden Gates of Heaven. He died without a struggle confessing the names of Jesus as his Saviour. Although we loved our darling boy so much, we would not wish him back to this weary world of sorrow & troubles ... You will be thankful to God that although his death was sudden, he realised & saw his position & implored & prayed for mercy as long as he was able to utter a word.

Such candid spiritual details sat easily with the physical:

> He lost a great quantity of blood by the bursting of a blood vessel. James said he did not think there was so much blood in a man as he lost. He told one of the boys previous to his death that he thought he was making too much blood by drinking so much milk.

According to Susannah, their parents, though affected, 'comforted themselves with the thought that it cannot be a great while till they meet him, where all is happiness and praise'.

Others, in the interchange of letters, exchanged various words of the psalmists: all stood in awe of God and accepted the death without demur or question. It was a passivity and acceptance elevated to joy in the description Mrs Newson (William's employer) gave of the death of the child of a friend:

> He was so sure of his soul's salvation — he told his mother in the afternoon "He knew he was a sinner but Jesus had died for him" & just a half hour before he died he pulled her to him & said "The pain is all away but I am not going to stay. I'm going away home to heaven". Oh, how sweet to be sure from God's word that sin is forgiven and that we are ready for the Lord Jesus whenever he may come!

Father. David Andrews senior, stern, but respected, loved. He died in 1902. (*Public Record Office of Northern Ireland*)

The genuine reality of such resignation to death, as God's will, speaks through what seems now — and was then — a kind of religious jargon, words of incantation that contrast strongly with the ordinary messages of the rest of such letters, news of crops and doings. The Bible and the stilted language of sermons dominated the language of death, in such a way as to remove it from ordinary discourse: a translation, change of gear readily made, by Bible Christians, hardly conscious they were doing so.

Yet, for all the apparent virtue of submission to God's will, it had its negative debilitating side. Was John's death a sign? A portent, revelation of the Almighty's power to put at nought the plans of men? Did God intend the Andrews brothers to succeed in this strange and forbidding land? The question did not surface, but the remaining brothers conferred in distress and confusion on the consequences of this disaster, which much more than deprived them of a brother. It threw into chaos their complex set of financial linkages and property acquisition understandings, and put into question their entire Australian plans. It refocussed their attention on what they also felt most keenly, responsibility for their aging parents and the farm in Ireland. Within months of John's death, they had decided that William must return to Ireland. David had disappeared (temporarily) in New Zealand. Of the five, only Hugh and James were left, enduring and barely surviving the economic trauma of the 1890s separately, but coming together again at the Tambo Crossing farm in 1899. There they were to quarrel and move apart: James dying in 1920, childless, with an adopted son; Hugh died in 1929: his son Jack worked the farm until 1961, when he moved to Bairnsdale. Their Tambo Crossing farm retreated towards the bush.

Vanished Empires? Hardly. Ordinary people with no great ambition, other than to lead decent God-fearing lives. They lacked the hubris and elan of the Catholics. Viewed in the broad sweep of their diminishing Australian history, their dogged courage seems like that of the defeated — endurance, tenacity, survival, the grim grasp of a bare handhold on a crumbling dry soil. Destroyed, one feels, by that death — John's. At the wrong time and in the wrong place. And by that enemy of all, work; work intensified by an economy gone mad and sour. And by the choice of stubborn and precipitous land which only slavery could master, and that badly and briefly.

'We Irish': it was a possessive phrase of William's. What did it mean? Perhaps a sense of ownership rather than a sense of belonging — or is that too harsh? Or did it simply connote the

Right: William and Susanna Andrews (at left) back at the Ballycroghan farm in Ireland in the 1890s. (*Public Record Office of Northern Ireland*)

Below: Protestant and Catholic Irish in Gerringong, New South Wales, cemetery share the vista of the Tasman Sea.

claim to be Irish while others — different others — were Irish as well? Whatever, it had the ring of pride and confidence. And for all that their religious cultures divided them, the great worldwide cultural manufacturer of the common denominator drew them together. The Ulster Irish adopted, as did the Gaelic, the American-created, pseudo-Irish culture that was popularly taken to be genuine in Australia, from 'Danny Boy' at the upper end of taste, to 'If you're Irish come into the parlour', at the bottom.

But as they moved together into the common musical suzerainty of Tin Pan Alley, both Presbyterian and Catholic, Ulster Scot and Gael, regretted the dying of traditional music, the end of an era in both homeland and colony, the replacement of the domestic and the amateur, by the imported and the commercial. Hearing from home in June 1891 that the family had re-employed Willie Boyle as a servant, William, in Australia, asked Susannah:

> does he ever give you a tune on the fiddle, if Mother is anyway well & the rest enjoying good health. You will be pleased to hear him occasionally, 'twill bring back old memories. I have not tried the fiddle for sometime, my evenings are so taken up otherwise.

So taken up otherwise. Like the evenings of that other, later, erstwhile Irish fiddler, Paddy O'Farrell. But when William returned to Ireland, did he return, in those long evenings, to the fiddle as well? Was he able to unlearn the colonial lesson that all life was work, resume that place and pace where music dwelt as a language necessary to humankind? Did he ever really return to the Land of Song?

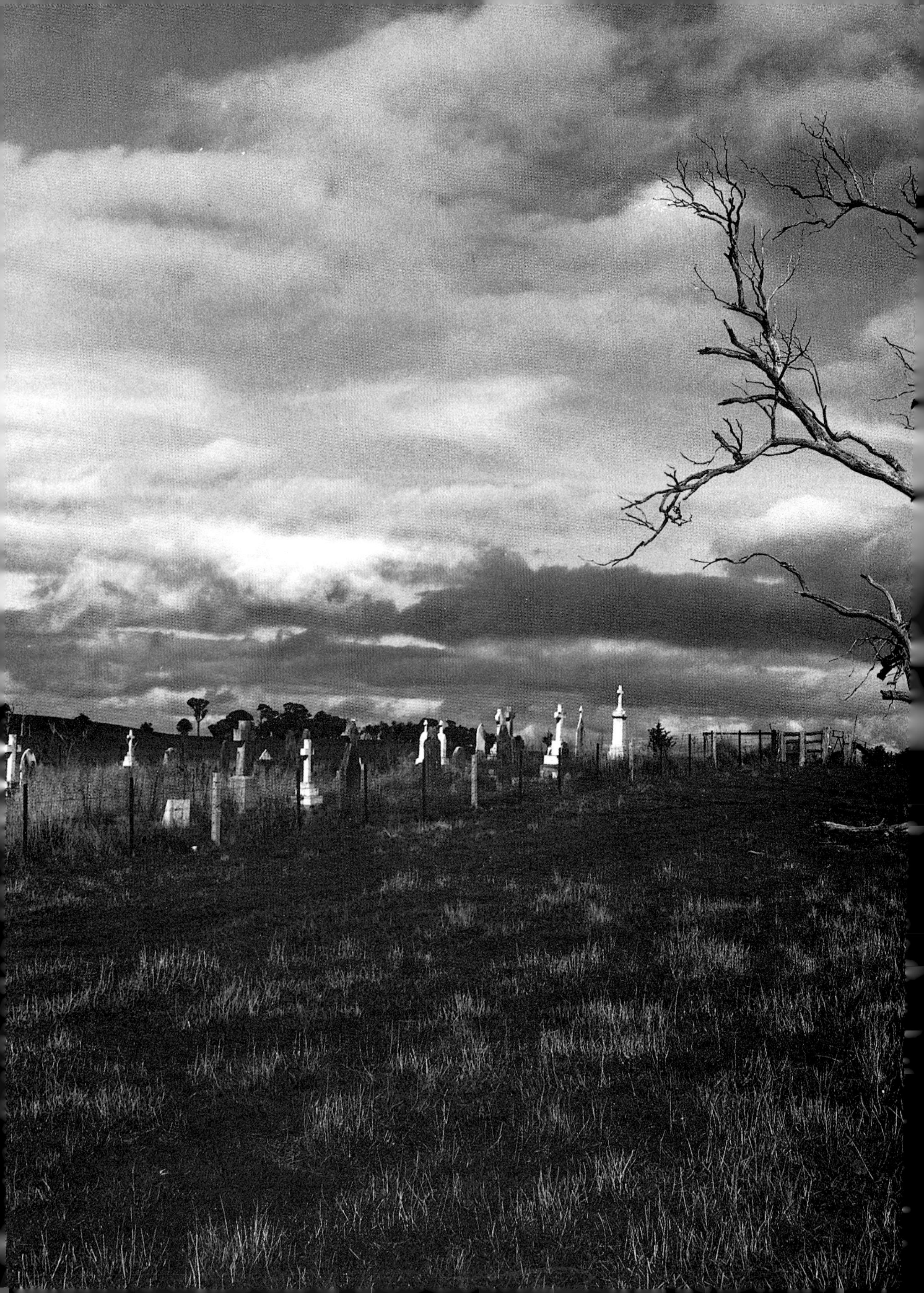

CHAPTER 7

THE FIRST GENERATION

Pat Hickey, born in Waimea South of Irish Catholic parents in 1882, was to become, in 1908, a key figure in the radicalisation of the New Zealand labour movement. Moving to Australia in the war years, he was prominent in the Victorian union and socialist movement, and later, after a further period in New Zealand, in the Victorian Labor Party: he died in 1930 just after pre-selection to a safe Labor seat. Hickey was the archetypal, blazing radical, pugnacious, full of hate and socialist doctrine, with an insatiable thirst for worker justice. In 1903, then barely twenty, he decided he must see the world in the kind of reverse migration from the colonies, which was to become de rigueur for the young in later more affluent times. His tour took in his ancestral home and Irish cousins. He found Dublin filthy, and demonstrating more poverty than any other city he had seen. Barefoot women and houses built of mud affronted him, as did his cousin's house — mud floor, straw roof, dogs and hens inside with the family. And they, incomprehensibly, were not regarded as poor, as they owned some land. Moreover, everybody treated him with deference, called him 'Sir' and doffed their hats. It was all too much.

The cemetery at Grabben Gullen, NSW, casually situated in an Australian nowhere, sheltered by dead trees

Hickey was angry and very uncomfortable in Ireland.

Next, America, where, in the western mining areas, he picked up the militant industrial and revolutionary socialism that was to be his radical stock-in-trade thereafter. Not that he was more at home in Utah: 'I do not like the Mormons and they do not like me'. And there he found the bugbear of colonials of Irish descent: he was categorised as Irish. At the same time he found that distinction virtually unique: 'Irishmen are conspicuous by their absence'. it may have been 'the Land of the Free' as he called it, but some (capitalists) were much freer than others (wage slaves), and the racial melting pot still contained many foreign lumps, which Hickey, for all his theoretical internationalism, intensely disliked. He had no love of 'foreigners'. He was glad to return to New Zealand, via some time in Australia, in 1906. Those two countries were to divide his future.

Hickey had found out what many of Irish colonial descent found out — some before him, but most after — that he did not like Ireland, nor feel at home there, but that nevertheless he was Irish in the eyes of others (outside Ireland) and he belonged in some discernible, and welcome, way, to the wider tribe of Irishmen. Even those whose Irish origins were very remote could often feel compelled to acknowledge or invent 'Irish' characteristics. Thus, non-Catholic and very remotely Irish (Australian for several generations) Democratic Labor Party leader, Jack Kane, rejecting an offer to drop Wilfred Burchett's libel case against him in 1974 remarked: 'I guess it's just the Irish in me . . . I want to go through with it. I want to get that bastard'.

But Kane's, and other's similar attributions to 'the Irish' in them, were not entirely accurate, even given the natural vagueness of the whole area. James Connolly, the Irish socialist and victim of the 1916 Rising executions, remarked in 1913: 'Ireland is a country of wonderful charity and singularly little justice'. The observation was apposite, its truth politically reflected in the weakness of labour movement and party in Ireland, both North and South. Ireland's concern for the individual and the nation left little room for anything in between, such as the thirst for communal justice expressed in trade unions and labour political parties. It was only in the colonies (not America, where the dominant Republican-Democrat dichotomy swallowed the Irish) that political structures allowed 'the Irish' in the Irish, free expression. And it was the lack of a modern and developed social consciousness in Ireland (among other things) that so affronted the colonial visitor of

Right: Sights to make colonial Hickey angry and uncomfortable. Children in Tempo, County Fermanagh, 1899. (*Ulster Museum. Langham Collection*)

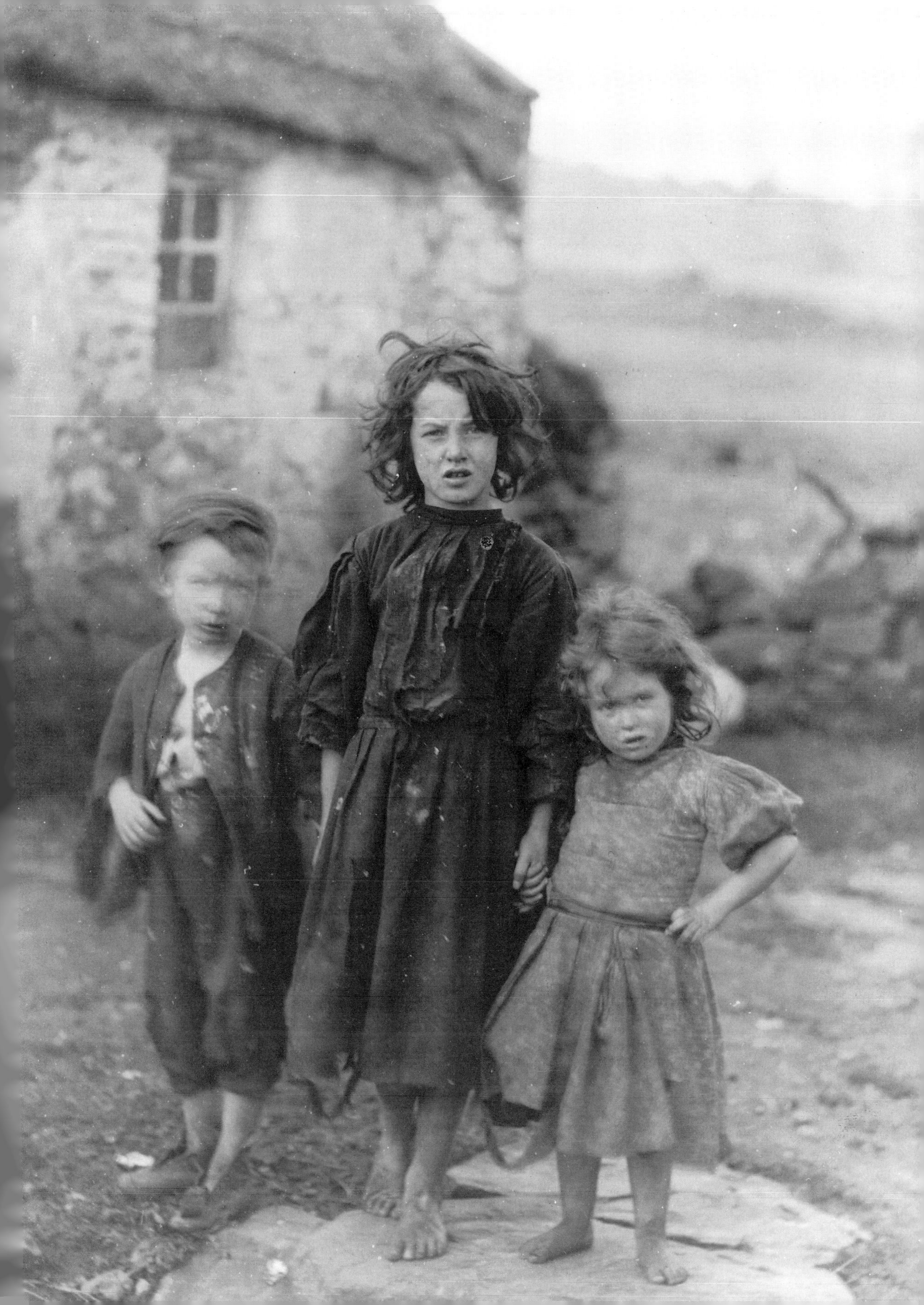

Irish descent, until well into the 1960s and 1970s. Used to the radical nature and wide achievements of their own social legislation and relatively classless environment, such visitors were wont to be ultra-conscious and highly critical of this aspect of Irish life. They would admire the intense warmth and genuine closeness of inter-personal relationships, and the depth of hospitality and other humane behaviour, but their own colonial society had accustomed them to the loneliness — and freedom — of space, and the superficiality of human contact necessitated by an obsession with personal independence. They preferred a common structure which took care of people, to a specific charity, in the widest sense, which did the same. To their taste Ireland was both claustrophobic and intrusive, both inefficient and — in curious ways at variance with the religious principles it espoused — to their mind, false.

Nor were such hostile judgments the upstart preserve of uncomprehending colonials. The best known of Australian Irish pioneering families, the Duracks, those *Kings in Grass Castles,* exhibit a consistency in this, from Irish born to colonial generation. Patsy Durack, family patriarch, had long been concerned about the differences between himself and his Australian descendants. Dame Mary Durack has captured the essentials of this contrast:

> At times he [Patsy] would shake his head over the Australian-born generation of his family unable to express himself clearly on where the difference lay between their attitude and his own.
> 'I will not criticize them for their stockwork or their bushmanship, for they were born to it and I was not, but in other things they do not seem to think beyond a day or a year. They will act upon impulse and make the law for themselves as they go along and hang what shall be the end result of it. They have been brought up in the faith but they do not turn to it for advice. They look only to themselves as though they were almighty God himself, which they are not.'

To this 'the young fellows' in question would reply with some scorn: 'We have been brought up in a country where a man has to rely on his own judgment. We have no time to be riding a thousand miles to find a priest and besides, we don't carry our religion on our sleeves like you Irishmen'.

Then, in 1896, Patsy Durack returned to Ireland, after forty-four years, to disillusionment. He had been generous among his Irish relations with remittances and passage money to Australia, but this seemed to have converted his persona into a mere revenue source and no one was interested in him or his colonial life. The place seemed to be full of poverty, apathy and procrastination, and obsession with the past. Things that could and should be done never were, easy improvements were neglected. Australia evinced no interest, only the question of how much money he had. It was profoundly depressing. He himself, Patsy Durack, no longer fitted Ireland. Nor, as a returning Irishman, was he exceptional in that experience.

Julia Moriarty's father left Ireland as a teenager at the turn of the century, for London, then, in 1910, for the New Zealand police. He returned to Cahirdaniel in 1950 — 'this is only where I was born. In fifty years nature herself has changed even the marrow of my bones. I do not belong here'. He asked Julia not to tell her mother, 'who lived in a pipe dream of a perfect country', despite reminders from friends that they had left Ireland because of the poverty: reality was no match for fond remembrance. Her mother's brother, Irish-born, went back to Ireland permanently, buying a farm, a step he regretted. When the river flooded it washed up waste on his property, from the TB hospital. He hankered after *Truth*, the colonial paper in various Australian and New Zealand cities, which would have got something done about the pollution: there was no *Truth* in Ireland.

As to the colonial Duracks, they had been convinced for many years, that their ultimate roots lay in France, not Ireland, and kept a critical distance from the Irish. Visiting Ireland in 1902, Michael Patrick Durack, like his father, was shocked by both the poverty and apathy he found, and surprised that the Irish were so distinct from the English and so bright and clever with it. Why on earth did they accept such degrading poverty, and why didn't they do something to change what was easily remedied — the prevailing disrepair and dirt? He kept quiet to his Irish friends about the cause which leapt first to his mind — the clergy and the church: he found the contrast between this poverty and the ecclesiastical opulence and comforts of the clergy, hard to stomach. Poverty was being taxed to sustain splendour, and the swarming clerical beneficiaries did nothing to brighten the lives of those off whom they lived. A good thing he kept quiet. In that very year Michael J.F. McCarthy created an enormous furore in Ireland by asserting the very same thing in his book *Priests and People in Ireland*. In McCarthy the impulse seems to have been anti-clericalism and hostility to religion: in Durack it was a colonial sense of justice, and a colonial estimate of the proper place and style of

The affluent home-coming emigrant stereotyped, for Irish consumption, in the *Wolfe Tone Annual* 1947.

the clergy and religion. Had he spoken out, it is doubtful if listeners would have made the distinction.

Nor did Durack have any previous conception of the intensity of the hatred for England, nor of the depth of religious antagonisms. He was simply not prepared for such raw and vehement emotions. Where would they lead? Surely to nothing good. Nor could he, participant in the British tradition of empire, share them, even in diminished stridence.

Against this, in contrast to all he found incomprehensible and repulsive, and which made him feel a stranger, foreign, there was much in Ireland that was wonderful and warm. He fell under its human spell. Obviously, he had lived all his life with the Irish in Australia. They were a pale reflection of what he discovered in Ireland, as a photograph was distinct from reality. But all in all, as Mary Durack has it, Ireland, to Michael Durack was an intriguing, beautiful but decidedly foreign land'. Besides, despite his parentage, his visit was no pilgrimage, but a detour in a visit whose main purpose was to attend the coronation of King Edward VII in London. And his stance was that of sightseer, first class, whose pastoral heritage was bigger than half the counties of Ireland. Ireland was a minor, if enjoyable, curiosity. His brother, J.W., was more at home on a 1907 visit, but still very much the colonial in the way of which his father had complained — before his disillusioning 1896 return.

Brian O'Higgins's famous Irish verse cards capture the spirit of Eileen Duggan's involvement with Ireland.

Of course, until very recently, the colonial descendants of Ireland seldom saw and judged Ireland for themselves. Only the affluent had that opportunity. The sources for their image were religious, either priests or nuns, or the Catholic press. Both carried a predictable bias and selectivity; more than that, however, there was a degree of unreality, discussed earlier in relation to the clergy, but strikingly illustrated by a lay influence of great longevity and personal goodness. The New Zealand poetess, Eileen Duggan, as a columnist ('Pippa') in the *New Zealand Tablet* for almost fifty years (1927–1972), had a remarkable influence on the descendants of Irish Catholicism in New Zealand. Her biographer remarks that it has been said that she was a woman of two countries — Ireland and New Zealand: she regarded herself as a grand-daughter of Ireland. While her achievement lay in locating such Irish and their descendants in a New Zealand environment, and, indeed, in an international Catholicism, she could find little in common with that other contemporary female figure of New Zealand Catholicism, the convert Maria Dronke, European, with a Jewish upbringing, whose Catholicism was totally non-Irish. The culture gap was too great. Yet, in what did this gap consist?

Dronke's cultural setting was contemporary European Catholicism. Duggan's was, as her biographer suggests, that of stories of the Great Irish Famine, a century earlier, retailed by her Irish parents, born in the 1860s in its aftermath. Of course, she had supplemented such childhood tales by wide adult reading, but the fact remained that this champion of Ireland, elected to honorary membership of the Irish National Club of Wellington in 1948, for her journalistic services to Ireland in New Zealand, had never been to Ireland. Essentially her devotion, what she communicated, was an idea, a tradition, a parental legacy, a vision refracted through literature and history. Perhaps, had she visited Ireland her view would have been no different. Perhaps the image disseminated by this gentle, spiritual woman was better, more uplifting and morally formative than any reality might have been. However derived, Eileen Duggan's Ireland was sustained and was disseminated by an older generation, mainly Irish-born, mainly priests and nuns: it gave that generation a sense of warmth and security in their origins. Communicated to the young, through Catholic schooling, it was counter-productive, force-feeding, which furthered neither the reputation of Ireland nor that of Miss Duggan, producing apathies and antipathies which endured into the present. Whatever the duality of its impact, the fact remains that her Ireland was a construct of the hopes of a pure and generous heart and soul. Was the reality her equal?

Visiting Ireland in 1951, the newly ordained Dominican Father P.M. Farrell (my brother Tim) was quite unprepared for the reality of the circumstances of his relatives; or for the care they had taken to disguise, or disinform — or was it merely not to mention — the facts of their existence to their colonial relatives, notably Mai, my mother, as all my father's family had left. It may be that this apparent deception was merely an accident of circumstance. Correspondence between Mai and her Irish sisters and brother had never been intense, though frequent at the level of superficial banalities, Christmas, marriages, births, and so on. Whatever the cause, as Patsy Durack had found half a century earlier, a great gulf of incomprehension and disinterest had grown to separate the two experiences, metropolitan and colonial. The main responsibility for this lay at the Irish end. They knew nothing of Australia or New Zealand, cared less and had lost any real feeling for those so distant who had departed so long ago. But problems also lay at the colonial end: it was inconceivable that those at home could have forgotten them, or did not know them still. Home was home. But of course it was not. Tim found little vestige of the antiquated dreamworld Mai had led him to expect. The remaining family was far from the semi-rural Borrisokane group of relatively carefree adolescents and young adults Mai and Chris had left in 1914. It had been dispersed, largely sucked into the drift to urban Dublin. It was also full of internal tensions, riven by competitive marriages among the girls, and deeply divided by the social pretences, felt senses of gradation, and minor but intense class consciousness endemic to Dublin life and location of residence, then as now. On top of that, some of the family had developed eccentricities of a kind frequently encountered in nineteenth century Irish Australia, but seldom encountered in the more modern colonial world.

All this came as a surprise to Tim; he was, in general, prepared for erosion by time and tide but was taken aback by the farrago of side, pretence and sheer oddity which accompanied the genuine kindness and hospitality turned on for his benefit. 'Turned on' was the operative description for the procession of performances; for, it soon transpired that the various family members normally saw very little of each other and harboured intricacies of mutual hostility and dislike, the entirety of whose causes Tim could only vaguely fathom and had no wish to pursue. He was soon out of patience with the whole weird imbroglio — as he saw it — but happy to relate cordially to its separate parts. A somersault of expectations and imaginative depictions was necessary to cope with this situation.

Orthodoxy had it — nationalist and clerical — that Ireland was the home of happy and holy families. Emigration was the destroyer of this paradise, driving exiles to lonely and fragmented lives on hostile and degraded shores. But the fact was that most of Mai's and Paddy's family that had left Ireland were in fairly constant communication, on reasonably good terms, and exchanged holidays amongst themselves on an annual if not more frequent basis. It was the Irish home-branch of the family that had fallen apart and lapsed into separate entities and factions. On any reasonable scale of observation and judgment, these were the unhappy and bitter ones. This went against all pious predictions and assurances, contradicted all the mythology, but was unmistakably so. This was only one such family perhaps, no basis for generalisation. Perhaps — though Patsy Durack's disillusionment with his Irish clan, when encountered face to face, comes back to mind. And of course the reversal in actuality of the propaganda image makes ample human sense. The migration process itself, its pressures and exigencies, drove emigrant family members together, not apart; for society, for money, for protection, for chain migration schemes, for companionship in a common, large enterprise. Emigration welded them together, and also demanded they come out of themselves to face the new environment, itself diverting, outward-going.

Those who stayed at home faced no such challenge: their failure to emigrate often the source of a sense of inadequacy and defeat, their energies forced inward on the world they knew and its closest boundaries, their remaining family. Its constrictions, close living, envy of fabled emigrant wealth, a sluggish, if not stagnant, Irish economy until recent times — all these things were more corrosive of family life than the perils of migration. Added to which, of course, was the destructive internal effect of emigration itself. For two centuries Irish politicians and clerics bewailed the cost of this to Ireland, in terms of the draining of its life-blood, sorrowing mothers, loss to religion, and such-like generalities. They seldom descended to specifics. In 1951 Tim encountered, in his own relations, such specifics. (In 1965 I noted another: our family of five Australian children was by far the largest, and double the norm, in the middle-class area of Dublin in which we were living.)

However, the occasion demanded an appropriate response from the Irish family. Tim was a priest, from countries distant and strange, and Mai's boy. Efforts must be made, whatever the feelings of awe and awkwardness.

So, Tim began his social rounds. The Dominican Priory was on the north side of the city, his first aunt to be visited was on the south: he was to stay with her for a few days. Given only a street number, he soon became completely lost and was taken pity on by a passing motorist, who drove him to the door. The door, to Tim's amazement and discomfiture, was that of an inner-city 'public house', 'the shop' the owners called it, very conspicuously painted and labelled 'The Green Bar', all of which had caused him to walk past it earlier without a glance. His anonymous driver was vastly amused, at Tim's stupefaction and at the destination of this respectable man of the cloth.

Tim in the garb of his order and in serious mode: Reverend Dr P.M. Farrell, O.P., S.T.L.

(Fifteen years later, passing this pub, which by then had changed hands, I innocently mentioned its family provenance to a University College colleague, who was similarly moved to a malicious guffaw. Was it some notorious watering hole, resort of policemen, informers, or other persons of ill moral repute?)

The message seemed to be that Dublin social propriety held it as a historical constant that it was beneath the dignity of priests, or university lecturers, to have, or at least acknowledge, such truck with the purveyors of alcohol at the common level (such an attitude in the colonies would have imposed family isolation on half the Australian-born priesthood.) However, there seemed nothing against drinking there. It was the students' pub, and a much more pleasant place than the appalling staff favourite across the street, which boasted ancient filth, wooden floorboards, and the most repellent and odoriferous urinal in all of Ireland. My reaction to this mysterious social pecksniffery was much the same as brother Tim's: in his parlance of 1951, what the heck?

Obviously our aunt was aware of the Dublin mores that governed the situation and, apparently, imposed a social gap and shame on publicans (and sinners, one cannot resist querying of the holy isle?). Why else should she maintain to the last moment the absurd pretence of hiding their trade behind a telephoned street number when Tim was bound to find this proclaimed, by the very nature of its business and a large sign? And why was this unknown, never mentioned, in dispatches to the colonies? One can only suppose that there was an Irish protocol to be followed of which the colonial was ignorant. That was, presumably, that the publican's trade was in the social nature of a disfigurement or disability, which in polite encounters should be ignored, not adverted to, and the pretence adopted that it did not exist. Tim's colonial naivety (and mine) led him to be unaware that this was the Irish game that ought to have been played to save the face of all parties. Instead, the innocent abroad was annoyed at what seemed to him a stupid and totally needless deception, which had brought him puzzlement and ridicule and caused embarrassment. The root cause of all this — the nuances and rituals of Irish social structures and snobberies — seemed to have passed completely over Tim's head, or been dismissed as of no account, in what he knew would be a brief impingement on the lives of these very odd and foreign people.

Meeting this first aunt, her husband and family, introduced him to some of the keys to the Irish family labyrinth. Most obvious was that Mai was family pet. He conveyed this back as

Tim and the author beholding Ireland: two faces of colonial amazement.

compliment, but a deeper look might have questioned what her leaving Ireland had done to family unity. Had Mai stayed, she might have bridged, in a way her divisive sisters could not, the substantial differences and tensions that grew within a group that was high-strung and competitive. Somehow Mai had been the hub of the family wheel, the stable central point to which the others related, sought approval from, wanted to please. With her gone, the structure fell apart, as family members failed to manage or contain within its boundaries, their differences in temperament, choice and destiny. They fragmented into individuals with such different locations in hierarchical Irish society as drove them further apart, worsening by dint of external social pressures and expectations, and traditional behaviour patterns, their tendency to become strangers to each other.

Colonial Tim had never encountered this before. True, the colonial family were much on the one economic level — not affluent, though in no way poor by Irish standards — but while there were relativities and gradations, these never obtruded into, or influenced, the basic closeness and amity of family relations in New Zealand. That occupation of different levels of poverty, or pursuit of bourgeois lifestyles, or particular employments, should be basically destructive of family unity and convert its members into virtual strangers, was a new experience to Tim: but he quickly grasped the rudiments of why it might be so. Conditioned in coming to Ireland more by Mai's nostalgic sentimentality, his experience converted him more to appreciating why Paddy had left.

The clan still had sufficient pride and vitality to assemble its forces; gingerly, and suspicious of itself. Tim, as innocent colonial and heedless priest, but also as foreign observer and intelligent man, was both aware and not aware of the consternation he was causing. His coming had confronted the dispersed and factionalised family with the colonial demand that it exist, jump about, perform in traditional fashion, be itself — or rather, as it could never be that again, be a pretend self. In turn, they expected a priest act, a grand clerical performance, which he was neither equipped nor disposed to give. He had camped in too many bush huts and dossed in too many rough beds to care much for side, but they were not to know that, and were confused by his informality and his refusal to take charge. He had, in fact, placed these people, strangers who happened to be family, in an impossible position. He lacked the lordly and demanding Irish-priest manner and was nonplussed by its expectation. His relatives were bewildered by his unfamiliar low-key portrayal of his priest role, blended with his position as nephew from foreign parts, and embarrassed that he had, in a sense, found them out. They knew his discoveries would be reported to Mai, placing them at a further disadvantage. Under Irish rules, Mai was already leagues ahead with a son a priest.

What they probably did not appreciate was the sharpness of the microscopic examination being focussed upon them, nor its heavily comparative colonial criteria. There were pluses and minusses but, on the whole, Ireland was weighed in the balance and found wanting. This went against the facts of parentage (though not any vigorous indoctrination from that source) but much more against the climate and mythology of the colonial Irish Catholic culture. The promotion of Ireland as paradise had one overwhelming danger. Direct experience of the actuality might sour an observer excessively, that is, induce an over-reaction from disillusionment. Tim contrived to avoid this by simply stepping outside what he saw and recounting his observations.

His publican aunt was thin and nervy, with a passion for 'nice' things, something of which her Dublin sisters were highly critical, to her face as well as behind her back. This explained much of the frosty and distant atmosphere which dominated the infrequent family encounters, one of which Tim's visit had compelled. Her critics detested what they dubbed her 'grand style', for itself, no doubt also out of envy, and because of what they deemed its affectation. What was she but a jumped-up pub-keeper's wife putting on airs (and serviettes, and 'American' salads) and display, pretending to be superior and the great lady. Exacerbating her apparent and actual remoteness, and the aura of being aloof, was the fact that she was completely deaf in one ear, wore no hearing aid, and hated people shouting at her. Her immediate household she comprehended largely by intuition and expectation of what they might be saying. Tim's conversation, in unfamiliar accents and on unpredictable topics, was largely incomprehensible to her. Afraid to speak loudly and embarrassed at constantly repeating himself, he retreated into frustrated silence, embellished by an inane grin of goodwill, to express his gratitude to a person both generous and anxious to be of help. He was reduced to speaking to her through the translation of other family members.

It was a bizarre situation, with elements of sadness and farce. The lonely social climber, lover of pretty things, besieged by deafness and her sisters' venomous hostility, hating the

Above: Main Street, Borrisokane, about the time of Tim's visit in 1951.

Left: Tim in colonial garb: in miner's gear for a visit in 1952 to the Brunner coal mine, just outside Greymouth.

occasional duty of serving in the bar, but good with the books, cared for and protected by a slow, considerate husband; the awkward, out-of-place guest relation, his position even more complicated by his priesthood, observing, judging, comparing, and reporting all this back to Mai, ex-member of this now derelict ménage. Reporting even down to comparative physical evaluations of the various children. Ellen's children 'are the best looking of all my cousins here — indeed they struck me as being in quite a different physical class from all the others. But then they have much better opportunities and environment than Norah's or Mary's kiddies'.

Norah and Mary. Visits to them, led by Ellen, were brief, awkward and bristling with sensitivities: necessary, but potentially explosive situations, volatile with past and present tensions. Tim reported: 'I began to realise that if I showed any interest in these politics I should very soon find myself on a triangular rack, so I allowed none of it to sink in.' The politics may not have sunk in, but the general scene did, deeply. Norah lived in the poorest quarter of Dublin — explaining Ellen's reluctance to visit, and the embarrassment of Norah. The area was industrial, their terrace house dingy and small, without bathroom or hot water. The street was the playground and on Sundays was full of loungers playing pitch and toss while the pubs were closed (during the 'holy hour' as the mocking tag

The kind of Irish church architecture that failed to inspire Tim: the Catholic chapel, Borrisokane.

had it). It was vintage working-class, dirty Dublin, and Tim's observations sounded like those of a nineteenth century slum-clearance reformer: 'The whole atmosphere is unwholesome and depressed'. And he noted the concomitants — illness, frail children, TB, infantile paralysis, deformity of all kinds, filth, smells: a shock to the New Zealander of 1951, hardly one to those to whom he was writing. This was the other side of Ireland's ability to stand still in time, which so charmed visiting romantics who did not see such areas, and were able to stay elsewhere in comfort. Norah's three children mirrored their environment. They seemed 'physically washed out and undernourished . . . very frail and carry the suggestion of a reddish rim about the eyes as if they had lived in a cave all their days on bread and jam and ice-cream with no sun': the imaginative ingredients of the description were of colonial derivation, but they made the point vividly enough. The older girl, under-developed, round-shouldered, and afflicted by recurrent styes, was destined for dressmaking, or to be a shop assistant. The younger girl, outgoing, bright, a keen Gaelic dancer, wanted to be a nurse, but she was behind at school and the cost of nursing training in Ireland was prohibitive for the poor. England beckoned. Here be battlers. Norah was all heart, 'a kind of community centre for the whole street. All in trouble came to Norah and there is plenty of it'. Her husband was quiet, colourless. Moving into optimistic clerical distancing gear — or was it a perception of grace? — Tim judged them a happy family with a native toughness and resilience, and a secure place in their own community.

Next visit. Mary had the reputation of being odd, even by Irish standards. She had long been prodigal with excessively candid personal observations, which had been too much for the sensitivities of Ellen, who delegated the task of Tim's guide to one of Norah's children. Ellen then supplied incorrect directions for the bus trip. Believing that everyone should have cars, buses were not Ellen's preferred mode of transport, and she affected vagueness about public transport movements. Being late at Mary's was reputedly a cardinal offence, likely to trigger off a tirade, irrespective of the reason or dignity of the personage. Half an hour in a bus travelling in the wrong direction ensured that Tim arrived for his 3 p.m. appointment at 4.30. But Mary was merely abrupt and that, simply a mannerism. A widow, fairly comfortable 'by Dublin standards' — Tim, deprived of a glimpse of the upper economic ranges of that city, had decided that these standards were low. Mary was a lonely and eccentric person, who, at the time, as an obligement to a friend, was managing a small suburban clothes shop: the responsibility was undermining her health. In the tradition, now gone, of giving significant sums of money as gifts to visiting priests, she gave Tim a generous £5, extracted from her store of money hidden, it was reputed, in various odd parts of the house. (This was a practice also followed in the colonies. Paddy had such caches, whether from distrust of banks, unwillingness to facilitate the taxman, secretiveness — I never knew of it — or mere convenience, is impossible to tell.) Mary's reputation for eccentricity may have been enhanced by her means of protecting her hoard — nailing down all windows in the house, a practice common enough now, but not then.

The colonial observer was being scrutinised and judged in return. Visiting that place of penitential pilgrimage, Lough Derg, Tim sent off a few postcards. He overlooked Mary, an omission later drawn to his attention by Norah.

Next, off to uncle John in Borrisokane, preceded, it transpired, by trepidations about the 'foreign priest', and fears that he might be one for ceremony and dignity they could not provide. Or rather, for John was affluent enough, could not be bothered providing, or saw no need. John was a widower, now newly engaged. He had been ravaged by TB, having had one lung removed, but was now completely recovered. Following his father, a contract painter and decorator, with a reasonable business and owning some property, he took absolutely no care of his personal appearance, diet, or domestic habitation, but was altogether a lovely man (a judgement of Tim's I can confirm personally). His scruffy and unkempt appearance soon faded in the comparative eye: to have been neat and well-dressed in northern Tipperary would have been the eye-catching eccentricity. John cooked for himself, to the constant rebellion of his stomach, on a small temperamental primus stove. His house had one usable room, the rest was an empty shambles, with bulging wallpaper and neither water nor sewerage. He had to go up the road to get water, but the house had no drains to dispose of it. Nor sewers. He told Tim he used a 'bucket system' for a WC, but, despite urgent searching of the tiny back yard, Tim could not find it, nor even a likely shed or cranny for its placement, were such a bucket to exist. There was no bathroom, although John had made provision for one when drainage and water were eventually — this was 1951 — laid on in Borrisokane. There was a door in the wall of an upstairs bedroom which opened on to a sheer twelve foot drop into the back yard. The bathroom would go there. In the meantime, John mostly lived and ate with (and used the bucket of) his friend in the bike shop. Eventually the new wife would fix everything up.

Yet, this ramshackle scene and life-style projected the reverse of depressing squalor. It was merely, to a colonial view, crazy. John owned a far better house immediately next door, which he rented, and a car, whose use he pressed on Tim. He took the week off work to show him around the district. In that tour he laughed and joked with all, so that his peregrinations were constantly and joyously tearful, with that strange watery mixture of delight and regret that only such favoured individuals can generate in their company. His passage anywhere was interrupted by stops to chat, and any journey was always of uncertain social duration. Charmer. Lightener of the load. For all the colonial obsession with missing and absent sewerage, there remained the suspicion that at the centre of this madhouse existence was a lesson on how life ought to be lived.

Tim saw this lesson and admitted its validity — in part, and not for him. He could appreciate, in that vein, that the great monastery at Mount Melleray was 'one of the really great monuments to the Faith of the Irish poor'. Yet, he seems to have forgotten that his own parents were part of that constituency, turning on the gawping colonial tourist act for Mai by waxing long and lyrical about the Tipperary scenery: 'How much you must have loved the pastoral beauty of your Tipperary'. Perhaps. Your Tipperary? Certainly not his. He made no identification with Ireland whatever. It was not his country and he viewed it as a beautiful, fascinating, and backward place he was passing through. Neither did he have any deep appreciation that his parents had been part of this place. His imagination put them there in roughly the same role as his own, but the fast motoring foreign priest of 1951 held a very different perspective on the view, from the girl and boy of 1914. The problem was that he could not envisage them as part of this odd place. He knew them in New Zealand and of New Zealand, and the family he had met in Ireland were eccentric strangers, who theoretically bore a relationship to him and his parents but, in practice, were foreigners and treated him as one. How could his parents have ever been an intimate part of this society? It was an imaginative lapse on his part, a failure to appreciate the cultural distance they and time had travelled, a lack of appreciation of the transformation the colonial environment had wrought. Mai could have become what her sisters were. That she did not, that her son should have such difficulty in placing her in her original context, is in part due to those traits of character which took her out of Ireland, in part to the new environment she came to occupy and, eventually, to reflect. Whatever the bonds of birthplace and family, she was not — she was no longer — one of these people, or a true inhabitant of that place.

And what about Tim's estimate of the heroic struggles of the Irish poor? His admiration was tempered by his having come to Ireland by slow transport, and walking, through the medieval heartlands of Catholic Europe — Italy, Austria, Germany,

France. That is, he had arrived in Ireland via the great monuments to the achievements of the Ages of Faith, and their contemporary residues in Christian civilisation, still war-scarred, but extraordinarily vital. To him, Ireland was an anticlimax: 'The architecture, like that of all Irish churches (with few exceptions) is quite uninspired and what is remarkable about them and worthy of admiration, is rather the spirit and the circumstances of their being built'. They were in the category of Dr Johnson's dog that walked on its hind legs — commendable for its walking style, but rather that it should walk at all. Such Irish spirit and circumstances were not things for emulation. Indeed, that was impossible, given that they were the product of history that had passed. Ireland was a 'despite' country. Its amazing and prodigious triumphs had been despite — to borrow from Father Faber's famous hymn — dungeon, fire and sword, and, of course, despite oppression and poverty and lack of opportunity.

To Tim, the 'despite' motif seemed not a good base for colonial building. Formed in his initial adult thinking by the neo-scholastics — French, notably Maritain, Dominican-trained in Rome in the originals of the scholastic tradition, notably Aquinas — Tim, as aspiring religious intellectual, could see no comparable Irish tradition which would command his respect. The 'despite' stance of confrontation of the world ill-suited the colonies, however natural it might be to the plight, or the former plight, of Ireland. A far better base of colonial operation would be, 'because'. A colonial religious position should be worked out and reasoned out, not flung offensively without thought in the face of those who were neither oppressors nor persecutors: but doing so, would make them so.

Each to his own Irish concerns. Tim gave no thought to Irish ancestry until he was compelled to do so, and then it was not his ancestry that concerned him. That was irrelevant to the problem to hand, which was the frustrating Irishness of those in power in his own Dominican order. They regarded him as a colonial, which was how he regarded himself, and the colonies were where he regarded his knowledge, experience and responsibilities as being situate and operative. Irish clerical authority in Australia regarded this as a disability. It knew best, for Ireland and Australia. Even into the 1950s, even the 1980s, the Irish image of Australia remained that inherited from a century before: Terra Nova, 'the Cannibal Isles', gold-rush primitive, oafish, uncivilised, inferior. The logic of Australia and New Zealand being Catholic Ireland's most distant missions generated and sustained the image of both nonentity and tutelage. All the stereotypes, even the cliche of geography — 'down under' — implied the subordinate. Such were the elements of a massive misunderstanding and incomprehension damaging to, and frustrative of, all the parties involved.

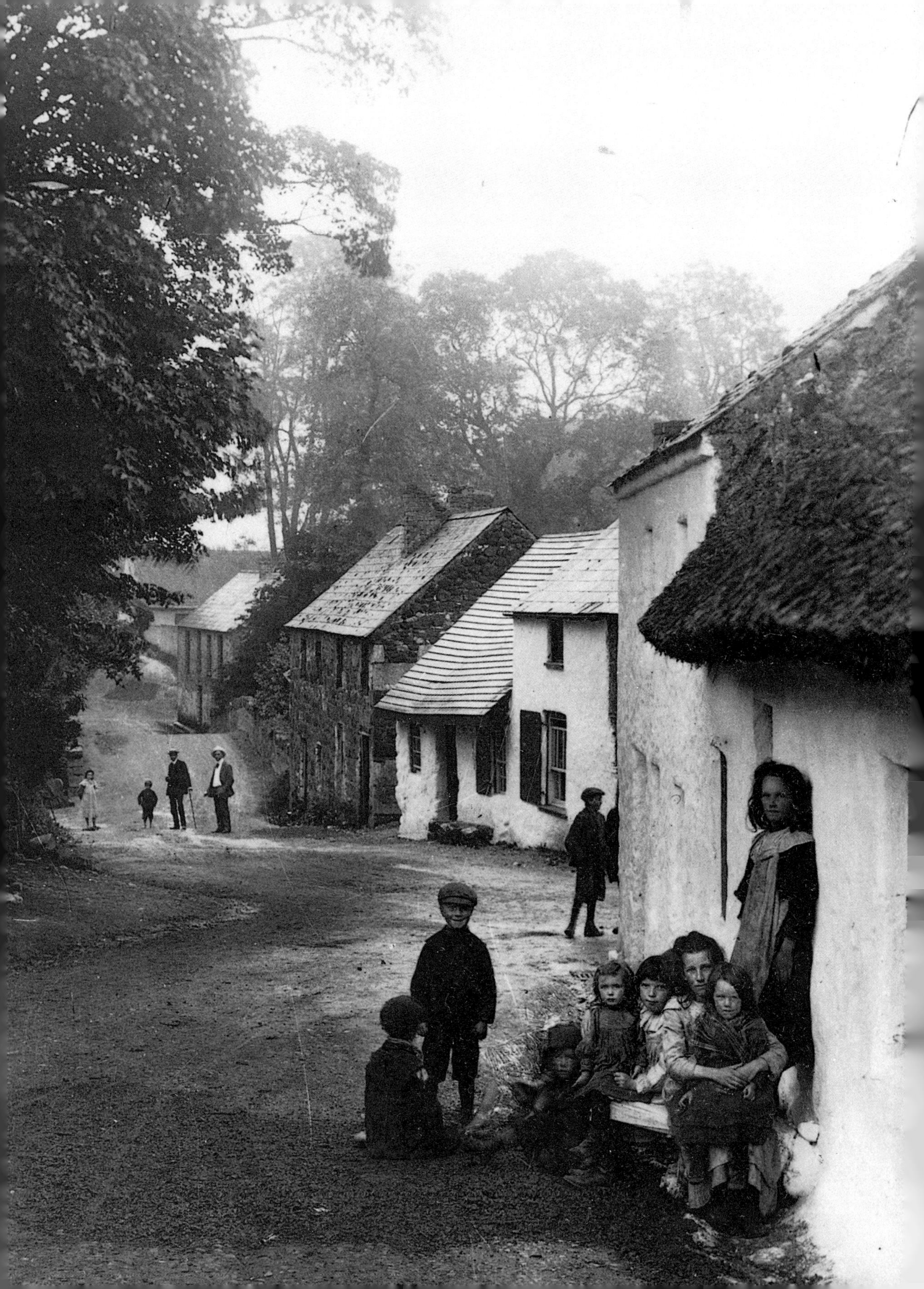

CHAPTER 8

DREAMS OF IRELANDS

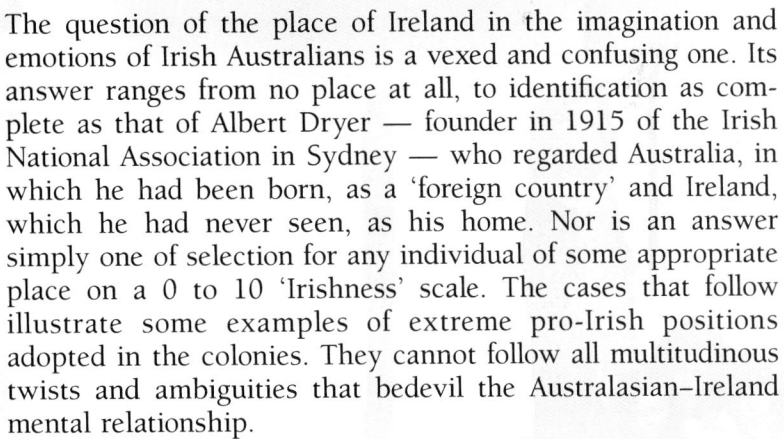

The question of the place of Ireland in the imagination and emotions of Irish Australians is a vexed and confusing one. Its answer ranges from no place at all, to identification as complete as that of Albert Dryer — founder in 1915 of the Irish National Association in Sydney — who regarded Australia, in which he had been born, as a 'foreign country' and Ireland, which he had never seen, as his home. Nor is an answer simply one of selection for any individual of some appropriate place on a 0 to 10 'Irishness' scale. The cases that follow illustrate some examples of extreme pro-Irish positions adopted in the colonies. They cannot follow all multitudinous twists and ambiguities that bedevil the Australasian–Ireland mental relationship.

For a glimpse of that complexity, what better entry point for exploration than the mind of a poet? In relation to Ireland, the Melbourne academic and poet Vincent Buckley called himself a 'loving outsider', and affirmed that Ireland was his 'imagination's home'. Yet, his autobiography acknowledges that he was only preponderantly Irish in ancestry, that his Australian-born father denied his Irishness and was blank about his origins.

Dreams of Ireland—pretty, picturesque—much photographed Glencoe, Country Antrim, 23 June 1906 (*Ulster Museum*)

The chapter in which he discusses this is entitled 'Self-conscious and Australian'. Yet, while his family had lost the link with Ireland, traces of that origin remained, in the Buckley case, expressed in a tradition of song, but were otherwise vague or buried. Vincent's own fascination with Ireland as a source country, issued in several long visits and eventually, in 1985, a book, *Memory Ireland,* whose 'hidden theme is Ireland's loss of its own memory, forced out by dispossessors, abandoned by ignorance, sold by jobbers, collapsed for lack of visible support, or simply leached away by the green misty weather'. At heart, the book is a kind of critical lament, contentious certainly, yet informed by dispositions of a learning process and true affection, if tinged at times with exasperation. As 'loving outsider' he sees himself on one level as Irish, but knows on another level he is not: he is Australian. Nor does he claim 'the full range of Irish virtues or vices', nor want to think with 'the extravagant evasiveness' of many Irish writers and intellectuals he knew. It is the book of a colonial intellectual, ambivalent in part, but basically a critique springing from perceptions not just of these things, too, in Ireland which were valuable, beyond price, and those things which were irksome to the colonial. Inevitably, these latter include inefficiency, tardiness, rapacity and a failure to perceive and preserve what he thought valuable in matters of religion, myth and spirit.

All of this seemed both perceptive and predictable to the informed colonial eye, and very much in harmony with colonial experience of, and reactions to, Ireland, both historical and contemporary. But the American Irish response to the book raises a general question which must be confronted. In a review headed 'Cantankerous Silliness' in the American *Irish Literary Supplement* of Spring 1986, Buckley was accused of indulging the grudges of 'a man who finds himself on the periphery of the Irish literary scene' and of revealing 'not so much a love of Ireland as a resentment against the British, the Irish literary establishment, writers from the North of Ireland, book reviewers, and land-lords. The "loving outsider" wishes he were inside'. Even allowing for the hagiographical attitude of many Irish-Americans towards things Irish, and their refusal to countenance any criticism of their idols, the comments raise valid questions. Does the outsider — even the word carries that implication — really wish he were inside? Is the identification with Ireland by many Irish Australians merely, or largely, a vehicle for their rejection of the English roots and establishment character of their own society? It would be a superficial analyst who could give a confident 'no' to these

More like the real thing — bare, hard, dirty. Main Street, Tempo, County Fermanagh, 1 November 1899. (*Ulster Museum, Langham Collection*)

questions in their generality. The acts of electing to live in a country, of giving one's time, energy and gifts to considering the operation of its society, suppose a kind of identification which carries elements of the wish to belong. But the wish to belong, to be an 'insider' can apply equally well to the country of one's birth. Many Americans might equally well find warmth towards Ireland hard to disentangle from a traditional dislike of Britain.

As to Vincent Buckley, a passionate Ireland enthusiast might find his *Memory Ireland* an infuriating book, in that it reflects an ambivalent expression of his ego, that drawn to Ireland but in love/hate. Such a Gaelophile would be much happier with Buckley's self-description in a television interview shortly before his death in 1988, as 'an Irishman living in Australia'. Yet, it is unlikely that many Irishmen would concede him that status, and no reader of his autobiography *Cutting Green Hay*

201

could have any doubt about the depth of his Australian commitment — nor of the family and cultural formation that involved him with Ireland. Involved with Ireland — the phrase is loose enough to cover ebb and flow, like and dislike, and fluctuation of the relationship with mood and time. It might cover as well, if not for Buckley then for others of similar heritage, the substitution of interest in Ireland for the culture of Catholicism rejected, an adult Ireland filling in for, as retrieval, lost Catholic boyhoods: the magic, but without the compulsions of the old gods.

The American critique alerts one to an important contrast. One might expect — or at least be open to expect — very different attitudes to Ireland from a man whose links had been deliberately broken by his ancestors, in favour of stressing an Australian identity, as was Buckley's case (and that of many other Australians), than from the predominant Irish–American experience. That experience was of those whose ancestors, at some distance, hailed from Ireland long ago, and whose Irish experience, or mythology, constituted a venerated, treasured, family tradition. Such is the predominant Irish-American experience. Far from being unique, or unusual, as Buckley implies, the uncommunicative Irish grandparent(s) is a common feature of Australian experience. He was heir, with much of the Australian and New Zealand progeny of the Irish, to 'denial of Irishness', 'blankness about origins' and an 'air of fatherless malaise'. For most, that was good enough, nothing much to bother about: but, for Buckley, poet, in adult maturity, it was unacceptable. He had been, as he saw it, cheated of a glorious past, deprived of imaginative and psychological substance.

The present American Irish seldom had a directly familiar experience of Irish culture, in the specific sense of its being filtered through immediate parenthood. By the twentieth century they tended to be the very American and proud exemplars of a multi-generation flow of imported Irish tradition, long established, heavily myth-laden and woven into a hybrid which gave them a firm sense of location in both places, however superficial and false might be their appreciation of contemporary Ireland. They were secure and happy in what might seem to others — notably the Irish themselves — romantic and sentimental illusions. Not so the Australian Buckley. He was saddled with elders who 'did not know or would not tell', who wanted to forget. To question why they should want to forget Ireland (a common reaction in my own family) hardly occurred to him, but the determination to do so presented itself to him as a radical deficiency: 'they were the inheritors of Anonymous Man'. Buckley's wish to inherit a rich past ran full tilt against his elders' refusal to give him one. This situation filled him with anger, even contempt, and imported into his quest for a lost Irish heritage, a set of confusions, resentments, twists and contradictions, which appear to derive from reactions to parental and other family relationships, as much as from anything he was to find out about Ireland. But is this true, and can the two be separated, Ireland and clan?

The simplest answer to the question he never asked is this: his ancestors wanted to forget and would not tell, denied him a glorious Gaelic past, because they did not have one to convey. All they had was something mean and painful to recall, and a sense of guilt for having left it. They were starting again, elsewhere. Buckley's plaint about his deprived Irish identity rested on his assumption of possession of the best quality ancestral stereotypes. He took for granted that his ancestors were 'basic conductors of social and mythic tradition', repositories of 'the mythic substratum of Irish religion' and veritable founts of potential folklore and song and stories, on all of which he missed out, because they died when was too young, or because they chose to clam up. South Australia's 150th Jubilee Oral History Project, for instance, indicates that he had wanted 'stories about the little people and the fairies' as he sat on his grandmother's knee, such as had been made available to others, as with reminiscences of the traditions of Irish life. But the question of the quantity, and especially the quality, of such oral legacy is highly problematic. Existing traces suggest a preponderance of banal generality. Buckley craved a skilled *seanchaí,* and such were rare enough in pre-modern Ireland. The nineteenth century, indeed the eighteenth, saw these talents, those of the hidden Ireland and the Gaelic poets, rapidly shrivel, retreat to the West, vanish. Buckley's complaint has a genuine basis, but the genesis of the lack may be in Ireland, not Australia. His grievance may be against Australian honesty, not any Irish suppression.

Moreover, the impressive structure of American Irishism has always harboured myths, of both love and hatred, and always had the marks of manufacture. Its content, when not locally political, has derived its poetical character — so enviable to the Buckley mind — first from that great edifice of recent intellectual Irish manufacture, the Gaelic revival, then from the literary and academic industries that have sprung up in America around W.B. Yeats and James Joyce. There is in all this

'the inheritors of Anonymous Man'.

activity and veneration a large element of recent myth construction, both Irish and American. In so far as it is American it fills the need for a past which they can appropriate and colonise, possess and cherish, fashion in their own image and likeness.

Hence their fury at Buckley, bringing colonial scepticism to hallowed ground. They cannot abide — as sacrilege — his penetrating sourness and partial rejection of his father's father's fatherland: or, I love and admire you, but no bullshit please. Nor do Americans comprehend Buckley's smouldering sense that his Australian forebears had been cheated, and in turn cheated him, leaving him, a poet, with a fragmentary past, which 'was a tissue of guesses, half-memories and misunderstandings'. Surely this is more or less a fair description of what most Irish-Americans, and not a few Irish Australians, are happy and content with? American Irish enthusiasm is prompted by gratitude at Ireland's giving them what they feel they lack — a rich and ancient identity, a noble history, in whose warm and dreamy waters they can bathe occasionally. They cannot understand that rough colonial impatience that dives through the misty dream-vapours in search of hard rock bottom.

Buckley desperately wanted the spiritual sustenance and poetry of the Irish dreams and the myths, but he was too hard-headed and too much the colonial bush sceptic to be fobbed off with the delusion and bombast that normally went with them for foreign consumption. And too proud and self-confident not to attempt, in love and deep concern, to diagnose what was wrong with Ireland as he saw it — strangely, loss of memory, of sense of the past, the very thing of which he believed himself cheated in Irish colonial boyhood. It was an instinctive perception which implied an obvious answer to that very question he had not thought to ask. To reiterate, he had been given nothing, because there was nothing to give. The aim to become Australian — with which he taxed his forebears, implying its home-grown thinness and banality, in contrast to alleged Irish richness — had produced in him an honesty and directness, a freshness of approach, a distaste for evasion and pretense, a touch of repudiation of the old world, and the impulse to make things new. But not without contradiction and pain and regret. Instead of upbraiding his ancestors for not bequeathing him a fortune that they did not possess, he might have thanked them for sparing him a diet of the thin gruel of their own real cultural sustenance.

Of course there is another side, the more well-worn, of this interpretive coin: the taunt of the pursuit of conformity, the aim of so many Irish in Australia to blend in and succeed in a society basically British. 'My parents', writes Dinny O' Hearn, 'while admiring wildness, preached conformity'. In fact, such Irish were wild enough. Their so preaching sprang from the defensive urge to limit their eccentricity and rebellion to what seemed more than enough — their socially aberrant and disadvantageous Catholicism. Given the Irish–Catholic equation commonly made, there is a case for suggesting that the cost of clinging to the faith of their fathers in Australia was the abandonment of most else culturally characteristic of their fathers. To their sons and daughters they gave what they judged more valuable than wildness, a place and opportunity in a new society and an education in which to breathe.

Vincent Buckley illustrates the complex zones of tension, ambivalence and confusion characteristic of some of the more intellectual levels of the Australia–Ireland relationship. But for other colonials, a very few, identification with Ireland was unquestioning and complete. Their cases are, from one view, strange, out of place; from another, reflective of a colonial culture lacking in such qualities as Ireland — or rather the dream of Ireland — might supply.

Reverend Brother Egbert was a New Zealand (Greymouth) born Marist Brother who had spent a month in Ireland in 1932. Long steeped in Irish political verse, an enthusiasm he seems to have caught from books rather than people — the Irishmen he knew in Wanganui in the 1920s were bookish rather than political (befitting the fact that many were ex-Irish policemen) — Egbert went to Ireland prepared with a programme of dramatic ways of identifying himself with such incidents in Irish history as had generated the popular poetry or oratory he had read. Thus, he recited 'Shemus O'Brien' in the very district (Glengall) which was the scene of the story. In Dublin, he boomed out (as near to the spot as possible) in his fulsome, old-fashioned, oratorical style, 'Emmet's Farewell Speech', and many other Irish poems as well, in appropriate locations. What the passing Dublin citizenry thought of these public declamations of their history by this portly religious, always in Homburg hat with elastic drawstring to permit easy retrieval in wind gusts, is not recorded. Probably they gave it not a thought: Egbert was in an acceptable tradition of Irish eccentricity. And these street performances gave him immense

Brother Egbert (seated in centre) on his Celtic tour in 1932: with Marist Brothers in Dundee, Scotland.

satisfaction. He had come from a land starved of history, to a country glutted with it, and encased in poetic words and song. Egbert was a singer, fully alive only when in song. Not that he sang well. Loudly, yes. But his being needed to escape that large frame and to roar, with joy, pride, sheer exuberance. Whereas others might embrace Ireland grimly, intellectually, as a cause, as a monstrous wrong to be righted, Egbert was firmly in the minstrel boy tradition:

> 'Land of Song!' said the warrior bard
> 'Though all the world betrays thee
> One sword at least, thy rights shall guard
> One faithful harp shall praise thee!'

Egbert was a latter-day warrior bard, excruciatingly out of place in New Zealand, but knowing, from his month in Ireland, that there was such a place as a Land of Song, and seeking as part of his life's mission to praise it, and to adapt it to his own colonial world. For all his veneration of Ireland, Egbert never lost sight of his actual location. His Ireland was a model for colonial emulation, a stimulus, part of a cultural continuum, a point of reference, a marker from which the colonies, or at least what was Catholic in them, could get true bearings.

He did not think (as Albert Dryer did) that Ireland had achieved perfection. Indeed, he was highly critical of what he believed were its short-comings, precisely because these marred the complete achievement of the possible ideal, so near and yet, infuriatingly, so far. Significantly, this criticism sprang from colonial principles and experience: Ireland would be indeed Heaven — if it had decent sewerage and a habit of hard work. So, Egbert's crusading sword was always two-edged; to carve out respect for Ireland, and to get Ireland to improve her act.

This crusade began on his Irish visit. He wanted to help Ireland, in particular to get it cleaned up a bit, and to jog the Irish into such practical action as he thought necessary to an appropriate image. He found particularly irksome the Irish failure to remove all the visible traces of the pre-1921 British imperial regime. He seems to have regarded this as supine dereliction; yet, with bewilderment, as incomprehensible. So, he sought out the Taoiseach, de Valera, at the Irish Parliament House, in regard to one of the most prominent of these vestiges of oppression, which stood outside the House itself. He urged de Valera 'to have removed the statue of Queen Victoria, who signed 49 Co-oercion Acts against Ireland and was very antagonistic to Ireland's demands'. Later he heard that the statue had been sold, an outcome he attributed to his own intervention. In fact, it had been removed for discreet storage by the Irish Board of Works, and was resurrected to grace the precincts of the refurbished Queen Victoria Building in Sydney, where, since 1988, it now reigns in full splendour. The building's restorers found, in the 1980s, that in the rest of Britain's ex-colonial world, the multitude of Queen Victorias in statue form had been subject to various nationalist indignities, and such as had survived complete demolition, lacked heads or arms or whatever, by discourtesy of liberating mobs. Only in Ireland had patriots not bothered much with such desecration, preferring the amusement that could be gained by retaining imperial symbols to be laughed at, and avoiding the labour and expense of removal. This kind of lazy ridicule was beyond Egbert's understanding or tolerance. The land should be purged of all evidence of the oppressor's yoke, even if it meant hard work and offence to Britain. On this theme he continued adamant, instructing the Irish diplomatic representative in Canberra in 1956: 'The Irish must combine more vigour with their native courtesy'. This was a polite way of putting the common colonial, and colonial Irish, belief that the Irish were bone lazy and should put themselves, their houses, and the country in decent order.

It is illuminating to note that it seems not to have occurred to Egbert, and the many well-wishers like him who persisted in issuing directives to the Irish as to how to conduct themselves, that Ireland was not their country and that its management was not their business. His assumption was that it was

The humorous journal *Dublin Opinion* took a light-hearted (and probably ironic) view of Victoria's eventual removal. She is remarking, under imminent threat of displacement, to a passing de Valera 'Begob, Eamon, there's great changes around here!' (*National Library of Ireland*)

also, in a way, *his* country, and that what it did or did not do, somehow reflected on him; it was, thus, taken together with his love, a matter of his legitimate concern. He was part owner of Ireland, from afar. And he, and colonials like him, were right. They were judged, within their own distant communities, by reference to Ireland, what it did, what it was, or could be represented to be.

So, the international Irish could never leave Ireland alone, praising and blaming, interfering, offering advice, expressing opinions, because, whether they liked it or not, they were part of the family. And the Irish, in Ireland, constantly misbehaved, in matters trivial or large, judged on standards important to the Irish and their descendants elsewhere. Those overseas 'Irish' could never grasp that an essential fact about Ireland, indeed one writ large in its history, was that it was untamed, and would remain so, resistant to all coercions, whether it be Britain's through major force, or mild critiques like Egbert's. Even Irishmen themselves could be blind to this wild but predictable fact. As a boy in the 1940s, Joseph Hone knew County Kilkenny as a self-contained, ordered society. Returning forty years later he discovered what was always so:

> There's a strong aura in Ireland — in the landscape and in the people — of much that will always be ungoverned, untutored, where any imposed order has the air of a temporary holding operation, a temporary clearing or civilisation won from a ragged and voracious nature.

Governors and instructors beware. Egbert, and a legion of other friendly tutors, would have rejected with anger the very notion of the 'wild Irishman', as an English-manufactured slur: and, in its extreme derogatory applications it was: but in its milder connotations — of being disposed to take its own uncontrolled, random, way — it was centrally implied as the basis of their criticism. The Irish were not sedately civilised, in the way these improvers thought they should be.

The matter of the retention of imperial symbols was important to Egbert, and many colonials (not only Catholic), because it related to their own sense of colonial identity and independence. Many were quite prepared to see these things in the casual Irish way. Symbols did not matter, realities of power did. But within Ireland itself there were those —many — who thought symbols did matter, and distant Egbert was far from alone in his obsession with names and objects. What he lacked was the Irish delight in occupying contradictory and evasive positions in these sacred areas. So, again to the Irish diplo-

'a temporary clearing or civilisation won from a ragged and voracious nature'. Corcomroe Abbey, in the Burren district of County Clare. (*Bord Failte Photo*)

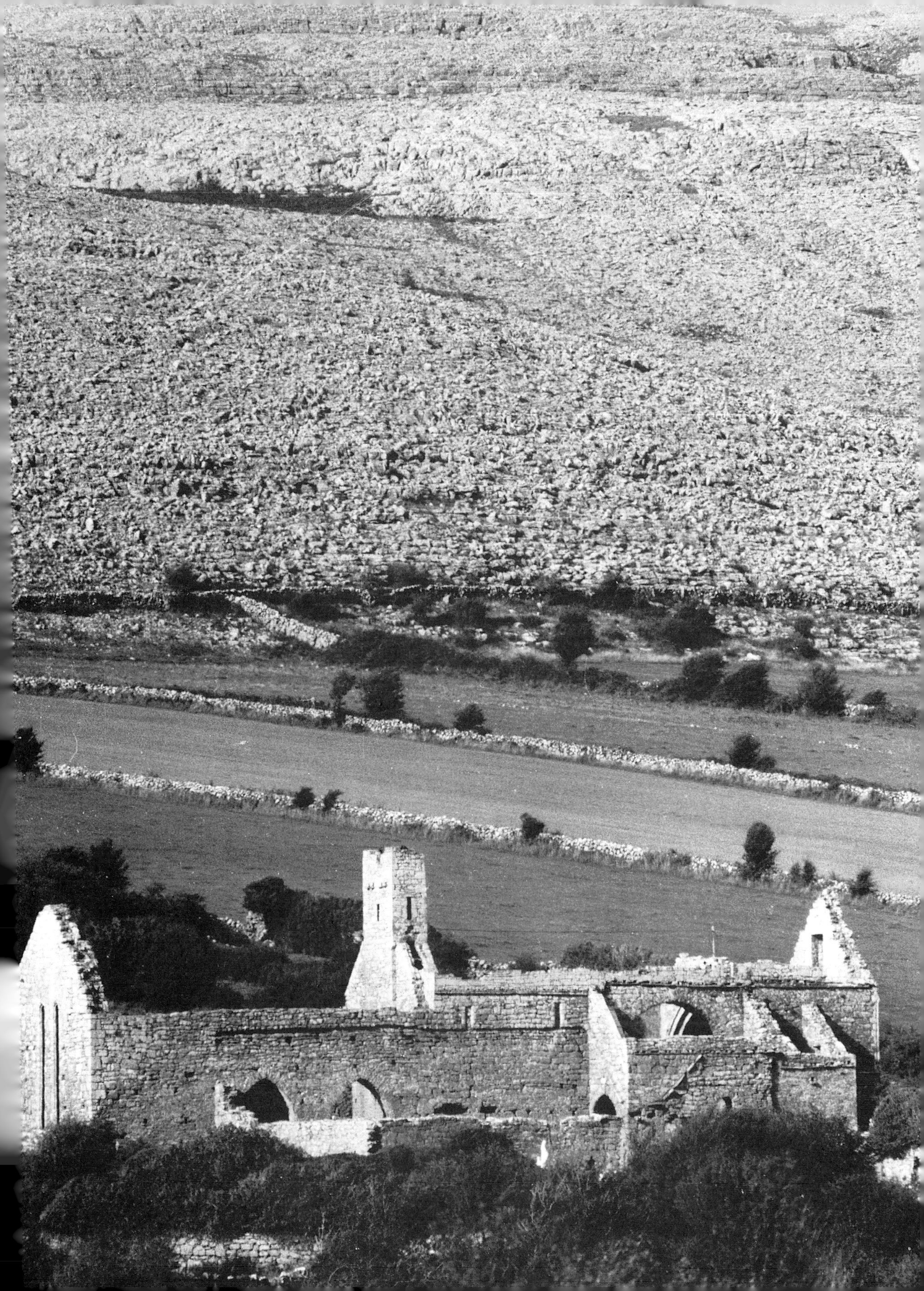

matic representative in Canberra in 1956, he expressed his views on another monument: the imposing Nelson's Pillar, which stood, until it was assassinated by a bomb in 1966, in front of Dublin's General Post Office, centrepiece of Ireland's 1916 Rising, and the place from which Padraig Pearse read the proclamation of a provisional Irish Republican Government. Wrote Egbert, 'I am hoping to hear of Pearse's Pillar'. It was an innocent hope in an Irish world, whose comic vulgarity made no exceptions for the subjects of national monuments.

In his classic portrait of Dublin, V.S. Pritchett supplies an anecdote to illustrate how the Parnell obelisk (the transference was predictable in this case) had been appropriated by the poorer classes as a useful anatomical euphemism in confessional situations 'Me Parnell'. The watery sculpture at the corner of St Stephen's Green was to be dubbed — in play on the famous ballad 'A Nation Once Again' — Urination Once Again. Ireland just would not take its revolution or its heroes seriously enough for colonial taste. Or rather, it took them very seriously indeed in its own way, with its own mixture of idolatry and derision, its own ability to perform an instant switch of focus from the noble profile to the feet of clay. Such inconsistency and contradiction simply did not register coherently with solemn, straightforward colonial Irish, schooled in British heroic forms and show (and bombast), into the belief that there was one proper and respectable way of doing national things. Rude jokery was simply inconceivable in regard to the nation's icons.

Subsequent to his transformatory Irish month, Brother Egbert applied himself industriously to writing pro-Irish articles in whatever press outlets he could find, under the pen-name Pawl Makshaen, which he believed to be the Irish form of his name — Michael Jackson. (Sadly — or was Egbert cheating a little? — the leading authority, MacLysaght, has MacShane, which Egbert's form sought to Gaelicise, equivalent to Johnson. Jackson was an entirely English name, numerous in Ulster since the mid-seventeenth century: whatever was Irish in Egbert was descended from the Cromwellians.) Egbert's writing was heavily laced with quotations, preferably from British sources, expressing criticism of British stupidity and perfidy towards Ireland. By the 1950s he had collected sufficient material to envisage a book to be entitled *Ireland, the Valiant and Virtuous,* a title which caught exactly the key themes of Egbert's admiration for his dream country. It embodied, like himself, a boisterous and holy pugnacity. This would be 'a book that would rejoice the mind and heart of every lover

The idea of Australasia helping Ireland was an old one; New South Wales assists Erin in the *Illustrated Sydney News*, 21 February 1880.

of freedom in the world'. Like every author of this kind of universally liberating text, he had the blurb already written in his heart.

However, there were problems. He had been compelled to cease his journalism. He explained to the Irish Embassy in Canberra in 1956: 'In later years I have had to cease press correspondence for fear of injuring the prospects of my growing family'. This is a curious reference from a celibate religious. Either he meant his own parents' other children, or more likely his religious family, the Marist Brothers — or maybe it was merely another instance of the self-dramatisation in which he constantly engaged. Indulged? No — engaged is the better description; for, Ireland's far-flung embattled heroes did see themselves genuinely as pitted against the forces of incomprehension if not of darkness, and as always, befitting the freedom fighter, victimised by authority for their beliefs.

Egbert probably saw the game of misleading the Irish Embassy (among other persons) as to his true religious status, as a necessary service to the cause. The married lay image was more an asset to the championing of Ireland than the predictable support of a religious. And the adopting of a role, a disguise, was somehow in keeping with the idea of secret service in the great game, suffering for Ireland.

Nevertheless it was like a stagy false beard. Everybody knew. And was meant to know — and to pretend not to know. But all the world was not a stage, and reality kept breaking through. Egbert had to cease his public crusading because it became an embarrassment and a liability in the discharge of his profession, teaching boys, as a Marist Brother.

Egbert's pro-Irish whimseys were tolerable in his Order as an eccentric, extra-curricular activity, but were no asset in the wider community, Catholic or otherwise. Even this was probably endurable to the Brothers, who were a remarkably tolerant lot, until it began to have a direct impact on the classroom teaching situation. By the 1940s Egbert habitually used all or most of his Latin periods to teach Irish history and verse. Or, more accurately, to teach a world view which integrated Irish, English and New Zealand loyalties and identity. My own Latin notebook began (copied out from dictation) with the complete words of 'God Save the King', then followed 'God Save Ireland'; then 'God Defend New Zealand', with the Irishness of its author, Thomas Bracken, much detailed and emphasised in later lessons. Then followed one of Egbert's own many compositions, which focussed this procession of wider loyalties down directly to our own locality and home:

> Oh the hills and dales of Fair Westland
> Are ever dear to me,
> From mountain's gleam by rushing stream
> To Greymouth by the sea.

... and so on, through eight similar stanzas, all performed with callisthenic exercises, in class unison, as a warm-up device in the bitter cold of winter classrooms.

Egbert's tuition produced school boys who could explode into 'All Hail, O'Connell, noble chief, Immortal liberator', with seven subsequent verses of equal passion and meaninglessness: nobody had any idea of who O'Connell was. Nor of what had happened in Ireland in 1798: it was nearly twenty years later before I realised the meaning of a fragment of verse lodged in my head from that time — 'how they braved the rack and the

Brother Egbert as teacher, Wellington 1916.

gibbet in the gloom of '98'. At the time, it was chanted gibberish. In such circumstances, neither did students learn much Latin, to my parents' annoyance. Ignorance of Latin might seem no problem in a coal-mining, saw-milling town, where many parents were unconvinced of its utility, but it was in the school curriculum and was examined, and parents were paying for the education of their children. If anything, a knowledge of Ireland was more pointless, futile and incomprehensible than that of a dead language. So, even in the days of unquestioning acceptance of religion and all its works, even among a parental group substantially Irish, Egbert's Irish enthusiasms, at the expense of other things, constituted a public relations problem. He knew this and tried to keep it within bounds. What he seemed not to know was that his efforts were totally counter-productive, even to his lessons in handball, that economical Gaelic game that needed no bat. The Irish dimension, to which he wished to introduce his students, remained to them an unintelligible joke. Why? Because it was so remote, foreign to

213

all colonial experience and cut across all dominant cultural influences. No other Brother had any interest in Ireland. Neither did any parent, at least publicly. Rugby, and rugby league, ruled, with cricket. England was the point of cultural reference, with Rome. St Patrick's Day was a Catholic, not an Irish occasion.

But a major reason was that the Ireland thing seemed merely another facet of the outlandish and amusing Egbert persona. So it was with other colonial Ireland enthusiasts on the margins of their own local histories. Ireland seemed a crank cause, promoted by odd-balls, and diminished to joke status by the patent ridiculousness of its advocates: Ireland itself seemed the ultimate Irish joke. As a man of religion, Egbert commanded respect and affection. Even to barbarian boys he was obviously good, kind, holy and good-humoured, and a good teacher. But his eccentricities were numerous and obvious, well beyond Ireland. He was round and fat — 'Eggy' — with a sonorous, mimic-inviting voice. And he rode everywhere on a fantastic bicycle, a monstrous balloon-tyred juggernaut, with a massive strengthened frame and a huge seat. It was unique, never elsewhere seen. Eggy had a power and integrity that made him no joke; and he was no fool. But he was an eccentric, whose madnesses were out of kilter with the local varieties, which were more physical and roughly hooligan. So he seemed of no account, and his pupils forgot his incomprehensible Irish ravings within minutes of being removed from their environs.

Egbert soldiered on. The matter of appropriate national anthems in the colonies had long — since 1921; (and even before) — been a vexed and contentious matter in Irish Australasian communities. Given the frequency and popularity of concerts of all kinds, it was a problem constantly encountered and seldom solved to the satisfaction of all concerned, as audiences held different degrees and points of loyalty and different ideas of what to do about it. (At a Sydney State dinner in 1988 in honour of the Taoiseach, Charles Haughey, various Irish sat down and refused to participate in the toast to the Queen, though Mr Haughey had no difficulty with the matter.) This was just the kind of insoluble symbol and loyalty problem Egbert loved to confront, applying his own brand of rigorous, impractical logic to its resolution. He noted that some Irish patriots boldly sang the Irish national anthem. In fact, in the colonies there long remained confusion as to what this actually was. As late as 1956 Egbert believed it to be 'God Save Ireland', although it was in fact, since 1926, 'The Soldier's

Song'. No doubt the 'God' had particular appeal for Egbert, but the reason why colonial Irish assemblages thundered out 'God Save Ireland' was that it had been long and better known and had an excellent tune and lyrics. By comparison, few outside Ireland knew 'The Soldier's Song' or warmed to its dirge-like qualities. The New Zealand Irish had access to a better anthem and a more acceptable tradition of usage to enable them to avoid singing 'God Save the King'. They sang 'God Defend New Zealand', happy in its Irish authorship.

Egbert held that all these should be sung, on all occasions, in the following order: first, 'God Save the King', to appease the enemies and critics of the Irish, Orangemen and the like; then, 'God Defend New Zealand' to affirm that Irish New Zealanders were loyal to the land of their birth or adoption; then 'God Save Ireland'. Quite apart from the predictable resisters to putting Ireland last, the ludicrous and impractical aspects of bellowing through this succession of choral tributes to all and sundry did not occur to Egbert, who loved singing and could not understand those who did not. Anyhow, he reasoned, by embarking on this anthem marathon, 'we are taking from our opponents the rod with which they wish to strike us'.

It could equally well be argued that this contorted device, and the placing of 'God Save the King' first, was a capitulation to the pressure of Ireland's colonial enemies. That Egbert did not see it so speaks not only for his conciliatory nature — he was always a benign and magnanimous warrior bard — but also of his real priorities, of his vision of the natural and proper order of things. He lived in a predominantly British colony, still linked in allegiance to the Crown. Yet, it was separate, independent, unique and itself, in so many vitally important ways that demanded loyalty and acknowledgement. And it contained his people, the Irish, as a minority, with their own distinct and different culture, history and traditions, which ought also to be recognised, affirmed and praised. Put thus, the logic of Egbert's hierarchy of loyalties seems impeccable, however cumbrous and long-winded the process of spelling them out in song might be. The hand-out sheet for audience participation at the St Patrick's concert in Wagga in 1929 began with 'Advance Australia Fair', followed by 'God Save Ireland', then 'Faith of our Fathers', then 'We Stand for God'. As to Egbert, the wonder is that, given his literary turn of mind, he did not pen some grand, single conflation, in which all these allegiances were happily reconciled.

Instead, he turned his frustration towards bringing into line the odd man out — Ireland. Britain and the colonies were easily reconciled as a loyalty package, and the great virtue and appeal to the colonial Irish of Home Rule from the 1880s, had been the way it had fitted Ireland into a happy trio. The events of 1916 and the years that followed had killed that as a possible solution, and from 1921 most Irish colonials had solved the problem by forgetting it. They simply allowed the matter of loyalty to Ireland as a nation, or state, to drop from their concerns or even interest. It was, after all, a member of the Commonwealth, if a restless and reluctant one. For a few (to say, like Egbert, would be to unduly complicate the picture) the problem remained that of sustaining a threefold loyalty, not allegiance, but loyalty — in the sense of love, affection, respect, admiration, ease of being associated with. Ireland was increasingly hard to live with for reasons even its best colonial friends were loath to utter. Not so Egbert, friend and warrior to the last. Bluntly, Ireland smelt.

He opened this delicate matter with the Irish representative in Canberra in 1956. From America, Australia and New Zealand he had heard a chorus of Irish — he meant of Irish lineage — people 'saying that Ireland's leadership of the world, in Faith, Morals and Freedom' — a staggering claim made constantly as a virtual aside by the true Ireland devotee, indeed the ethical basis of the cult — 'would be greatly heightened if Ireland also led in sanitation and sobriety'. That Egbert should concede without contest the drunkenness stereotype, hotly denied by some champions of Ireland on a sound factual comparative basis (the colonies themselves drank more heavily and with far less humour and grace), points to the extent to which he accepted the colonial image of the Irish. That the Irish were dreadful boozers was a Protestant dictum whose veracity was on a par with the Bible, the truth of a biased gospel Egbert took in from his environment and never bothered to question or deny. Again, the colonial Irish impulse is revealed. What is at issue is not the facts about the Irish, but what those hostile to them chose to assert or believe were the facts. Thus it was not so much the distant Irish as the reputation generated locally about them, the opinions and beliefs held in their regard by other colonials, that agitated their colonial champions like Egbert.

His views on Irish sanitation were much stronger, almost obsessional, and reeked of offended, perhaps over-sensitive, personal experience. Here his revulsion was not only at the actual situation, but at the inaction and laziness that allowed it to continue. Ireland, if she wished, could do a lot to clean herself up, in ways the colonial deemed basic by the 1950s (or 1930s), so as to render herself more socially acceptable to the overseas Irish. So it seemed to Egbert, who had no mind to consider the former dereliction of the colonies in such matters, until climate, plague and rapid urbanisation forced action and the concession that it was worth the expense. Nor did he consider the cost to a poor economy. No, it was simply intolerable that visitors should be repelled by the smell of the Isle of Saints. It seems not to have occurred to Egbert that filth was an aspect of anchorite holiness, or at least a concomitant of it, and that Job endured the dung-heap among his tribulations. Again, his colonial environment and conditioning were showing. Cleanliness was next to *Protestant* Godliness; that particular virtue was not always the top of the Catholic hierarchy of moral goods.

Practical as ever, Egbert had two solutions. First, a vigorous campaign to have every Irish home supplied (by whom and at whose cost, he did not say) with an indoor or outdoor, chemical or water, toilet. Second, that all cattle be debarred from the streets of towns, 'or at least that they should not be allowed to halt on their journey' — or allowed their natural functions while journeying? He might just as well have added, a national issue of soap, or an edict on more frequent washing to attack the fetid atmosphere of Dublin's winter buses. Such would have been hardly more practical than what he did propose. Even if toilets were provided, as they slowly were, those available to the public, and tourists, remained infrequent and noisome. Mere provision would not induce clean maintenance. Cattle fairs were traditional to the streets, and economies, of many towns. To alter these ancient customs was a large task, although accomplished by the government by the 1970s, more for the welfare of livestock and because of relation to better provision of stockyards, than for the reasons Egbert had in mind.

What was most remarkable in the colonial view of Ireland was the ignorance and unreality of such enthusiasts as Egbert: the incomprehension of Ireland's overseas friends was different in kind but hardly in degree from that of her enemies. Egbert's impatient application to Ireland of colonial standards and practicalities paid no regard to a very different history, values, economic resources and way of life. The stench of a rural Irish town from cattle dung, and other sources, was part of what traditional Ireland was. Surely God's pure rain would wash it all away? With sewerage provision as Egbert urged, came secularisation which he did not; perhaps not inevitably, but

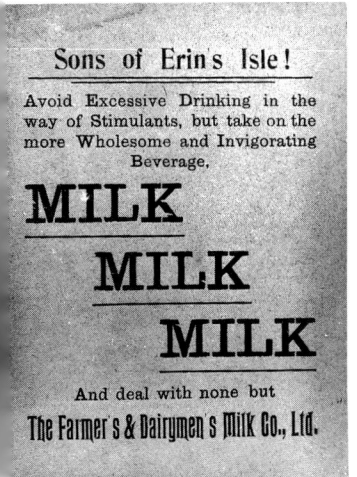

A concession to the stereotype in the Sydney St Patrick's Day Sports Programme for 1899: a milk company offers its alternative by implying the prevalence of drunkenness.

Fair Day at Ballineen, County Cork, with cattle in evidence. (*National Library of Ireland*)

part of the package nevertheless. And while Egbert's head was full of the doings (or reputed doings) of Irish heroes of great nobility and purity of heart, he had little real knowledge of Irish history at a level below myth and nationalist propaganda. Nor did he credit its inhabitants with any common sense or perception of their own problems. So, on the drink matter, Egbert was aware, no doubt through encountering members who wore the distinctive Sacred Heart lapel pin, of the existence of the Irish Pioneer Total Abstinence movement formed in Ireland in 1901. His question to the Australian Irish Embassy was, could there not be moderate temperance teaching and organisations for those not called to total abstinence? It was a question in total ignorance of the history of the Irish temperance movement, and of debate (and organisations) related to this very matter since the 1830s. Egbert, and well-intentioned colonial critics like him, were continually obsessed by what often amounted to inventing the wheel again for the Irish, and with becoming annoyed with the stupid Irish for not thinking of it themselves, which they had long ago, but unbeknownst to their would-be improvers.

Brother Egbert's forthright letter of instructions for Ireland's improvement, addressed to the Irish Embassy in Canberra in

1956, remained in my father's papers, stamped envelope and all. It probably came to my father with a covering letter leaving its forward posting to Paddy's discretion, which he exercised wisely to prevent Egbert seeming a crank and a fool. For all the appearances, he was at heart neither, but rather an ignorant, well-meaning enthusiast, totally won over to Ireland by a month's acquaintance, a tourist's skim.

Yet, his brief encounter was true love at first sight, uninformed and superficial only in essentials. Egbert fell in love with the essence of Ireland, its bewitching spell as dream country. It was his kind of place, holy, human, heroic, eccentric, fey and a bit mad. Nor was he beyond responding to the special place, flattery and respect it reserved for clerics and religious. Here the man of God got his due, not the suspicion and cold-shoulder of the publicly Protestant colonies. But like so many lovers, he desired to reform the beloved. And like so many energetic colonials he wanted to improve what existed,

Unobjectionable street activity? Clothes sellers at the May Fair in 1900, in Tempo, County Fermanagh. (*Ulster Museum*)

attend to the dodgy plumbing, put a bit of zip and order in the mess, and treat the wonderful Irish like the dear incompetent children they really were. They must be children, given their goodness and impracticality. How a little bit of intelligence, hard work and colonial know-how would transform their tumbledown, grubby, little country! Egbert could hardly restrain his impatience to get together with the Irish and clean things up. Make Ireland like the colonies, with their flush toilets, bathrooms, and no wading through cow-dung in the streets, and an atmosphere of hard work and things getting done, and a good breeze blowing through the whole scene: Egbert was a fanatic for fresh air. So, this quaint, rotund religious represents in his way the achievement of full circle; Ireland was being weighed in the colonial balance and found wanting, not up to scratch. For all Ireland's virtues and charm, it was not like home — and home was New Zealand.

Paddy, my father, knew Ireland better, despite the forty years he had been away from it. Despite or because. He knew its inertia, its ancient arrogance and contempt for upstart outsiders, its tolerance of dirt and disrepair if it be its own, its time-scale, which put a yarn and a laugh before being up and doing, its suspicion of Protestant rush and impatience. Egbert's schema for an Irish social revolution was best left reposing in Paddy's files, there to do no harm.

However, Egbert had also bequeathed to Paddy, amongst unfinished notes, some much more explosive material; rough drafts of astonishingly candid criticism of the Irish church. His basic inclination was theocratic, or at least in favour of a major clerical influence in social life, as a general theoretical principle — and he saw Ireland as the nearest approach to this desirable objective. Yet, his colonial liberalism and tolerance enraged him against the actualities of the Irish clerical scene:

> The only weakness in the scheme of clerical influence is that the mass of the clergy are not particularly cultivated or sophisticated. The C[atholic] C[hurch] & the C[lergy] of Ireland are both puritanical & narrow minded.
>
> To say this will naturally anger most Irish readers. It is none the less a regrettable fact. Its effects may be seen daily in such things as the inhuman treatment of unmarried mothers, in a stupid censorship, in the fanatical way in which such innocent amusements as dancing or the modest games of chance are controlled through the district courts where the Parish priest turns up to oppose, never once to support every other application for a licence. The indirect power of the church in the education system (there are only one or two schools not controlled by the clergy . . .

There the fragment ends, obviously moving towards completion of that litany of anathemas — social injustice, censorship, puritanism, indoctrination — which was the stock in trade of the usual enemies of Catholic Ireland. That such should also be the real opinions of this passionate friend of Ireland points to the fundamental impulse behind Egbert's surface eccentricity: Ireland was opportunity lost, the one best chance for a glorious amalgam of holiness and social harmony and freedom and Christian joy — squandered, thwarted, spoilt, shrivelled. Egbert was, in worldly terms, a dreamer, no realist: yet, in Christian terms he was a man of hope, in deep anger that the church to which he had dedicated his own life, should be, in its human shortcomings, itself an obstacle to the very principles of a perfect society to which it was dedicated.

Egbert was to continue his Irish crusade until his death, but he was increasingly conscious — for he was basically a very sensitive man — that other people found this tiresome, indeed evidence of paranoia. It was a painful irony that, while the unshakeable belief of the general community was that all Catholics were Irish and pro-Irish, in the same way that they were allegedly the property of the Pope, Egbert was convinced — and he had ample evidence — that the Catholic community was militantly anti-Irish. He took his conclusion too far, to the extent of seeing plots and malevolent purpose; but he was correct in discerning that most colonial Catholics wanted to forget Ireland. When pro-Irish elements would not let them, their reaction was to defend their position of simple neglect (leaving Ireland out of everything from sermons on the pioneers to school concert programmes) by mounting what seemed to be an attack.

In 1959, confiding in Paddy, Egbert singled out the *New Zealand Tablet* columnist J.C. Reid (who later became professor of English at the University of Auckland) as the only Catholic writer on Ireland — and that by insult. Egbert believed that this was deliberate policy, encouraged by the paper's Board of Directors, aimed at satisfying subscribers. Reid had expressed irritation at the Irish boast that they were the greatest Catholic nation on earth, a claim Egbert maintained nobody Irish had ever made. Perhaps his denial was a nice point of casuistry: *he* had made such a claim, but he was not Irish. More likely he had simply forgotten. In any case he was wrong. Such claims were the delight of sermonising Irish bishops, of whom Cardinal Moran's were the most extravagant and easily documented. Again, Egbert's basic and profound ignorance of Irish affairs stands revealed. Indeed, as is so often the case with such immoderate and generalised enthusiasms, his whole position relied on ignorance, on a very limited and selective acquaintance with present facts, and a narrow, heroic travesty of history. More — and again the syndrome is typical — it assumed convoluted ill-will, arrant self-interest, and nefarious plots behind those with a contrary view. It never looked for some simple explanation. Egbert could not understand Reid's irritation. It seems a natural colonial reaction to a mother-

Stereotype and Myth become Reality in Donegal, to be approached hand-in-hand. (*Bord Failte Photo*)

country's continued claims to power and superiority: Reid's impulses were not all that different in origin from Egbert's sanitary conclusions. But Egbert lumped it all in with the general anti-Irish disposition of Catholics, which had its roots in their fear of being discriminated against in employment, and claimed that it was this consideration which had the effect of keeping Irish priests quiet.

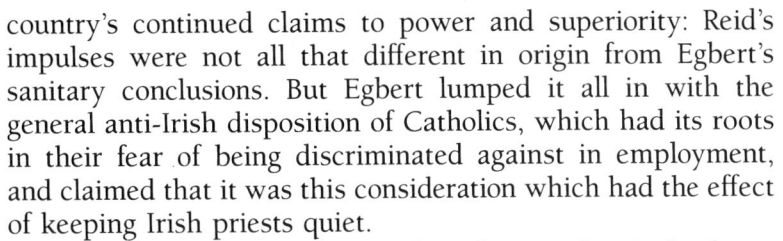

The silence of Irish priests in the colonies when Ireland was under attack puzzled Egbert. His search for an explanation again neglected the obvious — that such priests saw the issue as divisive of their flocks, and of no possible advantage, pastoral or personal. Nor did he understand that public silence did not necessarily denote private lack of feeling. Amongst themselves Irish priests fumed, and excoriated Ireland's critics, in a fashion Egbert would have found completely edifying, but they were not about to tell him that: he was a colonial outsider — again a position of exclusion which, given the purity of his loyalty as he saw it, would have been incomprehensible to him. Had he known of it. But if he had known of it, or even thought of it as a possibility, such subtlety might have merited inclusion in the charmed circle — or a more perceptive and cynical appraisal of what that Irish circle was about.

But none of that was Egbert. Incomprehension ruled. He could not understand Reid's impatience with the constant self-rectitude of the Irish, and their permanent posture as Britain's wronged. They *were* right. They *had* been wronged. That Reid, and many others, might accept these postulates, yet believe it was time the Irish stopped their martyr act and got on with the future, was beyond Egbert's imagination. Nor did he see that his focus was wrong. It was as always on Ireland, whereas Reid's was essentially colonial. Reid had tired of Ireland as a local Catholic albatross: he wanted it off his neck. Indeed, he demanded it off. What Egbert could never understand, in his vision of a harmonious Irish-colonial cultural amalgam, was that many, most, colonials could see no need to include anything Irish in it. He was dragging them back towards a past they had shed, had forgotten, never knew. Reid insisted on moving forward, away from origins, away from being shadows of Ireland or any other place, away from being a sub-category of some irrelevant Irish stereotype, towards being new — new colonials, New Zealanders, a distinct and distinctive people. With all that, part of Egbert would have heartily agreed. It was the part that did not, which constituted a problem wider than himself.

In New Zealand Egbert was a strange, isolated figure, irrelevant and virtually unique by the 1940s, even by the 1930s when he first took up Ireland's cause. However, it was the neutrality of Ireland in the 1939–45 world war which killed residual sympathy for Ireland. Few, if any, at that colonial distance, appreciated the anti-German, if not pro-British, character of that neutrality or could comprehend the good reasons which led de Valera as Taoiseach to take the position he did. Still, that was not entirely true. Some would have preferred Ireland to have taken a pro-German stance. Some had not forgotten 1916. When Paddy Bastic of Maroubra enlisted in the 2nd AIF in 1941, his Irish father said that he never thought he would see him in the King's uniform — a phrase which had little Australian meaning in the young colonial mood of that time or of that earlier Great War. His father instructed: 'Never kill any Germans — they are a great people': they had helped Roger Casement, traduced martyr of Ireland's 1916 Rising. Paddy agreed: he would kill only Japs. And Peter Bogan of East Maitland, fifth generation Australian, recalls his Australian father's action during the same wartime period. With some official form, which required a statement of nationality, he was confronted by a choice — British (born in Australia or British Isles), or alien. He crossed both out and wrote 'Irish'. Australian is what he was, but he would not concede that this amounted to 'British'. A trivial thing, but symbolic and expressive of a strain of rebellion and resentment that still lingered in the blood of a man whose ancestors left Ireland in 1841.

The threat to Australia and New Zealand from Japan in 1941 made the Irish issue a totally dead letter in those colonies; but, even before Japan entered the war, Paddy O'Farrell, as a prominent local, and justice of the peace, was a distribution point for British war propaganda literature. When Japanese invasion became a (remote) possibility, he became an air raid warden and an officer of the St John's Ambulance Brigade. Egbert was as serious as other teachers in enforcing the perplexing complexities of air-raid drill dispersion exercises for school pupils. Home was under threat: New Zealand was at stake.

But such local focus had been the case for twenty years. The Irish Civil War had almost totally destroyed the Irish cause in both Australia and New Zealand, to the degree where lack of interest was the best reaction to be hoped for by the handful of republican enthusiasts. They often encountered a venomous fury, particularly from Irish churchmen. According to Gerard Griffin, New Zealand's foremost Irish republican in 1923, that country's Irish born element was mainly composed of shoneens — that is, in his view, deserters to the British — and of 'men *from* Ireland' — that is, those who had left Ireland in all ways. They wanted to forget about it; it was a bad memory they wanted to erase from their minds. Griffin found the New Zealand Labour Party ignorant of what he regarded as the murder policy of the Irish Free State government, and determined to remain so. So, in Australia, was the Australian Labor Party. The editor of the *New Zealand Tablet,* Father James Kelly (nephew of Archbishop Kelly of Sydney), made it clear that he believed the Irish bishops knew what was best for Ireland — that was the prevailing colonial view — and that he would not listen to the lay theologians he associated with the republican position.

So, in New Zealand, from 1923, Irish republicanism was going nowhere. Nor was it in the bigger Australian scene, where such remnants of the movement for an Irish republic as had survived the attrition — rather annihilation — of the Civil War period soldiered through the 1920s and 1930s in a spirit which mixed futility with farce. They had run full tilt into the absolute local power of the Catholic priesthood and encountered an Australian Ireland totally dominated by the priest. Even before the Civil War debacle, such priests — with some spectacular exceptions — were not notably enamoured of Irish politics or current affairs.

On his release from detention in 1919, held as a member of the Irish Republican Brotherhood, that super-enthusiast for Ireland, Albert Dryer, thought to combine ideals and earning a living by opening an Irish bookshop in Sydney. His customers were mainly priests, but not sufficient a clientele to sustain a viable business. It lasted barely a year, and that at the height of the interest generated by the Anglo-Irish war of 1919–20. By 1923, the end of the Irish Civil war, interest in Irish republicanism had dropped to zero among priests, save for Daniel Mannix; and his singular and deviant republicanism counted for nothing on the ground, even in Victoria. The scene for republicanism in Victoria was set by the antics of R. O'Dea, deputed by the Irish Republican Association to make collections in country towns to aid such Irish republicans as were still holding out for the cause in Ireland, and gather protests against their treatment. His reception was typified by that accorded him in April by Archpriest McKenna of West Geelong who assured him most warmly that he would be the first to subscribe — towards ropes for the republicans' necks. Elsewhere he was accused of collecting money for murder and of stirring up strife among Catholics. Everywhere priests refused to see him and instructed their parishioners to do likewise: they did not need such direction; invariably they feared Irish contacts would prejudice their employment. O'Dea changed tactics. He embarked on a Victorian rail tour, stopping long enough in each place to lodge a protest telegram to headquarters on behalf of all the local Irish he never met. Like Lenin, he knew the moral obligations of the vanguard when the masses refused to act.

In Melbourne the republican movement centred on the Irish Republican Association from 1923, and from 1926 to 1946, the Tone–Pearse Republican Cumann, with W.F. Corrigan and Gerard Fitzgerald as key figures. Both were Australian born. Corrigan was the archetypal political romantic. His poetry, some published under a pseudonym in 1909, was about Man, roses, love, death, but also the bush. His romantic imagination was entirely captured by the 1916 Rising in Dublin — 'the greatest epic since the days of Leonidas in the Pass of Thermopylae'. His unpublished fiction 'Strands of Life' features a Pearse figure, the stranger Lindsay, superhuman rescuer in a shipwreck, who heroically perishes with the last of his rescued. Corrigan's cast of mind craved the visionary and heroic, the grand and the grandiose, which he believed Ireland exemplified. Yet, it was a cast of mind also fervently Australian: in 1973 he submitted three entries in the Australian National Anthem quest.

Gerard Fitzgerald was another generous idealist. He had volunteered to join the IRA in Ireland in 1920, but had been told, locally, to stay to help the Melbourne cause. He lived in the then closed world of deafness, never hearing the songs which caused his organisation so much trouble. Ill-health eventually forced his resignation.

From 1923, these two men — with Gerard Griffin in New Zealand — found that the Irish republican cause in the colonies shared the apathy and demoralisation that had overtaken the movement in Ireland. The Melbourne *Irish News* (Being the Truth from Official and reliable sources) ceased publication in April 1924. They found that the Irish-born were not interested, wishing merely to forget Ireland. The Melbourne Gaelic League, one of the related Irish groups, with substantially common memberships, had an entirely Australian-born membership in the mid-1930s of twenty. The Tone–Pearse Republican Cumann averaged twenty-three members throughout the 1920s, rising to a maximum of fifty-four in the early 1930s. When it was dissolved in 1946, five were present.

The almost entirely Australian-born character of this tiny group, of which very few had been to Ireland, gave its extreme Irish republican complexion an unreal and fanatically imitative and purist character, often to the degree of absurdity. They subscribed to the Irish republican journal *An Phoblacht* to which they contributed an occasional Australian letter, summarising their doings. These consisted of an annual pilgrimage (unlike Sydney's 1798 memorial, Melbourne had no graves of republican martyrs) to the grave of the *father* of Terence MacSwiney, the lord mayor of Cork whose hunger strike to the death in Brixton Prison in 1920 had so captured the imagination and sympathy of the Irish world. In 1923 the Gaelic League had erected a monument over this grave in the Melbourne General Cemetery. It was somehow pathetically fitting that this honour should centre on a grave of a previous generation to the republican one, an ordinary immigrant, and that the inscription be in mistaken Gaelic, not quite correct. After this pilgrimage, honouring the giants of the republican tradition, Tone, Emmet, the Manchester Martyrs, MacSwiney, with fewer and older devotees as the years ran on, there was 'Irish-Ireland' entertainment, as there was on other Cumann occasions throughout the year.

It was this entertainment, the core — indeed virtually the entirety of the organisation's activity — which created a host of problems and disputes, which themselves became the major business items at meetings and absorbed most energy and interest.

Corrigan and Fitzgerald were obsessed by what they saw as a vital need to maintain the purity of the Irish heritage as purveyed by the Cumann. Its very distance from Ireland increased the need for its Irish culture to be protected from contamination, so multitudinous were the dangers of corruption by commercialism or carelessness or sheer ignorance. Their Australian birth increased the misgivings and nervousness of the organisers on such points, issuing in an increasingly rigorous purism and censorship. Were their concert songs genuine, Irish enough? What were the correct steps, postures and hand placements in various Irish dances? What was an acceptable standard of dancing? Predictably, experts were at hand to offer any number of conflicting views, and to demand this or that be done, and to denigrate how it was done elsewhere, or here, or in Sydney, Melbourne, or Brisbane.

The outcome was a growing list of specified prohibited songs, reaching nearly twenty by the mid-1930s and growing. These included those with sexual innuendos, however mild

The grave of the father of Terence MacSwiney, in the Melbourne General Cemetery.

('Barney Brallaghan's Courtship', 'Katey's Letter') alcoholic reference ('I'm not myself at all') or anything unflattering of the Irish, or undignified ('The Bould Sojer Boy', 'St Patrick was a Gentleman'). But the ban also included classics of the drawing room genre. The prohibition of 'Oft in the Still Night' led on to rejection of all songs of Thomas Moore. Then went all the popular American Irish songs, 'The Kerry Dance', 'When Irish eyes are smiling', 'Kathleen Mavourneen', 'Killarney', and 'In the Garden where the Praties Grow'. A situation was rapidly being reached where there were no familiar 'Irish' songs not under interdict. Performers (who were paid a fee) came under disciplinary scrutiny as well as their repertoires. Objection was made in 1933 to a performer who had served in the AIF, a complaint which tested the patience of one member, who regarded it as farcical. Much else was occurring that courted that description. A demand was made for songs in Gaelic. Nobody knew any, and fewer could have understood them if they had. Performers were instructed to avoid dramatic gestures, or anything 'stagy' in elocution, or any songs of the 'shoneen' type — a broad gather-bag that. Even the Australian Irish corpus was suspect. Recitation of John O'Brien's 'Little Irish Mother' was rejected as an item in 1935. Strait-jacketed by these regulations, but needing the fees, performers tried to make the best of it. 'All Irishmen are sportsmen', pleaded Chas. J. O'Mara in 1934, 'and if they put me on and don't like my performance I won't take payment'. It was perhaps excusable in a republican group, but in 1946 members still did not know the official Irish national anthem, 'The Soldier's Song'. Though they had had it printed in Melbourne for their own use, nobody had learnt it. They still sang 'God Save Ireland'.

The situation of Irish dancing was no better, racked by problems of purity, even in the sense of the matter of modesty; some members regarded any dancing whatever as an insult to Irish maidenhood. But it was purity in the sense of cultural accuracy and integrity which was the major area of contention. Some disputed the traditionality of the female green cloak with hood. Others protested against the male brown pants and black cutaway cloak, as a relic of the stage Irishman. A major row erupted in 1936 over Pat Wynne's right to be called Grand Champion dancer of Australia. It was alleged by both Sydney and Melbourne dancers that he was a mere showman, not a master of the pure Irish dance. Acrimonious disputes developed in relation to correct technicalities in, for example, dancing the Blackbird. And for the local-born to consult the Irish-born was fraught with hazard. A Tipperary authority simply laid down that 'they can't dance in Kerry'. Priests asked to help with Gaelic language matters shied off.

The public face of Irish republicanism was no less censorious than its internal purges. In 1929 it objected direct to Archbishop Mannix (a suspect reactionary in their spectrum) about the presence of Boy Scouts in the St Patrick's Day procession. In the 1934 procession it objected to the St Patrick's Society Banner, which included a Union Jack, in the corner of the Australian flag. Its major public triumph of the 1930s was to kill the street trading, at the St Patrick's Day procession, of 'caubeen-ed', ghastly-looking models of an Irishman. How 'killed'? Probably by intimidation of the vendors. The Ballarat

Ignorance and the ape-image get free reign in Melbourne *Punch* in 1872: two cartoons which illustrate contemporary prejudice (below and overleaf).

MELBOURNE PUNCH. *July 18, 1872.*

THE IRISH EMIGRANT.

BRIDGET.—"*Shure, ma'am, I knows jography 'too, we waas taught it coming out*"
MISTRESS.—"*Indeed; then do you know how many hemispheres there are?*"
BRIDGET (*just landed*).—"*Shure, an' there's two, ma'am, Oirland and Australy!*"

St Patrick's Day celebrations of 1935 violated all the canons of purity espoused by the Cumann. The procession included the Base Hospital Display, the Benevolent Home Float, the Fire Brigade, and the Soldiers and Sailors Memorial Band. It was in fact a typical expression of Irish Australian assimilation, into these organisations, and they into the Irish community. The procession was followed by a race meeting at which the Catholic bishop presented a cup. What could be more mainline Irish Australian? And a good time was had by all. The rage and indignation of the Cumann at the gross decadence into which Irish culture had lapsed in Australia was effectively censored out by the *Irish Review*, A.A. Calwell's Melbourne Irish monthly. It published protest letters with all the criticism of the local scene edited out. And what could they do in a situation in which a public figure as eminent and as identified with 'Irishness' as the previous prime minister, J.H. Scullin, declared in the *Age* in November 1934, that 97 per cent of Australians were of British stock and proud of it?

Even while the Cumann was selling the republican *An Phoblacht* in the Melbourne streets (600 on St Patrick's Day 1926) and maintaining direct contact with the IRA in Dublin by buying sweep tickets, and commemorating the martyrdom of republicans by the Free State government, an increasing number of the tiny membership simply wanted their songs and dances (and unending, enjoyable arguments) and to support whatever party was the government in Ireland. It was all too far away and long ago, all too complicated and far too serious. And the Cumann's local politics were getting increasingly worrying and grotesque. It sent a delegate to the communist-inspired conference on War and Fascism in 1934 and opened up relations with the Melbourne Kuomintang in 1927. Private correspondence from Ireland about this time, reported to Corrigan that Ireland was obsessed with politics and *An Phoblacht* was full of that fixation. These politics were mostly incomprehensible at 12 000 miles distance and out of date anyhow by the time they reached Australia, which was the problem that had frustrated Irish activism in Australia since the foundation of the colony. For dedicated enthusiasts, all that was possible was cultural identification and replication, to a degree in keeping with the extent and kind of their Irish commitment, and to the extent of their ability to find out what was the pure, undefiled and genuine Irish cultural article.

For several years the group's minutes were inscribed 'Minuets', a word which, shorn of its stately connotations, neatly summarises the futile but energetic to-ing and fro-ing therein described. It does not do justice to the constant disputation and highly personal invective which these records glossed over. Nor does it reflect a movement which was not made, one which might have made a little difference — liaison with the Sydney Irish National Association where Albert Dryer, with similar views, laboured in similar isolation. State self-containment and rivalry ruled.

But on one issue and one occasion, the Tone–Pearse Cumann took a leading public role in Irish Catholic Melbourne, with resounding success. It was in full keeping with the character of the organisation — negative, the imposing of a ban — and demonstrated clearly the area where the purism of the Cumann coincided with the popular impulse in Irish Australia, which was towards vigorous defence of public reputation, the refusal to be treated as a farce — defence of Catholicism.

In November 1927, Hoyt's picture theatres in suburban Melbourne began screening *The Callahans and the Murphys*, based on a novel by Kathleen Norris: the film had generated protest in the United States as holding up the Catholic religion and the Irish race to scorn and ridicule. Australian Irish protests were made on an official level prior to screening, leading to the censor making cuts. These were insufficient to please the protestors, who took particular exception to a scene showing women drinking, and one showing a woman in bed with a flea-ridden dog, but generally to its being a 'low comedy and of a rather coarse type', as the minister for Trade and Customs described it under questioning in the federal House. The censor released the film as a legitimate farce, saying he believed people had enough sense of humour to regard it so, and accept it as inoffensive.

Not Irish Catholics. In Sydney the *Freeman's Journal* put it politely — the film was a clumsy and vulgar caricature of the Irish people, and should not have been shown in Australia after the storm it had provoked in New York. In Melbourne, in that suburban citadel of Irish Catholicism, Brunswick, they acted. A meeting of Catholic and Irish people was called to assemble in the grounds of St Ambrose's Church, directly opposite Hoyt's Empire, prior to the time of scheduled screening. An enormous crowd gathered, moving across to block all theatre entrances, excluding would-be patrons. Police arrived and, confronted with the size of the assemblage, summoned reinforcements. Three car-loads of extra police arrived and immediately set on the crowd with a baton charge. The crowd responded, and a major riot was narrowly averted by the intervention of three of the local priests: the Catholic press gave them the credit for averting wholesale bloodshed. Meanwhile, a large contingent of protesters had penetrated the theatre, grimly awaiting the screen appearance of Mrs Callahan and Mrs Murphy. They promised a repeat performance at any subsequent showing and complete disruption of any present one. The manager cancelled the showing. The next day a high-powered delegation, including Gerard Fitzgerald and A.A. Calwell, waited on the chief secretary. Later in the day MGM withdrew the film from further Australian screening.

It was a signal victory, but what it signalled was the power of Catholicism, rather than Irishism, in Victoria. It led on to the formation of the Associated Catholic and Irish Organisations of Victoria, a body which grew out of the protest committee. This consisted of the Catholic Federation, the

Milder stereotyping — but the stage Irishman is given a place in the front row. (*National Library of Ireland*)

Gaelic League, the Gaelic Athletic Association, the St Patrick's Society, the Irish National Association, the Irish National Foresters, the Tone–Pearse Cumann, the Catholic Women's Social Guild, Fianna Fail, the Celtic Club, the Hibernians and representatives from the *Tribune*: on a count of Irish-named organisations in Melbourne (there were nine), the pursuit of things Irish was in very healthy condition. But all of these were either tiny, Irish in name only, or moribund, and none could abide any of the others, even those who shared similar aims, such as the Cumann, the Irish National Assocation, and Fianna Fail. The Associated Organisations drifted on for a few years, stopping another denigratory film *Smiling Irish Eyes* in 1930, after being alerted from America. The reality was fragmentation, tiny membership in other than the benefit organisations — the Hibernians, and the Foresters, and the social Celtic Club — and apathy and acrimony. For anything Irish to happen in Melbourne, or anywhere else in Australia, it had to be Catholic, and it had to have the support and involvement of priests.

The question remains, why did these particular Australians and New Zealanders, of Irish descent, persevere in a cause almost totally deserted in their home countries, and with the allegiance of a dwindling minority in Ireland itself? The psychology of their reactions as eccentrics or true believers will remain obscure while their personal backgrounds are largely uncharted. Yet, some characteristics seem common: intelligence, idealism, the search for a sacrificial cause, contempt for the pragmatic and the temporising, high — impossibly high — principles, obsessive temperaments, and a background or parentage which swung all these dynamics into an Irish focus, not softened nor contradicted by too much reality. Most of these enthusiasts had never visited Ireland, and those who had, only briefly, long enough to encounter what they hoped for but not long enough to experience any of the negativities that abounded in that land of contrarieties. Take Father Forrest, MSC, the foremost Australian pamphleteer on the Anglo-Irish War, *Atrocities in Ireland, Ireland's Darkest and Brightest Year* (1920).

Michael Davitt Forrest, born in 1883 at Korong Vale near Ballarat, carried the pride, and burden, of his Irish ancestry in his given names. To be named after a living Irish patriot, greater in stature than Parnell, at the height of the Irish Land War, betokens a parentage ultra-conscious of commonality with what was happening in Ireland. Nearly forty years later as a priest, he was able to visit Ireland, at the height of 'the Troubles', to make that identification personal rather than nominal, by support for the cause of the Irish Republican Army. Returning to Australia in 1921, Forrest's championing of Irish republicanism put him at odds with his archbishop, Michael Kelly, and his religious order. He loved both controversy and Ireland, and fretted with the constrictions and smallness of his Australian situation, which he considered an inferior world for his talents. His importuning of his Order to return to Ireland led to a compromise. He was sent to America, beginning a series of restless clerical wanderings, back to Australia, to Ireland, but mainly in America, which reflected both his energy and his unhappiness. It is tempting to make the link between his instability, his core of dissatisfaction with his small impact, his reactive urge to bury his dreams of grandeur by immuring himself in the enclosed Benedictine Order (he tried twice), and the impossible Irish heroism imposed by the brand of his great name. Michael Davitt's was indeed an extraordinary penumbra within which to conduct a priestly life, and Forrest gave every sign of being both acutely conscious of this, and of inability to make more than intermittent sense of it. His name warred against his priesthood, to his disturbance and confusion.

Nor was W.F. Corrigan's parental legacy without a similar Irish complexity. His father, W. J., wrote melancholy poetry fixated on his breach with Ireland, the dearest place on earth, the land where his ancestors slept. These were familiar themes in Irish emigrant versifying, clichés even, but much more common in the tradition of American exile than in the more pragmatic Australian scene. It was a poetic output, where the heroism of Sons of Erin, bedecked with emerald green and sporting shamrock, could be honoured at the level of the Tug of War. Small wonder that his son, nurtured in such an intense, indeed emotionally overblown atmosphere, should cleave so passionately to real heroism, when it appeared in Ireland in 1916.

Brother Egbert in New Zealand, Dr Albert Dryer in New South Wales, W.F. Corrigan and Gerard Fitzgerald in Victoria, a scattered few elsewhere; these were a handful of marginal men, good men certainly, believers that the virtue they sought to prevail in human affairs was embodied in a place — Ireland. But their smallness of number, their isolation, their reputation as eccentrics and cranks, their tiny followings, all pointed to the fact that their Irish message meant nothing to the overwhelming majority of Irish Australians, who ignored them, from simple lack of interest and failure to see any relevance in what they preached. Preached. When laymen, or obscure individual brothers, preached Ireland, nobody listened. Inertia, or common sense, or concern for Australian affairs, imposed a perspective which reduced lay enthusiasts for Ireland to irrelevant nobodies. Not so the clerics. It was from clerical sources, and some Irish orders of teaching brothers and nuns, that the main push towards things Irish came. This was often not obvious, built into ordinary structures of communication, even unconscious. These sources, to the level of archbishops until the 1960s, were numerous, powerful, widespread, backed by the authority of religion, and in some cases very determined and deliberate in their championing of Ireland in Australia. The actual effect of such propagandising, or of mere presence, is debatable. The scepticism and dismissal accorded the lay champions suggests that similar dispositions may have underlain the traditional public deference accorded clerics. But by virtue of their office and role these clerics filled the cultural stage. Other acts were impossible until they had vacated it, by which time the theatres were emptying.

Obsession with Ireland could only retard and distort a constructive relationship and a considered appraisal of the new colonial environment. Those whose point of cultural reference and measure of moral and religious value was Ireland, led themselves and others into confusion and frustration. Assumption of Irish superiority in the things that mattered, led them quickly into a bewildering and profitless maze, as they tried to mould the colonies into Ireland's image and likeness. The task was impossible, because the assumption was not necessarily false; it was simply irrelevant, inapplicable to the situation. Ireland and the colonies were not on higher and lower rungs of the one ladder of merit, they were separate enterprises, one old, the other new. They were not a common ground for competitive comparison, but different endeavours in human history. To take Ireland as a paragon, a model, entailed a progressive compounding of errors.

First, it dictated that efforts must be made to tailor the colonies to be like Ireland, a coercive social programme that continually abraded against the realities of the local scene. To the extent to which the colonies were crammed into an ill-fitting Irish mould, it did violence to the true character and potential of the local impulse; it was, thus, bound to be eventually rejected and repudiated. To the extent to which such Irish pressure failed to do this generally, it narrowed its objectives to what was possible, and concentrated its energies on those elements of the Catholic population that could be brought to accept and obey; thus, it sealed them off from the wider population and created tension and division. Through all this ran a set of assumptions about Ireland and what was Irish. As the case of Brother Egbert illustrates, these assumptions were often outmoded, even false, worse still, fabricated, imaginary, fed by ignorance or superficial knowledge, and at best narrowly clericalist. Worse still again, these assumptions were run through with, and held together, sustained, by what amounted to primitive ancestor worship: cults of heroes in politics (first) and religion (second). In other words they expressed a form of social control, enshrined in a pantheon, around which eddied a multitude of tribal incantations in verse, song and prayer, and an underlying belief in blood superiority.

This powerful mixture held its own heady fatality for Ireland, and who would argue that it was out of place there? But the colonies were shores with their own fatality, weighted enough with their own brief, but radically different histories. They were to be twice burdened, the overlay burying for many years the more basic conquest. For, the Irish were insistent that (with minor exception) they were the source of the Christianisation of these southern colonial lands. They built on this undoubted fact a gamut of further propositions, some doubtful, others untenable, all mounting to a general law that these progenitors were invariably holy, wise, impeccable, ultimately beyond evaluation, let alone criticism — saints.

The backward Irish look, applied to the colonies, rested lovingly on the pioneers. It postulated their superiority and generated towards them and their culture, a reverence, sanctified by religion, which paralysed, made unthinkable, the search for the new and colonially appropriate. Indeed, for more than a century signs of such a search, seen as a kind of sacrilege against the Irish, were denigrated and suppressed. The mind-set that inspired Father Faber's hymn (*English* Catholic triumphalism) — Faith of Our Fathers living still, in spite of dungeon, fire and sword — became the habitat of too many of the clerical leaders of the colonial Irish. They lived in Ireland still. Their mental world was structured as in Faber's prison, copies of which they built for themselves and demanded others crowd in with them. What drama! What excitement! To stand siege against the devil and all his Protestant works. But where would the extras go, volunteers and conscripts, when the performance was over, when the fight had petered out and all the stage generals had died of old age or gone home? They would drift away lost into the secular desert, where nothing was.

For the second consequence of Ireland as model was the negative one: neglect of the reality of the colonies as places and problems. Indeed, the most corrosive and debilitating outcome of the cult of Ireland was an effect beyond the inhibition of constructive thought. It was to discredit the thought process itself, to damn intellectual life as religiously dangerous. There was no need for any locally focussed thought, save on practical questions of how to implement the Irish model. Any departure from what was determined, settled, by Irish experience and authority, was patently futile, misdirected, destructive. Such energies in the Irish camp as were directed towards comprehending or mastering the new environment found themselves in frustrative conflict with those who demanded a southern remake of Ireland — Ireland as measure of all things. The Irish obsession did untold damage, not only by default, but by outright opposition to the growth of a local consciousness of unique place, and by the need for the sensitising of the eyes and ears — and hearts and minds — to the imperative demands of a new world. And its legacy in defeat — so great was the force of the hubris that had once possessed it — was the falsehood that such a local consciousness was wrong, or did not much matter. Given that the day had passed when visiting giants had walked the land, the best that might be expected of the local pygmies who had succeeded them was that they follow the same footsteps, or those charted out in allegedly better places — America, Rome.

Worship of the past, and the men and women of the past, so central to the Irish obsession, may have been a dynamic in Ireland's own history, a galvanic inspiration for freedom and independence in historical circumstances where only the past had the resources on which to rest a springboard into a self-determining present. In the colonies it was to emerge as a frightened disposition, a flight from reality, a timid and craven succumbing to foreign if familiar gods, an easy avoidance of the present and daunting challenge of vacant lands, which was to build something new.

Imitation of Ireland, for all that it never worked, rendered itself down, true to the Irish tradition, to hero worship, which the attrition of death eventually reduced in time to deferential posthumous flattery of those dead giants. And then was revealed the fundamental flaw in the grandeur of the Irish obsession, the worm at the core of empire: that it was disgraced by its emptiness, its pretence, its cringing, terrified, laziness. Behind all the splendour, the noise, the tremendous salvific activity, was the man of the Gospel parable, with one talent, buried in fear that the Lord might think he had lost it. There was to be no risk-taking: the safe Irish road would be trod. For sure, the achievements of the journey on that road were prodigious, great buildings were raised up, many people were joined in common cause, God's word and sacraments were spread through the land. In all this marvel of doing, what was not done was not noticed. Who noticed the omissions when the list of commissions was so long and distinguished? But the void had been spanned by old imported bridges, sufficient for their day, but shaky in their skimpy foundations, eventually beyond repair, carrying dwindling and distrustful travellers. Who would build again, and, this time, tunnel to set their structure on foundation rock?

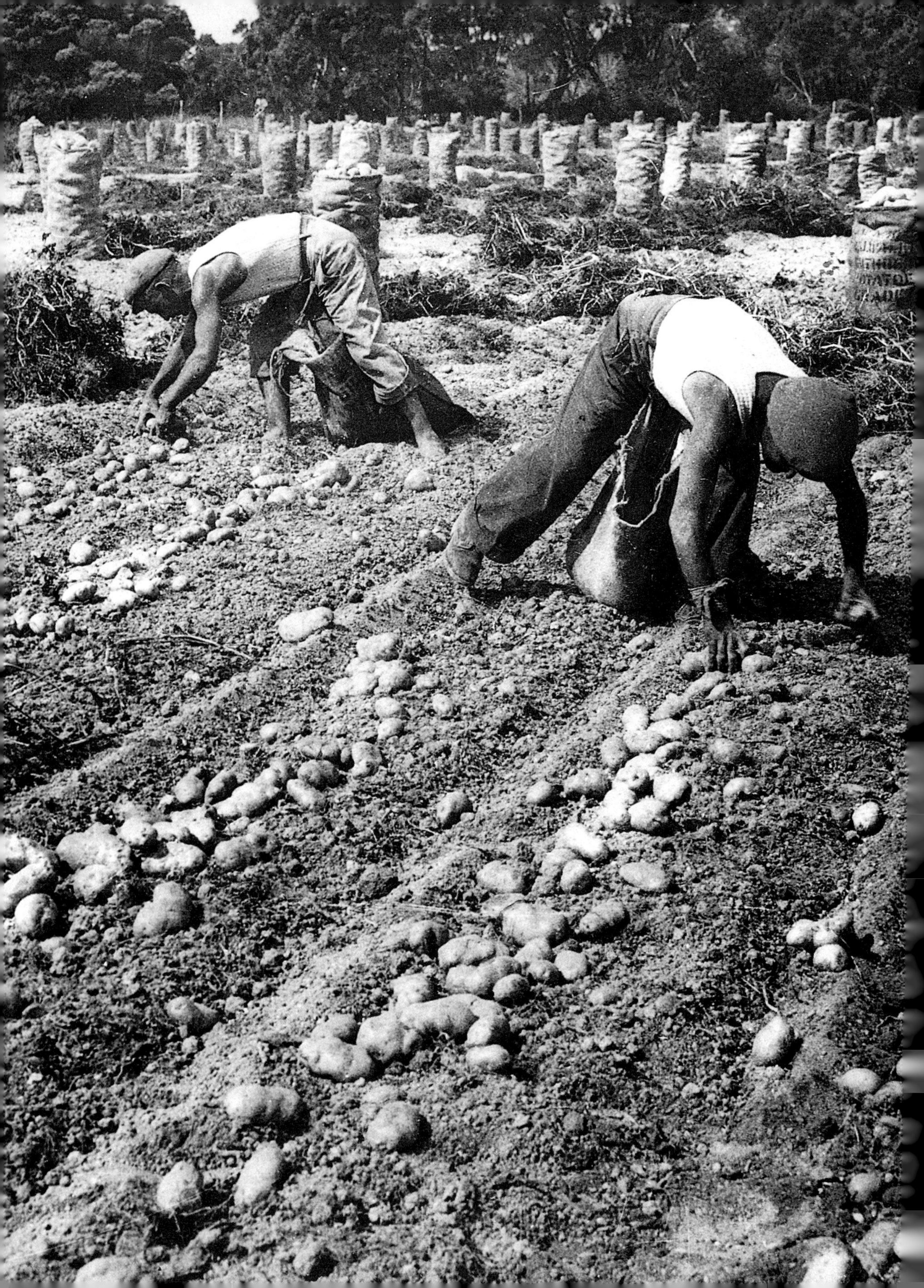

CHAPTER 9

POLITICS

According to Padraig Pearse, in his 1915 pamphlet *Ghosts,* the previous Irish generation, the generation that had produced my parents, had failed Ireland shamefully. It was desperately in need, from the nationalist viewpoint, of 'redemption', which he and his revolutionary colleagues offered them in 1916. Pearse's target was the leaders of the Home Rule movement. His strident, insistent message was that Ireland was a separate nation. If those inconsequential emigrants of 1913–14 from Borrisokane, Paddy Farrell and May Sullivan, were any indication, the general nationalist atmosphere had already percolated through to ordinary people in forms appropriate to their needs and character. In both cases their needs seem not to have been for high-powered injections of republican political enthusiasm (much less the fanaticism of Pearse) but for such more low-key and marginal emanations of a national ethos as would enable them to define and enjoy their own individual identity as persons. Irish nationalism has been usually comprehended and depicted in terms of organisation, movements, ideologies, big names, great events, and its objectives considered in relation to Home Rule, republicanism, independence and self-determination, as they affected the fundamental nature of the

Before mechanisation, some typical Irish farming work, picking potatoes in Western Australia c1940s. (*National Library of Australia*)

state. Grand themes. But to the ordinary Irish individual, those not indexed in the books of national or local fame, the manifestations of the Gaelic revival, of the new nationalism, appealed to them no less profoundly, but at an individual level, the level of making available to nobodies a sense of being somebody. The Gaelic language, by the very fact of its revived existence (not necessarily any mastery of it), together with what might be seen as its peripherals — Gaelic prefixes and forms of anglicised names — gave to ordinary people a sense of distinction and dignity they felt they lacked before. They would be no longer inferior on some English scale of racial merit, but themselves, on their own, different, terms. The brogue would no longer be a quaint joke, a humiliating secret given away with the first word, but of a piece with the name, and one's own language, a complete cultural entity.

Little matter that this was, with most ordinary people, a token acknowledgement. They had woken up to the fact that they had a great and different cultural legacy. It was enough to know, for the sake of pride and security and knowing who one was, that it existed. The scholars and the enthusiasts could be left to explore it. The ordinary person had neither the time nor training, nor perhaps wish, to know much more than it was there, that his or her feet rested on solid, ancient, civilised Irish ground.

Mai's cultural identity had a strong religious dimension. She left Ireland with a newly published (1913) prayer manual *Our Lady of Perpetual Succour and Ireland*, on which she had written the date of her departure (3 March 1914) and her name in English and Gaelic, in keeping with the nature of the book — alternate pages were printed in English and Gaelic. The careful, laboured, inscription of her name in Gaelic suggests no great facility in the language, but the book, a history of the devotion, plus prayers and pious practices, was in use until her death in 1970. Just when Mai, and her sister Chris, reclaimed the Gaelic 'O' to add to their 'Sullivan' (the Irish section of the family seem not to have done this) is uncertain, but Paddy added his 'O' in 1917, the minute book record of his Greymouth tailoring union beginning with 'Farrell' when he joined in 1916, and changing to 'O'Farrell' the next year. None of his brothers or sisters made a similar change, a situation which led to some confusion and comment in the years that followed. Of all the New Zealand Farrell family, Paddy seems to have been the only one who affirmed his Irishness in any public manner. To adopt the 'O' in 1917 was a provocative act, a very deliberate and aggressive proclamation of where his

Joseph Aloysius Lyons, son of an Irishman, Catholic, long time Labor politician, but on this occasion, despite the 'Irish' spirit of the photograph, triumphant leader of the United Australia Party, election day 1931. He was to be Prime Minister 1931–1939. (*National Library of Australia*)

loyalties lay in the Anglo-Irish conflict which had begun with the 1916 Rising.

Yet, the 'O' was not so different from Mai's move in the same direction. It was a declaration, a stance, a pride-in-identity matter, rather than any embracing of a revolutionary programme, or active commitment to any contemporary Irish cause. Indeed it was essentially an O'Connellite gesture, what Bishop Quinn in Brisbane did in 1875 in honour of the O'Connell centenary. That is, it was in central keeping with the Irish nineteenth century colonial tradition, which was, above all other things, O'Connellite — democratic, parliamentary, Catholic, a little radical, firmly Irish, but in a British context. All this was Paddy to the essence. Besides, it sounded and read a little better than the unadorned 'Farrell', dished out with contempt by English overlords: O'Farrell had that distinctive clan form and Irish aristocratic uppishness which the English so hated and the Irish so relished to assert. But in New Zealand there was no need for a crusade about it. The name (the Irish knew the significance and magic of names) was implicit confrontation enough; it carried a message beyond a mere individual label but that transmission was as much personal as national. Vestiges of Paddy's occasional peripheral involvement in Irish causes surface in his papers — a receipt dated 22 August 1921 for £17, from the Nelson Creek [Irish] Self-Determination Fund. Nelson Creek was a small gold-mining centre with a residue of Irish miners (they were often the last to leave exhausted diggings) and, evidently, Paddy had acted as one of their Greymouth collectors of money to be remitted to Ireland. And he was a member of the Hibernian Australasian Catholic Benefit Society from the early 1920 until his death, though that was more a colonial Catholic benefit organisation than an actively Irish one.

Irish heroes, icons? The sitting room walls carried the usual lace-curtain Victoriana, some local paintings, plus some holy pictures — the Sacred Heart. At some stage, there was also an amateur-ornamented photograph of Terence MacSwiney, lord mayor of Cork, who fasted to death in London's Brixton prison from August to October 1920, thus entering Ireland's gallery of heroes with claims both political and religious: his martyrdom united, or at least silenced, all Irish factions, lay and clerical. On the sitting-room mantelpiece, among the close assemblage of family photographs, was one in a solid silver frame — a young Archbishop Mannix. He was the only stranger in that company.

Paddy had encountered the great man in 1924 when he visited Greymouth: he is in the back row of the local Hibernians' group photograph with the archbishop. His admiration for Mannix was not for his Irish politics, but for his performance as a great churchman and champion of Catholics. Daniel Mannix was a star, to the same degree that film stars or sports stars currently dazzle the public gaze. Indeed, the visible Mannix was, in part, for public consumption, an act, and knew he was an act. He acted the Great Churchman. Whether he was or not, was irrelevant to the role. It was enough that the

Archbishop Mannix bottom left, Paddy O'Farrell top right, Father Long bottom right: Hibernians in Greymouth 1924.

image of his being so was needed by Catholics and he supplied that need: the reality — and magnification — lay in the eyes of the beholder. Despite his numerous public appearances, his very existence substantially consisted of iconography: on most public occasions glimpses of him were distant and fleeting, but everywhere was the intimacy of the ritualised likenesses. Paddy's solid silver frame had its equivalents in a multitude of other lesser forms displaying the ubiquitous archbishop — cards, badges.

Paddy admired a great act such as the archbishop's. As Mannix was part a living performance, so in his small way was Paddy, stern, impeccably dressed for occasions, with an aura of remote power held in reserve but it was on a far lesser plane than the archbishop's, and the role always flawed by his breaking up, a grin at his own pretentiousness. Nor did lowly performers have Mannix's enormous supporting cast.

The extent to which Mannix was theatre is a perception lost in the overlay of the serious religious issues and values involved: there is no necessary conflict or disrespect involved. Daniel Mannix had all the marks of the consummate actor. He carried on to the stage, wherever it was, the commanding presence of an aristocratic self-image, which he projected with all the aid of his poised physical bearing, superbly crafted lines deliberately underplayed, and a range of props: top hat or biretta, even a cape in the Victorian thespian tradition. In his study (the experience is mine, in 1960) piles of books and journals grew haphazard from the floor, the stage-set accoutrements of the man of learning. His enormous audience relished this performance, enjoying it because of its studied excellence as a role, and because it was constructed from, and deeply relevant to, real Catholic life. Here was leadership not merely as directional encouragement, but in projecting effortless superiority. The money given away in the legendary private walks was aristocratic largesse distributed in royal progress. The polite and polished insults to the secular authorities came from a source patently above them, with no care of their regard. Did he live so long so that God could teach him humility? The public arrogance of the younger Mannix was a total delight to ordinary Catholics like Paddy: the sheer style of the man was breathtaking. He behaved in every aristocratic way they thought he should, obeying no rules except his own. Here was no vanished king, but ancient chieftaincy resurrected, in a kingdom defined and populated by Irish colonial Catholicity.

Mannix's contribution to Australasian life was prodigious, on the grand scale the liberation he effected for his admirers far outweighs the cost in sectarian alienation. That was a deep poison that had to be drained at some stage. Better the assault of rough surgery than the unprompted and uncertain healing of time. No, the most culturally damaging, negative factor in the Catholic political scene was the least obvious — the interminable, slow longevity of the episcopal power centres: Mannix, Duhig, Kelly, Prendeville. As the greatest of these influences, Mannix's antiquity increasingly paralysed Melbourne Catholicism. It made it impossible for anything naturally Australian to grow freely: anti-Irish was no more natural or creative than pro-Irish. The point of reference remained Irish. Nor was Mannix's much-vaunted flexibility, openness, alertness, and encouragement of freedom and lay initiative of crucial importance. He was still there. His very presence, nothing he did or did not do, fixed the situation in time, preserved it in an aspic whose recipe was that of the early 1920s. For forty years beyond that vivid age of seeming giants, Mannix continued as centre of the Melbourne universe — and well beyond that universe to other adjacent worlds, such as that of Paddy O'Farrell. Time stood still as the great man ruled, secure in unthinking deference springing from his persona, authority, achievement, longevity. Stability it seemed, the protraction of a divine Irish benediction. Stagnation it was, nobody's fault: while the old Irish patriarch lived, his Australian household was condemned to the confines and immaturities of adolescence.

Mannix was the greatest, and the longest-lived of the Irish colonial icons, and it was at this level of distant veneration, acknowledgement of a superior but somehow kindred spirit, that Paddy wished to conduct his limited Irishness. For him (how many others?) Ireland could never lose its image of deprivation, of representing a denial of his own capacity, its tendency to evoke among a mixture of proud feelings, a tinge of resentment.

It was not only the few heroes that marked out the boundaries and nature of Paddy's Irish allegiance, it was the reverse icons as well, notably the British crown. Paddy's earliest New Zealand friend, George Phillips, the Waimate bootmaker, had displayed, behind his lavatory door, a large and lavish full-colour photograph of the coronation of King George VI in 1937, which had appeared as a supplement to a nationally circulating illustrated paper. I was innocent enough to ask

George why it was there, and affixed to the bottom half of the door. Not wishing to corrupt the young, George replied that he thought it was a good picture. That particular depiction of royalism in all its splendour had a wider appeal than to George Phillips. I encountered it in exactly the same position in the Christchurch home of Joe Keenan, married to an Irish friend of my mother's. Such sly digs at 'Britishism', semi-private half jokes (nobody had anything against George VI who seemed a nice family man, a bit weakish) were more the style of Paddy's Irish (and New Zealand) confrères than anything aggressively Irish, or any overt challenge to monarchy or the British system. Being Irish in Australia and New Zealand meant having a bit of a mild anti-British edge and not accepting Pommy bullshit: indistinguishable from being colonial, really. (In 1980, the English cricket captain Mike Brearley explained 'an element of hate' in his visiting team's reception, by referring to a correspondent who put it down to the large numbers of people of Irish Catholic origin in Melbourne and Sydney.)

But all that swagger was being Irish when young — being a cut above the dullard Brits, with their silly king and puffed-up humourless ways. Being Irish when old may have been another matter. Neither Paddy nor his brother Jack ever spoke of it. No indulgent reminiscences passed on to my mind, or that of my cousins. Why? Was it because of childhoods too painful; because it was a closed chapter, too distant or profitless to recall or was it too painful for another reason: not to talk of it was one way to attempt to banish its loss from the mind. Banished to colonial emptiness by self-executed decree: was this the way the older mind worked? Certainly, the older female mind carried some of this element, the aching desire to return; frequently talking of it, what it might be like, knowing it would be different, but hoping it — dream or whatever it was — might come true. And Mai holding Paddy vaguely responsible for its not; then me, visiting Ireland without her. But Mai's Ireland was cluttered with people, alive and dead, the home of a legion of ever-present memories, part frozen in 1914, but part the subject of ever-present curiosity about the lives of this one and that. How had they got on in the great competition of life? Wouldn't she be a surprise to them! What fun! And wouldn't the old, bygone, village reassemble, just for the occasion, for the moment; and would not life become whole, complete, unfragmented, again? The words carry their own contradiction, and fatality and foolishness, which may be why an older Paddy never wished to utter anything that might seem like them.

Yet, times and experience differed radically, and both personal fates and the particular atmosphere of various phases of emigration coloured the individual's view of his two worlds. Four houses down Puketahi Street from the O'Farrells lived the O'Neills, originally from Kerry. Thomas had come to New Zealand because of the West Coast gold rushes. With a good claim at Rimu, in the 1870s, he had persuaded his brother Patrick, then in Australia, to join him. Patrick's wife thought the climate would be better than Australia's heat. They had six children. But Thomas, having captured his brother's labour, exploited him, paid him a pittance, which reduced his wife to constant tears, and wrung from Patrick spasms of home-sick verse, which the family preserved. It took the form of protracted and detailed dream visitations to the places of his childhood — and laments for his present situation.

> When I woke from my dreams my vision was o'er
> Alas I was exiled in New Zealand's wild shore
> The pangs of my sad heart no words can portray
> As the tears flow for green Erin, so far far away
> To my home in Castlegregory, I return with a sigh
> And reflect, o'er the days, that are now long gone by
> May God, who has made Thee, so verdant and gay
> Drive misrule and oppression, from Thee, far far away.

The vogue for such sentimental emigrant verse did not pass with the Victorian age, but its natural environment was more the nineteenth century rather than the twentieth. It is difficult not to discern the growth of a hardening process, the introduction of a certain matter-of-factness, even a casual air, in Irish emigration before the end of the century. In the exodus around the Famine, and in the years that immediately followed it, the keynote was that of high emotion, even trauma, and the process of separation was loaded with drama and sentiment, and the trappings of the romantic agony in verse and literature generally. However by the 1890s, the 1880s even, emigration had become such an accepted part of the fabric of Irish life as to become ordinary, no great stimulus of major emotion or poetical outpourings. A quiet revolution in attitudes and expectations separated the outlooks of the old and new generations: the older O'Neill brothers, a few doors down the street, were from a markedly different Irish mental climate from the younger Paddy O'Farrell. It may be that the O'Neills tended to be exiles while Paddy was an escapee, and it may be that such roles reflected not so much Ireland, as changes in the cultural climate of the whole European world, but whatever differences they harboured in their vision of Ireland, their colonial outlooks seemed much the same — pragmatic, hard-working, Catholic, neighbourly, permanent residents, belonging.

What of those who came from the same Ireland, but the city, and a higher social class? Dr Arthur Hanrahan came to Australia in 1910, as assistant to the medical officer in charge of Kapunda Hospital in South Australia. He returned to Ireland in 1912 to marry, then returning to Australia to private practice. He died back in Ireland in 1919. On a superficial view, from mere appearances, taking into account his language and style, Hanrahan seemed the archetypal West Briton: his parents were 'Mater' and 'Pater', he played all sports, especially tennis, was musically accomplished in the classical tradition, and very well read. Against this he regarded Orangemen as 'awful rotters', and was a devout Catholic, with strong friendships within the Jesuit and Dominican Orders. He professed a strong and romantic Irish nationalism, moving quickly in 1916 from support of Home Rule to republicanism. He was in many respects socially the typical imperial English gentleman, but cast in an Irish and Catholic mould.

The Hanrahans came from an elite Dublin world, far removed from the countryside, or rural life. Their natural environment was the heavily English-oriented one of upper class, big house, Dublin gossip, friends, clothes, servants and lifestyle. In Adelaide, they gravitated to the 'Switzers' of that city, the best store. And they moved in a professional medical world, which related them to priests as equals (a most unusual and restricted Irish situation), and those priests from the 'best' orders. The Hanrahans took an easy place among Ireland's 'Irish' natural leaders and opinion-makers of the Home Rule years; a group of the well-educated and affluent, who spoke the same class-language and were often related. Membership of this élite carried over advantageously to the colonies. Dr Hanrahan's setting up private practice in Sydney in 1918–19 was facilitated by an Irish network, led by priests: 'you may rely on our using all our influence on your behalf' wrote Father Patrick McGrath, SJ, in 1917. Father McGrath was much impressed by 'the good example both of you are setting in this degenerate age of limited families'. Hanrahan had delighted his clerical friends by choosing an Irish wife.

Was this the reason that this network not only favoured Hanrahan, but was determined to keep Australians out of the competitive medical world? Hanrahan was frightened 'lest some Australian would jump in and queer our pitch'. Were they less reliable in Catholic family matters? Or thought by Irish clerics to be so? To this network, Irish lineage was everything. If Irish birth could not be called on as proof of good character, parentage could be sufficient. 'Tho' born out here, his parents were Irish' — thus was validated Father Frank Connell SJ, 'His mother is a Nenagh woman and very nice' — so Dr Willie Doyle of Glebe Point passed muster. To clerical influence was added religious. Doyle assured Hanrahan that the Irish Lewisham nuns 'work tooth and nail for their Hon[orary] Staff to put work in their way'.

Hanrahan's Irish nationalism was romantic, emotional, and very intense. For nationalist purposes he lapsed — or is the word blossomed — into a poetic patriotic jargon. Thus, in a letter back to Ireland just following the 1916 Rising he wrote: 'St Patrick's children should be true to him now of all times . . . Our hearts are with you in Dark Rosaleen who once again raises her noble brow purified and yet more ennobled from purging fires which have seared her soul'. Hanrahan's was another of those imaginations fired by the popular revival of ancient Irish history, particularly by the writings of Alice Stopford Green, whose *Irish Nationality* had so mesmerised colonial Irish devotees — Hubert Murray, Hugh Mahon, Albert Dryer. Of Joyce's smaller *History of Ireland,* Hanrahan wrote in September 1911: 'It . . . rouses my national pride in my country. I can only hope that the future suns may dawn in such another famous Ireland'. A famous Ireland was a dream of the romantic literary classes, whose nationalism tended to be a contagion caught through reading rather than reality, and whose Ireland was a very different place from that of their servants and the countryside.

That other, peasant Ireland, Hanrahan tended to regard, in his West Briton persona, as quaint, and with amused affection. In South Australia he looked for evidences of the importation of the loveable and pious lower Irish orders he knew at home. He found them, remarking in September 1913: 'I went to Benediction and devotions. Lots of Mrs Boyles with 'bee' bonnets and real old Irish saints with 'Baldoyle' beards gobbling up their prayers and shaking their heads'. The observation was entirely without contempt. In his own house Hanrahan gave out the rosary and litany every night. The same with colourful Irish turns of phrase: his wife remarked — 'old Mr Brady says (when you have told him something) "Well, Well, the devil a doubt!" — the latter has become a habit with Artie'. The mimicry was in good part, a kind of bemused wonderment at such antique and colourful turns of phrase, but it also betokened a major class distance and a profound culture gap. A similar gulf was revealed by the behaviour of the two Irish servant girls they had brought out to South Australia. Dr and Mrs Hanrahan regarded these as devoted family retainers, but they soon discovered, when these girls promptly left, that they had an uncle in Sydney; their chief prompting for expressions of loyalty and affection had been to ensure that they got their passages paid to Australia. Surprising to the Hanrahans — they were an idyllic and unworldly couple, who thought only within their own notions of truth and honour — this was an old ploy, and a continuing one, brought into and adapted to modern times by marriages of convenience, false sponsorships, and the multitude of ways in which immigration regulations might be cleverly exploited or circumvented by lies and trickery. That they should be gulled by the underclass of their own nation saddened the Hanrahans but did not diminish their faith. Indeed, it reinforced their belief in the need for the new, pure Ireland in which such things would not be.

Hanrahan's nationalism goes beyond the category of colonial dream. Here is an Irishman, a brief sojourner in Australia as it was to happen, whose ideas are part of the reality of Irish politics. Yet, his politics seem more dream-laden than the visions of the Ireland-distant colonial dreamers. Small wonder that delusion and romance prevailed in Australia when it was rife in its purest and most extravagant form in Ireland itself.

Arthur Hanrahan's nationalism filled a romantic and psychological need in him as it did for the colonial dreamers. For him, as for them, Ireland was or would be the incarnation of nobility and virtue. Even more than them, he changed gear into a worshipful language to celebrate the nation. He and his wife rejoiced in symbols. In 1913 they decorated their Christmas cake with green shamrocks and a motto in Gaelic. They were much moved by pressed shamrock sent from home, delighted by Limerick lace they found being worked in the Good Shepherd institution for girls in Melbourne, enchanted by the brogue and Dublin accents they might encounter socially or hear in the street. Beyond any enthusiasm the colonies might produce, the Hanrahans conducted a constant love affair with Ireland and all things Irish. They lived in a state of Ireland-infatuation.

Yet, it was also a natural nationalism, in the sense of being the then orthodoxy of their social group. For instance, Hanrahan knew beforehand one of the Irish delegates of 1911

The Irish lace making model for Australian emulation. A class in Ardara, County Donegal. (*Ulster Museum*)

to Australia, Richard Hazelton, whom he admired: they had met casually at a dance in Dublin. Mrs Hanrahan knew Willie Redmond, son of the Home Rule Party leader. When Hazelton came to Kapunda, Hanrahan proposed the motion opening the subscription list: he was an ardent, starry-eyed, and passionately righteous Home Ruler:

> It makes my blood boil at times when I think of the mess England has made in her Irish administration. Why, all over the world we are treated differently, even from the Chinese, as we have the stamp of a conquered nation on our brows. I know it because I have experienced it since I came out here. Ireland, once given a parliament for her own affairs and treated as a nation and not as a nigger country, and the Race will change all over the world.

The myth of Home Rule as a panacea for all Ireland's ills, and for the international repute of Irishmen, was not unusual nor was the personal dimension of humiliation Hanrahan felt. Much more than the ordinary immigrant, it was persons in his class and position that felt the stigma of inferiority and the hurt of being regarded as outsiders. The structures of his level of society in the colonial world were heavily English in character, and his Dublin upbringing and class had steeped him in attitudes and values which accepted the essential framework of that English way of looking at the world, both in its decencies and prejudice. His whole gentlemanly being — honourable, high-principled — rebelled against the notion and feeling of being treated as a member of 'a nigger country'. This sense of outrage took him straight on without hesitation to support the 1916 Rising, 'its brave heroes who have died for the cause of Ireland', and to embrace republicanism without further thought — and to oppose conscription in Australia as tyranny.

The Hanrahans' sense of honour was also outraged at the scurrilous attacks on Catholics that accompanied the conscription campaign, at 'that old wretch Billy Hughes', and at the hypocrisy of public expectations. Mrs Hanrahan wrote to Ireland in May 1917: 'Here they are hoping Catholics will join up and fight for those who attack their religion and all they hold most sacred. Then when they are in a tight corner palaver us and hold out fresh promises which they never intend to keep'. This was a disposition that made them great admirers of Dr Mannix (whom they met in April 1919), Father Lockington, SJ, and the leaders of Sydney Irishism — Neal Collins and Fathers Tuomey and Maurice O'Reilly. But not Albert Dryer, although Hanrahan became an inaugural member of the Adelaide Irish National Association, the organisation Dryer had founded in Sydney in 1915. Hanrahan's was a clerical and socially upmarket Irish world, into which Dryer and his lower Irish orders did not fit, despite common objectives and enthusiasms.

As to enthusiasms, even Hanrahan's wife believed, in January 1919, that 'He has Sinn Fein on the brain. I tell him he has 2 wives at present "Sinn Fein" and me!'. His child, born in February 1919, was christened 'Ciaran Proinsias'. 'One feels so proud to be Irish', he wrote to his mother in February, urging her to learn Irish, at least sufficient to say the rosary. 'Let all share in the rehabilitation of our ancient nation after her 700 years of slavery.'

Bliss in that Irish dawn to be alive — for those who could reach, and afford, that level of exaltation. The disposing con-

Home Rule as dental treatment, from the Melbourne Hibernian Society's *Official Report*, 1913.

A specimen of the type of anti-Irish and anti-Catholic propaganda that incensed the Hanrahans.

AUSTRALIANS, AWAKE!

Are You Blind to What is Going On?
READ THIS, AND **ACT!!**

ARCHBISHOP MANNIX ADVISES THAT AUSTRALIA SHOULD DO NO MORE.

"Speaking at the opening of a bazaar at Clifton Hill, Archbishop Mannix said: 'Conscription was a hateful thing, and almost certain to bring evil in its train. He held the conviction that Australia had done her full share—or more than her full share—in the war, and as a peace-loving people, they would not easily give Conscription a foothold in this country.'"—"Age" report, September 18.

FATHER O'KEEFE THREATENS TO FIGHT IN CIVIL WAR.

Preaching in Bowen (Q.) on October 15, Father O'Keefe said: "I hope that the hands will wither of all those who vote for Conscription; that God will turn all those from voting for Conscription. If Conscription is granted there will be Civil War in Australia, and I will fight with the rebels to the last drop of my blood."

QUEENSLAND MINISTER FIHELLY.

Mr. J. Fihelly, M.L.A., Minister for Justice in Queensland, spoke to the Queensland Irish Association on September 2:—

"No Irishman should have the impertinence to apologise for the rebels. . . The opinion was held by many young Australians that every Irish Australian recruit means another soldier to assist the British Government to harass the people of Ireland. . . England was the home of cant, humbug and hypocrisy. . . A good deal was heard about the case of Captain Fryatt and Nurse Cavell, accompanied by denunciation of the Germans, who, after all, had only done such things against alien enemies, whereas England had murdered people whose compatriots were fighting for her by the hundred thousand. . . If they thought of contributing to local patriotic funds, they should instead, for the immediate present, divert the money to relieve the distress in Ireland. . . Irishmen should stick to their brethren. The shooting of Fryatt by the Germans was no worse than the shooting of Skeffington."

IRISH REGIMENTS CALL FOR IRISH HELP IN VAIN.

The appeal for help sent in October from the front by Major W. H. K. Redmond (brother of the Irish Nationalist Leader) fell upon deaf ears. He said: "It would be a thousand pities and almost a betrayal of Ireland's heroic dead if the Division which brought so much honour to the Irish name ceased to be Irish."

IRELAND FAILS TO GIVE VOLUNTEERS TO THE WAR.

Lord Derby, Under-Secretary for War, last week gave the following figures showing the numbers of Irishmen who had joined the army between April 24 and October 12—nearly six months:—

Ulster	3556
Leinster	3081
Munster	1749
Connaught	469
	8855

or less than 1400 per month!

ONLY TWO-AND-A-HALF PER CENT. IRISH FIGHTING FOR BRITAIN.

Mr. Asquith, Prime Minister of Great Britain, last week said that 105,000 recruits had joined in Ireland since the beginning of the war. This was only two and a half per cent. of the population. It was a low percentage compared with the rest of the Empire.

In the face of these figures and facts, who can wonder that Major Redmond was driven to make a despairing appeal for recruits, or that the appeal should fail?

WHAT IRISHMEN DO IN THE WAR—TAKING THE BRITISHER'S JOB.

ditions appear to be the unquestioned assumption of complete Irish identity, substantial reading in the romantic literature of Irish nationalism, close familiarity with day-to-day events in Ireland, some acquaintance with the leading actors in the dramas of Irish politics, and the conviction that Irish events were important to them personally. In Australia and New Zealand these conditions were filled in the main by clerics, and, as in Hanrahan's case, by a few professional men. And at the other end of the economic spectrum, by a few working men, natural rebels or idealists.

The Hanrahan family and friends with a home-made Irish republican flag, Hanley Bridge, South Australia, January 1919.

For most ordinary immigrants, committed to the colonies, Ireland counted (though often merely as a symbol of their own oppressed plight). But it was well down the list of priorities. Those priorities included, for many, but by no means all, Catholicism; though that, too, had a symbolic dimension, related to social standing and community regard. But was religion the first priority? The clergy would have liked to have thought it was, but the reality was, of necessity, less edifying. In most cases, the first priority of the unprivileged was work, the pay and conditions of that work, and the place that work occupied in the recognition and power structures of the new colonial society. Hence the gravitation into the labour movement: a twentieth century escapee from Ireland was not likely to accept a mere duplication of his old situation twelve thousand miles away, especially as even Ireland, from 1916, had proved itself capable of self-exertion towards bettering its lot, if only then politically.

Work: the free selector at home — free to work — every illustration shows some work activity. (*Illustrated Australian News* 10 June 1882).

Work. Work was not only the centre of the immigrant world it was its meaning and its nemesis. Land of opportunity: opportunity to work. From a land where work was scarce, pay low, and pace slow, the Irish came to a place where might be glimpsed the golden edge of distant fortune. Hard work might, with a little luck, open the door to a truly good life, an inconceivable possibility to the ordinary man or woman in Ireland. But at a price: work was not merely the dire necessity, but the big temptation. Yet not always, or all at once. The nineteenth century seems — and it is more than the illusion of nostalgia — to have been more spacious, to have had more time, for sport, for travelling around, for socialising. But both economy and expectations were to change. Take the north coast of New South Wales. Originally settled from the 1860s by Irish who grew corn and potatoes: the corn was a seven-month crop, the potatoes a major burden only in the picking. Short periods of intense work —and then all kinds of fun; rowing and sailing on the river systems, odd sports like weight-lifting and dumb-bell swinging. Time off for the picnic races, the trip to the beach, or a yarn at home and a smoke. Life, its needs and amenities, were simple. The introduction of dairying in the early 1900s eroded all that with its seven-day-a-week regimen dragging in wives and daughters, who were to rebel in favour of the city and secretarial work, it eventually undermined the old sense of community, then its very existence, as the old died and the young failed to take their place.

Other typical Irish work — on railway construction, Greymouth — Runanga 1901–1902.

But for many Irish, early on, work became their idol and purpose, the gold-rush mentality protracted, and applied as a general disposition. Get rich quick, that is what they were here for. Besides, there was nothing else to do but work, or if there was, it was frivolous, non-productive, not exchangeable for material benefit. Work became a trap. So, swiftly, within half a lifetime of any one man, work — plentiful, well-paid, never-ending colonial work — eroded their old world and picked, shovelled and hammered it to an end. It was work that killed their joy, silenced their music, foreshortened their fun. It stole all their waking time, sapped their energies, undermined and destroyed their health. It was work that killed them, in spirit and in fact: it was work that dimmed, extinguished, buried, the light of Ireland's colonial empire. That it glowed so long spoke for the waves of new recruits, dazzled by colonial prospects and brimful of energy and hope, willing to put shoulders to wheels and sing while doing it. Desires and regrets: the opposing pull of these two emotions was never stronger than in emigrant situations. But their frustrative counter-action has been noted in observing Ireland itself, by a Frenchman whose words seize on its essence while conveying its poetic obscurity: 'Placed between memory and hope, the race will never conquer what it desires and it will never discover what it regrets'. Perhaps. More likely it — or rather individuals who give 'race' its name — has done both. And in conquering what it thought it desired, found it hollow and a deception. And in discovering, at journey's end, what it regretted, knew it to be truly worthy of regret.

And work — what for? The cliche assumption has it that it was to give the children an education, to buy for them an easier life than their parents, a profession, status. True, but not as true as myth would have it, or as early, or within the broader society. Initially, the Irish rose within their own narrow society. It also had an extra career dimension not valued outside it, that is, the religious life. Those who valued, wanted and could afford higher education were few until the 1950s, even the 1960s. Indeed, into the 1960s (the profession was accountancy, the information from Sydney), Catholic sources had a list of firms to which there was no point applying for jobs: and experience added others that would say 'We don't employ people of your kind/background'. The Irish Catholic response to this, from the 1930s, was to set up their own firms — obviously, but this was not the initial stimulus — in competition. These, naturally, employed Catholics, who had nowhere else to go. As to medicine and law, these professions tended to pass on their Irish Catholic elements by descent. Medical fathers who held qualifications from the Royal University of Ireland, ensured that sons followed them in the profession. So did Irish immigrant lawyers, but the usual Irish Catholic pathway to the law was not university, but entry from matriculation as articled clerks, and admission through Solicitors' Board examinations.

In part the restraint was money. It was also failure of vision and imagination. To some extent, to a peasant people, however respectful of learning, the very idea of sending their children to university was an absurdity. In part it was the terror induced by the Depression, children whisked out of school as soon as they could get a job. It was also the schooling. Between 1868 and 1920, 162 Irish Christian Brothers came to Australia, in a prodigy of commitment and missionary zeal. Their historian says their Irish influence was strong. The mentality appropriate to Ireland's social structure and outlook was transported to Australia; results, not culture. Catholic educational horizons did not go past the public service and evening commercial colleges. At the highest ecclesiastical level, save for Mannix, there was suspicion of the intellect, distrust of universities as enemies of the Faith. In the main, the ordinary worker worked to live, to survive, with little ambition, in a close, boundaried, sub-world.

'Smoko'. Jack Farrell's son and son-in-law take a break for tea on his Hunter farm c1950.

Paddy O'Farrell came to Greymouth early in 1916. He immediately joined the Westland Tailoring Union, or to be exact in the then new syndicalist jargon, the Westland Tailoring Industrial Union of Workers, a small organisation with a strong and independent female section, then pressing for a forty-four hour week. By May he was on the committee; in the July elections he became president; in March 1917, secretary: obviously the union needed new and energetic officials in campaigns which were both industrial and political — pressing for a war bonus (1918 rates were £4 2s 6d for men, £2 for women) and for repeal of the Military Service Act, which gave New Zealand conscription. In 1916 Paddy also became a foundation member of the local branch of the newly formed New Zealand Labour Party. He had arrived in the area a little late for those landmarks in New Zealand socialist and industrial history: the 1908 Blackball strike, which first successfully challenged the arbitration system and the 1913 Grey by-election which put the first socialist in parliament, the Australian, P.C. Webb.

However, the Grey district, with its coal mines at Blackball, Brunner and Runanga, had seen the birth of revolutionary socialist industrial militancy, which had led on nationally to the formation of the 'Red' Federation of Labour in 1912 and the Labour Party in 1916. By that time, the brightest of the local stars — Pat Hickey, Bob Semple, Paddy Webb — had moved to the national stage, there to join the other labour luminaries, Harry Holland, Mickey Savage, Peter Fraser, and other lesser destined names. Nevertheless 'the Coast' remained the birthplace of New Zealand labourism, and stalwart in devotion to its principles.

Those principles were, in fact, none too extreme: unionist rather than revolutionary socialist. Hickey, with his fiery Americanism, and that 'noisy larrikin' from Australia, Semple (great entertainers in their different ways), both seem to have taken with them a good deal of the colour as well as the wild radicalism. What remained in Grey was dour and tough as it had always been with miners, with a dash of cautious and highly non-doctrinaire 'Irish' right wing, centred around Webb, his Australian parliamentary successor Jim O'Brien, Mick Daly of the local labour newspaper, Paddy O'Farrell, and a range of others with Irish names, but often of Australian birth.

So, what is to be made of stern notices of meeting, emanating from Runanga, the local power-house of labour, addressed to Paddy as 'Comrade', as was the then fashion of the inter-

Above: Paddy's thirty-year path to work: Kear's tailoring shop was opposite the railway station.

Right: The slogans which adorned the Miners' Hall in Runanga (opened December 1908) proclaimed the spirit and legacy of Grey district labourism.

national brotherhood. He was a most unlikely comrade, as were most of his labour colleagues. Mick, Jim, Paddy were the natural forms, so that 'Comrade' became a distancing title, an ideological declaration rather than an affirmation of bond and common cause. The Grey Labour Party, whatever the intensity

Left: Miners in front of State Mine, Runanga: Bob Semple arrowed.

Below: And the Runanga boxing team (trainer Bob Semple, future Labour cabinet minister, on left) also embodied an aspect of the message of Grey labour.

of disputes and rows, worked on the assumption that its affairs were those of family and friends, not of an army of dedicated fanatics. 'Comrade' as a form of address swiftly drifted into the exclusive possession of the few local communists, whose point and pride was to affirm their internationalism, their anonymous membership of the great indistinguishable mass of the world's workers. 'Comrade' was the equivalent of 'soldier'; it was depersonalised, universal. Whereas, the Grey Labour Party was just that, Greymouth, local: a group of people who knew each other well, had other allegiances, notably family, and church, and who came together partly in belief, partly in self-interest. It was a serious organisation, no doubt of that, and took itself seriously, but its style and atmosphere was radically different from that of the 'Comrades'.

To personalise the point, in the 1940s and 1950s, of the few Greymouth communists, Jack Doyle — the name betrayed his origins and his 'comrade' label stuck most awkwardly over the real Jack beneath — was the most enduringly energetic. His distinctive mode of cycling, leaning forward grimly into whatever the gales that lashed him, with bulging eyes and total dedication to piston-like pedalling, encapsulated his confrontationist political attitude. He and his velocipede were hurtling with total commitment towards the beckoning final barricades, which, sadly for Jack, ever receded into the revolutionary distance. Paddy and he maintained a wary acquaintance. Doyle had the humourless intensity of the totalitarian zealot, a narrow Padraig Pearse of a man rather than a big James Connolly. He was a man whose intolerance and devotion to what he saw as principle made him an outsider — and in Paddy's view, a maverick wrecker, a troublemaker, a political liability, but still exasperatingly part of the local scene — bloody Jack Doyle.

It had been Irish nationalism that had brought Jack and his brother initially from Napier to the West Coast. Both were radicals, anti-British and anti-conscriptionist, and they had heard, by word of mouth in Irish and socialist circles in the North Island, that the West Coast was the place to go to evade conscription and make common cause with others of Irish background. Specifically, the Donnellan timber-milling family of Nelson Creek had set up a refuge for such men, a bush hut near their home, which at various times held up to thirteen men on the run. These men were fed by the Donnellans and spent their time fossicking for gold in the area. Around the Doyle brothers at this time swirled a variety of lively stories: were they in fact army deserters; engine driving at Inchbonnie under assumed names; the object of police searches, going bush, captured, Mrs Faolain of Greymouth's Golden Eagle Hotel summoning the Donnellans to the rescue, unsuccessfully. Fact and myth, truth and tall story, entwined like the supplejack vines of the impenetrable West Coast bush, or the tangled traceries of the ornamentation of Irish monkish manuscripts. In telling the story, fifty years later, a lifetime of secrecy, caution, the necessities of duplicity and cunning, the habit of silence, still choked and twisted Jack's devious narration.

Doyle's was the aberrant, obstinate Irish style, so much at home in colonial communist parties, hot-headed, uncompromising, in rebellion against the authority and power of the Catholic church, arrogant, lonely, suspicious, painfully serious in devotion to communism's saints. The Labour Party had no room for such purists, either socially or politically. Such communists believed that the colonial Labour parties (J.H. Scullin was attacked on this point in 1932) were simply part of the imperialist exploitation and repression of Irish workers, a proposition regarded as farcical rubbish by Labour supporters of Irish descent.

Paddy O'Farrell was in the traditional right-wing Labour style, relaxed, pragmatic, a behind-the-scenes master in the arts of prudence and arrangement who was renowned for sound political advice, a believer in the power of words, of rational discussion and the press. He was a firm exemplar of the maxim made famous later by the most 'Irish' of recent American politicians, speaker of Congress, 'Tip' O'Neill: 'All politics is local', the theme of successful, expatriate Irish politicians worldwide. In Australia it was a theme pursued by the Irish city and town politicians, often working from a hotel base, like Dan Minogue and Paddy Stokes in Surry Hills, New South Wales. Stokes based his Sydney lord mayoralty on the promise to his horny-handed bar patrons that he would give them work: they remodelled Hyde Park. Minogue promised he would give them an Irish voice in Canberra, which he did, for many years, and on every possible Irish issue. Paddy O'Farrell's faith lay in the power of the workers' press. He was an early director of New Zealand's first and only Labour daily newspaper, the *Grey River Argus,* established privately from 1865, in which local labour organisations took over a controlling interest in 1919, his own tailoring union buying shares in 1923. This enterprise, sounding high-powered and efficient — labour's strong propaganda arm — was always on the verge of financial collapse and even physical disintegration, housed in an old building beset by floods and the vibrations of its ancient presses. But it became a key meeting-place for local labour activity, and its board contained the leaders of the movement. Jim O'Brien, Labour candidate in 1919, and member for Westland 1922–25, 1928–47, was an early chairman and manager of the *Argus* — and close friend of Paddy's.

O'Brien had good labour credentials. Arriving in New Zealand from Australia in 1904, he had worked as coal-miner and engine-driver at Runanga, been imprisoned in 1917–18 for sedition in relation to his opposition to conscription, was prominent in the union movement, in organising co-operative societies, and in both Runanga and Greymouth borough councils. And he knew the national luminaries of the emerging labour movement. He was not quite a placeman in the hostile sense of that description, but he was also no ideologue and, when elected, liked his parliamentary job: he was the archetypal, solid local member for a worker constituency. And he depended heavily on Paddy in the electorate. Throughout the 1920s Paddy was a key figure in Labour electoral organising,

O'Brien's West Coast background: the Dunollie section of Runanga about the time of his arrival from Australia in 1904.

to the extent that in December 1931, O'Brien, who had just scraped in in the national election of that month, wrote to him personally: 'without your assistance, and that so freely given by a few others, Westland would have gone to the Tories'. What O'Brien at least half meant, was 'But for you I would have lost my seat', which was human enough, but in his case, an emphasis perhaps closer to him than abhorrence of Toryism. His letter to Paddy was no general circular to helpers: 'I am afraid that the language is too cold to lend itself freely to feeling that, now and then, comes from our hearts'. O'Brien, a warm man, was genuinely grateful, and Paddy was glad to help. He knew O'Brien's limitations; none too sharp, a bit pompous, but somehow in the same Irish mould, with the subtleties and insights rubbed off by the unrefined colonial minting. It would have been O'Brien who organised the award to Paddy in May 1937 of the King's Coronation Medal, to be worn in commemoration of that event so colourfully displayed on the back of his friends' lavatory doors. The medal remained in its little red box. O'Brien was not sensitive to the anti-English elements that simmered quietly below the surface of Irish minds like Paddy's; not exactly hostility, but suspicious reserve, points of principle and behaviour not to be yielded to the English by decent Irishmen.

Nor did O'Brien have any comprehension of the cynical deviousness and devilment that went together with, and in no way vitiated, Paddy's deep commitment to labour politics. As local party president Paddy proposed a toast to the labour movement at a function in 1940, in which he declared that his political creed was 'the principle that some people must share the burdens of others and that all must combine in helping their fellows'. Unless misreported (a constant hazard, given the local reporting talent available to the *Argus*), this manifesto was so entirely unobjectionable as to bear the interpretation both that he believed in it and that it plumbed the depths of banality and meaninglessness into which he occasionally descended, to enliven (for himself only) those many dull or preposterous gatherings in which he was compulsorily involved. Paddy strongly believed that very few people paid real attention to anything said, particularly at public meetings in draughty halls, or ever read carefully what was written. It was therefore a waste of time — indeed, positively misleading because it would inevitably be misconstrued — to say any-thing clear or precise. Better — less trouble and more amusing — to make harmonious expected noises, which an audience would vaguely translate into what they wanted or thought they ought, to hear.

Paddy applied this same technique to written character references for jobs, documents for which he was often asked. The case he cited to me was of a parent of his acquaintance who sent his son for such a reference. The boy was unknown to Paddy save as an obviously lazy dullard, but it would be unkind and needlessly trouble-making to send him away. Paddy therefore supplied him with his 'unknown wage warrior' reference. This said something to the effect that young Houlihan would, no doubt, be suitable in any employment which a potential employer had any reason to believe he had the ability to perform — or, effectively, make up your own mind and be it on your own head. Yet, the wording was sufficiently high-flown, fatuous, and stereotyped, as to seem to mean much more, though what, who could say? There were never any complaints, and Paddy's references were highly valued.

Labour politics, however, was more than a narrow game, taken seriously by ideologues like Jack Doyle, or those it employed, like Jim O'Brien, MP. For those on the periphery, like Paddy, it was both a serious pursuit and a source of amusement, a contradiction which the professionals could neither understand nor abide. It was also a social world of the usual sort, with a bit of entrepreneurial capitalism, between friends, on the side. Like-minded persons of whatever political persuasion will be forever scheming schemes and letting each other in. In 1931 Jim O'Brien, together with a group of other Irish colonials who had a little money to invest, launched a venture which would make their fortunes: Paddy took a small share of the action.

The wealth of the area (such as it was in depression circumstances) then came from coal and timber; but, historically, since 1865, it had been gold. The curious spell of that metal lingered, given economists' veneration, and its traditional enticement to Irish gamblers. O'Brien and his friends — sawmillers Arthur Donnellan and James Flaherty, carrier Terry Deere, ex-MP and successful Christchurch coal-merchant, P.C. Webb, coalminer and land-holder, Dick Spencer (brother of Kate, who worked with Paddy in Kear's tailoring shop), with architect William Hill — all persons of Irish origin and middling substance, decided to pursue the rush in its then modern form. They bought a large gold dredge, and formed the Brian Boru Gold Dredging Company, with capital of £27 000. The name suggests homage to Irish history, but in fact this generation of Irish colonials had no interest in such talismans, in

An Australian example of the gold-dredging boom. The Araluen, New South Wales, dredge in the early twentieth century. (*Braidwood Historical Society*)

evoking the heroes of their cultural tradition (of which most of them were ignorant). The name was a fortuitous legacy from Irish miners in the 1880s, who did value such things, and had so named the ground about to be dredged. The newly formed company acquired the idle 'New River' dredge, which itself was in part a reconstruction of the 'Ahaura' dredge, both of which had proved unpayable. This direct history, and the fact that the West Coast was littered with forsaken dredges, might have warned the directors and shareholders of the Brian Boru: but, of course, they would be the lucky ones. Reality dawned slowly as the leisurely buckets chomped expensively into ground which was often auriferous, but not sufficiently so to pay the bills, just enough to whet the appetite for the real strike — tomorrow. Eventually the Brian Boru fell silent. It was a better name for a pub, which indeed it was in Greymouth as in so many other Irish-oriented places. There, illusions could be less expensively sustained.

Paddy never learnt to abandon his vicarious gold-seeking, to the chagrin of his sister-in-law Chris, critic of those in situations she had never entered: 'Mai, why did you marry Paddy? He'll never amount to anything' — meaning he would never have any money. But he did have money, to spend on racing and gold-dredging shares, which is what he wanted it for. A clean-out of his workroom cupboard spilled forth to my delighted juvenile eyes an avalanche of share certificates, with wonderful ornate engravings, pictures of formidable dredging machines, all encrusted with gold embossing. Surveying the pile on the floor, Paddy enunciated what he called his first law of gold dredging investment: the more gold lavished on the printing of the share certificate, the less is in the ground to be dredged. Up to that revelatory point, I had thought these impressive documents denoted real wealth and had been awed by my father's casual storage of this treasure, of which I was secretly aware. To a child the truth was no deflation nor, I suspect, to Paddy. They looked grand, they breathed the air of romance and dreamed possibilities, they witnessed to bigness, money laid out on great financial enterprises. Something again of Fitzcarraldo, visionary — or is it mad — myth and symbol of sublime craziness, which purses the lips of contemptuous penny-pinchers, but lifts the hearts of venturers, spenders, men of risk, cloud-collectors.

And sometimes the risk paid off. Sometimes Paddy got out when the going was goodish: in September 1936 he sold 1000 shares in the Nemona Gold Dredging Company for £81. And sometimes the failed company's leases or equipment were bought by new dredgers and a little of original investment retrieved. One survived long enough to be bequeathed to me, the Kaniere, at a total share worth of £4 7s 6d.

Dredging was the long gamble, racing the short. Sudden death. But a full week's entertainment: post-mortem media coverage dwindled by Tuesday, form and predictions mid week, placing bets with illegal SP book-makers Friday and Saturday (exciting activity), tips arriving any day or hour, by any means — mail, men on bicycles, knocks on the back door, later, telephone. Here was a predictable weekly ritual, interspersed by moments of high drama as word came urgently from those who knew. Paddy (and millions of others) loved horse racing, or rather, betting on horse racing, not caring much for horses, but for the occasion, the tension. He enjoyed the infrequent local meetings, which meant dressing up for a day's outing, but meetings elsewhere in New Zealand, several each Saturday, suited his work pattern better: he could drop his tailoring to listen to the races by radio. His was one of the earlier radios in the town, but the technology of the day, plus the Southern Alps mountain barrier, meant that afternoon reception from distant cities fluctuated from faint to absolute silence, in rhythmic waves. Paddy could never see the humour in the usual situation: clear calls of the start dwindling to nothing as the post was reached, leaving him to wait, sometimes for hours, for results summaries. When large wagers were at stake, his frustrated rage, in the face of such crucial silence, could be terrible, more terrifying to behold than in any other family circumstance.

Paddy transfixed by racing results c1952: the radio is an S.T.C. (Standard Telephones and Cables of Australia).

Whatever the size of these wagers, or their outcome, they seem not to have affected the family economy. Nor were there rows about it. My conclusion is, that it was 'surplus' money, earned above subsistence; its use was not so much 'gambling' in an uncontrolled sense, as a kind of high risk investment on a par with the gold-dredging. When it did not come off, then life continued as usual, instead of being transformed as had been hoped. Meanwhile, a kind of agonised fun had been had and tension injected into dull lives. Besides, Mai gambled too; or rather, loved to attend race meetings, to dress up, and for the excitement. In the years before Paddy's death, in 1959, they frequently went to the races together, in mad drives across the Southern Alps in Eddie McDonald's car, leaving at 3 a.m. and back at some similar time the following day, after attending some obscure country meeting in Canterbury in which McDonald, who owned horses, had one running. Why 'mad'? Because of the weather and the roads, adventure was as certain to occur as it was unpredictable in exact nature. McDonald was a prosperous merchant, who drove his giant, luxurious Packard roadster with a touch of Mr Toad's imperious ego and erratic prowess: he was short-sighted, wore a Panama hat, constantly smoked large cigars, and drove at speed. He was in fact a lonely widower, finding in Paddy an unexpected friend, but he looked a rich but dubious character from Graham Greene's South American novels. This entourage, with him at the helm and Paddy and Mai and perhaps others as passengers, plus picnic hampers and assorted bottles of spirits, tended to make its own right of way against lesser vehicles (satisfyingly English in their puny motoring inferiority), but there were snow and ice, floods, washouts, flat tyres, breakdowns, trees and boulders on the road, all to be negotiated, usually in pitch dark.

What happened on these long journeys five or six hours each way, I can reconstruct from similar related experience: motoring in this headlong fashion, hurtling into the unknown dark, so exhilarating in large and powerful American cars built expansive and generous to extravagant purpose. Race-ward bound, sad or satisfied in return, was a culture in motion — Irish, religious, colonial in its adventure and zest, and wild setting. The rosary would be said, all fifteen decades, plus a variety of litanies, in unison, with a fixated intensity well beyond normal church practice. Such a journey, with its edge of physical terror, was a profound religious experience, plunging at eighty miles an hour, or crawling through watercourses, in a tunnel of dark bush, headlights bright, but drowned in the

A programme for the Melbourne Racing Fraternity's 30th Annual Mass, 1988.

rain or lost in a starry wilderness. And trailing into the blackness a common brave chant celebrating the life and death of Christ, fellow believers in the shared intimacy of their speeding capsule. Here was happiness: companionable wayfarers, uncomplicated for the long moment by thought of responsibility. Salved from sin by their prayerfulness, these mad riders had small hold on earth. Heaven would welcome them, if such was God's will (a blown tyre, a washed away bridge): innocent racegoers off on a spree. It never happened, and the rosaries and litanies, and jokes and stories and gossip and racing hopes and failures, long continued their orbit across the Southern Alps.

This semi-sacred journeying, this Irish pilgrimage to the playgrounds of the pagan God of Chance, were a special extra benefaction granted Paddy and Mai, through friendship, in their later years. Dressing up for the local meetings was a significantly lesser delight. What was at the heart of all this? The obvious. The thrill of the wager was its own escape from life and work both dull and dreary. It was a decision made in a world where most of the decisions had been made by others. Here was a small bid for freedom. Moreover, a win meant the triumph of one's own judgment, and a blessing of luck. A big win meant a liberation from wanting a new hat or a pair of binoculars. With a win came a good feeling, vindication; and the windfall gain, merited not by work but somehow by character, a benefaction from above. The risk and the previous

An Australian country race meeting: Braidwood 1918. An occasion for formal best wear. (*Braidwood Historical Society*).

losses were worth enduring for that moment of pure elation, the release of tension in victory. Were the Irish more subject than others to diminish their victories and self-estimates to the level of the outcome of some horse race? Yes, the despised of the earth had their priorities right. They knew that joy was fleeting, rewards few and unenduring; and the nature and ritual of racing (foot racing as well) encapsulated what they knew of life, and how they liked to live it. Paddy loved excitement, hated a dull life; racing — and risk-sharing in gold dredging — was how he escaped into the world of action and large affairs.

Politics filled a similar role in his life, that is, not as an avenue for ambition, or the pursuit of public name, but as an entry into a wider arena of human affairs and as an outlet for his skills as negotiator, conciliator, manipulator, and local party wise-man. Accepting a justiceship of the peace in 1943 was in the same tradition: in New Zealand, that position, which was honorary, entailed serving as magistrate in cases usually minor, but sometimes as serious as manslaughter. In 1948 he was appointed to the local State Housing Allocation Committee, another thankless public service in times of serious housing shortage.

Constant nightly meetings, or work: such was the regimen. In 1947 his health collapsed, and he contracted tuberculosis, 'the sickness' as the Irish called it, appropriating a scourge, not entirely, but characteristically, their own. For the last ten years of his life (he died in October 1959, aged 67) he lived in semi-retirement, going out seldom, but his home increasingly the centre for advice-seekers and political scheming and conversation.

Yet, the heart went out of Paddy's involvement with Labour politics in 1947 with the death of Jim O'Brien. They were men of a kind, of a common religion and culture, of a generation. The personalised bonding of friends, so much at the core of Irish-style political operations, died with O'Brien. Seeking to maintain the easy magic by collecting money for a new building for the *Argus* as a memorial to O'Brien was no substitute for the reality of being loyal to Jim, nor was he really a sufficient figure to sustain a myth. The obvious heir to his safe Labour seat was J.B. Kent, whom Paddy neither liked nor trusted. Kent, a Scot, came from the British Keir Hardie tradition of labour politics. He claimed to have known the famous anarchist Kropotkin. So what? What had Kropotkin to do with a right-wing Irish-flavoured Grey labour movement? Paddy — the O'Brien men generally — did not want Kent; but who else?

Not himself: he was a back room man, and not well. The house became again the focal point for callers who walked briskly, or brought their bicycles around the back for anonymity. At last, the only alternative to Kent was determined, Bob Ware, clerk in the local Post Office, office-holder in the local party. He came to see my father.

Paddy held normal court outside, even when raining: it was the phase of TB treatment when fresh air therapy was in vogue. He sat on the edge of a small table, on a not much bigger open back verandah, his guest perched further along the edge. The situation was private and commanded a view of the back garden, the Marist School, the Greymouth gorge and, usually, the incessant rain. A gravel path around the side of the house, and a heavy gate kept deliberately noisy, announced any other visitors long before they appeared. Paddy chose this bleak site partly because of the fresh air, partly because (he said) it shortened the conversations of the long-winded, and sorted out the hardy from the feeble, but also because it avoided cluttering up the workings of a very small house and thus annoying Mai. (In fact it annoyed Mai anyway, as it excluded her from company and conversation which she enjoyed. But more complex still, Paddy's political visitors were likely to have clammed up and avoided what they came to discuss if Mai had been present. Possibly because he was used to working with tailoresses, Paddy related easily to female party members, of which there was a considerable, and able, number; other males were less able to cope with this.) Paddy's back verandah privacy arrangements were the equivalent of similar devices elsewhere, of which the walk across the paddocks would have been the favoured country course. A Tasmanian variant was the wood heap out the back, providing elevated seating with an all-round view of whoever might approach.

I walked in from school to glimpse what was the end of the O'Brien Irish empire. Paddy and Ware were sitting on the back table. Ware was crying. He simply was not equal to facing the revolution in his life parliamentary membership would entail, and as he talked to Paddy the utter impossibility of his rising to meet the challenge bore in on him until he wept, not in rage, or frustration, but in sheer misery. He had come to Paddy distraught, pressed by Kent's enemies and by his own feeling of responsibility, but paralysed by his own sense of inadequacy, plus his wife's utter fright at the prospect. Ware was a nice man, at home behind the Post Office's brass grille that separated him from his customers; a man of the bicycle and bus when politicians had entered the age of the car. He put on his bicycle clips — that bygone part of the ritual of leaving — and left, thanking Paddy, comforted, a happy man. As Paddy reported it to Mai, here was a hopeless case, whose inadequacy deserved respect, not pity, as the maximum of which the man was capable: he would be a disastrous parliamentarian. Kent would have the seat.

Kent had enough sense to continue to consult Paddy, and Paddy offered advice when he was asked for it. But the visits were awkward and infrequent. It was not so much that Kent could look after himself, as that he was carried along by the momentum of tradition. The 'Irish' age which Paddy had helped make had passed and it was a bitter disappointment to him that the best it could produce by way of legacy and heir was Bob Ware — or its translation into another labour culture, that of Keir Hardie's Britain, diluted into the colourless pragmatism of J.B. Kent.

Yet, for all that they contained an Irish, or Irish-descended element, the labour parties and trade unions of Australia and New Zealand were the most powerful of colonial anti-Irish solvents. While the media or labour's enemies would have it otherwise, the implications of labour's operations, politically and industrially, were consistently anti-Irish in effect. They eroded the possibility of Irish coalition and militated against support for Irish issues.

Labour organisations 'colonised' the Irish in several important ways. First, they cut across, transcended, all religious divisions. The movement might have factions and conflicting tendencies, but it would not entertain sectarianism. A consequence was to broaden Irish Catholic acquaintance and friendship outside their religion. Obviously the accidents of neighbourly encounter worked to the same effect, and some parents deliberately offset the segregation of the Catholic school system by ensuring that their children joined community groups where they mixed with all others: my sister was in the Girl Guides. But labour organisations, party and unions, added powerfully to this assimilatory effect by joining persons of all religions or none in common cause: many of Paddy and Mai's friends were from the labour movement, and not Catholic.

A revealing contrast may be drawn with the Hanrahans in South Australia, whose social focus remained Irish. Lacking

J.A. Lyons points to first principles (on the side of an aeroplane in the 1930s.) (*National Library of Australia*)

more than the formalities of doctor–patient relationship to draw them into the local community, they existed above it. So, their intimate circle was closely Irish, even in Kapunda. In effect, they were camped in Australia, mixing with other expatriates and sustained socially by Irish visitors. The local born were invariably described as 'colonials', if their antecedents were not known. If they were of Irish descent, it is the original family county or town which is used to fix them into the familiar Irish world. The demand that such persons be 'placed' in Ireland was almost obsessive, contrasting with the colonial's locational anonymity and casual disregard for antecedents. As for themselves, the Hanrahan's self-insight was clear: 'If I possibly can I will settle down in Ireland. I think we are both too thoroughly Irish to live in exile from our dear native land'. Too thoroughly Irish. It was an honest disclaimer of local Australian attachment and might have been made, to mutual benefit, by other professionals who came to do Australia service, notably those in the field of religion.

Labour's service to the Irish did not end with its contribution to personal assimilation. Labour organisations drew the Irish and their energies into colonial concerns and immediate local matters, establishing and imposing priorities in which Ireland held no place. In contradiction to the false 'Irish' image foisted upon the Australian Labor Party, if there is one factor responsible for the weakness of the Irish issue in colonial politics (contrast America, with its weak political labour movement), it is the nature and power of that party. Nor can there be found any meaningful Irish consciousness among prominent Labor Party personalities of Irish descent: witness the bewilderment of Labor Treasurer, Paul Keating, when receiving the title of 'Irishman of the Year' in 1987. Or to cite the most prominent Catholic historian of Australian Labor, Bede Nairn: his biography of New South Wales premier and Labor legend Jack Lang, notes a vague and undefined 'Irishism' in seven brief references. The context indicates that it was hardly more than a paranoia in the mind of opponents, in the same class as Bolshevism, with which it shared the conservative hate list.

To the extent that Labor 'Irishism' had any reality at all, it consisted, in the early 1920, of a general sympathy towards things Irish among those in the Labor Party with Irish-derived names and Catholic origins (but not necessarily religious practice). Similarly, Nairn's (much more frequent) reference to 'Tammany' (Tammany Hall being the headquarters of the American Democratic Party in New York), which has an American Irish connection and connotation, is simply his shorthand for the 'skulduggery' and 'dirty tricks', which became 'a fine art' in the labour movement from 1916. There was nothing exclusively Irish about it, though the Irish names then prominent in New South Wales — McGirr, Dooley (who was Irish born) and so on — were among those adept at such manipulation. Frank Farrell makes the same general points in regard to the federal Labor leader and prime minister, J.H. Scullin. His 'Irishness' (by descent) and Catholicity, were 'privatised beliefs and emotional attachments that contributed little to his day to day thinking'. To be precise, briefly, from 1916 to 1922, the Irish issue — in Ireland — was modestly significant to Australasian labour, as a matter of general socialist principle via James Connolly's involvement, and as a matter highlighting the right of a small nation to independence.

By the late 1940s, the political sway of the Irish, such as it was, had run its natural course, surviving on both sides of the Tasman only in old men — Big Jim Roberts, born Cork 1881, uncrowned King of New Zealand according to the labour movement — or in Irish names about Australasian business: Australian labour abounded with them and still does. These men, the Irish names that explode out of the cataclysmic labour Split of the 1950s, had nothing to do with Ireland, or things Irish in any political sense, unless it be vestigially in their association with the Australian Catholic church. But was their political style 'Irish', or their ideological stance, or their modes of political behaviour?

In a sense the very question is meaningless and unprofitable. Who can disentangle what was 'Irish', from the complexity of what was universally 'political', and why bother to do so, save for some unworthy denigratory purpose? Such has indeed been pursued, to the discredit of the investigators, and to their neglect of that area where historical parallels both real and revealing do exist. Briefly but crucially, in the mid 1950s, the authorities and habits of the Irish political tradition surfaced for a last time in Australia, in a fashion both anachronistic and decisive. The story is all there, for those with the exploratory comparative historical equipment to look, in the substantial literature of the Split. The Split was that division in the Australian Labour movement which followed the charges made by the federal Australian Labor Party leader, Dr Evatt, in October 1954, that Catholic Action, in the form of industrial groups and 'The Movement', a Catholic social studies group led by B.A. Santamaria and supported particularly by Archbishop Mannix, sought to take over control of the Labor Party. The story is particularly encased in the published memoirs of B.A.

Santamaria, and of Jack Kane, one of the founders of the post-Split Democratic Labor Party, accounts which reveal their astonishment, bewilderment, at what took place. And what took place was a replay with local variations of what had occurred in Ireland in the period of the political ascendancy of Charles Stewart Parnell between 1886 and 1891. There had taken place then a crucial confrontation on the question of who should lead the Irish, and where and how they should be led. Then, the clerical assumption that a religious people should be religiously led, had been implicitly challenged and denied, as the 1880s progressed, by the Irish Home Rule Party led by Parnell. The power, influence and authority of priests was being rapidly eroded and replaced by that of politicians, and the fall of Parnell in 1891 and the subsequent collapse and fragmentation of his Home Rule Party, was regarded by most bishops and clergy as providential, a divine blessing to enable the return of the Irish to the control of the church.

That Australia, fifty years later, should be host to similar dramas, of which all the actors were unconscious of Irish precedent, is hardly surprising. In the 1950s the clerical role in Irish politics was a hostile and ancient, general cliché with Ireland's and Catholicism's enemies; but historical research had not then supplied in any neutral and credible form, the detail of the actualities behind Irish political and religious scenes. More, quite contrary to the image of devious malignancy conferred on them by their enemies, Australian Catholic lay leaders were ignorant, naïve and indeed innocent, particularly in regard to the potential political ambitions, manoeuvring and unscrupulous tactical resource inherent in the actions and attitudes of some of their own clergy. Central to this curious variation on classic Irish themes were, of course, the clerical descendants of the Irish church: not at all Mannix (the genuine maverick Irish article) but the colonial clones, ignorant, as Mannix was not, of Irish history and therefore prone, given their inherited Irish impulses, to repeat it. These clones were also victims of the illusion they had helped to manufacture, that Catholic Australia was like Ireland, a presumption akin to skating on thin ice, where surface and appearance belie reality.

Cardinal Gilroy and Bishop James Carroll sought to frustrate and destroy the Movement (citing fear that it would generate sectarianism) in their determination to maintain the Cahill New South Wales Labor government, with which they had strong links, with a view to securing State aid for Catholic schooling. But the essential issue, as Kane came later to discern, was that certain New South Wales bishops could not stomach an official and influential Catholic body under, not their control, but that of a Melbourne layman, Santamaria. It was the elements of the Parnell crisis over again. Who should lead the Catholic people? Should it be bishops or politicians? The means these New South Wales bishops (and, to be even-handed, some of those bishops who opposed them, and supported the Movement) used to impose their will were in the Irish historical tradition, beginning with Cardinal Cullen in the 1850s. There was insistence on clerical authority and lay obedience, appeals for loyalty to the bishops and for Catholic solidarity, claims that bishops knew best, and a range of less high-flown political ploys, pre-arranged motions, secret arrangements, disinformation, deviousness generally. Such tactics were entirely successful in their short-term purpose.

Australia lacked the strain of sceptical anti-clericalism that had developed, as the other side of the deference, in Ireland. There, the long abrasion between the church and the militant republican tradition stretched vigorously from 1798 through the major upheavals of Irish history into the IRA present. Australia was virtually innocent of this, to the degree of being notably more Irish than Ireland itself, in matters of submission and loyalty to the clergy. The fundamental reason for this went back to the beginnings of settlement. Irish priests and people in Australia were invariably on the same political side, initially in regard to religious liberties, thereafter in a series of major public issues: immigration, education, conscription, support for the Labor Party, and the long sectarian war. Historical experience and tradition had tutored the Australian Catholic laity in the habit of unquestioning acceptance of clerical political judgment and decision, to a degree well beyond that prevailing in Ireland, itself a very different political environment. By the 1950s, with a laity increasingly well-educated and politically experienced, this subservience was an astonishing anachronism, unnoticed because buried beneath continuing political harmony. The Labor Split put the clerical-lay alignment to the test. This was crucially the case in New South Wales, because that State's episcopal leaders were committed to a political position of support for existing Labor forces, from which a significant section of the laity, associated with The Movement, diverged, on the ground that Labor was compromised by association with communism.

On 30 September 1956, at a meeting of 700–800 people at the Sacred Heart Monastery Kensington New South Wales, Bishop Carroll engineered lay support for the episcopal position, but not by argument or normal political means. The approach adopted was that of the assertion of episcopal authority and the reiterated demand for 'loyalty to the bishop'. This was accepted by many reluctantly, by others against their wishes and better judgment, and by a very few, not at all.

The immediate consequences of this appeal to religious authority were momentous. It sounded the death knell of The Movement and achieved the political objectives of the New South Wales bishops, and the continuance of the State Labor government in power. The long-term consequences were, arguably, even more momentous — damage, to the point of destruction, of episcopal authority as a whole. As a basis for political action, an appeal to religious loyalties, personalities, and solidarities, was, in the ultimate, self-destructive. As a tactic, it could only be used once, in circumstances of surprise. Once used, it unmasked itself as clericalism in politics of the most antiquated and caricatured 'Irish' kind, placing those over whom it was exercised in the role of ignorant priest-ridden peasants. The disbelief of the Melbourne elements that this is what in fact what was happening, their incomprehension, is understandable. It went against all the notions of harmony and trust between priests and people which were assumed to be at the heart of the Australian Catholic tradition. And were. Always excepting, of course, that element in Irish clericalism which had rippled below the surface of Irish affairs well before Parnell destroyed himself — the fear that lay politicians would undermine the authority and interests of religion. That subterranean element had long existed particularly in New South Wales, appearing most powerfully in Cardinal Moran. It was a highly politicised, and deeply Irish-grounded, authoritarian paternalism, which saw clerical insight, charisma and power as an essential influence for good government; and it regarded the laity in politics, as in religion, as ill-informed and irresponsible, and as needing clerical direction and control.

The Kensington meeting of 30 September 1956 marked the last, anachronistic but powerful, throw of the Irish clerical church in Australia. It went with a highly destructive, profoundly damaging, bang. The detonation wrought unconfined havoc well beyond any intention or foresight, reducing all subsequent episcopal efforts to exercise authority, legitimate religious authority, to a whimper. Even in the manner of its going, through the crude, aggressive, incompetence of its inheritors, that vanished kingdom left a powerful legacy of ruin.

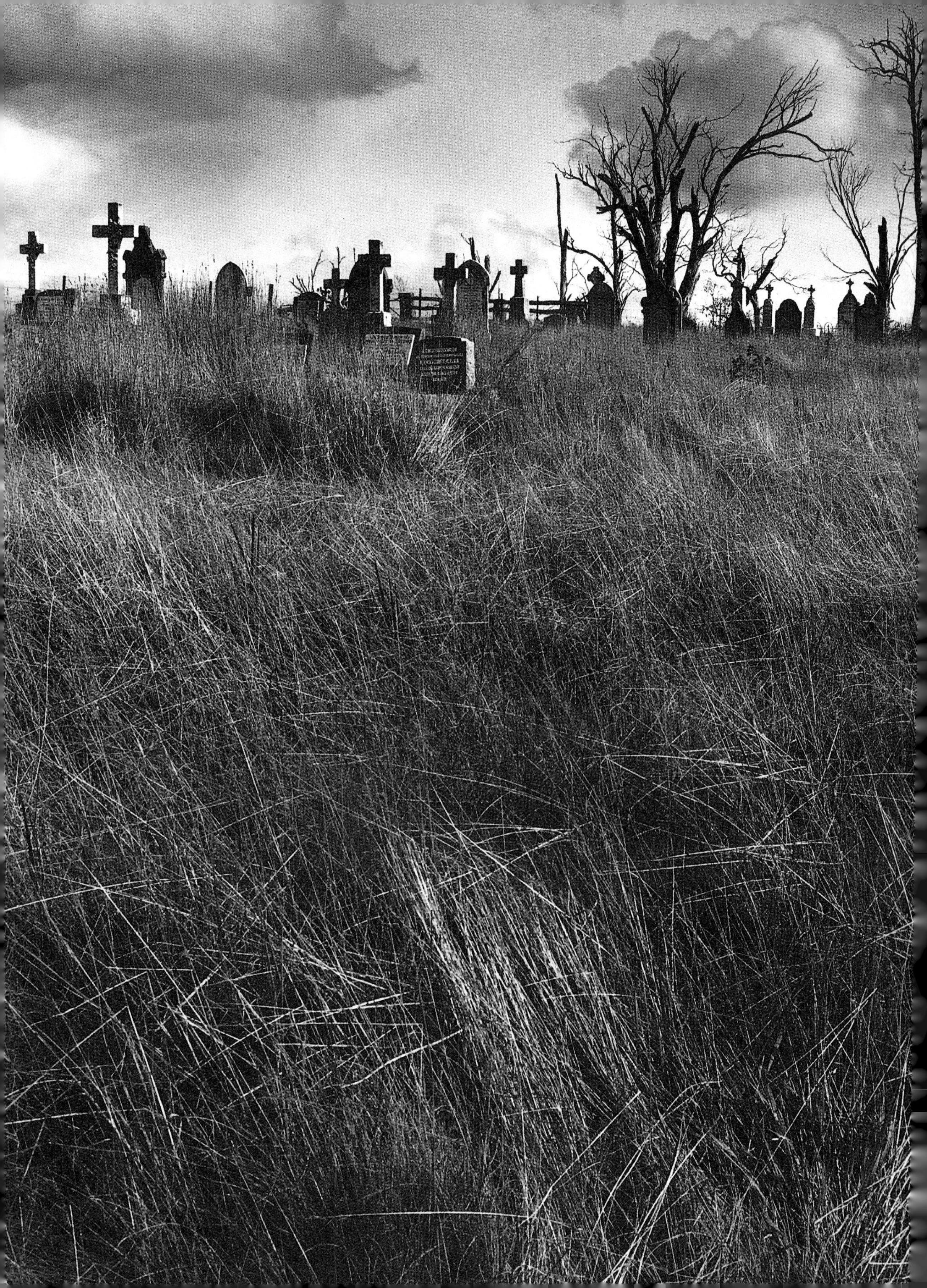

CHAPTER 10

DEATH

Hallo Death. My first clear extended memory of an event (as distinct from mental snapshots confused by old photographs) was that of watching the passing to the Greymouth cemetery of my sister's funeral. I was then in Montessori pre-school, and being cared for, during the ceremony, by a family friend: I was not taken to the burial, just to see the hearse pass, destination obscurely heaven-ward. Mary's passing in 1939 was in a confusion of cultural traditions: the post-Victorian (too traumatic, children not admitted), Irish Catholic (priests, prayers, piety), and practical colonial (park the kids with kind friends, and don't quite know what to do or how to react: from the new land, nothing comes naturally.) Taking place fifty years ago, in a remote Irish colonial enclave, it offers a point at which to examine that confusion and collapse of old mainstays, assess what support they still gave, and to pose again the intimate questions; how did these outcast Irish think, feel and behave as they trooped along the corridors of death?

Emigration was a death already. It was so regarded in Ireland with its wake-like farewells, so hinted by the designation of the destination of the emigrants — the New World. Letters

Days withered like grass? Lonely death in the colonies

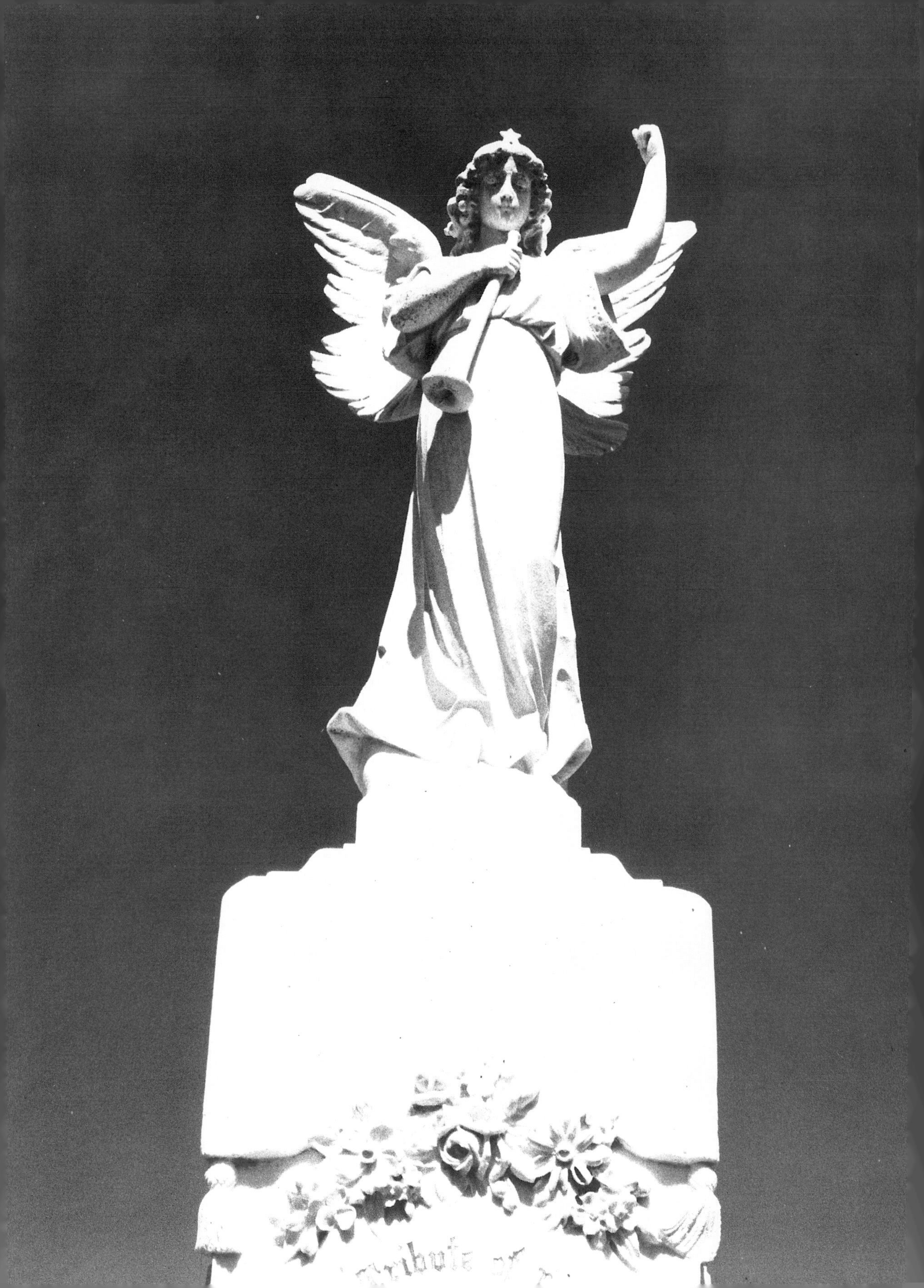

maintained contact with the Old World, as did newspapers and new arrivals, easing the grief of parting but also emphasising its fact. The emigrant had died to much of his or her former self, shed that skin, painfully. The emigrant's new life was based on the assumption that it would be better, successful. It was also a gamble, full of risks of all kinds. And for that the emigrant was mentally prepared, at least in theory, save for the ultimate disaster, death. Emigration separated the exile from the normal, natural actualities, the necessary drama of close family death, the child in sickness, the old in age: it substituted death by letter, death reported, not seen, not experienced; it reduced to a sudden shock of written information, a process which normally took time, and which was accompanied for those present by shared ritual, by cushioning, familiarising human circumstances. To see it in another way, distant death, particularly of parents, deprived the emigrant of one of life's great — in the sense of awesome, mysterious — experiences. To the extent that parental death marked the child's entry into full adulthood — or had emigration already done that? — absence from the traditional deathbed diminished the scope and span of life; it constricted, inhibited, falsified emotional range, demeaned the survivors and deprived them of finality. The fracture of traditional society's continuums imposed by emigration was nowhere more profoundly disruptive than in matters of death; yet, perhaps nowhere more understated or (it is hard to avoid the word) buried, such was the emotional suppression and avoidance both contrived and allowed by distance.

Death in the colonies? The usual emigrant was young, his or her company young, and encounters with close death infrequent, and usually through accident. For all these reasons the emigrant was particularly vulnerable to the death of the beloved, those who formed part of his or her newly created world; who, indeed *were* that world. In emigrating they had died to themselves; that they should be required to bear also the ultimate loss of what they had made new, was often insupportable. Their fragile buildings of the heart broke and fell. In the hour of such death — and its urgent and inescapable demands prefigured their own — they needed home, needed a secure, rooted sense of belonging, but they were homeless. All they possessed was a sense of profound loss. Often it pulled them apart, or into false hardness of heart.

The original Australian Irish world coped with this situation with a distinctive coming together of its elements: to recreate through the structures and rituals of religion as much of the consolations of the old culture as could be mustered against an Australian environment that threatened to crush them with its stark indifference. The Australian nineteenth century was full of Irish funerals which pretended they were taking place in Ireland. With, even, reversals of the theme. In 1847 it took almost six months for news of the death of the great Daniel O'Connell — the Liberator — to reach Australia. Sydney Irish Catholics promptly assembled at a requiem mass, complete with catafalque. This led some to believe that a French corvette, then in port, had brought O'Connell's body to enable his colonial admirers to 'wake' him. A woman who believed the catafalque contained O'Connell's remains went about enquiring where he was to be buried, so she might attend. Such simplicity was serious, but these earlier Irish also harboured goonery, which had its butt in death, as in all else. The

A Masonic funeral at Gundagai, New South Wales, 1903. Ritual dispersed, swallowed up, made empty, by distance and the land's expanse. (*National Library of Australia*)

Melbourne Catholic *Advocate* of 22 August 1875 included in its 'Wit, Wisdom, and Humour' column the following:

> An Irishman leaning against a lamp-post as a funeral procession was passing by, was asked who was dead. "I can't exactly say, sir, but I think it is the jintleman in the coffin."

Natural or contrived idiocy on this solemn subject was dwindling fast as Irish Australia moved towards religiosity, respectability and the dilution of its old culture in the twentieth century. Even in the 1870s a confused cultural erosion was evident. The combination of the comforting Victorian notion of death as sleep, and the Christian one of the dead as belonging to God, merely on loan briefly to their loved ones, lent itself to the device of the declamatory grave-stone, in which the dead instructed the living in ways which reflected an imaginary dialogue that took place with the bereaved. Firm words on stone had an authority that eased broken hearts and put perspective on disaster. Thus, at Michelago, New South Wales, a small distance from the snowfields highway, is one of many such reminders and injunctions:

The McNamara children instructing from beyond their grave at Michelago, New South Wales.

> In memory of Bridget McNamara who died January 8th 1879, Age 2½ Years   Also Catherine McNamara   Died January 27th 1879   Age 18 Days
>
> > Parents Dear do not weep
> > We are not dead but here to sleep
> > We are not yours but Christs alone
> > And He thought Fit to take us home.

But if cultural solidarity was shaky and waning in the midst of effusions of sentimental Victoriana, it still existed strongly amongst the Irish-born particularly. So, when in May 1919, four-year-old Michael Hanrahan died of diphtheria in Lewisham Hospital, his mother could write 'our very own little Mick is safe with God', and both his dying and his funeral were surrounded by Irish religious: the child himself could say the 'Hail Mary' in Irish, taught by his Gaelic-enthusiast father. But the old edifice of certainty and acceptance was cracking, with time and, in this case, with new temptations — the idea that with science and medical skill it might be possible to defeat death. For the boy's father was a doctor, an immigrant of 1910 to South Australia, with an excellent professional reputation, and to help his son he had summoned Sydney's leading specialists. Father and doctor, the child's death came, as his

Lourdes remembered in Australia, in the grounds of the Redemptorist monastery, Galong, New South Wales. Other countries' shrines, experienced by imitation.

wife put it, as a 'stunning blow' to Arthur Hanrahan. Did he ever recover? Just over a year later, in June 1920, he was dead of cancer, aged thirty-four. He died in Ireland. Diagnosed in Sydney as beyond surgical aid, he determined to leave at once, visit Lourdes to open himself to a cure if God willed, and to die in Ireland. He wished his five remaining children to be educated there. In South Australia in 1913 he had watched an Irish medical colleague wait too long. Similarly diagnosed, he too decided to return to Ireland to die, but by the time he had decided to make the booking, the disease had so gripped him that his greatest fear had become that of dying without the company of a priest, without the last rites. The dilemma both agitated and paralysed him. Would he die priestless on board ship before he reached his own home place? Distraught, distressing to others, he would not venture travel. Mrs Hanrahan gave him a life of the Little Flower and a miraculous medal; no pity or patronage from health, but a gesture in the humane tradition of a shared religion. Ethel and Arthur Hanrahan rang true. Their Irishness, their Catholicism, decency and bravery in the face of death, all this was all of a piece. So was Arthur's wish to die in Ireland, holy ground, his. (Natural, too, was his children's desire, eventually fulfilled, to return to Australia.) But it was a wish he could indulge — too loaded a word — say, fulfil; as was the trip, the supplication for a miracle, to Lourdes. He had the means to do so. What of those who did not? With that multitude the wish also remained, an unsurfaced impossibility. They lived and died in the knowledge that they would, at least in this world, forever lack Irish completion.

The distance between 1919 and 1939 in Irish colonial history is immense. This is the period in which Irish cultural hegemony fell apart and declined into increasing irrelevance. Ireland, with its Civil War, had fallen into disgrace, then into a somnambulant stagnation. The colonial Irish, for the first time in their history, were left gradually to their own slim resources, of self-meaning, un-nourished (save in residual make-believe) by that gigantic, galvanic, Irish grievance. Such colonials were hardly at the point of having left-over lives to kill; but yet they were at that point of integration where they might be dragged back by their emptiness or regrets over what they had long ago forsaken, or drawn forward by the energies and ignorance of their colonial children into the new world, quick and clean. For my sister to die just then, at fourteen, was disaster. It drove my parents, not together, but apart in spirit; it swung my mother into an introverted and sour piety, in which her natural gaiety became increasingly submerged. Mary had been my mother's pet and pride, not in an indulgent so much as a friendly outgoing way, small housekeeper when mother was ill, always bright feminine company.

The nub of the matter was this. Mary contracted meningitis, following a chill caught at a children's birthday party: she was a party girl. The local immediate, unanimous, and continuous, medical opinion was that her death was a matter of a short time. God was besieged without avail. Then it was suggested to my father than he charter a special aeroplane to land at the small, local aerodrome to take Mary to better care, recovery, somewhere — Dunedin? My mother fixed on this idea as the salvific — or was that only later, when it did not happen? A special plane was a prodigious, unheard of resort at the time

Mary and the author, 1939.

and my father was willing to bankrupt himself, but professional advice held it futile and foolish. All that could be done anywhere was already being done in the Greymouth hospital. At that stage of medical resources no doubt it was, but as a desperate last resort, a gesture relevant not to Mary's death but to Paddy's and Mai's life, such an irrationally induced bankruptcy — at least it would have occasioned major (for us) debt — may have been a very wise investment.

Conditioned to accept authority, religious and medical on a par, my father reluctantly let the idea drop. The rebel in him, and that element which was mad, proud, and in pursuit of impossibilities, capitulated to the doctors, and to community opinion watching from the wings. (Who do these O'Farrells think they are? A special plane indeed! Let them accept the will of God like the rest of us.) To say my mother never forgave my father for Mary's death is a distortion and exaggeration of what happened. He never forgave himself for his failure. To do what? To be himself, to tell the doctors to go to hell, order the bloody plane, and be the bit of a mad bugger Mai had married. Of course it was all too difficult, even organising the mechanics of such a rebellion. And who would lend him the money for such a hare-brained extravagance: silly O'Farrell pleasing his scatter-brained wife again?

But my mother's animus sprang from just that failure to confront the impossible. The romantic in her yearned for derring-do on behalf of her dying daughter — and herself. Cautious acceptance of disaster by her husband was not her idea of how things should be, not when the marvels of modern science and technology were at hand to transport and transform. To the emigrant of her temper, all things were possible thereafter. Once the original bonds of home were broken, who was to say where one might not fly? Early commentators on the Bible saw Eve as the lighter principle, resembling the birds, dreaming the mystery of flight. Flighty? The word holds far deeper meanings of femininity than its common derogatory usage conveys. My mother identified with the angels in her peripatetic approach to the world, conducting her own rebellion against the leaden fact that she was not a creature of the air and sky. Perhaps the neglected plane, as symbol of the solution to this death, worsened her sense of entrapment and betrayal. As agent of this process, as failed facilitator, my father was bound to shoulder the blame.

All these private tensions and emotions eddied under the surface of a complex, public, cultural drama centred on Mary's dying. News of her illness, and that she was not expected to

Flighty? In Gippsland, de Courcey O'Donovan part-Irish, part French, attempted to fly with home-made wings. No inventor, his simple wish, all his life, was to fly like the birds.

live long, activated a network of prayers and letters New Zealand-wide, prompted by the dispersed relatives and friends of the family speaking to their local religious sisters. Sisters of Everything, Mercy, Marists, Brigidines, rained letters on Greymouth hospital. A whole convent school class at Ngaio in Wellington — where she had never been — wrote her individual letters, prompted by Julia Greaney's friendship with their teacher, Sister Raphael, who herself wrote: 'You will have such merit for bearing your suffering patiently for our dear Lord. And you will do so much for sinners if you offer some suffering for them: I wish you would say a little prayer for me and for the little ones here — that they may be always good'. Always good — the fond and pious hope of those nuns who knew themselves, their direction, and what goodness was. As for Sister Raphael's pupils, their concerns bounced healthily out of their letters to this unknown Catholic playmate — tests, the holiday for the Assumption, that their basketball bladder had perished, leaving them with only rounders: religion or its trappings were too integral to mention. That professional laywoman Julia Greaney wanted Mary to offer up her sufferings for the foreign missions, the salvation of black babies, the main subject of a five-page letter. But even Julia, expert though she was, could not keep the lachrymose pious act up for long, and her stream of letters to this young friend, her god-child, whom she loved, soon moved to new fashions in hats, notably the new pan-cake style. Such hats, she thought were both ridiculous and amusing. She resolved to buy one, just for fun.

Even the loquacious Julia was eventually defeated by the actualities of the situation — impending death — lapsing into repetition, the weather, and her inability to get grapes to send. Aunts, cousins, were tongue-tied. Mary was a constant visitor to their farms. Madge wrote from Willowbridge to remind her that the prime minister, Michael Savage, was also in hospital and that her husband Sam had a 'flash' pony for her to ride next Christmas holidays. She sent a box of Pears soap. Love and loss showed through silly jokes (all the relatives joked to avoid the pain) from Annie, and impatience that her own children dodged school when they could. Yet one of those children chose the occasion of this necessity to write — these were letters of farewell — to follow up on a conversation they had once had, these fourteen-year-olds, on *when* New Zealand would be taken over by atheistic communism in the form of the left wing of the Labour Party; strange echo of the depth of the then fears of Catholic adults, as early as 1939. Most of her correspondents were more at home with football as a topic.

It was all unbearably sad. Pencilled on the backs of the envelopes of this avalanche of kind mail were lists of goodies for my mother to bring next visit: grapes, apple tart, two raspberry buns, a jug of iced water, some sausage rolls, more soap — all the ingredients of a *Girls Crystal* picnic. That was her favourite reading, that very English public school reflection of gym-dresses and hockey, clean living and the traditional honourable standards and virtues. Nothing Irish or Catholic about it. Hers was a *Girls Crystal* illness, save for its end, with flowers and mail and visitors and kind, starched nurses, plus a Catholic dimension of visiting priests and nuns, with cheerful messages of jolly good show and home soon.

Back to that Catholic dimension. The sick, especially the young, innocent sick, were deemed closer to God; indeed, in their way, privileged, a source of awe and point of reference particularly for those professionally conscious of their own duties to God. Hearing on convent grapevines of her plight, unknown nuns (who even had her name wrong) beseeched Mary to talk to the 'Little Flower', that recent French saint, the enclosed Saint Thérèse of Lisieux, who had died in 1897 at twenty-four, to be canonised in 1925, and who so dominated the Catholic female religious imagination from nearly the beginning of this century. Devotion to the Little Flower was characterised by sweetness personified, virtually always the child, with passionate devotion to 'the Little Way' (small things done right for God), constantly sick, doomed with tuberculosis, a tragic joyful paragon of virtue and prayer. Indeed the overwhelming dominance of this devotion marked the decline and fall of the Irish tradition of strong, heroic ancient saints as they were virtually abandoned by the Irish themselves, to embrace this epitome of French bourgeois emotionalism. Tough Irish spirituality, nurtured on combative, aggressive saints, set in a context of indomitable religion-inspired nationalism, narrow and self-centred in its locational base, was drowned in the sea of international popular sentiment which welled up around this extraordinary obscure Carmelite nun. Ordinary people, particularly women, the world over, identified with this strange transformation of obedience and submission and pain — and lack of human consequence — into love and joy and triumph over self. The ordinary Catholic world of little people took her for their own.

And particularly nuns, for Thérèse was one of their own, a shift in the spiritual allegiance of this powerful educative force which did much to bring to an end its former Irish character. Saint Thérèse had canonised pain and weariness, submission and oppression, frustration of the self, conditions experienced by many religious women. More, she had created a romance with sickness and death, which many of her devotees, half in love with easeful death themselves, were incapable of resisting. The spiritual lessons of the Little Flower (supernaturalising the whole of daily life) were too refined and subtle, too rooted in a foreign culture, too bound up in the lachrymose monstrosities of religious art, to be readily comprehended by many of her followers. They took them to extremes of morbidity, or imposed them as ideals of passivity or quietism on personalities naturally at variance with their introverted religious style. Some nuns were obviously in search of Little Flowers growing — or rather, dying — elsewhere.

So, Mary (Thérèse was her second name) was bombarded with the Little Flower. 'St Thérèse takes a special interest in young people who are sick', instructed Sister Carmella from Wellington. 'She likes them to offer to her, their pains and weariness for priests and souls in general. I hope you have already a great devotion to her. If not you must become friends from now on'. Friends they became — or at least to appearances this side of Heaven, associates. The reverse of Mary's memorial card featured an Italianate depiction of the Little Flower, assumed into heaven, her solemn, mournful expression a strange contrast with the happy smile Mary offered in the photograph on the other side. The banalities of popular religious art were, perhaps, some protection, insulation, from the reality of the loss of that impish grin.

More 'art', good-intentioned, no less banal: Sister Teresita composed a special poem:

> Dear Marie O'Farrell, I hear you are ill
> But you will not quarrel with God's Holy Will
> He knows what is useful to body and soul
> This is the leaven if you would reach the goal
> The goal is heaven, as you know my child,
> Where no one may enter e'en slightly defiled.
> Life is the road where we're journeying all day,
> And illness a pearl you find on the way,
> So we must embrace what has come from high
> God is the donor who always stands nigh.

But the Carmelites, Saint Thérèse's own order, went much further. They raised the possibility, even expectation, of miracles. Or failing that, of course, that better life with God, away from this tear-stained earthly exile.

Miracles? Dear, dear God, what a thought — but it must

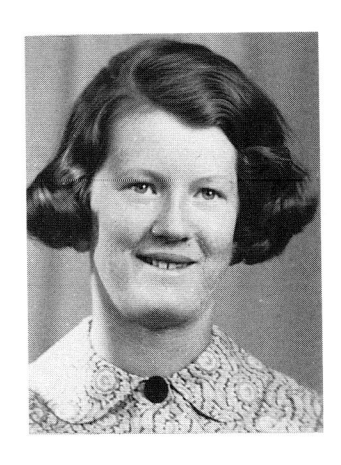

The Little Flower — on the back of Mary's memorial card.

have been present, unvoiced, in Catholic minds before the Carmelites spoke it, said the words of ultimate astonishing hope. A stream of cures had been attributed to Saint Thérèse; they were the 'shower of roses' she had promised. Then suddenly, in a weather freak virtually unprecedented in Greymouth before or since, fell snow, heavy, brilliant, pure, soft, drifting past hospital windows for Mary to report to distant correspondents, and for my mother to wonder if . . . What did this striking aberration of nature, this sparkling departure from God's ordinary order of dull Greymouth rain, portend? To the drama of anticipated death was added this white mantle, eerie, changing sights and sounds, and converting primitive colonial-uncouth Greymouth into a shadow of the Ireland of youth where snow was usual enough. Signs and wonders. Like so many Irish, my mother was open not only to the possibility of miracles, but to superstitions less worthy of credence or divine inspiration. Some years later, after that dreamed of miracle of life had been denied, our street was re-numbered, changing the number of our house from 10 to 13. This caused my mother much agitation and unease, and animus against the authorities that contrived it, at the behest, she thought, of those presently encumbered with 13, who were seeking to escape its dire influence. She contended that the change merely confirmed our house's capacity for attracting bad luck. My father was compelled to seek (unsuccessfully) a reversal of the decision, and our relations with the new possessor of number 10 were cool for some time thereafter. Eventually the number became a family joke, even with my mother, but it was a deliberate one, with an edge of consciousness, humour pitted against a vague sense of threat. Best to avoid ladders and black cats, though we had both.

The nuns were Irish, or of Irish descent; their strident, dictatorial religiosity good hearted and generous, but warped by their departure from the tough, ascetic spirituality of their national origins upon their voyages into the bottomless and dangerous psychological waters that eddied around the cult of the Little Flower. That name disguised the essential foreignness of the concept of Saint Thérèse of Lisieux, whose accents and pronunciation so baffled colonial tongues. Curiously, the French-derived order of the Marist Brothers was very different in its Australasian manifestation. They were all colonials at that time and place and, to various degrees, family friends and visitors. Brother Philip's pet name for Mary was 'Wonderful'; hers for him was 'Beautiful'. His hospital letters were full of fun, 'cheergerms' he said. Here's a specimen: Mary was not as

Good luck? The site of 13 Puketahi Street is now occupied by a children's playground.

bad as the little girl who swallowed a nib. 'She had to drink ink. Yes, ink. Why? To make her right (write), of course'. He offered good advice 'People make themselves sick by worrying'. And he described to her his amazement at the making of toffee-apples (toffee-coated apples with a stick through the core to hold), a sticky delicacy for fund-raising bazaars he had never seen before his transfer from Greymouth to Christchurch. Ah, innocent days of a remote Greymouth world before the invasion of the money-making toffee apple, harbinger of so many of civilisation's other discontents. Had Mary ever seen one, he queried. Probably not. He knew her favourite colour — red, and not blue. He reminded her of his teasing her, and her fits of laughter — 'and then run, run, and run, until you got the stitch'. This was a younger Mary, before he had left, red-haired, a wild and speedy runner, a passing hazard to the elderly, a flash of joy to the light and clear of heart, as Brother Philip was. No diatribe here on the agonies of Saint Thérèse or the offering up of suffering, or on submission to God's holy will. One religious line only in a long letter: 'pray to our dear Lord and His Holy Mother to look after you'.

What was real in all this correspondence was what reflected a colonial childhood: running, toffee-apples, perishing basketball bladders. Real, too, was the sense of solidarity with family and neighbours. What was real in its religion was not its morbid French gloss, but its basic, matter of fact, strength of faith. Thus, from Aunt Annie ('I'm still as fat as ever — 13.3 only') a warm and hasty note, as complex in its impulse as it was simple in its sentiment' 'God love you Mary. Say a Hail Mary for me. I'm a bad fellow and don't pray much'. Annie, like so many others, was beset by her large and unruly family, whose disruptive doings she confided to Mary. Colonial diet, sunlight, space, freedom from drudgery, made Australasian childhood by this time a much more exuberant experience. Without the supervisory assistance (or cramping interference) of grandparents, together with the demands of what still amounted to some kind of pioneering, parents were often compelled to let children, like cattle, run wild. Or free, and independent, depending on one's perspective. Failing the structures of grandparents or close family living, neighbours and friends became important social props, in ordinary living and emergencies — and these props were chosen not by shared race or religion, but more by the accidents of proximity and workplace. So, Mary's mail included letters of real affection and concern from neighbours' children, young adults now in distant cities, but remembering the friend they had known well.

Friend. All these letters were directed to a young adult, not a child, with allowances perhaps, and a touch of childhood nostalgia in some, but no condescension, nor juvenile stereotyping. Mary was Mary, an individual very much herself, already an accepted part of a community, which valued its own elements and instinctively reacted in a basic human way to what it saw as a threat to diminish its existence. The colonial settlement saw itself as pitted against the facts of its newness and came close together to affirm that it would not be swept away, nor would its roots die without struggle.

What was Irish about this? The heritage of faith of its Catholic elements (the pious overlay was increasingly French, international), a few children's names — Kieran, Brendan, Patrick (family names, not assertively Irish) — some of the religious personnel, but the junior ranks of that were increasingly colonial. So, by this time, the end of the 1930s, not much above ground: the foundations were solid Irish, but the cultural building proceeding on them, such as it was, was colonial.

The drama — imagined aeroplanes, yearned for miracles, a visitation of snow, letters, messages, enquiries, all in the shadow of impending world war — lasted a bare month: Mary died on 26 August 1939. In flowed the clichéd condolences. 'Deepest sympathy in your sad bereavement', it being first on the list of the Post Office's packaged messages; but what else was there to say? (I suppose the hordes of kind callers uttered much the same: it was a community never lavish with words.) On the fringe of the clichéd signals conveying the desolation of family and friends, there were quaintly stern, formal motions from tiny Labour Party branches, even from fourth-grade football clubs that my brother had played against in rough mining townships.

Not a reference to God or religion in any of them, but every evidence that my family had moved out into a community well beyond anything Irish, or Irish colonial, and that that community was determined to acknowledge their — and its — loss. Mary was not Irish, and in that curious reversal of loyalties and origins that such colonial children imposed, by their vivid fact, nor were my parents Irish for this purpose or occasion. They were bereaved human beings, being comforted and consoled by a community far looser and fragmented than any they had left; but one conscious of the elements that made it and instinctively anxious to affirm that basic human solidarity, beyond race or religion, that allowed it to survive and operate. Marooned on the outer edge of colonial space, like an outpost in some desert, they stuck together against the common enemy of all men, all women — death. And they would both acknowledge and repudiate its dominion in unison.

There was no 'wake'. Those I attended as a child were few, and were sober body-viewing and prayer-sessions rather than anything resembling the traditional Irish occasion. There was only one attempt to pull the occasion back into a traditional Irish framework, that of Father Matt Fogarty, then in Geraldine. He linked Mary's death with that of my mother's mother, aged eighty, in Borrisokane a few months before. It was a meaningless linkage; the one was agonisingly real, the other was not, merely a distant report. 'In the midst of your tears', he wrote, 'you have many real consolations. They are all gone to join the Saints of Ireland in their celestial home beyond the miraculous skies'. The Saints of Ireland? Father Fogarty was out of date with his allegiances. Mary was in the colonial and French sections of Heaven. And he issued, as was his habit, instructions to fit the occasion: 'No tears above her grave be shed but sweetest flowers be flung, for blest are those who pass away in childhood's happy years'. But there were ample tears, and for years to come. My mother's official line was that God and the Little Flower wanted her loved one. Every personal letter assured her that Mary was an angel happy in Heaven, an innocent advocate for them with God. But my mother was not Job, the model offered by Brother Philip. Nor did she appreciate the reiteration by nuns that life was very short and that she would soon be re-united with Mary. On the contrary life without Mary was drab, lonely — and long. As indeed it was to be — thirty years.

So Mai escaped again from that dreadful barbarous Coast, that had taken her beloved, this time to stay with friends at Wright's Bush, near Invercargill. Perhaps she had thought the Coast's response to her grief harsh and distant: it was merely the colonial style, non-intrusive, tongue-tied. In Wright's Bush she received, via letters sent on, a whiff of the true Ireland, or at least her Ireland, hard-hearted and self-absorbed condolences from her Irish brother and sisters, far tougher propositions than herself, addicted to inter-family quarrels and no-speaks, and possessing aggressive views on anything from hairdressers to birth control. Their letters did not advert to the death of their mother. Of the Irish family only the two sons and their wives had been present at her funeral, which the Nenagh *Guardian* reported as 'of very large dimensions'. The several daughters still in Ireland did not attend. The one who had five children informed Mai that her only son 'will remain so, as I'm going to have a rest now for a while. I'm sick & tired of having children every year' — cheering sentiments to convey to the bereaved. Nieces wrote banal letters from hospitals in England, where they were employed in a tradition that had been established in the war Mai had left behind in 1914. These Irish letters were steeped in mean gossip, and in assurances, as from her brother, that Mary was far better 'away from the wicked world. As it's but a vale of worry and trouble. Everybody meets trouble at some time. I have met my share ... I take it all as the will of God ... I hope now you will not worry over your loss'. And again the refrain: 'It only means a short time for us all'.

Obviously, the sorrows of Ireland, as registered by her brothers and sisters, were on too grand a scale for Mai's petty grief to be of much account. And the constant self-pity, the passive invoking of the will of God, and paeans to the brief vanity of all human existence, all went against the vigorous colonial spirit, and the character of those lay Irish who had gone to the colonies. The same letter of condolence from one of her brothers — or rather of instructions to be like me and not worry about it — reported that her sister Chris, who was then visiting England and Ireland, was urging him and other members of the family to emigrate: 'And I am inclined to go if we knew how things are'. How things are? What a question. To ask the question was to refuse to go, because it could be answered only by going to find out for oneself. The timid stayed home, as her brother did, and accepted 'things' as they were, and were long known to be. Like God's will — though how that could be known with such consuming arrogance, and meek submission is a mystery indeed. But the phrase was only an evasion, an excuse for inaction, an avoidance of human involvement.

The Irish family's reaction to Mary's death and my mother's grief seems callous. It was natural enough, given that Mai had died to them many years before, made her choices, taken her chance and left them to theirs. By definition she must have been, until now, better off, and what had happened had evened up the scales only a bit. Besides, while the death of a child in Ireland was a sad thing, the social and cultural context was very different. These Irish had no comprehension that the death of the colonial child struck at the very heart of the migration enterprise, destroyed what it sought most to build, not a fortune, or some holding of land (the images which dominated the home Irish view of the emigrant world), but new people, that unique and very personal creation. With the immigrant's child died the investment of human dreams and ambitions, generous ambitions which went beyond the self to

The colonial family, with Mary, and plus Paddy as photographer, about 1936.

the launching of a new generation which was not Irish, or at least not in any of the old ways, but a human venture which was exciting and absolutely theirs. Unspoken musings these, high-flown, but closer to the heart rather than the mind came the matter of company: in an unfamiliar lonely world the child was companion, society, guide. Oscar Handlin, in his *Children of the Uprooted* contends, with American reference, that such offspring always 'grew up in strangeness', becoming Americans, with a widening gulf between themselves and parents. But this postulates that parents remained committed to the old society and had not opted for the new. Paddy and Mai, in so far as the facts of origin would permit, had opted for the new, and the relationship with their daughter was close and easy. If problems were to come — and their sons' experience suggests not — they were in a future death had denied.

Despite her avowals that Mary was with God and the Little Flower, Mai deeply resented that Mary had been taken from her, her growing friend, her — unthinkable in Ireland — Girl Guide as well as Child of Mary, an easy colonial duality. The aeroplane illusion took hold. Paddy was bitter too. In December he clipped from the local paper a report of the convent school's production of the sacred drama 'Catherine of Alexandra' (nothing Irish about that). Mary was to have taken part. 'Did any of her school mates remember?' he wrote. An avenue closed, a future dimension of parental enjoyment cut off. But Mai's was the far greater loss. In the colonies each family built its own world from nothing, an achievement neither possible nor necessary in Ireland. For those first in each line, this was a prodigy of resource and courage, normal, matter of fact as it may seem. Mary's death annihilated much of Mai's comfort and dreams — no girl, no female companionship, no future marriage, condemned alone for ever in the rough world of men, on that barbarous Coast, the closest women kind neighbours, and those curious single relatives, intrusive domineering women who played bossy male roles — her sister, Julia Greaney.

And so Mary's room became, not, thank God, a shrine, but a part of life closed off. Her room was shut, door always closed, cleaned and dusted but never used, home to the bereaved dolls and teddy bears. Mothballed clothes filled the wardrobe, foremost the Girl Guide uniform: presumably she had been buried in the Child of Mary cloak and veil. It was a very small house, but it was twenty years before guests impinged on it and then only indirectly. I slept there, while they had my room. It was a happy place to sleep in, still and at peace, like a good death.

But death it was, and from behind that closed door, a strange neutrality at the corner of one's eye as one passed, death slipped out on Sundays to rule the atmosphere, structures and timetables of the house for long after. Gone was the frequent family photography. And the bush picnics. Sunday was mass, dinner, and the cemetery visit. Kennedy's bus ran a cemetery service, out at 2, back at 4.30. The cemetery was about two miles from the house, on a low cliff above the Tasman sea, with a startling view along the coast on a clear day, down to Mount Cook. It, too, was a happy place, breezy, open to sea and sky, with an occasional eerie cranny. It possessed a confusion of adult impacts to subdue a small boy, carrying the flowers, along with his mother (Paddy, father, seldom came). There were monuments to local disasters, the greatest, the deaths of sixty-five men in the Brunner mine in 1896, sculpted replicas of small angelic children (Mary's grave was plain), ruin and weeds, and the sweet smell of decay as wreaths and flowers rotted on new graves and old graves collapsed slowly under the weight of the continual deluge of West Coast rain. It was sociable enough coming and going, as many others kept their Sunday appointment with the dead, as one might visit hospital or home, bringing flowers. Little talking, nothing loud, converse with both dead and living, and with God, the mixture expected, accepted, understood. Children not unruly, in Sunday best, the place and its strange smell sufficient to keep them quiet. Dotted across the scene were those kneeling in silent prayer as we did ourselves, rough concrete on knees, both affirmation of the welcome pains of life, and penance in preparation for death. Then home for tea, happy, shriven, after visiting Mary, the family again somehow completed. Then, of course, Rosary, Sermon and Benediction.

So the dead reached back into life, demanding their quiet due, and linking their world with ours. Nothing morbid about it, it was more normal than neglect. Something Irish about it, or was it merely the legacy of a belief widely Catholic, Christian, international? Surely international: the visit to the cemetery is a substantial section of the classic treatment by Philippe Aries of western attitudes to death *The Hour of Our Death,* and the Greymouth pilgrimage a tiny copy of such visitations worldwide. Yet, if the practice was universal, the cultures who followed it had their own beliefs and reasons and emphases. At its European romantic height, the cult of the cemetery had connotations of both preserving the sacred and indulgence of nostalgia. It was the place where the living went to remember. And so in distant Greymouth. But there, and in a thousand other graveyards where the Irish communed with their dead, was the faintest echo of that Celtic idea that had captivated Proust, captive souls awaiting the liberation of recognition. It was a traditional Irish notion that harmonised with the Christian continuum of earthly life, then purgatory, then heaven. So, that difference in cultural emphasis.

Mai's visits were not for remembrance, they were visits — to pray, but also to converse. The grave was the appropriate ritual centre; the visit, the proper ceremonial occasion and form, as it was in general society. For, it was fact above all other earthly facts, that those who had died were alive and with us still, elsewhere. They were still what they were before, daughters,

Without Mary.

The view from the family grave — appropriately, across the plot that was colonial home to some of their closest friends and acquaintance; Irish priests and nuns.

friends, none of that altered by being with God. Would it not be wrong to ignore or neglect them, even if one could, inhuman not to include them in our lives? Was this Irish? No. In so far as it proceeded logically from the basic postulates of Christian faith, it was merely common sense. But also yes: Mai's faith was originally Irish; what it was after a quarter of a century in New Zealand (she always preferred the Marist Order and her son became a Dominican) is an open question. The other party to the cemetery conversations was not Irish: Mary belonged where she lay and no one thought otherwise. Mai? Those images of flight. She had once flown, in 1914, knew what flying was like, knew its cost. She hankered for it, not Ireland. Her ground was with Mary, the colonial, with the tiny part of a remote world she had herself created. By her death in 1970, it was merely a distant and irrelevant accident that she had come from Ireland long before. Few knew it, nobody cared: she, like Mary, came from Greymouth.

A long bridge is the image such emigration conjures up, a bridge on which Mai's and Paddy's journeying had taken them to the other side. There they were increasingly committed, and increasingly it ceased to matter from where they had come. Their children were colonial Irish, by matter of the fact of parentage and residuum of environment, but little else. They were colonial by allegiance, natural assumption, and, when they were forced to think about it, by clear preference. Colonial Ireland did not die with Mary, too soon — the 1930s were still a space of life between, and the bridge still stood, a strong enough structure still. Nor, half a century later, with the death of Tim in 1980, was it quite dead, almost casually as if his passing had not occurred, inadvertent: no — bits of the structure remained. But without doubt or question, colonial Ireland dies with me and with my like — the transitionals.

Transitional to what? To a land of cultural chaos and the walking dead? To fragments, and ghettoes of uncommunicating materialist minds? Or, are we to break the spell that immobilises the past, liberate its colonial, pioneering greatness from the shackles of its sins and negligences, and return it to life with us?

BIBLIOGRAPHICAL NOTE

This guide does not repeat details of sources adequately identified in the body of the text. The O'Farrell family materials cited, remain within the author's possession.

AUSTRALIA

Substantial bibliographies are appended to the author's three books *The Irish in Australia* (1987), *Letters from Irish Australia 1825-1929* (1984), and *The Catholic Church and Community, An Australian History* (1985), all published by New South Wales University Press in Sydney. Since 1987, the following relevant general material has appeared; entries on the Irish in James Jupp (ed) *The Australian People*, Angus & Robertson (1988); *A New History of Ireland* Oxford 1989) Vol.V, 'Ireland under the Union'. I. 1801-70, W.E. Vaughan (ed), with chapters on emigration by David Fitzpatrick, and the 'Irish in Australia and New Zealand' by Patrick O'Farrell; Edmund Campion *Australian Catholics* (Penguin 1987); Colm Kiernan (ed) *Australia & Ireland 1788-1988. Bicentenary Essays* (Dublin 1986); O. MacDonagh and W.F. Mandle (eds) *Ireland and Irish Australia: Studies in Cultural and Political History* (Croom Helm 1986) and *Irish-Australian Studies* (Canberra, A.N.U. 1989). Several Irish journals produced Australian Bicentennial numbers. Among them were; *Familia. Ulster Genealogical Review* Vol.2, No.3, 1987; *The Old Limerick Journal*, No.23, Spring 1988; and *Journal of the Cork Historical and Archaeological Society*, Vol.XCIII, No.252, Jan-Dec 1988.

NEW ZEALAND

Little has been written generally on the Irish in New Zealand, but see D.H. Akenson, *Half the World from Home. Perspectives on the Irish in New Zealand, 1840-1950* (forthcoming Victoria University Press). Both Australia and New Zealand are part of the reference in Akenson's *Small Differences. Irish Catholics and Irish Protestants.* (McGill-Queens Univ. Press 1988). Michael Bellam, whose 'The Irish in New Zealand' appeared in *Familia* Vol.2, No.1 (1985) has projected a book on that subject. *Familia*, Vol.2, No.5 (1989) is a special issue on the Irish in New Zealand. See also R.P. Davis, *Irish Issues in New Zealand Politics 1868-1922* (Univ. of Otago 1974) and David McGill, *The Lion and the Wolfhound: The Irish Rebellion on the New Zealand Goldfields* (Grantham House, N.Z. 1990).

IRELAND

The author's two books on Anglo-Irish relations, *Ireland's English Question. Anglo-Irish Relations 1540-1970* (Batsford, London 1971) and, *England and Ireland since 1800* (Oxford 1975) form the basis for his approach to the Irish background. The best recent general histories are R.F. Foster, *Modern Ireland 1800-1972* (Penguin 1988) and for the twentieth century, J.J. Lee, *Ireland 1912-1985. Politics and Society* (Cambridge 1989).

CHAPTER 2
KINGS DEPOSED

An earlier version of this chapter, appropriately source-noted, was given on 2 October 1987 as the University of New England's Annual Russel Ward Lecture in Australian History.

For the Irish background to this and other chapters see my *Ireland's English Question*. Professor Robert Reece has written extensively on Frank MacNamara, see, for example, 'The Convict as Poet' in *Ireland's Own,* Jan. 1988. For the 'Hidden Ireland' concept applied to Australia, see my 'In Search of the Hidden Ireland'. *Journal of Religious History,* Vol.12, No.3, 1983. For Edward Ryan and the Irish in south-western New South Wales, see Malcolm Campbell 'The kingdom of the Ryans: aspects of Irish Australian society in south west New South Wales, 1816–1880' Ph.D. thesis, University of New South Wales, 1989.

CHAPTER 3
IDIOCY AND DEVILMENT

Bruce S. Elliott's book is *Irish Migrants in the Canadas. A New Approach* (Belfast 1988). For treatment of female migration relevant to the time of my mother's departure, see Janet A. Nolan *Ourselves Alone: Women's emigration from Ireland 1885—1920* (Kentucky Univ. Press 1989). For Tipperary background, W. Nolan and T.G. McGrath (eds) *Tipperary: History and Society: Interdisciplinary Essays on the History of an Irish County* (Dublin 1985). W.F. Mandle's book, *The Gaelic Athletic Association and Irish Nationalist Politics 1884-1924* (Dublin 1987) covers the hurling context.

The history of Waimate County and Borough is detailed by William Greenwood, *Te Waimatemate* (Timaru n.d. c1983). Greymouth's history tends to be treated in the wider context of the Westland province. The classic work is E.I. Lord, *Old Westland* (Christchurch 1939), but R.A. Kay (ed) *Westland's Golden Century 1860-1960* (Greymouth 1960) is more diverse and up-to-date, at a popular level. At the scholarly level see the standard work of P.R. May, *The West Coast Gold Rushes* (Christchurch 1962) and the six excellent essays ranging to 1918, *Miners and Militants. Politics in Westland,* edited by P.R. May (University of Canterbury 1975).

CHAPTER 4
PRAYER-WORLDS

See Catriona Clear, *Nuns in Nineteenth Century Ireland* (Dublin 1987), and for the best example of a case history of nuns in Australia, Madeleine Sophie McGrath, *These women? Women religious in the history of Australia — the Sisters of Mercy Parramatta 1888-1988* (N.S.W. Univ. Press 1989). Barry Gustafson's biography of Michael Joseph Savage is entitled *From the cradle to the grave* (Penguin N.Z. 1988). Devotion to Mary in Ireland is surveyed by Peter O'Dwyer, O. Carm. *Mary: A History of Devotion in Ireland* (Dublin 1988). The story of Matt Talbot is accessibly told in John Saward, *Perfect Fools. Folly for Christ's Sake in Catholic and Orthodox Spirituality* (Oxford 1980).

CHAPTER 5
— AND PRIESTS

See Kevin Condon, c.m. *The Missionary College of All Hallows, 1842-1891* (Dublin 1986). There is, as yet, no history of the Dominican Order in Australia. For the Augustinians, see Michael A. Endicott, O.S.A. *The Augustinians in Far North Queensland, 1883-1941* (Brookvale N.S.W 1988). Jules Lemire's observations are from the translation by Sam Boland, C.SS.R., part of which, in quotation and paraphrase, forms the basis of 'A Liberal Catholic looks at Australia' *Australasian Catholic Record* Vol.LX, No.3, July 1983. Achille Lemire's remarks are a translation by Clare O'Farrell from his *From Ireland to Australia. Memories and Impressions of Travel* (Lille 1890). The quotation about the IRA is taken from P.R. Hay 'Labor vacates the bush. The eclipse of working class values in Victoria's Western District' *Labour History* No.54, May 1988.

CHAPTER 6
COLONIAL IRISH: THEMES

There is an excellent history of the Catholic diocese of Christchurch (which included Greymouth) 1840-1987 — Michael O'Meeghan, S.M. *Held Firm by Faith* (Christchurch Catholic Diocese, 1988), and a relevant unpublished thesis, Neil Vaney, 'The Dual Tradition, Irish Catholics and French priests in New Zealand: The West Coast expereince' M.A. thesis, University of Canterbury, 1977. See also Joanna Bourke 'Women and poultry in Ireland 1891-1914' *Irish Historical Studies,* Vol.XXV, No.99, May 1987.

CHAPTER 7
VARIATIONS: THOSE OTHER TRADITIONS

For Ulster Protestant emigration and settlement world-wide, see Rory Fitzpatrick, *God's Frontiersmen. The Scots–Irish Epic.* (Peribo, Chatswood N.S.W. 1989). For Australia in the period discussed, see Richard Broome, *Treasure in Earthen Vessels. Protestant Christianity in New South Wales Society 1900-1914* (Queensland Univ. Press 1980). The additional Andrews family papers used here are held, together with the Andrews papers used previously in *Letters from Irish Australia,* in the Public Record Office of Northern Ireland, Belfast.

Hickey's activities are widely covered in New Zealand labour history writing, including my own. The account here is derived from the latest source, Erik Olssen, *The Red Feds. Revolutionary Industrial Unionism and the New Zealand Federation of Labour 1908-1913* (Auckland O.U.P. 1988), which has an extensive bibliography. The history of the Duracks is given in Dame Mary Durack's two splendid books *Kings in Grass Castles* (London 1959) and *Sons in the Saddle* (London 1983).

Vincent Buckley's books are *Cutting Green Hay* (Penguin 1983) and *Memory Ireland* (Penguin 1985). For the New Zealand Marist Brothers, see P. Gallagher, *The Marist Brothers in New Zealand, Fiji and Samoa, 1876-1976* (Christchurch 1976). The W. F. Corrigan Papers 1900-1969, on Irish republicanism in Melbourne from 1920s to the 1940s, are held in the National Library, Canberra, and — in part — the Mitchell Library, Sydney. 'Michael Davitt Forrest MSC [1883-1970]' is the subject of an article by John F. McMahon, M.S.C. in *Annals* Vol.100, No.4, May 1989. For Albert Dryer, see Patrick O'Farrell 'Dreaming of Distant Revolution: A.T. Dryer and the Irish National Association, Sydney 1915-16', *Journal of the Royal Australian Historical Society* Vol.69, Pt.3, Dec. 1983.

See John Hutchinson *The Dynamics of Cultural Nationalism. The Gaelic Revival and the Creation of the Irish Nation State* (London 1987). The Hanrahan letters are in the National Libraries of Australia and Ireland. The politics of the Grey district workers are studied in two unpublished theses of the University of Canterbury, P.J. O'Farrell 'The Workers in Grey District Politics, 1865-1913' (1956) later expanded into 'Vanguard in Politics. Labour in the Grey District 1865-1913' (unpublished Ms, 1965), and Len Richardson 'The Workers and Grey District politics during wartime, 1914-1918' (1969). As a relatively small and less successful venture, the *Brian Boru* gets only passing mention in J.H.M. Salmon's *A History of Gold Mining in New Zealand* (Wellington 1963). John O'Hara's *A Mug's Game* (N.S.W Univ. Press 1988) is a history of gaming and betting in Australia. Bede Nairn's biography of Lang is *The 'Big Fella'. Jack Lang and the Australian Labor Party 1891-1949* (Melbourne Univ. Press 1986). B.A. Santamaria's memoir is *Against the Tide* (Melbourne 1981), Jack Kane's, *Exploding the Myths. The political memoirs of Jack Kane* (Sydney 1989).

See Monica Furlong, *Thérèse of Lisieux* (Virago, 1987) and Guy Gaucher, *The Passion of Thérèse of Lisieux* (English translation, St Paul Publications, Homebush, 1989).

CHAPTER 8
THE FIRST GENERATION

CHAPTER 9
DREAMS OF IRELANDS

CHAPTER 10
POLITICS

CHAPTER 11
DEATH

INDEX

Aborigines xv, 2, 67, 107, 108
accountancy 259
Act of Union (1800) xv
Adelaide 250, 254; *see also* South Australia
Aden 165
Adoration of the Blessed Sacrament 77
Advocate (Melbourne) 285
aeroplanes 116, 173, 287–8, 294, 298
Age (Melbourne) 231
All Hallows College Drumcondra, 98–9, 106, 116–18, 127, 132
Alphonsus, Sister Mary 139
Amazon river 138
America; American xiv, xix, xxi–xxii, 2, 15, 23, 34, 41, 67, 98, 136, 160–1, 163, 177, 180, 190, 200–4, 216, 228, 232–3, 234, 261, 264, 275, 297; Latin, 138, 270
An Phoblacht (Dublin) 227, 231
Andrews, David 167, 170, 176
Andrews family 42, 165–7, 170–2
Andrews, Hugh 167, 172, 176
Andrews, Jack 172–4, 176
Andrews, James 167, 171–2, 175–6
Andrews, John 167–8, 175–6
Andrews, Susie 172–4
Andrews, Suzannah 167, 175, 177
Andrews, William 165, 167–8, 170–2, 175–7
Anglicanism xiv, 100, 119
anglicisation 60, 61, 84, 121, 135, 136
Anglo-Celtic xxix
Anglo-Irish xv, xvii, 5, 44, 111, 170
Anglo-Irish war 225, 234, 243
Agnes, Sister 54
Annals of the Four Masters 3
anthems, national 212, 214–15, 226, 229
Apostleship of Prayer 87–8
apparitions 93, 95
Araluen, NSW 90
Arch-confraternity of the Blessed Sacrament 87–8

architecture 129, 196, 267
Aries, Philippe 299
Argentina 23, 137
Armagh 27
Arno, NZ 48, 143
Arthurs Pass NZ, 48
Asdee 13
assimilation xiv, xxii
Associated Catholic and Irish Organisations of Victoria 232–3
Aubrey, Pere 155
Auckland, University of 221
Augustinian order 106, 109
Austria 195
Australasian Catholic Record 132
Australian Imperial Forces 172, 224, 229
Avon River, NZ, 39

Bairnsdale, Vic. 176
Ballantynes 31, 48
Ballarat, Vic. 111, 113, 167, 229–30, 234
Ballinderry 26, 27, 28, 43, 50, 52, 54, 99
Ballychroghan farm 167, 170, 172
Bangor 167
Barnawartha, Vic. 168
Barrytown, NZ 155
basketball 283, 289
Bastic, Paddy 94–5, 224
Bath, Lord 3
Bathurst, NSW 146
Beban family 149
Bega, NSW 108, 116, 117
Belfast 43, 119
Benalla, Vic. 82, 83
Bendigo, Vic. 13
Benedictine order 106, 107–8, 235
Bible 76, 136, 165, 176, 216, 288
'big house' 44, 47
Birr 50, 57, 58
birth control 295–6

Blackball, NZ 142, 261; strike (1908), 260
Blainey, Geoffrey 16
Bogan, Peter 224
Bolshevism 275
bookkeeping 80
Boorowa NSW 124
Borrisokane 26, 41, 50, 53, 54, 55, 58, 59, 61, 71, 74, 80, 87, 99, 186, 194–5, 241, 295; kurling team 38, 80, 139
Botanical Gardens, Sydney 95
Botany Bay 5
Boy Scouts 229
boxing 67, 114
Boyle, Willie 177
Bracken, Thomas 43, 212
Braidwood, NSW 90
Brearley, Mike 248
Brian Boru Gold Dredging Company 267–8
Brisbane 139, 227
Britain; British xv, xxi, 5, 9, 25, 26, 105, 106, 136, 162, 200–1, 207, 208, 215, 21 223, 224, 225, 231, 243–4; army 5, 60; crown 247–8
Brixton prison 227, 244
Brunner, NZ 147, 148, 261, 299
Brunswick, Vic. 232
Buchan, John 136
Buckley, Vincent 199–205
Buenos Aires 110, 114
Burchett, Wilfred 180
Bustard, Arthur 150–1
Byrnes family 44–7
Byrnes Peter, 43–7, 80
Byrnes Sam, 47, 289

Cahill government 277
Cahirdaniel 183
Calcutta 110, 138
California xxi, 18
The Callahans and the Murphys 232

305

Calwell, A.A. 230, 232
Canada 23, 41–2, 74
Canberra 207, 210, 211, 216, 218, 264
Canterbury, South 23, 24, 28, 32, 33, 34, 41, 43, 48, 74, 140, 142–3, 143, 152, 155–6, 157
Canticles, Book of 140
Cape Province 114
card-playing 48
Carew, Dean 154
Carleton, William 48
Carlow 108, 124
Carmella, Sister 291
Carmelite order 290–2
Carnegie Public Library, Greymouth 136
Carroll, Bishop James 277–9
Casement, Roger 224
Castle Hill rebellion (1804) 5, 10
Castlebar 124
Castlegregory 249
catechism xxiii, 125
Catholicism; Catholic church; Catholics xxv, xvi–xvii, xix, xxii, xxiii, 7, 9, 13, 20, 42, 47, 76–7, 84, 90, 92, 95, 102, 136, 157, 170–1, 175, 176, 177, 184–5, 190, 196, 202, 205, 206, 214, 220–1, 231–4, 235–7, 245–7, 254, 257, 264, 274–9, 281, 290–4, 298–301
Catholic Action 276
Catholic Church in Australia, The xiv
Catholic Federation 232
Catholic Truth Society publications: Irish 71–4; Australian 111
Catholic Women's Social Guild 233
cattle fairs 217
Celtic belief xxiii, xxvi, xxix, 299
Celtic Club, Melbourne 233–4
cemeteries 281, 298–300
censorship 220, 227, 232–3
Charleville, Qld. 119
children 191–3, 220, 283, 285–301
Children of Mary 87, 88, 298
Chile 137
China; Chinese xxix, 15, 72, 253
Christchurch, NZ 31, 39, 43, 48, 53, 71, 155, 248, 293
Christian Brothers 260
Clancy, Father 117
Clare 95
'Clare Hill' 95
Clark, C.M.H. 9
Cleary family 57, 61
Cleary, Paddy 57
Clonmacnoise 72
coal mining 48, 140 213, 261, 165, 167
Cohen, Judge 95
Collins, Neal 254
colonial; language 58, process of becoming xiv–xv–xvii, xviii, xx, xxv, xxvi, xxvii, xxix, xxx, 52–3, 57, 95, 103, 106–7, 109, 114, 116, 120, 123–4, 128, 132, 136–8, 142, 144, 145–7, 154, 157, 174, 195–7, 199–205, 206–8, 215, 220–1, 223, 236–9, 248–50, 281, 287, 293–4, 296; term xvii–xix
commercial colleges 80, 260
Common Cause 114
communism 114, 132, 231, 261–4, 278, 289
concerts 214, 215, 221, 227, *see also* music, songs

Condon, Father Kevin 116
Congresses, Australasian Catholic 132
Connell, Father Frank, S.J. 251
Connolly, James 180, 263, 276
Connolly, S.J. 10
Conrahan, Mr 88
Conroy, Peter 13
conscription 132, 254, 263, 265, 278
convents 58, 60, 82, 290–2; *see also* nuns
convicts xxvii, 2, 3, 5, 10, 12, 15–18; emancipation 5, 17
Coonamble NSW, 117, 126
Cooper, James Fenimore 136
Corcoran family 5
Cork 12, 50, 227, 244, 276; fun of 36, 57, 138
Corkery, Daniel 10, 12, 15, 16
corn 258
Coronation medal 266
correspondence 168–70, 281–3, 288–94
Corrigan, W.F 226–7, 231, 235
Corrigan, W.J 235
Costello, Mick 28
Crago and Tremain 146
cricket 214, 248
Cromwell, Oliver 7, 105, 210
Crosin, Mr 66
Cullen, Cardinal Paul 84, 98, 108, 126, 278
Cullen, L.M 10
Cunningham, Philip 5
Cunard line 44
Curtain, Paddy 148
cycling 214, 263, 273–4

dairying 258
Dalgetys 34
Dalton's flour mills 146
Daly, Mick 261
dancing 55, 56–8, 60, 82–3, 84, 87, 116, 193, 220, 227, 229, 231
Darcy, Les 114,
Davis, Thomas 139
Davitt, Michael 235
death xxiii, 47, 57, 73, 87, 88, 163, 167, 175–6, 272, 281–301
Deere, Terry 267
Democratic Labor Party 180, 277
Denniston NZ, 142
Depression 160, 260, 267
de Valera, Eamon 111–13, 114, 207, 224
de Vere, Aubrey 132
Dillon Peter 137
domestic economy 146, 155–7, 194
Dominican order 89, 99–100, 102, 185, 187, 196, 250, 300
Donnellan, Arthur 267
Donnellan family 263–4
Dooley, James 276
Dowling, Patrick J. xxi—xxii, 8
Doyle, Dr Willie 251
Doyle, Jack 263–4, 267
dreams 18, 67, 107–8, 149, 167–8, 183, 185, 199–238, 248, 249, 252, 296
dress 36, 39–41, 229
dressmaking 28, 73
drinking 35, 47, 48, 52–3, 63, 66, 69, 73, 74, 92, 147–8, 149, 154, 188, 216, 218, 228, 232,
Dronke, Maria 185

Dryer, Dr Albert 199, 206, 225, 231, 235, 251, 254
Dublin 10, 38, 41, 50, 55, 61, 98, 108, 109, 114, 123, 135, 179, 186, 187–8, 190, 191–3, 205, 210, 217, 231, 250, 252, 253, 254
Dublin Opinion 103, 136
Duggan, Eileen 139, 184–5
Duhig, Archbishop Sir James 247
du Maurier, Daphne 87
Dunedin 287
Durack family 62, 182, 183
Durack, J. W 184
Durack, Dame Mary 145, 182, 184
Durack, Michael Patrick 183–4
Durack, Patsy 182–3, 185, 187
Dwyer family 5

earthquakes 51, 151
education, higher 259–60
Edward VII 184
Egbert, Brother 205–224, 235, 236
elections 265–6; Grey (1913) 260
Elliott, Bruce S. 41–2
emigrants; emigration; dreams of 48, 50, 51, *see also* dreams; process and phases xxvi–xxviii, 2, 23–8, 31–2, 34–35, 41–2, 44, 54, 55, 57, 60, 62, 69, 71, 84, 102, 135–8, 161–3, 167–70, 176–7, 186–7, 248–50, 254, 281–3, 288, 296–7, 300–1; schemes 3, 32, 34, 41–2; as traitors xxi, 16, 59; *see also* immigrants
Emmet, Robert 205, 227
employment 28, 48, 53, 57, 95, 223, 226, 259–60, 267; *see also* work
Endicott, Father Michael 106, 107
England; English xix, xx, xxix, 2, 3, 3, 6, 7, 9, 12, 13–15, 16, 18, 20, 27, 39, 55, 61, 66, 73, 74, 76, 94, 104, 197, 110–11, 124, 126, 136, 139, 142, 157, 160, 183–4, 193, 210, 214, 237, 242, 244, 250, 253, 254, 255, 270, 290
Enlightenment xv
entertainment 148–9
Euromanga, Qld. 64,m 65, 66
Europe, Europeans xv, xxvi, 7, 20, 121, 126, 185, 195–6, 249, 299
Evatt, Dr H.V. 276
Egypt 165

Faber, Father 196, 237
Fabian, Sister 80
family; families; Irish 5, 6, 13, 15, 20, 25, 32–3, 41–3, 44, 47–8, 50, 61–3, 97, 185–97, 202, 250–2, 295–7; colonial 62–3, 113–14, 140–2, 157–63, 187, 189, 202–3, 249, 251, 269–70, 283, 287–301
famine 25, 121, 163; Famine, Great (1845–50) xxvi, 3, 41, 84, 100, 108, 135, 163, 185, 249
Fanning, Ronan 102
Faolain, Mrs 264
farming 32–4, 36, 41–4, 47–8, 75, 76, 82, 167, 170, 183
Farrell, Anne 33
Farrell family 52–3, 50, 168, 170, 242; *see also* O'Farrell
Farrell, Frank 276
Farrell, Hannah 28, 31, 32, 43, 44, 47, 48, 59, 60, 140, 143, 289, 293

Index

Farrell, Jack 31, 32, 33–4, 36, 41, 43, 44–7, 49, 53, 143, 153, 155, 157, 248
Farrell, Rev James, S.J. 31, 32, 97–8, 99, 132
Farrell, Madge (Byrnes) 31, 32, 33, 34, 47–8, 51, 75, 289
Farrell, Matthew 25, 31–32, 33, 34, 51, 55
Farrell, Father Matthew Timothy, O.P. (Tim) 89–90, 99–103, 155, 185–96, 301
Farrell Michael 23, 24, 24–34, 36, 43, 44–7, 49–50, 51
Federation xxviii, 132
Fenianism, 98
Fianna Fail 233
fighting 34, 35–6
films 232–3; *see also* motion pictures
fire 73, 150
Fitzcarraldo syndrome 138, 269
Fitzgerald, Mr 13
Fitzgerald, Gerard 226–7, 232, 235
Fitzgerald, Seamus 12
Flaherty, James 267
Flanagan, engine-driver 30
Flight of the earls (1607), 20
Fogarty, Father Matthew 25, 38, 53, 80, 99–100, 102, 295
Fogarty, Mick 88
Fogarty, Pat 55
Fogarty, Tom 58
Folk-Lore Commission, Irish 15
folk songs 12, 82, 84; *see also* songs
football 289, 294, *see also* rugby
Forrest, Father M.D. MSC, 234–5
France; French xx, 72, 77, 98, 113, 128, 137, 153–5, 157, 173, 196, 259, 284, 290, 292–5
Fraser, Peter 261
Freeman's Journal (Sydney) 232

Gaels; Gaelic xv, xx, 3, 5, 6–7, 10, 16–20, 84, 170, 177, 201, 203, 210, 213, 229; Athletic Assoc (Ireland) 38, 99, (Melbourne) 233; dancing 193; *see also* dancing; football; language 12–15, 123, 229, 241–2, 252, 254, 285; League (Ireland) 60, (Melbourne) 226, 337, 344, revival 38, 72, 73–5, 121, 135, 242
Galong, NSW 5, 20
Galsworthy, John 138
gambling 220, 267–72
gardening 142, 146
Gaughan, K. 73
Geelong, Vic. 225
George VI 247–8
Geraldine, NZ 295
German, Germany xiv, 174, 195, 224
Gill, S.T. 41
Gilroy, Cardinal, Sir Normam 127, 277
Gippsland, Vic. 42, 167
Girls' Crystal 290
Girl Guides 274, 298
Glebe Point NSW 251
Glin, Co. Kerry 5
gold rush; mining xix, 13, 18, 26, 48, 84, 90, 131, 244, 249, 259, 263; dredging 267–71
Good Shepherd institution, Melbourne 252
Goulburn, NSW 108, 145
Greaney family 152
Greaney, Julia 90–3, 157, 160, 289, 298
Greek; Greece xiv
Green, Alice Stopford 251

Green, W. Spotswood 43
Greene, Graham 270
Greenhill, Bill 147–8, 155
Greenhill, Mrs 151–2
Grey River Argus 264–6, 272
Grey, Zane 136
Greymouth, NZ 48–9, 51, 71, 73, 80, 94, 98, 137, 140, 142, 143–57, 205, 212, 242, 244, 260–73, 288–9, 292–300
Griffin, Dean David 108
Griffin, Gerard 224–5, 226
Griffith, NSW 83
Guardian, (Nenagh) 295
guardian angels 78
Guinness 53
Gunning, Dean 116

Hacket, James 55
Haig, General 173–4
handball 213
Handlin, Oscar 297
Hanrahan, Dr Arthur 123, 250–6, 274–5, 285–7
Hanrahan, Mrs Ethel 252–4, 285–7
Hardie, Keir 272, 274
Haughey, Charles 214
Hazelton, Richard 253
Heenan, Dr 58
Hertzog, Werner 138
Heyer, Georgette 87
Hibernian Australasian Catholic Benefit Society 157, 233, 244
Hickey, Pat 179–80, 261
Higgins, John 13
Hill, William 267
history; historians xv, xvii, xix, xxiii, xxv, 1, 2, 3–5, 7–10, 16–17, 20, 47, 106, 110, 116, 117, 155, 203, 205–6, 218, 222, 251, 260, 267–8, 277–8
Historical Studies (Melbourne) 17
holidays 41, 186
Holland H.E. 261
holy water 72–3
'home' 50, 54, 123, 158, 160, 163, 167, 283
home brew 39, 52–3
Home Rule 121, 171, 172, 216, 241, 250, 253, 254, 277
Hone, Joseph 208
Hopkins, Gerard Manly 85
hospitals 27, 38, 119, 183, 250, 285, 289, 292, 296, 299
hotels 64, 66, 84, 187–8, 190, 191–2, 264, 268
Houlihan, Tom 27
Hoyts, 232
Hughes, Robert 17
Hughes, W.M. 254
humour 30, 34–6, 62–9
Hunter, NZ 33
hurling 38
Hutchinson, Bishop John 106, 109
Hyde Park, Sydney 264
hymnody 85

illness 144, 168, 170, 226, 287, 290–3
Illustrated London News 71
immigration xxviii–xxix, 9–10, 20, 57, 88, 187, 278; hostility to Irish 9; regulations 252; *see also* emigrants
Immigration Department, (NZ) 32

Inchbonnie, NZ 263
indulgences 88
Invercargill NZ, 295
Ireland; Irish; colonial spiritual and clerical empire xv, xix, xx, xxi, xxiii, xxi, 104, 106–11, 128, 132–3, 162, 246, colonial criticism of 179–97, 200–8, 216–23; as dream world 90–3, 167, 183 184–6, 199–238, 252; *see also* dreams; hidden concept of, xv, 6, 7–9, 10, 12–13, 15, 20; *see also* kingdoms, Irish, in labour movement in Aust. and NZ 274–9; nationalism xxi, 16, 20, 26, 343, 38, 60, 98, 116, 121, 127, 139, 163, 207, 210, 241–2, 250–6, 263–4, 290; stereotypes of 2, 6, 7, 10, 12–13, 20, 33, 34, 39–41, 42, 50, 60, 75, 182, 105, 107, 180, 217, 223.
Irish in Australia, The xvii, xxi, 5
Irish Board of Works 207
Irish Civil War 127, 224, 225, 287
Irish Free State 225, 231
Irish Literary Supplement 200
Irish National Association 199, 231, 233, 254
Irish National Club 185
Irish National Foresters 233
Irish neutrality 224
Irish News (Melbourne) 226
Irish Republican Army 127, 226, 231, 234, 278
Irish Republican Association 225, 226
Irish Republican Brotherhood 38, 225
Irish republicanism 224–234, 241, 250, 254, 278
Irish Review (Melbourne) 230
Italy; Italians 109, 195

Japan; Japanese 224
Jesuit order 31, 34, 97, 99, 123, 132, 250
Jews xiv, 185; harp, 82, 83
Job 217, 295
Johnson, Amy 116
Johnson, Dr. dog of 196
Joyce, James 203
Joyce, P.W. 251

Kaiata, NZ 148
Kane, Father Robert, S.J. 111
Kane, Jack 180, 277–8
Kapunda, S.A. 250, 253, 275
Kealty, Willie 28
Kear, George 48, 150, 267
Keating family 157
Keating, Jack 92–3
Keating, Paul 275
Keenan, Joe 248
Kelly, Archbishop Michael 224, 234, 247
Kelly Country, family 35, 66–7, 82
Kelly, Eva, ('Eva') 139
Kelly, Father James 225
Kelly, Ned 67, 82
Kennedy family 61
Kennedy's bus 298
Kent, J.B. 272–4
Kerry 5, 12, 13, 229, 249
Kiama, NSW 67
Kilkenny 12
Kilmovee 93
kingdoms, Irish xv, xxvii, 1, 3, 5, 6, 7, 16, 21; *see also* Ireland

307

Kingston, Maxine Hong xxix
Knock 72, 93
Koroit, Vic. 44
Kropotkin, P. 272
Kuomintang 231

labour; labouring; men xix, 5, 18, 36, 47–8, 113, 165, 170, *see also* work; movement (Aust. and NZ) 9, 179, 257, 265, 274–9 (Irish) 180, 264; parties (Aust. and NZ) 21, 65, 82–4, 140, 157, 158, 179, 225, 260, 262–7, 272–9, 289, 294; press 264–5; Red Federation of 261
lace 252
Lack, John xxviii
Landsdowne Lord, 3
Lang, Jack 275
Langan, Tom 5
Lanigan, Bishop William 108
Larmer, J. 6
larrikins 35, 261
Latin 212–13
Launceston, Tas. 108
lavatories 75, 102, 247–8, 266
law 256–60
Lecky, W.E.H. 3
Lemass, Sean 100
Lemire, Father Achille 113
Lemire, Father Jules 113, 128–31
Lenin, V. I 226
Letters from Irish Australia 1825–1929 xvii, 42, 167
Lewisham, NSW 251, 285
Limerick 1, 74, 87, 252
Lisieux 89
Listowel, Co. Kerry 13
Lockington, Fr. W. S.J. 254
London 39, 55, 158, 183, 184, 244
Long, Monsignor James 71, 98, 103, 132
Longford 26
Lough Derg 194
Lourdes 72, 286–7
Luther, Martin 88

McCarthy, Michael, J.F. 183
McCaughey, Sir Samuel 83–4
McDonald, Eddie 270
McEnroe, Venerable Archdeacon, J. xix
McGirr, J.J.G. 276
McGrath, Father Patrick, S.J. 250
McKenna, Archpriest, 225
McKenna, Mary T. 73
MacLysaght, E. 210
McNamara children 285
MacNamara, Francis 12
MacSwiney, Terence 227, 244
Macky, Rev. Dill 172
madness 27, 28, 48, 63, 88
Mahon, Hugh 251
Maitland, NSW 224
Makikihi, NZ 48
Mallow 13
Manchester Martyrs 227
Mandle, W.E. 38
Manly movement, xx, 127
Mann, Tom 142
Mannix, Archbishop D. 111, 114, 121, 127, 132, 225, 229, 244–7, 254, 260, 276, 277
Maoris 48, 138
Marist Brothers 53, 205, 211–14, 273, 292–3

Marist Fathers, 153–5, 300
Maritain, J. 196
Maroubra, NSW 94, 224
marriage 25, 28, 30, 31, 32, 33, 34, 41–2, 47, 51, 53–4, 55, 58, 59, 61, 73, 74, 80, 139–147, 152–4, 158–160, 185, 250
mass 95, 116, 119, 154, 155, 284
Massey, William Ferguson 83
Masterton, NZ 44
Marxism 9
Mayhew, Henry 39
Maynooth 116
Mayo 50, 93
Meagher, Monsignor James 71
medicine 88, 123, 143, 250–6, 259–60, 285, 286, 287–8
Melbourne, Vic. 121, 167, 199, 226, 34, 247, 248, 252, 278–9
General Cemetery 227
meningitis 287
Mercy, Sisters of 54, 80–1, 87, 124, 139, 289
Messenger, John C. xx
MGM (Metro-Goldwyn-Mayer) 232
Michelago, NSW 285
Military Service Act 260
Minogue, Dan 264
miracles 291–2, 294
Mitchel, John, Fund 121
Montessori 281
Moore, Bishop James 111
Moore, Thomas 84, 228
Moran Cardinal P.F. 106, 108, 109, 110–11, 114, 123, 124–6, 128, 132, 154, 221, 279
Moran, Maggie 55–62
Mormons 180
Moriarty, Bishop David 98
Moriarty, Julia 39, 44, 105, 136, 183
Morrissey, D. 35
Morven, NZ 43
motion pictures 149, 232–3
motoring 147–8, 187, 193, 194–5, 270–1
Movement, The 276–9
Mount Melleray 195
Moy, River 13
multi-culturalism 9–10, 301
Mulford, Clarence E. 136
Mungret College 31
Munster 12
Murphy, Jack 154
Murray, Frank (Wampoo) 65
Murray, Hubert 251
music 57, 82–5, 15, 177, 250, 259, *see also* songs

Nairn, Bede 275–6
Nation (Dublin) 139
Napier NZ, 263
Naughton, Joe 55
Nelson Creek, NZ 244, 263
Nelson's Pillar 210
Nenagh 26, 27, 50, 80, 251, 295
New South Wales; bishops 277–9; north coast 258; northern 67; south west 5, 6, 67
Newfoundland 110, 114
New York 110, 160, 232, 275
New Yorker 136
New Zealand, emigration to 74, 147, 163
New Zealand Tablet 139, 184–5, 221, 225
News Weekly 127
newspapers, labour 264–5

Newson, Mrs 175
Ngaio, NZ 289
Norddeutscher–Lloyd line 44
Norris, Kathleen 232
Northern Ireland 127
nuns 53–4, 58, 60, 61, 78, 80–2, 90, 117, 124, 125, 142, 235, 289, 290–2, 295, Lewisham 251, *see also* convents
nurses; nursing 27, 55, 58, 193

O Braon, Donal 13
O'Brien, Frederick 136
O'Brien, Jim 261, 265–7, 272–4
O'Brien, John (Fr P.J. Hartigan) 229
O'Brien, Sinead 117, 126
O'Connell, Daniel 20, 212, 243–4, 284; centenary appeals 121
O'Connor, Frank 138
O'Dea, R. 225–6
O'Donnell, Red Hugh 20–1
O'Doherty, Kevin Izod 139
O'Farrell family 157, 249; *see also* Farrell
O'Farrell, Mai, (O'Sullivan) 28, 41, 53–9, 61, 71–4, 78, 80, 84, 85–7, 89, 90, 92–3, 102–3, 138–53, 155, 157, 160, 167, 185–6, 188–91, 195, 241–3, 248, 268, 270–1, 273, 274, 287–301
O'Farrell, Mary 281–301
O'Farrell, Paddy (Patrick Vincent) 23, 25, 26–8, 30–4, 38–9, 48, 51–5, 57, 59, 61, 82, 84, 89, 90, 92, 97, 99–100, 102–3, 132, 136–58, 160, 163, 167, 177, 186, 189, 193, 219, 221, 224, 241–9, 260–74, 287–8, 292, 297–300
O'Hearn, Dinny 205
O hEiageartaigh, Padraig 34–5
O'Mara, Chas, J. 229
O'Neill brothers 249–50
O'Neill, 'Tip' 264
O'Reilly, Father M. 254
O Suilleabhain, Eoghan Rua 12
O'Sullivan, Christina 53, 55, 56–9, 61, 75, 80, 87, 158–9, 186, 242, 268, 296, 298
Oamaru, NZ 43
Oceania xx
Opera House, Greymouth 148–9
Orange, NSW 146
Oral History Project, Jubilee, South Australia 203
Orange Lodge, Order xv, 43, 67, 171, 172, 215, 250
Our Lady of Mount Carmel 93

Palestine 165
Pambula, NSW 113
Paris 158
parliament 243, 253, 265, 273–4
Parnell, Charles Stewart 234, 277–9; obelisk, 210
Patrick, Sister 54, 80–2, 85–7
Pearse, Padraig 60, 210, 226, 263
penal system 17–18
Philip, Brother 292–3, 295
Phillips family 155
Phillips, George 147, 247–8
photography 34, 38, 39, 51–2, 281, 298
piano 82
piety 72, 75, 76–7, 87–9, 251, 287; *see also* prayer
pigs 44

Pioneer Total Abstinence movement 218
Pius X 72
Pleasant Point NZ, 43
Plenary Council, Australian (1885) 109, 125
Plunkett, Nicholas 1, 2
poetry 139, 199–205, 226, 235, 249, 251, 291; Gaelic 6–7, 10, 12–15, 18, 31, 34–5, 203
Polding, Archbishop Bede 107–8, 123, 129 123, 129
police 26, 32, 34, 49–50, 66, 67, 93, 183, 188, 205, 232, 264
politics 20, 35, 39, 53, 65, 84, 231, 244, 252, 264, 266–7, 274–9
possum 41
potatoes 44, 155, 163, 258
poultry 146–7
poverty 179, 183, 191–2
prayer 60, 76–7, 88–9, 251, 270–1, 293, 299; books 87, 242; see also piety
Prendeville, Archbishop R. 247
Presentation Sisters 117
Presbyterianism 172, 177
priests; priesthood xx, 13, 31, 32, 38, 53, 61, 71, 73, 78, 80, 89–90, 95, 97–107, 113–14, 116–30, 142, 172, 175, 183–96, 225–5, 234–9, 247, 251, 277–9
Pritchett, V.S. 210
Propaganda College, Rome 110
Protestants, Protestantism xvii, 2, 7, 9, 13, 41–3, 74, 87, 88, 92, 104–5, 113, 119, 126, 136, 160, 216, 217, 219, 220, 237
Proust, Marcel xxiii, xxvi, xxix, 299
public service 260
Pukekohe, NZ 32, 34
Puketahi Street, Greymouth, 51, 145, 149, 249
Punakiki, NZ 148
Purgatory 88

Queensland 62, 63, 66–7, 107, 109, 119
Quinn, Bishop, J. (Brisbane) 243

rabbits 33, 41, 153
races, racing 36, 48, 63–4, 66, 148, 160, 230, 258, 268, 269–72
radio xix, 92, 269
railways 30, 48, 84, 113, 135, 145, 151, 226
Rangiora NZ, 25, 53
Raphael, Sister 289
reading 71–4, 87, 103, 135–9, 185, 205, 225, 251, 266
Reaskavalla, Tadhg 13
rebellions; (1798) 5, 98, 212–13, 227, 278; (1848) 139; Castle Hill 5, 10; see also Rising 1916
Redemptorist order 119
Redmond, Willie 253
Reformation 7
Reid, J.C. 221, 222–3
Reid, Mr 167
religion 60–1, 71–2, 75–8, 85–7, 92, 94, 149, 152, 176, 182, 183–4, 242, 270–2, 276–9, 294; teaching of 78, 80, 82, 87; structures of 94
Renaissance 7
Revington, Mrs A.M. 51
rifles 41, 52
Rimu, NZ 249
Rising, Irish, (1916) xv, xxvi, 34, 55, 104,
180, 210, 216, 224, 226, 235, 241, 243, 250, 251, 254, 257
Riverview, NSW 97
Rockett, Billy 13
Roberts, Jim 276
romance 55, 57, 58–9, 61, 87, 123, 135, 139–40, 145, 192, 292, 226, 249, 250, 252, 256, 269, 288, 291
Rome 89, 102, 106–10, 196, 214, 238
rosaries 76, 251, 254, 270
Roscrea 50
Ross, Edgar 114
Royal Irish Constabulary 26
Royal University of Ireland 260
rugby 214
rugby league 214
Runanga, NZ 142, 261, 265
Rutherglen, Vic. 84
Ryan, Edward, (Ned) 5, 20, 123
Ryan family 5, 6
Ryan, John Nagle 5
Ryan, Rev. Dr Paddy 114

Sacred Heart of Jesus 87, 88, 218, 244
Sacred Heart Monastery, Kensington, NSW 278–9
St Ambrose's Church, Brunswick, Vic. 232
St Bridget 124
St Columbkille's Church, Sydney 95
St Dymphna 72
St John's Ambulance Brigade 224
St Joseph's Church, Launceston, Tas. 108
St Mac Arten 72
St Patrick, ship 138
St Patrick's Cathedral, Melbourne, Vic. 129
St Patrick's College, Manly NSW, 128
St Patrick's Church, Boorowa, NSW 124
St Patrick's Day 62, 93, 214, 215, 229–30, 231
St Patrick's Society, Melbourne 233
St Stephen's Green 210
St Therese of Lisieux, (Little Flower) 87–8, 89–90, 92, 139, 286, 290–3, 295, 298
St Thomas Aquinas 789, 196
St Vincent's Hospital, Dublin 38
Salvation Army 119
sanitation 191–2, 194, 216–18, 220, 223
Santamaria, B.A. 127, 276–8
Satan 88
Savage, Michael Joseph 82–4, 261, 289
Scanlan, Pat 63
scapular medals 54
schools 47, 80, 113, 116, 126, 185, 212–14, 220, 273, 274, 277, 281, 289, 298
Scots xix, 157, 177, 272
Scullin, J.H. 231, 264, 276
sculling 39
sectarianism 247, 274, 278
Semple, Bob 261
servants 95, 251–2
sewerage 149–50, 194, 195, 207
Shackleton, Sir Ernest 136
Sheehan, Canon 135
Shinrone 58
shooting 42
Sillon movement 72
sin 60, 87, 140, 271
Sitwell, Osbert 136, 139
Skehan, Dinny 63–4
Skehan, Mary 64

Slattery, Father 113–14
Smiling Irish Eyes 233
socialism 20, 84, 127, 179, 180, 260–1, 263
solicitors 260
songs 87, 177, 200, 206, 210, 214–15, 227–9, 231; see also folk-songs, music
South Australia 250, 251–2, 274, 285
Southern Alps 48, 51, 145, 269, 270–1
Spain 105, 137
Spencer, Dick 267
Spencer, Kate 145–6, 158, 267
Split, The 276–9
sport 42, 66, 83, 114, 145, 250, 258
Stack, Father Maurice 13–14
stage-Irish 73, 153, 229
state aid, to education 277–8
State Housing Allocation Committee, NZ 272
Stations of the Cross 75, 76
Stokes, Paddy 264
Suez 165
Sullivan Family 42–4, 50, 74, 161, 185–97, 242, 295–7; see also O'Sullivan
Sullivan, Kit 160–1
Sullivan, John L. 67
Sullivan, 'Son' 61
superstitions 292
Surry Hills, NSW 93, 264
Sydney 5, 12, 99, 106, 127, 172, 207, 214, 227, 231–2, 259; Irish 95, 254, 264, 284; Stadium 114
Synan, Mother 117
Synge, J.M. 50

tailoring 26, 28, 31, 38–9, 48, 53, 147, 158, 242, 269, 273; union 242, 260, 264
Tailor and Cutter 39
Talbot, Matthew 92–3
Tambo Crossing, Vic. 167, 172, 176
Tammany 275–6
Tasman Sea 137, 153, 298
Tasmania 273
Templeton, Jacqueline xxviii
temperance 218
Temuka, NZ 74
Tench, Captain Watkin 15–16
tennis 250
Teresita. Sister 291
Thurles 124
Timaru, NZ 43, 74
timber milling 48, 90, 140, 263, 267
Tin Pan Alley 177
Tipperary 5, 23, 26, 38, 41–2, 50, 60, 74, 90, 154, 194–5, 229
toffee-apples 293
Tone-Pearse Republican Cumann 226–33
Tone, Wolfe 227
Total Abstinence Association 124
Totara, NZ 145
Tracy, Honor xx
transportation 2, 3, 5, 12, 16, 18
Trench, W. Steuart 3, 6
Tribune, (Melbourne) 233
Truth 183
tuberculosis 97, 183, 192, 194, 272, 273, 290
Tully family 62, 63, 39
Tully, Frank 63,
Tully, Maria 63, 64
Tully, Pat 62–3, 67, 69, 118–19
Tully, Patsy 63, 64, 66
Tully, Sarah 145

309

Tuomey, Father, P. 254

Uluru, N.T. 93
Ulster Protestants xv, xvii, 25, 83-4, 111, 165, 170-1, 174-5, 176-7
Undset, Sigrid 138
Union Jack 108-9, 229
unions, trade 140, 142, 145-6, 157, 179-80, 260-1, 265, 274
university 260
University College, Dublin 188
Utah 180

Valparaiso 93
Vancouver 93
Vanikoro 137
Vatican 155; Vatican II 77
Venezuela 137
Victoria xix, 13, 44, 66, 84, 167, 225-6, 232; north east 35, 82; south west 127
Victoria, Queen 110-11, 207
Victoria, Queen, Building 207
violence 66-7

violin 57, 82, 83, 157, 177

Waimate, NZ 28, 33, 43, 44, 47, 48, 53, 143, 147, 153, 155, 247
Waimea South 179
Wagga Wagga NSW 215
wake 281, 284, 295
Wanganui NZ 205
war 20, First World xvi, xxix, 31, 55, 57, 58, 61, 151, 172-4, 179, 224, 260, 296; Second World 224, 294
War and Facism conference 231
Ware, Bob 273-4
Watchman (Sydney) 172
wealth 33, 158, 160, 183, 187, 267-9
Webb, P.C. (Paddy) 84, 260, 261, 267
Wellington, NZ 39, 102, 105, 136, 158, 160, 185, 289, 291
Welsh 157
West Briton 250, 251
West Coast, NZ xix, 32, 140, 153, 154, 249, 261, 263, 264, 268, 295, 298, 299

Western Australia 167
White Australia policy xxviii
White, Harry 143
Wilde, Lady 139
Willowbridge, NZ 43-8, 75, 289
women 60, 62-5, 73-4, 80-2, 119, 139-40, 145-7, 158-60, 186-90, 229, 248, 258, 273, 287, 288, 290-1, 298; *see also* nuns
Women's Christian Temperance Union 23, 24
Woolloomooloo, NSW 95
work 30, 44, 47-8, 57, 152, 158, 163, 167, 176, 177, 207, 257-60; *see also* employment
Wright's Bush, NZ 295
Wyndham Land Act 25
Wynne, Pat 229

Yackandandah, Vic. 167
Yanco, station 83, 84
Yeats, W.B. 38, 203
Young, Arthur 3
Young Ireland Reader 113